D1639670

2

LEARNING AND COGNITION IN AUTISM

CURRENT ISSUES IN AUTISM

Series Editors: Eric Schopler and Gary B. Mesibov

University of North Carolina School of Medicine
Chapel Hill, North Carolina

AUTISM IN ADOLESCENTS AND ADULTS
Edited by Eric Schopler and Gary B. Mesibov

BEHAVIORAL ISSUES IN AUTISM
Edited by Eric Schopler and Gary B. Mesibov

COMMUNICATION PROBLEMS IN AUTISM
Edited by Eric Schopler and Gary B. Mesibov

DIAGNOSIS AND ASSESSMENT IN AUTISM
Edited by Eric Schopler and Gary B. Mesibov

THE EFFECTS OF AUTISM ON THE FAMILY
Edited by Eric Schopler and Gary B. Mesibov

HIGH-FUNCTIONING INDIVIDUALS WITH AUTISM
Edited by Eric Schopler and Gary B. Mesibov

LEARNING AND COGNITION IN AUTISM
Edited by Eric Schopler and Gary B. Mesibov

NEUROBIOLOGICAL ISSUES IN AUTISM
Edited by Eric Schopler and Gary B. Mesibov

PRESCHOOL ISSUES IN AUTISM
Edited By Eric Schopler, Mary E. Van Bourgondien, and Marie M. Bristol

SOCIAL BEHAVIOR IN AUTISM
Edited by Eric Schopler and Gary B. Mesibov

LEARNING AND COGNITION IN AUTISM

Edited by
Eric Schopler
and
Gary B. Mesibov

University of North Carolina School of Medicine
Chapel Hill, North Carolina

PLENUM PRESS • NEW YORK AND LONDON

Library of Congress Cataloging-in-Publication Data

Learning and cognition in autism / edited by Eric Schopler and Gary B.
Mesibov.
      p.   cm. -- (Current issues in autism)
   Includes bibliographical references and index.
   ISBN 0-306-44871-8
   1. Autism in children. 2. Cognition disorders in children.
3. Learning disabilities. 4. Autistic children--Education.
I. Schopler, Eric. II. Mesibov, Gary B. III. Series.
   [DNLM: 1. Autism--in infancy & childhood--congresses.
2. Cognition--in infancy & childhood--congresses. 3. Learning
Disorders--in infancy & childhood--congresses. 4. Education,
Special--congresses.   WM 203.5 L438 1995]
RJ506.A9L43 1995
618.92'8982--dc20
DNLM/DLC
for Library of Congress   94-44014
                                                              CIP

ISBN 0-306-44871-8

© 1995 Plenum Press, New York
A Division of Plenum Publishing Corporation
233 Spring Street, New York, N. Y. 10013

10 9 8 7 6 5 4 3 2

Printed in the United States of America

To our teachers, whose understanding of our students enables
both to learn from each other

Contributors

MARK H. ALLEN, Neuropsychology Research Laboratory, Children's Hospital Research Center, San Diego, California 92123

ANDREW S. BONDY, Delaware Autistic Program, 144 Brennen Drive, Newark, Delaware 19713

GRETCHEN BUTERA, Department of Special Education, West Virginia University, Morgantown, West Virginia 26506-6122

LISA CAPPS, Department of Psychology, University of California at Los Angeles, Los Angeles, California 90024

ROGER COX, Greensboro TEACCH Center, Greensboro, North Carolina 27401

GERALDINE DAWSON, Department of Psychology, University of Washington, Seattle, Washington 98195

DEBORAH FEIN, Department of Psychology, University of Connecticut, Storrs, Connecticut 06268; and Laboratory of Neuropsychology, Boston University School of Medicine, Boston, Massachusetts 02118

UTA FRITH, Cognitive Development Unit, Medical Research Council, London WC1H OBT, United Kingdom

LORI A. FROST, Pyramid Educational Consultants, 5 Westbury Drive, Cherry Hill, New Jersey 08003

TEMPLE GRANDIN, Department of Animal Science, Colorado State University, Fort Collins, Colorado 80523

LEEANNE GREEN, Department of Psychology, University of Connecticut, Storrs, Connecticut 06268

FRANCESCA HAPPÉ, Cognitive Development Unit, Medical Research Council, London WC1H OBT, United Kingdom.

SANDRA HARRIS, Graduate School of Applied and Professional Psychology, Rutgers University, Piscataway, New Jersey 08855-0819

CARL HAYWOOD, Peabody College, Vanderbilt University, Nashville, Tennessee 37203

KATHY HEARSEY, Division TEACCH, Department of Psychiatry, School of Medicine, University of North Carolina at Chapel Hill, Chapel Hill, North Carolina 27599-7180

STEPHEN JOY, Department of Psychology, University of Connecticut, Storrs, Connecticut 06268; and Albertus Magnus College, New Haven, Connecticut 06511

ANGELA KILMAN, Neuropsychology Research Laboratory, Children's Hospital Research Center, and California School of Professional Psychology, San Diego, California 92123

LAURA G. KLINGER, Department of Psychology, University of Alabama, Tuscaloosa, Alabama 35847

LYNN KERN KOEGEL, Autism Research Center, Counseling/Clinical/School Psychology Program, Graduate School of Education, University of California at Santa Barbara, Santa Barbara, California 93106

ROBERT L. KOEGEL, Autism Research Center, Counseling/Clinical/School Psychology Program, Graduate School of Education, University of California at Santa Barbara, Santa Barbara, California 93106

ALAN LINCOLN, Neuropsychology Research Laboratory, Children's Hospital Research Center, and California School of Professional Psychology, San Diego, California 92123

CATHERINE LORD, Department of Psychiatry, University of Chicago Hospital, Chicago, Illinois 60637

GARY B. MESIBOV, Division TEACCH, Department of Psychiatry, School of Medicine, University of North Carolina at Chapel Hill, Chapel Hill, North Carolina 27599-7180

HELMER MYKLEBUST, Emeritus Professor of Psychology, Neurology, and Psychiatry, Northwestern University, Chicago, Illinois 60611

SALLY OZONOFF, Department of Psychology, University of Utah, Salt Lake City, Utah 84112

ERIC SCHOPLER, Division TEACCH, Department of Psychiatry, School of Medicine, University of North Carolina at Chapel Hill, Chapel Hill, North Carolina 27599-7180

MARIAN SIGMAN, Neuropsychiatric Institute and Hospital, University of California at Los Angeles, Los Angeles, California 90024-1759

LYNN WATERHOUSE, Trenton State College, Ewing Township, New Jersey 08625-0550

NURIT YIRMIYA, Department of Psychology, Hebrew University of Jerusalem, Mount Scopus, Jerusalem, Israel 91905

Preface

This volume, like the other eight in the Current Issues in Autism series, grew from our annual TEACCH conference. The book is not, however, simply a compilation of conference proceedings. Instead, selected conference participants whose work has already achieved national and international recognition were asked to develop chapters around their presentations. Other recognized experts in areas relevant to the conference theme were also asked to contribute chapters. Although we were not able to include all of the workers who have contributed to the theme, this volume represents our best effort to pull together for our readers the most current knowledge and state of the art practices.

Although aspects of cognition, learning, and behavioral motivation have been touched on for relevance to autism in other books in this series, the growing integration of behavioral and cognitive theories has greatly enriched our educational interventions on behalf of autism. While this volume does not include all the fascinating facets of this recent integration, we believe that it offers useful information to teachers, parents, and researchers on some of the progress produced by their interaction.

ERIC SCHOPLER
GARY B. MESIBOV

Acknowledgments

As with the other volumes in our Autism Series, this book would not have seen the light of day without the help of many dedicated people. First, we are grateful to Helen Garrison, who organized the conference that gave us the mandate for this book. As the audiences continue to increase, her organizational skills have stayed right up with the new demands. Thanks also to Vickie Weaver, whose expert secretarial assistance and good cheer have been most valuable, and to Suzanne Orr, just beginning her work as Editorial Assistant, who has reviewed each chapter with a natural intuition for the nuts and bolts of good writing.

Like all of our projects, these books would not be possible without our superb TEACCH colleagues, who are too numerous to name. Not only do they apply their clinical insights and know-how to the topic of cognition and learning, they also consistently use the new material provided by these chapters to enrich the families and students who are looking for the latest information.

We especially appreciate the contributions of the families who struggle with the special problems of autism every day. Their energy in behalf of their children and their cooperation and participation in our program consistently inspire all our learning efforts.

Finally, the School of Medicine at the University of North Carolina at Chapel Hill, and especially the Department of Psychiatry under the capable leadership of David Janowsky, have provided the environment that cultivates and nurtures scholarly pursuits of this kind. We are also most grateful to the members of the North Carolina State Legislature, who have continued to support both services and scholarly research aimed at understanding and ameliorating the disadvantages of autism and related developmental disabilities.

Contents

Part I: Introduction and General Issues

Chapter 1

INTRODUCTION TO LEARNING AND COGNITION IN AUTISM   3

Eric Schopler and Gary B. Mesibov

Introduction   3
Cognitive and Social Deficits   4
Strengths in Cognition   5
Intervention Strategies   6
Overview of Chapters   6
References 10

Chapter 2

COGNITIVE FUNCTIONING IN AUTISM: AN OVERVIEW 13

LeeAnne Green, Deborah Fein, Stephen Joy,
and Lynn Waterhouse

Introduction 13
General Intellectual Functioning: Strengths and Weaknesses 14
Early Cognitive Development 16

Perception and Attention   16
Executive Function   18
Language   19
Memory   22
Social Cognition   22
Summary and Conclusions   25
References   26

Chapter 3

VERBAL AND NONVERBAL COGNITIVE PROCESSES   33

Helmer K. Myklebust

Introduction   33
Language Disorders   33
Language and Meaning   39
Nonverbal Learning Disabilities   43
Brain Status and Cognitive Dysfunctions   47
Conclusions   50
References   50

Chapter 4

RELATIONSHIP BETWEEN AUTISM AND LEARNING DISABILITIES   57

Roger D. Cox and Gary B. Mesibov

Introduction   57
Early Conceptualizations of Autism   57
Adjustments in Autism Definition   58
Early Conceptualizations of Learning Disabilities   61
Exclusion Principle   63
Similarities between Severe Learning Disabilities and Higher
    Functioning Autism   64

Differences between Learning Disabilities and Autism 66
Clinical Implications of Learning Disabilities versus Autism
    Diagnoses 67
References 68

Part II: Thinking and Learning

Chapter 5

MOTIVATING COMMUNICATION IN CHILDREN WITH AUTISM 73

Lynn Kern Koegel and Robert L. Koegel

Introduction 73
Motivational Treatment 74
Motivation and Social-Communicative Interactions in School 82
Summary and Conclusions 84
References 85

Chapter 6

THE ASSESSMENT AND INTERPRETATION OF INTELLECTUAL
ABILITIES IN PEOPLE WITH AUTISM 89

Alan J. Lincoln, Mark H. Allen, and Angela Kilman

Introduction 89
Assessment of Intelligence: The Wechsler Scales 91
Assessment of Autistic Individuals with the Wechsler Scales 92
Sequential and Simultaneous-Processing Abilities 99
Memory Functioning 107
Practical Considerations for the Assessment of Intellectual and
    Cognitive Abilities 110
Conclusions 112
References 114

Chapter 7

A FRESH LOOK AT CATEGORIZATION ABILITIES IN PERSONS
WITH AUTISM.. 119

Laura G. Klinger and Geraldine Dawson

Introduction.. 119
Categorization in Normal Development........................ 122
Categorization in Autism...................................... 124
Processes Underlying Categorization in Autism.................. 128
A Fresh Look at Categorization Abilities in Autism 132
Conclusions.. 133
References 134

Chapter 8

HOW PEOPLE WITH AUTISM THINK........................... 137

Temple Grandin

Introduction.. 137
Autism Subtypes 138
Visual Thinking 141
Implications of Visual Thinking 144
Emotions and Empathy 148
Sensory Problems and Attention 150
Summary.. 153
References 154

Part III: Social Cognition

Chapter 9

SOCIAL AND COGNITIVE UNDERSTANDING IN
HIGH-FUNCTIONING CHILDREN WITH AUTISM 159

Marian D. Sigman, Nurit Yirmiya, and Lisa Capps

Introduction 159
Sample Description. 162
Social Understanding. 163
Cognitive Abilities 170
General Discussion. 172
References. 174

Chapter 10

THEORY OF MIND IN AUTISM 177

Francesca Happé and Uta Frith

Introduction 177
Addressing Causes at Different Levels 178
The Puzzle of the Triad. 179
The Theory-of-Mind Hypothesis 179
Testing the Hypothesis 181
Further Experimental Evidence 183
Arguments and Artifacts. 183
Fine-Cuts Technique. 187
Puzzles That Remain 189
Practical Implications of the Mind-Blindness Theory 192
References. 194

Chapter 11

EXECUTIVE FUNCTIONS IN AUTISM 199

Sally Ozonoff

Introduction 199
Identifying Primary Deficits of Autism 200
Executive Functions and Autism. 200
Toward a Unifying Model of Autism: Prefrontal Dysfunction? 205
Implications for Treatment and Educational Remediation 214
Summary 214
References. 215

Chapter 12

FACILITATING SOCIAL INCLUSION: EXAMPLES FROM PEER
INTERVENTION PROGRAMS. 221

Catherine Lord
Introduction. 221
Principles Underlying Peer Intervention. 222
Peer Tutor/Buddies Program 226
Integrated Social Groups/Daycamps. 232
Conclusions. 238
References 239

Part IV: Education and Treatment

Chapter 13

STRUCTURED TEACHING IN THE TEACCH SYSTEM 243

Eric Schopler, Gary B. Mesibov, and Kathy Hearsey

Introduction. 243
Autism Characteristics 244
Guiding TEACCH Principles. 245
The Four Major Components of Structured Teaching 246
Other Structured Teaching Concepts. 263
Summary and Conclusions 266
References 267

Chapter 14

COGNITIVE EDUCATION OF YOUNG CHILDREN WITH AUTISM:
AN APPLICATION OF BRIGHT START. 269

Gretchen Butera and H. Carl Haywood

Introduction. 269
Characteristics of Children with Autism 270

Bright Start 275
Application of Bright Start to Children with Autism 283
Summary 287
References. 289

Chapter 15

EDUCATIONAL STRATEGIES IN AUTISM. 293

Sandra L. Harris

Introduction 293
The Context for Instruction. . . . . : . . . 294
Enhancing Social and Interpersonal Functioning. 295
Developing Speech and Language 299
Managing Disruptive Behavior 302
Summary 304
References. 305

Chapter 16

EDUCATIONAL APPROACHES IN PRESCHOOL: BEHAVIOR
TECHNIQUES IN A PUBLIC SCHOOL SETTING 311

Andrew S. Bondy and Lori A. Frost

Introduction 311
The Delaware Autistic Program 311
Behavior Management. 320
Communication Training 321
Approaches to Integration 326
Parent Involvement 327
Outcome Measures. 327
Conclusions 330
References. 331

INDEX 335

I

Introduction and General Issues

Introduction to Learning and Cognition in Autism

ERIC SCHOPLER and GARY B. MESIBOV

INTRODUCTION

From the perspective of social policy our understanding of autism is summarized in the *Diagnostic Statistical Manual of Mental Disorders* (DSM-III-R) (American Psychiatric Association, 1987). Some would argue that progress in research knowledge is also reflected in the several versions of DSM. These can be summarized as follows: In DSM I and II, autism was not identified as a distinct disorder (1950–1968). Both research and working hypotheses were formulated around Freudian assumptions. These have no significant empirical research support, and proved to be erroneous and ineffective in the long run. The next revision, DSM-III (1980), included autism, defined by the four criteria carried over from Kanner: (1) impaired social relationships, (2) delayed and deviant communication, (3) restricted interests, and (4) onset before 30 months. Autism was largely hypothesized to be a cognitive disorder (Rutter, 1983), with operating definitions often related to the discrepancy scores between performance and verbal subtests of the Wechsler Intelligence Scale for Children (WISC). The next revision, DSM-III-R (1987), identified 16 criteria for autism, resulting in a more

ERIC SCHOPLER and GARY B. MESIBOV • Division TEACCH, Department of Psychiatry, School of Medicine, University of North Carolina at Chapel Hill, Chapel Hill, North Carolina 27599-7180

Learning and Cognition in Autism, edited by Eric Schopler and Gary B. Mesibov. Plenum Press, New York, 1995.

complex diagnostic decision process. The greater complexity was helpful in accommodating more complex research formulations on the study of social reciprocity, new methodologies, and neurobiological correlates from neuroimaging studies.

Although changes in diagnostic systems are a useful way to understand conceptualizations of autism, none of the revisions of DSM brings us as close to the cutting edge of knowledge as the operational definitions applied in the chapters of this volume. This book offers discussions of research in autism that reformulate characteristics of the syndrome around social cognition. Although social learning and cognitive difficulties are not explicitly identified in the formal definitions of autism, these unofficially recognized dimensions are closely linked to problems of learning and educational intervention inevitably present in these youngsters.

The autism syndrome has generated intriguing research on both the similarities and the distinctions between cognitive thinking and social thinking. The two areas inextricably bound to each other through communication and language, cognitive functions that are social by definition. Throughout this volume the reader will become familiar with deficits of cognition or social understanding. For the autism disorder they provide new operating definitions usable for empirical research, and therefore offer a new handle for understanding the autism syndrome. Perhaps even more exciting is that these cognitive and social functions not only help to clarify the deficits of autism but also some of the functions spared from impairment that provide the basis for special skills and educational interventions.

COGNITIVE AND SOCIAL DEFICITS

Even the higher functioning students with autism often have problems with perceptual organization and relating stored information to incoming sensory experiences. Such organizational and sensory problems are clearly linked to other cognitive deficits. For example, attention deficits frequently manifest themselves in impaired auditory processing. The presence of such deficits may further inhibit executive function, cognitive problem solving, and verbal reasoning. Yet each of these concepts can also be studied independently.

Currently the autism features studied with greatest interest are the problems of social knowledge, comprehension, and reciprocity. When specific social rules are conveyed, many higher functioning autistic people are able to understand such information. On the other hand, when social rules have to be applied flexibly, as in complex social interactions based on a variety of signs and signals, even higher functioning people with autism are at a serious disadvantage.

Nowhere is this problem demonstrated more clearly than with the catchy phrase that autistic children lack a "theory of mind" (Baron-Cohen, Leslie, & Frith, 1985). This term refers to the basic human social ability to attribute thoughts and feelings to oneself or others, enabling us to empathize, communicate, imagine others' hopes, and also to deceive or outsmart opponents. Although the concept was first applied to autism by Baron-Cohen et al. (1985), it bears a resemblance to "listening with a third ear" or Freud's "observing ego." A crucial difference between the "theory of mind" and Freud's formulations, however, is that Baron-Cohen et al. have clearly supported their hypothesis with a heuristic experiment, one in which the subject is required to take the perspective of another. This experiment was not definitive for autism because correct responses varied with developmental age and other conditions. However, it did generate new experimental concepts and a substantial body of research knowledge. The "theory-of-mind" blindness found in autism also explains difficulties with symbolic play and problems of joint visual attention, which is the capacity to shift attention to another person's signal and to follow an abstract process flexibly. Not only were these concepts amenable to cognitive research (see Chapter 9 by Sigman, Yirmiya, & Capps; Chapter 2 by Green, Fein, Joy, & Waterhouse; and Chapter 6 by Lincoln, Allen, & Pianentini), but they also have been confirmed by neurological research in which cerebellar function is studied with event-related potential technology (Couchesne, 1991).

Social-cognitive functions are also involved in communication. Communication problems in autism include problems not only with verbal expression but also with prosody or emotional meaning, complex gestures, and reliance on word sequence rather than semantics.

STRENGTHS IN COGNITION

It is well known that several high-functioning people with autism show remarkable memory and attention for numbers, calendar dates, musical notes, and other specific facts. Likewise, the high-functioning group is able to learn rules, including a number of social rules. In Chapter 8, Grandin, who is autistic, explains this as her capacity to take and store in her memory different cassettes that she can use for playing out various social situations. Another of the cognitive strengths in autism is in visuospatial skills, with related abilities and relative strengths in visual-discrimination learning, puzzle solving, and sorting into categories. Research in classification skills is reviewed in Chapter 6, along with the possibility that autistic subjects may have some difficulty with this function.

Strength in visual-processing skill is of special interest in that it is documented with references in the chapters by Green et al. (Chap. 2), Lincoln et al. (Chap. 6), and also by introspection in Chapter 8 by Grandin. It has support in neurological reports from studies by Courchesne (1991). It is noteworthy that visuospatial processing refers to a perceptual-cognitive strength found not only in high-functioning individuals, but in the entire spectrum of autism as well. It therefore has a very special potential for contributing to educational intervention.

INTERVENTION STRATEGIES

Both the deficits and peak skills with autism in the areas of social interaction, communication, and restricted interest have been formulated into operationally defined cognitive concepts. This has produced the new empirical knowledge reviewed in the chapters in this volume and, more important, it has permitted the application of this new knowledge to intervention. Perhaps most noteworthy and generally applicable is the case of visual-processing skills. This is of special interest to us because, in the TEACCH program, visual-processing skills have been the foundation of our basic structured educational approach for more than 15 years. Visually structured teaching, discussed in Chapter 12, has been especially effective both for preventing behavior problems and for promoting independent learning and work skills. It has been useful in helping students to generalize what they learn in school to adult work settings. Visual-processing skills are also central to the picture-exchange system used in the Delaware statewide program (Chap. 15), another example of how observations of practical experience in teaching autistic children is verified by independent empirical studies.

OVERVIEW OF CHAPTERS

This volume is divided into four related parts, with chapters grouped to elucidate each area. The first part, General Issues, includes chapters concerned with general issues and concepts that recur either explicitly or indirectly throughout the book. Part II, Thinking and Learning, refers to issues of motivation and cognition, including the ability to group or categorize. Although our emphasis is on an empirical perspective, we have also included a subjective discussion of thinking in autism seen from the inside through the eyes of an engineer. Part III, Social Cognition, contains four chapters in which the authors try to distinguish cognitive functions central to social interaction from those not so involved. The lively discussions in this section have practical as well as theoretical importance. Part IV, Education and Treatment, presents state-of-the-art examples of how the cognitive impairments and strengths in autism are used in educational intervention for promoting both development and adaptation. The most far-reaching component to date appears to be the application of visual-processing strengths in autism through structured educational programs.

Chapter 2 by Green et al. leads off with a lucid overview of the cognitive deficits and strengths associated with autism, and the continuum over which they manifest themselves both behaviorally and with developmental changes. This helps to account for the heterogeneity found in autism, widely regarded as one of the most clearly defined diagnostic categories in the DSM series. It also explains the fascination and commitment to increase understanding of the autism syndrome shown by the authors of the subsequent chapters.

From his extensive contributions to the knowledge of learning disabilities, Helmer Myklebust surveys an array of learning disabilities in Chapter 3. He presents the interesting argument that because some autistic children have learning disabilities, and some children with learning disabilities have autistic characteristics, these conditions do not necessarily form a neurological continuum. Confirmation for this proposition is based on the different neurobiological loci for the problems. At the most general level, left and right brain hemispheres serve different functions, with the left mainly responsible for verbal learning and the right controlling nonverbal learning. The chapter is accordingly divided into disorders of language and nonverbal learning disabilities.

Chapter 4 by Cox and Mesibov takes an apparently opposite view, presenting the argument that autism and learning disabilities can be found on a continuum of disabilities. Although this appears to be a contradiction to the Myklebust position, it can be better understood as a difference in perspective. Cox and Mesibov make their comparisons between autism and learning disabilities based primarily on their behavioral appearance rather than on the site of neurobiological lesion. These two chapters can coexist conceptually and are best compared for their usefulness in educational interventions.

The chapters in part II deal with the issues of thinking and learning. In Chapter 5, the Koegels discuss the role of motivation. Motivation has long been recognized educationally as part and parcel of any learning enterprise. But from the traditional perspective of behavior theory, the Koegels' notions present a rather new challenge. Reinforcers are provided for a range of task-oriented behaviors or attempts to communicate rather than only for correct responses. Likewise, the goal of improving motivation leads the teacher or therapist to reevaluate cognitive obstacles in terms of environmental considerations such as using natural consequences, and interspersing maintenance or mastered tasks with new and more difficult ones.

Lincoln, Allen, and Piacentini (Chap. 6) present measures for assessing cognitive functions. They recognize that childrens' passing any item on a psychometric assessment offers a sample of their ability. However, if the children are unsuccessful, they do not necessarily lack the required skill; instead they may lack a concept of what is asked, the needed attention or motivation.

Their assessment information is clearly presented and based on a conceptualization of three interacting blocks of basic functions. The first includes arousal and attention, involving various subcortical structures such as the cerebellum and the reticular formation. The second involves impaired memory and sequential processing and possibly also the effects of subcortical dysfunction. The third block involves representational capacity, inferential ability, verbal reasoning, context recognition—all involved with impaired executive function discussed by Ozonoff in Chapter 10 and related to prefrontal lobe function.

In Chapter 8, Grandin ties together pieces of information provided in the preceding three chapters by examining introspective thinking processes in autism as inferred by her own experience and her reading of the scientific literature. This chapter reflects the remarkable intelligence recently documented by Oliver Sacks (1993) in an outstanding feature article in *The New Yorker* magazine.

The chapters in part III describe social cognition. Sigman, Yirmiya, and Capps, in Chapter 9, review their studies of cognitive functioning in autism. They examine problems in cognitive understanding of people, especially social understanding. They are also interested in the question of whether social unrelatedness in autism comes primarily from a lack of interest in other people or rather from a failure to understand them. The chapter includes thoughtful discussions of these important issues and creative research efforts to resolve critical issues.

The authors document not only how hard people with autism work at interpreting social information but also how difficult a task it is for them. They conclude that the logical understanding of social and emotional processes is very difficult for these clients. Especially surprising to the authors were the clients' severe problems with conversation. Difficulties with the cognitive components of perspective-taking activities were also unexpected and should be the subject of further exploration.

The theory-of-mind difficulties of people with autism have already been described. In Chapter 10, Happé and Frith provide a cogent description of this influential theory, describing the early experiments that identified this important concept and its implications. The inability of people with autism to take multiple perspectives and "think about thoughts" might be the most significant and handicapping of their disabilities, especially with respect to social relationships.

Readers will enjoy this firsthand account of the theory of mind. They will also admire the clever experiments that led to its formulation. The theory of mind is an important historical reason why cognitive theories in autism research are so much more prevalent today than they were in years past. This chapter explains how and why.

In Chapter 11, Ozonoff examines a slightly different aspect of cognitive functioning in autism: executive functions. Although these are related to theory-of-mind formulations, Ozonoff has identified slightly different deficits. Executive functions are behaviors thought to be mediated by the frontal lobes: planning, impulse control, inhibition of prepotent but incorrect responses, set maintenance, organized search, and flexibility of thought and action. These skills share the requirement of disengaging from the immediate environment or external context and guiding behavior instead by mental models or internal representations.

Ozonoff outlines recent studies of executive function in autism. She integrates behavioral research with neurological theorizing, arguing that prefrontal dysfunction might be a viable candidate for explaining the underlying impairment. More research is definitely needed, but this chapter sets some important directions.

In Chapter 12, Catherine Lord applies cognitive principles in her social skills training program. She provides practical guidelines for designing social experiences in schools or communities. Lord masterfully integrates cognitive theory with practical suggestions resulting in carefully planned and nicely implemented social skills training programs. Data are presented on the efficacy of this approach. Readers interested in providing supervised peer experiences for children and adolescents with autism will find many helpful suggestions from her peer-tutor program and after-school social groups.

The last part of this volume focuses on education and treatment. Schopler, Mesibov, and Hearsey describe Division TEACCH's structured teaching approach to working with students with autism. Emphasizing the development of cognitive abilities and use of visual skills, structured teaching is an innovative model for people with autism of all ages. The authors carefully present the different aspects of structured teaching with concrete and practical examples, while also highlighting the implications of this approach: It provides a way of helping students with autism to generalize their skills to community and vocational settings.

Structured teaching is an important demonstration of the efficacy of cognitive formulations. Similar to Lord, these authors demonstrate the practical application of this new direction. Researchers will find these cognitive principles provocative and practitioners will find many concrete and helpful suggestions to enhance their work.

Butera and Haywood, in Chapter 14, advocate a cognitive education program designed to help preschool-age handicapped students. They carefully review relevant cognitive principles and cleverly demonstrate how they can be of assistance. Clinical examples nicely highlight the practical application of their work in preschool settings. Professionals working with this population will find their suggestions extremely useful and relevant.

Chapter 15 by Harris is a comprehensive and effective review of educational strategies in autism. Starting with the context for instruction, she reviews critical components of educational programs including communication training, social skills training, and the management of disruptive behavior. Harris's clear and lucid style enables the reader to understand complex trends and issues in the field. The chapter ends with an excellent review of aversive techniques.

The volume ends with Bondy and Frost's description of the behavioral techniques they use in the Delaware Autistic Preschool Program. Focusing on communication, they have developed a systematic and highly effective picture-exchange communication system used with all of their students. This communication training program is effective for students with autism at all levels of functioning and offers new and helpful suggestions for professionals in the field.

Bondy and Frost also review the Delaware statewide system and how it meets a wide range of communication, educational, and behavioral needs. Approaches to parental involvement and social integration are also highlighted.

In summary, the book presents a clear, thoughtful, and comprehensive introduction to cognitive approaches to understanding and working with people with autism. After general issues are described, careful discussions of thinking and learning, social cognition, and education and treatment follow. Readers of this volume will find thorough descriptions of these techniques as well as concrete examples of their many applications.

REFERENCES

American Psychiatric Association. (1980). *Diagnostic and statistical manual of mental disorders.* (3rd ed.). Washington, DC: Author.

American Psychiatric Association. (1987). *Diagnostic and statistical manual of mental disorders.* (3rd ed., rev.). Washington, DC: Author.

Baron-Cohen, S., Leslie, A. M., & Frith, U. (1985). Does the autistic child have a "theory of mind"? *Cognition, 21,* 37–46.

Courchesne, E. (1991). Neuroanatomic imaging in autism. *Pediatrics, 85,* 751–796.

Kanner, L. (1943). Autistic disturbances of affective control *Nervous Child, 2,* 217–250.

Rutter, M. (1983). Cognitive deficits in the pathogenesis of autism. *Journal of Child Psychology and Psychiatry, 24,* 513–531.

Sacks, O. (1993, December 27). A neurologist's notebook: An anthropologist on Mars. *The New Yorker, 70,* 106–125.

Cognitive Functioning in Autism

An Overview

LEEANNE GREEN, DEBORAH FEIN, STEPHEN JOY,
and LYNN WATERHOUSE

INTRODUCTION

Autism is a syndrome that is defined primarily in behavioral terms, but is universally associated with cognitive deficits of varying degrees. Theorists over the last 30 years have argued over the primacy of cognitive versus affective and behavioral symptoms. Regardless of how this debate is ultimately resolved, an understanding of cognitive processes in autism is prerequisite to a full understanding of how the syndrome develops, and is necessary for designing effective strategies to ameliorate these cognitive deficits. In normally developing children, cognitive development proceeds in concert with affective development, within the context of social relationships. The study of cognition in autism may contribute understanding not only to children affected with this syndrome, but also to the ways in which

---

LEEANNE GREEN • Department of Psychology, University of Connecticut, Storrs, Connecticut 06268. DEBORAH FEIN • Department of Psychology, University of Connecticut, Storrs, Connecticut 06268; and Laboratory of Neuropsychology, Boston University School of Medicine, Boston, Massachusetts 02118. STEPHEN JOY • Department of Psychology, University of Connecticut, Storrs, Connecticut 06268; and Albertus Magnus College, New Haven, Connecticut 06511. LYNN WATERHOUSE • Trenton State College, Ewing Township, New Jersey 08625-0550.

Learning and Cognition in Autism, edited by Eric Schopler and Gary B. Mesibov. Plenum Press, New York, 1995.

skills are generally performed well by the autistic subject (Rumsey & Hamburger, 1988). A recent large-scale study of autistic, developmental language disordered and mentally retarded children (Rapin, in press) confirmed the sparing of visuospatial functions and quantitative concepts in nonretarded autistic children. Furthermore, quantitative skills loaded with visuospatial skills on factor analyses for all groups, suggesting similar relationships among nonverbal cognitive abilities for autistic and nonautistic children.

Within the verbal domain covered by the WISC, the Digit Span subtest, which relies on short-term memory, produces relatively higher scores than other verbal subtests (Sigman, Ungerer, Mundy, & Sherman, 1987). Not surprisingly, the Comprehension subtest, which assesses social knowledge and open-ended verbal expression, typically poses the greatest difficulty for autistic children. The Comprehension, Similarities, and Vocabulary subtests comprise areas of relative weakness for autistic children, even in comparison to children with developmental-receptive language disorder, which suggests that the cognitive deficits of autism cannot be accounted for solely by language impairment, at least language impairment of the same type as that characterizing language-disordered children (Bartak, Rutter, & Cox, 1975). Intellectual level as well as profile of abilities may be sustained across the lifespan, since IQ in autistic children has been found to be relatively stable over time (Freeman et al., 1991).

Rutter (1983) has suggested that the typical intellectual profile of autistic children reflects a basic cognitive deficit in the sequencing and abstraction of information. Sequential processing has been demonstrated to be relatively deficient in autistic children, in comparison to their simultaneous-processing abilities, as assessed by the Kaufman Assessment Battery for Children and selected WISC subtests (Allen, Lincoln, & Kaufman, 1991). Nonretarded autistic children have been found to do well with the rule-learning aspects of abstraction, but have significant difficulty with more complex processes, such as those involving reasoning (Minshew, Goldstein, Muenz, & Payton, 1992).

Of course, not all autistic individuals are mentally retarded, and even some of those who are retarded display exceptional abilities in certain areas of functioning, especially rote memory, calendar calculations, mathematical calculations, music, and art (Rimland & Fein, 1988; Waterhouse, 1988). Studying nonretarded autistic individuals offers the opportunity for researchers to delineate features and possible etiological factors that are unique to autism and not the result of more general cognitive impairment. Neuropsychological testing in autistic individuals of average and above-average intellect has revealed areas of relative strength in attention, associative memory, and the rule-learning aspects of abstraction, but deficits in tasks of abstraction involving cognitive flexibility, verbal reasoning, complex memory, and complex language (Minshew et al., 1992). Regardless of intellectual level, autistic individuals reveal deficits in conceptual problem solving, metarepresentational ability, pragmatic aspects of communication, joint attention, symbolic play, and recognition of emotions (Yirmiya & Sigman, 1991). The few studies that have examined individual differences in profiles or single abilities (Fein, Waterhouse, Lucci, & Snyder, 1985; Prior, Dahlstrom, & Squires, 1990) found that somewhere between one-half to four-fifths of samples of autistic children fit the "typical" profile or deficit. It must be concluded, therefore, that within the spectrum of children with autistic disorders, there is great heterogeneity, both cognitively and behaviorally.

EARLY COGNITIVE DEVELOPMENT

Some investigators have applied the Piagetian framework to the understanding of early cognitive development within autism (Curcio, 1978; Serafica, 1971). The attainment of object permanence (Piaget, 1952) is necessary for the child's internal representation of mother, which must underlie the continuing development of social relationships. Autistic children generally develop adequate Piagetian sensorimotor performance for the overall mental-age level (Sigman et al., 1987), and display adequate knowledge of object permanence and object use (Curcio, 1978; Serafica, 1971; Sigman & Ungerer, 1981). However, autistic children show a specific deficit in their use of objects to represent another object, as in symbolic play (Sigman & Ungerer, 1984; Ungerer & Sigman, 1981). As suggested by Sigman and colleagues (1987), the development of symbolic use of objects within play depends on social involvement, and it is within this realm of processes dependent on social experience that autistic children are most severely impaired.

PERCEPTION AND ATTENTION

Autistic children's attention to features of the environment has been variously described as oblivious (Wing, 1978) or as overfocused or overselective (Kinsbourne, 1989). Their abnormal responses to sensory stimuli are well documented and have been characterized by avoidance of stimuli and by attention to unusual stimulus features (DeMyer, 1976; Goldfarb, 1961; Hermelin & O'Connor, 1970; Ornitz, 1974; Rimland, 1964; Rutter, 1966). These observations have generated much speculation regarding autistic children's basic perceptual abilities and attentional processes.

It has been suggested that these apparent abnormalities in responses to stimuli are not adequately explained by hypotheses of dysfunction of lower level sensory–perceptual processes, but rather that the data seem to support the hypothesis of impairment at higher levels of processing (Frith & Baron-Cohen, 1987; Hermelin & O'Connor, 1970). A recent neuropsychological study of high-functioning autistic individuals revealed normal performance on standardized tests of attention but deficits in higher level processes such as reasoning, which led the authors to conclude that autism involves an abnormality in complex-information processing, and not a fundamental deficit in attention or information acquisition (Minshew et al., 1992).

Experimental studies show that autistic children have abnormal visual fixation patterns (O'Connor & Hermelin, 1967) and typically fail to display normal ear advantage in dichotic listening tasks (Prior & Bradshaw, 1979). In particular, autistic children's attention has been characterized as overselective, such that only one of several given cues, or only part of a given cue, is attended and responded to (Fein, Tinder, & Waterhouse, 1979; Lovaas, Schreibman, Koegel, & Rehm, 1971). The tendency for overselective attention *per se* is not specific to autism; it has also been demonstrated in nonautistic mentally retarded children (Anderson & Rincover, 1982; Koegel & Lovaas, 1978). Frith and Baron-Cohen (1987) have suggested that autistic children may show a specific kind of overselective attention, namely, impairment of attention to stimulus features which, for other children, are usually salient or meaningful. In support of this notion, autistic children show unusually good performance on the Embedded Figures test; their selection of different, less typically salient and meaningful features of the patterns presumably enables them to override the gestalt (Frith & Baron-Cohen, 1987).

Autistic children are able to learn simple discriminations of stimulus features such as line position, length, and dimensionality; however, their performance is greatly impaired when attempting discriminations of stimuli that are symbolic, and therefore more "meaningful" (Hermelin & O'Connor, 1970; Maltz, 1981; Prior, 1979). Other studies show that autistic children selectively attend to stimulus features which are less typically salient or characteristically social than those attended to by nonautistic children. (Fein et al., 1979; Frith & Baron-Cohen, 1987; Prior, 1979; Schwartz, 1981; Waterhouse & Fein, 1982).

Other theories to explain the overselectivity have been advanced by Kinsbourne (1989) and Dawson and Lewy (1989), who suggested that narrowed attentional focus and stimulus overselectivity result from overactivation of brainstem mechanisms of arousal. From this perspective, stereotypies and avoidance of social stimuli are understood as adaptive mechanisms used by the autistic child for purposes of de-arousal.

Courchesne et al. (1994) have proposed that disruption of neocerebellar coordination of the rapid shifting of selective attention causes stimulus overselectivity and other autistic features. Courchesne & colleagues (Courchesne et al., 1994; Townsend, Courchesne, & Egaas, 1992) have demonstrated impairments in the ability to shift attention between modalities, and selective impairment in shifting spatial attention on invalidly cued trials. Wainwright-Sharp and Bryson (1993) confirmed that autistic children have problems disengaging and shifting within the visual modality. Other attention mechanisms may be less disturbed: Garretson, Fein, and Waterhouse (1990) showed that autistic children's capacity for sustained attention is consonant with their mental age, but only when they are given tangible incentives. Garretson (1985) also found that self-stimulation (rhythmic, repetitive behavior) was associated with lapses in attention for the normal children, but not for the autistic children. In fact, the autistic children who showed such repetitive behavior performed better on the sustained-attention task than those who did not. These findings may suggest that the ability to sustain attention to externally imposed tasks can be normalized at least for a short time with adequate incentives, and that forcing the children to suppress noninterfering self-stimulatory behaviors may be counterproductive.

Abnormalities in the functional, neurophysiological processes of attention in autistic individuals have frequently been studied through examination of middle to longer latency components of the event-related potential (ERP). The various components are believed to correspond to particular attentional processes, specifically, the detection and classification of stimuli, orientation to novel stimuli, self-generated attention, selective attention, and the maintenance and shifting of attention. Studies have suggested that autistic individuals have abnormalities in all of these processes (Ciesielski, Courchesne, & Elamasian, 1990; Courchesne, Lincoln, Kilman, & Galambos, 1985; Courchesne et al., 1989; Courchesne et al., 1994; Dawson, Finley, Phillips, Galpert, and Lewy, 1988; Novick, Vaughn, Kurtzberg, & Simon, 1980). In general, findings suggest that autistic children are not at all oblivious to their environment. They are able to attend to stimuli adequately for successful performance on some tasks; however, they may possess abnormal mechanisms for selecting and shifting objects of focal attention.

EXECUTIVE FUNCTION

Autism has also been hypothesized to be a syndrome of dysfunction of higher level executive functions, which are regulated by prefrontal cortex (Damasio & Maurer, 1978; Ozonoff, Pennington, & Rogers, 1991). These functions include the formation of abstract concepts and problem-solving strategies, subordination of individual cognitive processes to a goal, self-monitoring and self-correction, maintenance of reinforced response strategies and switching of unreinforced strategies, and inhibition of impulsive responses. Deficits in these functions have been tested in autistic subjects through the use of neuropsychological instruments that are sensitive to frontal damage, including the Wisconsin Card Sorting Test, Rey–Osterrieth Complex Figure, the Trail-Making Test, and the Tower of Hanoi. Autistic individuals, including high-functioning autistic adults, appear to show significant impairment on these tasks, and are especially prone to perseverative errors (Ozonoff et al., 1991; Prior et al., 1990; Rumsey & Hamburger, 1988; Szatmari, Bartolucci, Bremner, Bond, & Rich, 1989). Ozonoff and colleagues (1991) have proposed that executive functions are selectively impaired in autistic individuals, as their presentation in some respects is like that of patients with damage to prefrontal cortex, particularly dorsolateral and orbitofrontal lesions. Several features of autism, such as response perseveration, insistence on sameness, stereotypies, restricted range of interests, and the failure to plan, self-monitor and inhibit inappropriate responses, appear to resemble symptoms observed in frontal patients. It has been argued by Ozonoff and others that executive system/frontal lobe dysfunction may cause impairment in second-order cognitive representation, leading to specific social-cognitive deficits, such as impaired theory of mind (to be discussed). A recent paper by Bishop (1993) reviewed executive-system findings in autism, and analyzed the adequacy of arguments for a causal role of executive-system deficit in the development of autistic cognitive and behavioral impairment. Bishop concluded that, although executive-system impairment has been demonstrated in autism, it probably is insufficient to account for documented deficits in social cognition, because such deficits are not shown by other clinical groups with impaired executive system functions, and because autistic children fail to show comparable difficulty when second-order representations do not involve social material.

LANGUAGE

Perhaps the most distinctive cognitive feature of autistic disorder is that of language impairment. It is also undoubtedly the one area of cognitive dysfunction that best exemplifies the necessary, dynamic interdependence between social and cognitive development. Language deficits in autistic children were traditionally studied with regard to unusual features, such as echolalia. Current research focuses on the development of crucial aspects of language, including phonology, grammatical morphology, syntax, semantics, and pragmatics.

Despite delayed onset of speech, verbal autistic children show a normal order of acquisition of speech sounds and typical phonological errors. However, they do appear to depend on relatively immature phonologic processes, and tend to display mastery of speech–sound systems at late stages of language development (Bartak et al., 1975; Bartolucci & Pierce, 1977; Bartolucci, Pierce, Streiner, & Eppel, 1976; Paul, 1987; Tager-Flusberg, 1981). Acquisition of morphemes is also normal with regard to order, but is delayed in development in autism (Waterhouse and Fein, 1982). Autistic children also tend to display less frequent usage of varied morphemes, that is, they seem to use the same morphemes repeatedly (Tager-Flusberg, 1989), which has been interpreted as a deficit in semantic usage of grammar in connected language (Paul, 1987; Tager-Flusberg, 1989; Waterhouse & Fein, 1982).

Verbal autistic children have also been found to possess fairly well-developed syntactic structures in spontaneous language, despite their tendency for echolalia. Length and complexity of sentences may be comparable to those of children of similar cognitive and verbal developmental level, and are not marked by abnormal grammatical constructions (Bartolucci & Pierce, 1977; Cantwell, Baker, & Rutter; 1978; Paul, 1987; Tager-Flusberg, 1981, 1985b; Waterhouse & Fein, 1982). They do appear to rely on perseveration of grammatical structures, which Waterhouse and Fein (1982) have suggested to be alternatives to repair and recoding strategies whenever a particular structure is not readily available to the child. Results suggest that while acquisition of structures is relatively normal, autistic children fail to use the structures and may instead rely on echolalia.

Language comprehension appears to be greatly impaired relative to expression (Rapin, in press; Waterhouse & Fein, 1982). As distinct from children with developmental-receptive language disorder, autistic children may tend to emphasize syntax rather than semantic content in their comprehension of connected language, for example, by relying on interpretation of word order without regard for semantic relations (Paul, Fischer, & Cohen, 1988). Lexical development and use of different word classes by autistic children are comparable to those of children of similar verbal and intellectual ability; however, their vocabulary within each word class is relatively diminished (Cantwell et al., 1978; Lord, 1985; Prior & Hall, 1979; Tager-Flusberg, 1981). Waterhouse and Fein (1982) have suggested that autistic children are not utilizing their available vocabulary as readily as children of similar verbal and intellectual level. While deficits in relational meaning in autistic children have been thought by some researchers to reflect a basic cognitive deficit in semantics (Fay & Schuler, 1980; Hermelin & O'Connor, 1970; Menyuk, 1978; Schwartz, 1981; Simmons & Baltaxe, 1975), others have found evidence that may suggest it is the functional use of acquired conceptual knowledge, and not the understanding of concepts that is impaired (Rapin, in press; Tager-Flusberg, 1985a, 1985b, 1989). These deficits may be sociolinguistic in nature, and reflective of pragmatic impairment (Rapin, in press).

Socially functional, or pragmatic, language use and communicative ability are by far the most impaired aspects of language in autism, and are reported to be strong differentiators between autistic and other groups of children (Rapin, in press). Although autistic children are able to produce some degree of functional language (Prizant, 1983; Prizant & Duchan, 1981; Prizant & Rydell, 1984; Wetherby, 1986; Wetherby & Prizant, 1985; Wetherby & Prutting, 1984), they are unable to use it appropriately for the sharing or requesting of information (Paul, 1987). Conversational skills, including interaction with listeners, initiation of topics (Baltaxe, 1977), turn taking, and use of referents (Fay & Schuler, 1980), are generally absent or limited in autistic children.

In a recent large-scale study (Rapin, in press), autistic children with nonverbal IQs in the normal range were found to exhibit a very uneven pattern of language skills. They showed particular deficits in functions requiring comprehension, open-ended expression of ideas, verbal reasoning and rapid word retrieval, and relative strengths in written language and the labeling of visual stimuli. While functional use of receptive language was found to be consistent with scores for formal measures of receptive language, functional use of expressive language was worse than almost all expressive test scores.

In summary, autistic children display normal, but delayed, acquisition of grammatical morphology and syntax, and relative strength in acquiring grapheme–phoneme correspondence for writing and the decoding aspect of reading. They tend to fail to use meaning to guide their comprehension and their expression of acquired morphemes, grammatical structures or vocabulary. Even in autistic children with fairly adequate language development, interactive communication, conversational behavior, and speech prosody are deficient (Paul, 1987). The potential impact of fundamental deficits in social capacity on cognitive functions is perhaps nowhere better demonstrated than in the linguistic profile of the autistic child.

MEMORY

Several authors have proposed that autism is a syndrome of hippocampal dysfunction, with memory particularly affected (Boucher & Warrington, 1976; DeLong, 1992). Early studies of this hypothesis found that only a subset of autistic individuals displayed memory deficits (Boucher & Warrington, 1976). The relative sparing of cued over free recall found by Boucher & Warrington has not been replicated by a recent investigation (Minshew & Goldstein, 1993). Like the amnesic patient, the autistic individual has relatively normal short-term and procedural memory. Generally, rote learning (e.g., of word pairs), is not substantially impaired (Boucher & Warrington, 1976; Minshew & Goldstein, 1993; Prior, 1979; Sigman et al. 1987). However, memory for verbal material is, in general, selectively deficient relative to recall of nonverbal material (Fama, 1992; Prior & Chen, 1976). Incidental memory for faces has also been found to be deficient in autism, relative to memory for objects (Hauck, 1992).

Memory deficits, as measured by many of these studies, are obviously closely related to language ability, especially its semantic aspects. The use of meaning in memory might be expected to be particularly deficient in autism. Supporting this, autistic children with normal nonverbal IQs, compared to language-disordered children, showed increasing impairment as material became more and more meaningful (Digit Span to Sentence Memory to Story Memory) (Rapin, in press). Other recent findings, however, suggested that semantic encoding of verbal material by high-functioning autistic adults is unimpaired (Minshew & Goldstein, 1993); yet, as was found by Tager-Flusberg (1992), independent use of semantic strategies for recall is deficient.

SOCIAL COGNITION

Many processes presumed to be purely cognitive are part of a larger dynamic system of affective and affiliative processes, for example, the emotional component of encoding of memories, and the involvement of social interaction in the development of language. Certain aspects of cognition may be seen as inherently social, such as the comprehension of affective and social cues. Three main areas of study have contributed to the understanding of social cognition in autism: (a) the awareness and comprehension of mental representations of others; (b) the recognition of human features and behavior; and (c) the processing of affective stimuli.

Many autistic individuals appear to lack the ability to attribute beliefs and other mental states to people, and as such have been said to lack a theory of mind (Baron-Cohen, 1988, 1989a, 1989b; Baron-Cohen, Leslie, & Frith, 1985; Leslie & Frith, 1988; see Chap. 10 in this volume for a more complete discussion). A theory of mind permits one to understand that others may possess their own unique perspectives, knowledge, feelings, and perhaps even false beliefs. Compared to normal and mentally retarded children who are 3 years of age or older, autistic children have difficulty with tests of this capacity (Baron-Cohen, 1990). Early manifestations of the child's theory of mind in normal development include pretend play and joint visual attention and gesturing both of which are significantly disrupted in autistic children (Leslie & Happé, 1975; Baron-Cohen, 1990; Leslie, 1987). Autistic children typically show a specific deficit in joint attention, even in early stages before the acquisition of language, which could be interpreted as a deficit in intersubjectivity (Rogers & Pennington, 1991), the inability to share emotional experience through gestural communication (Curcio, 1978; Wetherby & Prutting, 1984), or the failure to understand the presence of another's frame of reference (Baron-Cohen, 1990). Autistic children also fail to engage in symbolic play, reflecting either disruption of social relations or the inability to make symbolic abstractions (Sigman & Ungerer, 1984). Other functions that are believed to require theory of mind are empathy and pragmatic communication, both of which are necessary for the development of successful social relations, and are severely impaired in autism. As such, Baron-Cohen and colleagues (Baron-Cohen, 1990; Leslie & Frith, 1988) have proposed that the failure to develop second-order mental representations is the single cognitive deficit that is responsible for the primary symptoms of autism. The theory-of-mind hypothesis has been specifically criticized for failure to account for autistic social deficits that arise in infants prior to hypothesized emergence of theory of mind, and lack of universality among autistic social deficits presumed to be dependent upon absence of theory of mind (Klin, Volkmar, & Sparrow, 1992). Theory of mind is a phenomenon one would certainly describe as a social aspect of cognition; the possibility remains that the autistic child's absence of theory of mind is dependent upon an earlier failure to attend to the social environment. Researchers are beginning to try and separate social from nonsocial aspects of metarepresentation: they have found autistic children to be consistently more impaired in comprehending false beliefs than false maps (Leslie & Thaiss, 1992), false photographs (Leekam & Perner, 1991) or false drawings (Charman & Baron-Cohen, 1992). This result may support the importance of the social content rather than the cognitive demands of metarepresentation as crucial to the autistic deficit.

In recognition of the role of affect in the development of social behaviors, Fein and colleagues (Fein, Pennington, Markowitz, Braverman, & Waterhouse, 1986; Waterhouse & Fein, 1989) and Hobson (1990a, 1990b) have proposed that failure of basic internal socioaffective processes is primary in the etiology of autistic social-cognitive, and thus social-behavioral deficits.

Studies of social cognition have revealed that autistic children often rely on superficial aspects of appearances rather than facial characteristics when classifying or describing pictures of people, and have difficulty in recognizing typical age or sex-appropriate behaviors and contexts (Hobson, 1987). These deficits suggest a lack of awareness of social environment and failure to use or comprehend socially salient stimuli, at least with regard to features of other individuals.

Autistic individuals appear also to have difficulty with the processing of affective stimuli. Hobson and colleagues (Hobson, 1986a, 1986b; Hobson & Lee, 1989; Hobson, Ouston, & Lee, 1988a, 1988b, 1989) have found the verbal and nonverbal communicative cues of autistic children to suggest that they are deficient in comprehending affect. Autistic children are also deficient in matching emotions to pictured contexts (Fein, Lucci, Braverman, & Waterhouse, 1992; Hobson, 1986a), in differentiating facial emotional expressions (Sigman et al., 1987) and in matching pictured facial emotional expressions to situations (Fein et al., 1992; MacDonald et al., 1989), gestures, and vocalizations (Sigman et al., 1987). Compared to children of similar nonverbal ability, autistic children have difficulty matching pictured affects and comprehending affect terms (Braverman, Fein, Lucci, & Waterhouse, 1989; Ozonoff et al., 1990). However, autistic and non-autistic children of similar verbal ability were found to display the same level of impairment in many of these affect-processing tasks, suggesting that these features may not be uniquely characteristic of autism or may be impaired only to the same degree as language (Braverman, Fein, Lucci, & Waterhouse, 1989; Ozonoff, Pennington, Rogers, 1990; Prior, Dahlstrom, & Squires, 1990).

In summary it appears that early cognitive abilities involving comprehension and processing of affective and social stimuli are disrupted in autism. The degree of deficit, however, is still unclear. The findings of Ozonoff and colleagues (1990), Prior and colleagues (1990), and Fein, Lucci, Braverman and Waterhouse (1992) suggest that these deficits are milder than may have been thought. Furthermore, a question still remains as to whether these deficits originate from impairments in affective responsivity or from a cognitive failure to handle certain kinds of information.

SUMMARY AND CONCLUSIONS

Studies of cognition have revealed substantial heterogeneity within the autistic population. It may be that there are specific cognitive or behavioral "types" of children (e.g., Wing's [Wing & Attwood, 1987] three types of autism, classified according to social behavior) that correspond to specific biological etiologies (Gillberg, 1992), or it may be that the children vary along specifiable dimensions without falling into "types." Patterns of individual cognitive deficits and variability along cognitive dimensions need to be identified and related to behavioral patterns and, ultimately, to biological markers.

Despite this heterogeneity, certain patterns of cognitive strength and weakness do emerge as characteristic of a majority of autistic children. Autistic children have specific impairments in the selectivity and shifting of attention, executive functioning, abstraction of information and reasoning, language (particularly the social aspects), and social cognition. Relative preservation of function is present in visuospatial and sensorimotor abilities, as well as in the ability to sustain attention. Within the language domain, there is relative preservation of grammar and phonology, and of the acquisition of written language.

Here, we are reminded of the importance of distinguishing between deficits that are specific to autism and those that are the product of general cognitive delay. In addition, we must distinguish between deficits that are epiphenomenal consequences of autistic impairment and those that are central to autism.

Examination of the aspects of cognition that tend to be selectively disrupted in the majority of autistic children suggests that many of their most prominent cognitive impairments can be directly related to their social deficits. The areas of relative strength for autistic individuals, namely visuospatial and sensorimotor abilities, represent what are probably the least socially dependent aspects of cognition. Abilities related to communication, social cognition, and play obviously must develop in a social context. Likewise, the concept of the mind of oneself or another must develop within the context of social relationships.

These issues have highlighted a fundamental debate regarding the relative importance and interrelationships of affect, cognition, and the social context in determining psychological phenomena. Cognition and affect should be understood as developing interdependently, both at the neural and the psychological level, as symptoms that are inextricably woven within our development as fundamentally social beings. Perhaps the appropriate question is not whether socioaffective mechanisms filter cognitive abilities or whether cognition determines socioaffective functioning, but at what point in their dynamic interdevelopment the deficit arises, and how the mutual disruption proceeds as the child develops.

ACKNOWLEDGMENTS

The writing of this chapter was supported in part by National Institute of Neurological Disorders and Strokes 20489 to Autism and Language Disorders Collaborative Project Preschool Study Group, of which authors Fein and Waterhouse are members.

REFERENCES

Allen, M. H., Lincoln, A. J., & Kaufman, A. S. (1991). Sequential and simultaneous processing abilities of high-functioning autistic and language-impaired children. *Journal of Autism and Developmental Disorders, 21,* 483–502.

Anderson, N. B., & Rincover, A. (1982). The generality of overselectivity in developmentally disabled children. *Journal of Experimental Child Psychology, 34,* 217–230.

Baltaxe, C. A. M. (1977). Pragmatic deficits in the language of autistic adolescents. *Journal of Pediatric Psychology, 2,* 176–180.

Baron-Cohen, S. (1988). Social and pragmatic deficits in autism: Cognitive or affective? *Journal of Autism and Developmental Disorders, 18,* 379–402.

Baron-Cohen, S. (1989a). Are autistic children "behaviorists"? An examination of their mental–physical and appearance–reality distinctions. *Journal of Autism and Developmental Disorders, 19,* 579–600.

Baron-Cohen, S. (1989b). The autistic child's "theory of mind": A case of specific developmental delay. *Journal of Child Psychology and Psychiatry, 30,* 285–297.

Baron-Cohen, S. (1990). Autism: A specific cognitive disorder of "mind-blindness." *International Journal of Psychiatry, 2,* 81–90.

Baron-Cohen, S., Leslie, A., & Frith, U. (1985). Does the autistic child have a "theory of mind"? *Cognition, 21,* 37–46.

Bartak, L., Rutter, M., & Cox, A. (1975). Comparative study of infantile autism and specific developmental receptive language disorder: I. The children. *British Journal of Psychiatry, 126,* 127–145.

Bartolucci, G., & Pierce, S. J. (1977). A preliminary comparison of phonological development of autistic, normal, and mentally retarded children. *British Journal of Disorders of Communication, 12,* 134–147.

Bartolucci, G., Pierce, S. J., Streiner, D., & Eppel, P. (1976). Phonological investigation of verbal autistic and mentally retarded subjects. *Journal of Autism and Childhood Schizophrenia, 6,* 303–316.

Bishop, D. V. M. (1993). Annotation: Autism, executive functions and theory of mind: A neuropsychological perspective. *Journal of Child Psychology and Psychiatry, 34,* 279–293.

Boucher, J., & Warrington, E. (1976). Memory deficits in early infantile autism: Some similarities to the amnesic syndrome. *British Journal of Psychology, 67,* 73–87.

Braverman, M., Fein, D., Lucci, D., & Waterhouse, L. (1989). Affect comprehension in children with pervasive developmental disorders. *Journal of Autism and Developmental Disorders, 19,* 301–315.

Cantwell, D. P., Baker, L., & Rutter, M. (1978). A comparative study of infantile autism and specific developmental receptive language disorder: IV. Analysis of syntax and language function. *Journal of Child Psychology and Psychiatry, 19,* 351–362.

Charman, T., & Baron-Cohen, S. (1992). Understanding drawings and beliefs: A further test of the metarepresentation theory of autism: A research note. *Journal of Child Psychology and Psychiatry and Allied Disciplines, 33,* 1105–1112.

Cieselski, K. T., Courchesne, E., & Elmasian, R. (1990). Effects of focused selective attention tasks on event-related potentials in autistic and normal individuals *Electroencephalography and Clinical Neurophysiology, 7,* 207–220.

Courchesne, E. (1989). Neuroanatomical systems involved in infantile autism. In G. Dawson (Ed.), *Autism: New perspectives on diagnosis, nature and treatment* (pp. 119–143). New York: Guilford.

Courchesne, E., Lincoln, A. J., Kilman, B. A., & Galambos, R. (1985). Event-related brain potentials of the processing of novel visual and auditory information in autism. *Journal of Autism and Development Disorders, 15,* 55–76.

Courchesne, E., Lincoln, A. J., Yeung-Courchesne, R., Elmasian, R., & Grillon, C. (1989). Pathophysiologic findings in nonretarded autism and receptive developmental language disorder. *Journal of Autism and Developmental Disorders, 19,* 1–18.

Courchesne, E., Townsend, J. P., Akshoomoff, N. A., Yeung-Courchesne, R., Press, G. A., Murakami, J. W., Lincoln, A. J., James, H. E., Saitoh, O., Egaas, B., Haas, R. H., & Schreibman, L. (1994). A new finding: Impairment in shifting attention in autistic and cerebellar patients. In S. H. Broman & J. Grafman (Eds.), *Atypical deficits in developmental disorders: Implication for brain function* (pp. 101–137). Hillsdale, NJ: Lawrence Erlbaum Associates.

Curcio, F. (1978). Sensorimotor functioning and communication of mute autistic children. *Journal of Autism and Childhood Schizophrenia, 8,* 281–292.

Damasio, A., & Maurer, R. (1978). A neurological model for childhood autism. *Archives of Neurology, 35,* 777–786.

Dawson, G., Finley, C., Phillips, S., Galpert, L., & Lewy, A. (1988). Reduced P3 amplitude of the event-related brain potential: Its relationship to language ability in autism. *Journal of Autism and Developmental Disorders, 18,* 493–504.

Dawson, G., & Lewy, A. (1989). Arousal, attention and the socioemotional impairments of individuals with autism. In G. Dawson (Ed.), *Autism: Nature, diagnosis and treatment* (pp. 49–74). New York: Guilford.

DeLong, G. R. (1992). Autism, amnesia, hippocampus, and learning. *Neuroscience and Biobehavioral Reviews, 16,* 63–70.

DeMyer, M. K. (1976). Motor, perceptual-motor, and intellectual disabilities of autistic children. In L. Wing (Ed.), *Early Childhood Autism* (pp. 169–193). Oxford: Pergamon.

Fama, R., Fein, D., & Waterhouse, L. (1992, February). *Verbal and nonverbal short-term memory in autistic children.* Paper presented at International Neuropsychological Society, San Diego, CA.

Fay, W., & Schuler, A. L. (1980). *Emerging language in autistic children.* Baltimore: University Park Press.

Fein, D., Lucci, D., Braverman, M., & Waterhouse, L. (1992). Affect comprehension in children with pervasive developmental disorders. *Journal of Autism and Developmental Disorders, 19,* 301–315.

Fein, D., Pennington, B., Markowitz, P., Braverman, M., & Waterhouse, L. (1986). Toward a neuropsychological model of infantile autism: Are the social deficits primary? *Journal of the American Academy of Child Psychiatry, 25,* 198–212.

Fein, D., Tinder, P., & Waterhouse, L. (1979). Stimulus generalization in autistic and normal children. *Journal of Child Psychology and Child Psychiatry, 20,* 325–335.

Freeman, B., Rahbar, B., Ritvo, E., Bice, T., Yokota, A., & Ritvo, R. (1991). The stability of cognitive and behavioral parameters in autism: A twelve-year prospective study. *Journal of the American Academy of Child and Adolescent Psychiatry, 30,* 479–482.

Frith, U., & Baron-Cohen, S. (1987). Perception in autistic children. In D. J. Cohen & A. M. Donnellan (Eds.), *Handbook of autism and pervasive developmental disorders* (pp. 85–102). New York: Wiley.

Garretson, H. (1985). *Sustained attention in infantile autism.* Unpublished doctoral dissertation, Boston University, Boston, MA.

Garretson, H., Fein, D., & Waterhouse, L. (1990). Sustained attention in autistic children. Journal of Autism and Developmental Disorders, 20, 101–114.

Gillberg, C. (1992). Subgroups in autism: Are there behavioural phenotypes typical of underlying medical conditions? Journal of Intellectual Disability Research, 36, 201–214.

Goldfarb, W. (1961). Childhood schizophrenia. Cambridge, MA: Harvard University Press.

Hauck, M. (1992). Social memory in infantile autism. Unpublished master's thesis, University of Connecticut, Storrs, CT.

Hermelin, B., & O'Connor, N. (1970). Psychological experiments with autistic children. Oxford: Pergamon.

Hobson, R. P. (1986a). The autistic child's appraisal of expressions of emotion. Journal of Child Psychology and Psychiatry, 27, 321–342.

Hobson, R. P. (1986b). The autistic child's appraisal of expressions of emotion: A further study. Journal of Child Psychology and Psychiatry, 27, 671–680.

Hobson, R. P. (1987). The autistic child's recognition of age- and sex-related characteristics of people. Journal of Autism and Developmental Disorders, 17, 63–79.

Hobson, R. P. (1990a). On acquiring knowledge about people and the capacity to pretend: Response to Leslie (1987). Psychological Review, 97, 114–121.

Hobson, R. P. (1990b). Concerning knowledge of mental states. British Journal of Medical Psychology, 63, 199–213.

Hobson, R. P., & Lee, A. (1989). Emotion-related and abstract concepts in autistic people: Evidence from the British Picture Vocabulary Scale. Journal of Autism and Developmental Disorders, 19, 601–624.

Hobson, R. P., Ouston, J., & Lee, A. (1988a). What's in a face? The case of autism. British Journal of Psychology, 79, 441–453.

Hobson, R. P., Ouston, J., & Lee, A. (1988b). Emotion recognition in autism: Coordinating faces and voices. Psychological Medicine, 18, 911–923.

Hobson, R. P., Ouston, J., & Lee, A. (1989). Naming emotion in faces and voices: Abilities and disabilities in autism and mental retardation. British Journal of Developmental Psychology, 7, 237–250.

Hutt, S., Hutt, C., Lee, D., & Ounsted, D. (1965). A behavioral and electroencephalographic study of autistic children. Journal of Psychiatric Research, 3, 181–197.

Kinsbourne, M. (1989). Cerebral–brainstem relations in infantile autism. In G. Dawson (Ed.), Autism: Nature, diagnosis and treatment. New York: Guilford.

Klin, A., Volkmar, F., & Sparrow, S. (1992). Autistic social dysfunction: Some limitations of the theory of mind hypothesis. Journal of Child Psychology and Psychiatry, 33, 861–876.

Koegel, R., & Lovaas, O. I. (1978). Comments on autism and stimulus overselectivity. Journal of Abnormal Psychology, 87, 563–565.

Leekam, S. R., & Perner, J. (1991). Does the autistic child have a metarepresentational deficit? Cognition, 40, 203–218.

Leslie, A. (1987). Pretense and representation: The origins of "theory of mind." Psychological Review, 94, 412–426.

Leslie, A., & Frith, U. (1988). Autistic childrens understanding of seeing, knowing, and believing. British Journal of Developmental Psychology, 6, 315–324.

Leslie, A., & Happé, F. (1989). Autism and ostensive communication: The relevance of metarepresentation. Development and Psychopathology, 1, 205–212.

Leslie, A., & Thaiss, L. (1992). Domain specificity in conceptual development: Neuropsychological evidence from autism. Cognition, 43, 225–251.

Lincoln A., Courchesne, E., Kilman, B., & Elmasian, R. (1988). A study of intellectual abilities in high-functioning people with autism. Journal of Autism and Developmental Disorders, 18, 505–524.

Lord, C. (1985). Autism and the comprehension of language. In E. Schopler & G. Mesibov (Eds.), *Communication Problems in Autism* (pp. 257–281). New York: Plenum Press.

Lovaas, O. I., Schreibman, L., Koegel, R., & Rehm, R. (1971). Selective responding by autistic children to multiple sensory input. *Journal of Abnormal Psychology, 77,* 211–222.

Maltz, A. (1981). Comparison of cognitive deficits among autistic and retarded children on the Arthur Adaptation of the Leiter International Performance Scales. *Journal of Autism and Developmental Disorders, 11,* 413–426.

MacDonald, H., Rutter, M., Howlin, P., Rios, P., Conteur, A. L., Evered, L., & Folstein, S. (1989). Recognition and expression of emotional cues by autistic and normal adults. *Journal of Child Psychology and Psychiatry, 30,* 865–877.

Menyuk, P. (1978). Language: What's wrong and why. In M. Rutter & E. Schopler (Eds.), *Autism: A reappraisal of concepts and treatment* (pp. 105–116). New York: Plenum Press.

Minshew, N., & Goldstein, G. (1993). Is autism an amnesic disorder? Evidence from the California Verbal Learning Test. *Neuropsychology, 7,* 209–216.

Minshew, N. J., Goldstein, G., Muenz, L. R., & Payton, J. B. (1992). Neuropsychological functioning of nonmentally retarded autistic individuals. *Journal of Clinical and Experimental Neuropsychology, 14,* 749–761.

Novick, B., Vaughn, H. G., Kurtzberg, D., & Simon, R. (1980). An electrophysiologic indication of auditory processing defects in autism. *Psychiatry Research, 3,* 107–114.

O'Connor, N., & Hermelin, B. (1967). The selective visual attention of psychotic children. *Journal of Child Psychology and Psychiatry, 8,* 167–179.

Ornitz, E. M. (1974). The modulation of sensory input in autistic children. *Journal of Autism and Childhood Schizophrenia, 4,* 197–215.

Ornitz, E. M., Brown, M. B., Mason, A., & Putnam, N. H. (1974). Effect of visual input on vestibular nystagmus in autistic children. Archives of General Psychiatry, 31, 369–375.

Ozonoff, S., Pennington, B., & Rogers, S. (1990). Are there emotion perception deficits in young autistic children? *Journal of Child Psychology and Psychiatry, 31,* 343–361.

Ozonoff, S., Pennington, B., & Rogers, S. (1991). Executive function deficits in high-functioning autistic individuals: Relationship to theory of mind. *Journal of Child Psychology and Psychiatry, 32,* 1081–1105.

Paul, R. (1987). Communication. In D. J. Cohen & A. M. Donnellan (Eds.), *Handbook of autism and pervasive developmental disorders* (pp. 61–84). New York: Wiley.

Paul, R., Fischer, M. L., & Cohen, D. J. (1988). Brief report: Sentence comprehension strategies in children with autism and specific language disorders. *Journal of Autism and Developmental Disorders, 18,* 669–677.

Piaget, J. (1952). *The origins of intelligence in children.* New York: Norton.

Prior, M. (1979). Cognitive abilities and disabilities in infantile autism: A review. *Journal of Abnormal Child Psychology, 7,* 357–380.

Prior, M. R., & Bradshaw, J. L. (1979). Hemisphere functioning in autistic children. *Cortex, 15,* 73–81.

Prior, M., & Chen, C. (1976). Short-term and serial memory in autistic, retarded, and normal children. *Journal of Autism and Childhood Schizophrenia, 6,* 121–131.

Prior, M., Dahlstrom, B., & Squires, T. (1990). Autistic children's knowledge of thinking and feeling states in other people. *Journal of Child Psychology and Psychiatry, 31,* 587–601.

Prior, M. R., & Hall, L. C. (1979). Comprehension of transitive and intransitive phrases by autistic mentally retarded and normal children. *Journal of Communication Disorders, 12,* 103–111.

Prizant, B. (1983). Language acquisition and communicative behavior in autism: Toward an understanding of the "whole" of it. *Journal of Speech and Hearing Disorders, 48,* 296–307.

Prizant, B., & Duchan, J. (1981). The functions of immediate echolalia in autistic children. *Journal of Speech and Hearing Disorders, 46,* 241–249.

Prizant, B., & Rydell, P. (1984). Analysis of functions of delayed echolalia in autistic children. *Journal of Speech and Hearing Research, 27,* 183–192.

Rapin, I. (ed.) (in press). Preschool children with inadequate communication: Developmental language disorder, autism, mental deficiency. *Clinics in Developmental Medicine.*

Rimland, B. (1964). *Infantile autism: The syndrome and its implications.* New York: Appleton-Century-Crofts.

Rimland, B., & Fein, D. (1988). Savant skills in infantile autism. In L. Obler & D. Fein (Eds.), *The Exceptional Brain* (pp. 474–492). New York: Guilford.

Rogers, S. J., & Pennington, B. F. (1991). A theoretical approach to the deficits in infantile autism. *Development and Psychopathology, 3,* 137–162.

Rumsey, J., & Hamburger, S. (1988). Neuropsychological findings in high-functioning men with infantile autism, residual state. *Journal of Clinical and Experimental Neuropsychology, 10,* 210–221.

Rutter, M. (1983). Cognitive deficits in the pathogenesis of autism. *Journal of Child Psychology and Psychiatry, 24,* 513–531.

Rutter, M., Bartak, L., & Newman, S. (1971). Autism—a central disorder of cognition and language? In M. Rutter (Ed.), *Infantile autism: Concepts, characteristics and treatment* (pp. 148–171). London: Churchill Livingstone.

Schwartz, S. (1981). Language disabilities in infantile autism: A brief review and comment. *Applied Psycholinguistics, 22,* 25–31.

Serafica, F. (1971). Object concept and deviant children. *American Journal of Orthopsychiatry, 41,* 471–481.

Sigman, M., & Ungerer, J. A. (1981). Sensorimotor skills and language comprehension in autistic children. *Journal of Abnormal Child Psychology, 9,* 149–165.

Sigman, M., & Ungerer, J. A. (1984). Cognitive and language skills in autistic, mentally retarded, and normal children. *Developmental Psychology, 20,* 293–302.

Sigman, M., Ungerer, J., Mundy, P., & Sherman, T. (1987). Cognition in autistic children. In D. J. Cohen & A. M. Donnellan (Eds.), *Handbook of autism and pervasive developmental disorders.* New York: Wiley.

Simmons, J., & Baltaxe, C. (1975). Language patterns of adolescent autistics. *Journal of Autism and Childhood Schizophrenia, 5,* 333–351.

Smalley F., & Asarnow, R. (1990). Brief report: Cognitive subclinical markers in autism. *Journal of Autism and Developmental Disorders, 20,* 271–278.

Szatmari, P., Bartolucci, G., Bremner, R., Bond, S., & Rich, S. A follow-up study of high-functioning autistic children. *Journal of Autism and Developmental Disorders, 19,* 213–225.

Tager-Flusberg, H. (1981). On the nature of linguistic functioning in early infantile autism. *Journal of Autism and Pervasive Developmental Disorders, 11,* 45–56.

Tager-Flusberg, H. (1985a). Basic level and superordinate level categorization in autistic, mentally retarded, and normal children. *Journal of Experimental Child Psychology, 40,* 450–469.

Tager-Flusberg, H. (1985b). The conceptual basis for referential word meaning in children with autism. *Child Development, 56,* 1167–1178.

Tager-Flusberg, H. (1989). A psycholinguistic perspective on language development in the autistic child. In G. Dawson (Ed.), *Autism: Nature, diagnosis and treatment* (pp. 92–109). New York: Guilford.

Tager-Flusberg, H. (1991). Semantic processing in the free recall of autistic children: Further evidence for a cognitive deficit. *British Journal of Developmental Psychology, 9,* 417–430.

Tager-Flusberg, H. (1992). Autistic children's talk about psychological states: Deficits in the early acquisition of a theory of mind. *Child Development, 63,* 161–172.

Townsend, J., Courchesne, E., & Eggas, B. (1992). Visual attention deficits in autistic adults with cerebellar and parietal abnormalities. *Society for Neuroscience Abstracts, 18,* 332.

Ungerer, J. A., & Sigman, M. (1981). Symbolic play and language comprehension in autistic children. *Journal of the American Academy of Child Psychiatry, 20,* 318–337.

Wainwright-Sharp, J. A., & Bryson, S. E. (1993). Visual orienting deficits in high-functioning people with autism. *Journal of Autism and Developmental Disorders, 23,* 1–13.

Waterhouse, L. (1988). Speculations on the neuroanatomical substrate of special talents. In L. Obler & D. Fein (Eds.), *The exceptional brain: Neuropsychology of talent and special abilities* (pp. 493–512). New York: Guilford.

Waterhouse, L., & Fein, D. (1982). Language skills in developmentally disabled children. *Brain and Language, 15,* 307–333.

Waterhouse, L., & Fein, D. (1989). Social or cognitive or both? Crucial dysfunctions in autism. In C. Gillberg (Ed.), *Diagnosis and treatment of autism* (pp. 53–61). New York: Plenum Press.

Wetherby, A. M. (1986). Ontogeny of communication functions in autism. *Journal of Autism and Developmental Disorders, 16,* 295–316.

Wetherby, A. M., & Prizant, B. M. (1985). Intentional communicative behavior of children with autism: Theoretical and practical issues. *Australian Journal of Human Communication Disorders, 13,* 21–59.

Wetherby, A. M., & Prutting, C. A. (1984). Profiles of communicative and cognitive–social abilities in autistic children. *Journal of Speech and Hearing Research, 27,* 364–377.

Wing, L. (1978). Social, behavioral, and cognitive characteristics: An epidemiological approach. In M. Rutter & E. Schopler (Eds.), *Autism: A reappraisal of concepts and treatments* (pp. 27–46). New York: Plenum Press.

Wing, L., & Attwood, A. (1987). Syndromes of autism and atypical development. In D. J. Cohen & A. M. Donnellan (Eds.), *Handbook of autism and pervasive developmental disorders* (pp. 3–19). New York: Wiley.

Yirmiya, N., & Sigman, M. D. (1991). High-functioning individuals with autism: Diagnosis, empirical findings, and theoretical issues. *Clinical Psychology Review, 11,* 669–683.

Verbal and Nonverbal Cognitive Processes

A Comparison of Learning Disability and Autistic Children

HELMER R. MYKLEBUST

INTRODUCTION

A body of knowledge has developed regarding both learning disability and autistic children; however, in making comparisons we cannot conclude that because some autistic children have learning disabilities and some learning-disabled children have autistic symptoms that these conditions should be viewed as comprising a single diagnostic category. Because some children have more than one disability does not mean that their limitations derive from a single cause.

LANGUAGE DISORDERS

Interest in learning disabilities is pervasive throughout the world, with several disciplines making contributions. There are many children who are not mentally retarded, autistic, mainly emotionally disturbed, or deaf or blind, who have no severe motor problems, but who cannot learn as normal children do. Some of these learning-disabled children are bril-

HELMER R. MYKLEBUST • Emeritus Professor of Psychology, Neurology, and Psychiatry, Northwestern University, Chicago, Illinois 60611

Learning and Cognition in Autism, edited by Eric Schopler and Gary B. Mesibov. Plenum Press, New York, 1995.

liant intellectually but are thought to be stupid because they cannot master specific academic tasks, such as learning to read, or certain nonverbal tasks, such as learning to tell time or find their way from one place to another. When the concept of learning disabilities was first introduced, we thought only verbal processes were involved. A few years later, we realized that nonverbal cognitive processes also can be impaired. In some children the cognitive dysfunction might entail only an aspect of verbal learning, such as dyslexia, and in others it might entail only a nonverbal aspect of learning, such as size judgment or way-finding; some children have both verbal and nonverbal disorders of learning (Myklebust, 1975; Rourke, 1989). It seems that nonverbal cognitive disabilities are more often confused with autism, mental retardation, and emotional disturbances.

The brain comprises two major systems, the right and left hemispheres. These systems are functionally different, with the left hemisphere mainly responsible for verbal learning and the right hemisphere for nonverbal learning. Hence, the variation in the types of learning disabilities; illness and injury may damage both hemispheres or only a single function of one hemisphere. Progress is being made in understanding how the brain processes verbal and nonverbal information (H. Damasio & A. Damasio, 1989). More knowledge has been acquired about how the brain processes verbal information because it has been known for more than a century that if individuals sustain damage to certain areas of the left hemisphere they may lose ability to speak, to comprehend what is said, to read or write (Broca, 1864; Jackson, 1876). We can ascertain whether the cognitive disturbances are primarily verbal, primarily nonverbal, or both. These assessments reveal that some children may function normally when receiving information but be unable to function expressively. Likewise, some children may function well both receptively and expressively but be unable to gain meaning or to store information. If they are able to store information in memory, they may be unable to retrieve it. In many children it appears that these cognitive dysfunctions are specific and do not overlap (Gaddes, 1980; Myklebust & Morinaga, 1990).

When differentiating between autism and learning disabilities, it is significant that learning disabilities as originally conceived did not include the mentally retarded. This distinction was clearly stated in the original definition (Kass & Myklebust, 1969). Accordingly, we have limited our studies to those who fall at the level of 90 IQ or above on either verbal or nonverbal tests of intelligence (Killen, 1975; Myklebust, 1968; Myklebust & Boshes, 1969). The reason for defining learning disabilities in this manner was to avoid confusion between generalized impaired cognition and cognition impaired because of specific brain dysfunctions when general intelligence is average or above. We limit the designation of learning disabilities to those who have a discrepancy between intellectual potential for learning and actual achievement. When we proposed the Learning Quotient we were attempting to quantitatively differentiate level of attainment from potential (Myklebust, 1968). To designate a child as being dyslexic when the intelligence level is below that required for learning to read is to confuse and mislead. An outcome of the confusion that has arisen regarding learning disabilities has been discussed by Haywood (1989). He pointed out that the designation "slow learner" has all but disappeared in many schools. Where are these children? They are classified with the learning disabled, which explains why the "incidence" of learning-disabled children has proliferated, with disadvantages to both groups. There is a psychology and neurology of cognition for the mentally retarded that serves as the basis for their education. Likewise, there is a psychology and neurology of learning for learning-disabled children; the cognitive abilities and functions for these two groups vary one from the other. These differences must be reckoned with if we are to provide the most advantageous remedial programs (Gaddes, 1980; Myklebust, Bannochie, & Killen, 1971; Rourke, 1989, 1991).

Childhood Aphasia

The verbal disorders include aphasia, dyslexia, dysgraphia and dyscalculia. Of these, the most incapacitating is receptive aphasia. Spoken language, the most basic of the language systems, is universal and evolved long before the written form; it evolved first phylogenetically and it developed first ontogenetically. This sequential relationship between the spoken and read language forms is pertinent because there is growing evidence that the brain is prestructured to learn auditory language before the visual-read form (Myklebust, 1983). There are other developmental hierarchies. For example, comprehension of what is said precedes use of the spoken word expressively. These developmental relationships help us understand why an inability to comprehend what is said is more debilitating than an inability to speak; receptive disorders are more incapacitating than expressive disorders (Gaddes, 1980). These reciprocal relationships in language development are critical to evaluation of learning disabilities in relation to autism. Authorities stress that it is common to see nontalking preschoolers who are presumed to be deaf when in fact they are autistic, aphasic, pervasively mentally retarded or selectively mute (Frith, 1989b; Myklebust, 1954; Rutter, 1971). Our first question when we see mute children is, can they comprehend? If they cannot comprehend we do not expect them to be able to utter words meaningfully.

Childhood Dyslexia

There is much interest in childhood dyslexia, as well there might be—it is a problem of great importance to many children. Research has shown that no matter what form of written language is used, in the Western World or in the Orient, the incidence of failure in learning to read is the same (Hsu, 1988; Stevenson, 1985). For alphabetical languages, it is the left brain hemisphere that is specialized for learning to read (De Kerckhove & Lunisden, 1988). For character systems, such as those used in the Orient, there are similarities but also differences. Jones and Aoki (1988) have shown that *kana*, a system of phonetic characters, and *kanji*, a logographic system (nonphonetic) are processed differently in the brain. The left hemisphere is mainly responsible for processing *kana* whereas *kanji* is processed mainly on the right hemisphere. Kawamura, Hirayama, Hasegama, Takahashi, and Yamamura (1987) presented similar evidence with an excellent example from neurosurgery, as did Sasanuma (1981). Exciting results also were presented by Morinaga (1981), who used our Letter Completion Test (unpublished) and found that the errors made by Japanese school children were of two types: errors in *kana* and errors in *kanji*, with some children making errors of one type but not the other. From these results we postulated that there are two primary types of dyslexia in Japanese, one involving the phonetic–auditory aspects of the characters (*kana*), and the other involving the ideographic (visual) characters (*kanji*).

These results are of interest because they contribute to knowledge about brain–cognitive processes in learning to read, no matter what written form is used. These data support the hypothesis that dyslexia is of two primary types, those involving auditory-cognitive processes and those involving visual-cognitive processed, with subtypes of each. Only a presumption a few decades ago, this postulation is being confirmed by a wide range of research studies around the world (Flynn & Boder, 1991; Rourke, 1991). No longer can we assume that dyslexia occurs only in alphabetical language systems, and no longer can we attribute all reading failure to poor teaching, poor effort on the part of children, poor cooperation on the part of parents, or only to emotional disturbances.

This body of knowledge regarding childhood dyslexia is related to differentiation between learning disabilities and autism in many ways, including the nature of autism itself. Dyslexic children are not autistic; some are brilliant and have become world-renowned persons. A further question is whether many or most autistic children are dyslexic. Some authorities have proposed that they are (Bartak, Rutter, & Cox, 1975; Rapin, 1991). Whether some autistic children should be categorized as being aphasic or dyslexic depends upon one's concept of the nature of autism. Frith's (1989b) point of view is revealing. She observed that specific language disorders should be applied diagnostically only when the potential for language has been demonstrated. Rutter (1991, personal communication) stated, "I don't actually see it as helpful to regard autistic individuals as having aphasia, dyslexia, and so forth."

Dysgraphia

Studies of written language have added to knowledge of learning disabilities and to understanding of language development in normal children. Using the Picture Story test, we found that in children the written word develops year by year from 6 through 17 years of age (Myklebust, 1965, 1973). An illustration of this growth is the number of words written per sentence. By 17 years of age the average is 17 words, showing a developmental gain of about one word per year; this finding has remained consistent for more than 50 years. Kirk's (1985) evidence on the maturation of graphic skills shows the complexity of this language process. Written language is the last language system to be acquired; comprehension of auditory language develops first, followed by expressive auditory (spoken), then receptive visual (reading), and last the expressive visual (written; Myklebust, 1978).

Dysgraphia, like most of the language disorders, was first recognized in relation to brain lesions in adults, but definition continues to be difficult, especially when applied to children. Some authorities continue to limit dysgraphia to classic apraxia, as was done initially in the diagnosis of language disorders in adults. Coltheart and Funnell (1987) used this designation to include spelling and other errors in writing. We differentiate between dysgraphia and writing errors related to dyslexia (Johnson & Myklebust, 1967). Dyslexic children have difficulty with spelling and their errors are characteristic, depending upon whether their dyslexia is mainly of the auditory or visual type (Flynn & Boder, 1991). Spelling errors are not caused by dysgraphia. When children cannot write well, our first concern is whether they can read. If they are deficient in reading, this limitation is reflected in their writing (Myklebust, 1965). We conclude that writing deficits that result from dyslexic involvements are not due to dysgraphia; they are a reciprocal disability that derives from dyslexia. When given remedial assistance, as the child learns to read he also learns to spell, although at a slower rate; limitations in spelling persist, although less severe, after ability to read is well established.

Some autistic children learn to use written language meaningfully, but some write without expression of meaning, in a manner comparable to their use of the spoken word. When evaluating these children, we use the developmental–hierarchical approach—as we do with other children. If auditory language has not developed, there is little possibility that read language will be acquired normally, and without reading there is little possibility for development of meaningful use of written language. When cognitive limitations preclude language development the designation of dysgraphia seems unwarranted.

Dyscalculia

Although frequently overlooked, dyscalculia is a learning disability that causes hardship for many children. As a cognitive dysfunction it is a severe handicap. Henschen (1925) first used the term *dyscalculia* and related mathematical disabilities to dysfunctions in the brain. We showed that many learning-disabled children are deficient in ability to calculate (Myklebust & Boshes, 1969). Out of 50 tests of cognitive function, arithmetical ability was fourth in accuracy in differentiating learning-disabled from normal children. Cohn (1971) found that dyscalculia was a difficult cognitive disturbance that often persisted into adulthood. He emphasized the importance of distinguishing this condition from memory disorders. Badian (1983) found that there are subtypes of dyscalculia, including alexia and agraphia for numbers, anarithmetica and attentional-sequential dyscalculia, and mixed types.

The work of Deloche and Seron (1987) illustrates the progress being made in understanding childhood dyscalculia. Developmental psychology covers a wide range of cognitive processes in learning to calculate, such as perception, the language processes involved in counting, decoding of rotational systems, and cultural and social factors. It is important to distinguish between reading numbers and the names of numbers, because some children can read digits but not words. This observation is supported by Sugishita, Iwata, Toyokura, Yoshiaka, and Yamada (1978), who showed that digits differ from words and that phonographic aspects of numbers differ from the logographic. Hemisphere involvement also was studied by Gazzaniga and Smylie (1984), who found that the left hemisphere serves the purpose of calculation, whereas the right hemisphere identifies numbers—and that number processing is dependent on the language areas of the brain. Rourke's studies (1989) show that mathematical-cognitive processing correlates with severe nonverbal cognitive functions related to right hemisphere operations.

In assessing dyscalculia in children we evaluate both receptive and expressive cognitive processes, being mindful of the role of meaning. Some autistic children are successful in performing arithmetical operations such as addition, subtraction, and multiplication, but their performance is ritualistic, involving little conceptualization of quantitative values. This type of isolated, nonintegrated skill behavior is similar to their endeavors in other areas, as in echolalic responses, perfect pitch, repetition of TV commercials, and reading without meaning. Input- and output-cognitive processing should be appraised visually and auditorially. Brainerd (1987) used such an approach and showed that encoding is the most critical factor in diagnosis of childhood dyscalculia; retrieval and processing operations are secondary. Hartje (1987), among others, observed that spatial and orientation disorders are associated with ability to calculate; hemi-inattention is related to dyscalculia of the visual-spatial type but rarely with anarithmetica and dyscalculia due to alexia or dysgraphia. Spatial dyscalculia is seen as an inability to align numbers in proper order and in carrying while computing.

Caramazza and McCloskey (1987) stressed the complex nature of ability to calculate, stating that there are three basic cognitive functions that must be operational: (a) ability to process numerical symbols and the arithmetical processes needed to perform them; (b) ability to retrieve the needed operations from memory; (c) ability to execute these operations. Disruptions of any one of these functions might result in dyscalculia. Some learning-disability children perform calculations well *if* they are informed beforehand of the processes involved. These processes entail input, output, and integrative-cognitive systems. Most dyscalculic children function successfully in other areas of academic learning and socially, notwithstanding the fact that some are deficient in other aspects of nonverbal learning, such as spatial orientation, telling time, and way-finding. They do not manifest autistic qualities. This does not mean that some higher level autistic individuals may not have dyscalculia as another disability. If so, it seems, as in other aspects of academic learning, it is important to make a dual diagnosis—autistic and dyscalculic, because autism and dyscalculia seem to be separate entities, not overlapping conditions.

LANGUAGE AND MEANING

Language development has been an area of focus in evaluating and treating autistic children (Baltaxe & Simmons, 1983; Paul, 1987; Prizant and Schuler, 1987). These studies vary, sometimes making no reference to definition of language, or to verbal-symbolic behavior and the cognitive processes involved. Rapin (1991) suggested that diagnostic designations such as dysphasia are valid in the classification of autistic children. We have raised the question of how useful these designations might be. If the child is pervasively limited cognitively, classification on the basis of specific learning disabilities may not be helpful to the child, or to the child's family.

In achieving verbal behavior the child can be described as going through five stages developmentally (Myklebust, 1978). Inner language is acquired first. The cognitive processes involved at this crucial level are not well understood, but they seem to be largely nonverbal because they entail imagery that precedes acquisition of word meanings. Only after nonverbal meanings, such as the image of mother, have been acquired do words become meaningful. The processes involved in acquiring meaning, verbal and nonverbal, are referred to as the development of *inner language*. This level of cognitive development is especially pertinent to the concept of autism. Inner language processes consist of associating verbal symbols (spoken words) with a specific unit of experience. This vital language-development process, in normal children, proceeds from birth to approximately 8 or 9 months, at which time the infant begins to understand words, cognitively associating a word with a nonverbal experiential unit, such as relating the spoken word "mommy" with a certain individual who has become familiar through imagery.

As the child begins to comprehend spoken language, the second stage of development has begun. Further study is essential but it seems that the cognitive deficit seen in many autistic individuals falls at this level. Because they do not gain meaning from daily-life experience, there is no basis for acquisition of words to represent experiences symbolically. In the psychology of language development, inner language provides the basis for verbal–symbolic learning. Neuropsychologically both brain hemispheres are involved, as are interhemispheric processes (H. Damasio & A. Damasio, 1989; Rourke, 1991). As language develops further, the auditory form develops first and the left hemisphere becomes dominant for the cognitive processing involved (Benson, 1983). In some children, because of neurogenic dysfunctioning, the capacity to comprehend what is said does not develop normally. If other development is progressing well, it is these children who are designated as having receptive aphasia. Deficits in auditory comprehension have a reciprocal impact on inner-language development, making receptive aphasia a disability of major consequence. Bartak et al. (1975) compared children with autism to those having receptive aphasia and found that those with autism were more generally deficient in language behavior, including all sensory modalities. Perhaps this difference can be explained by the fact that those with autism have an inability to acquire meaning—inner language. Receptive aphasics develop inner language, albeit with modification, through visual, tactile, and motor learning even though auditory–verbal symbolic representation is limited. They are not devoid of meaning as is commonly observed in autistic children (Myklebust, 1954).

After children have acquired a minimum of inner- and auditory-receptive language they are developmentally prepared to begin to use auditory expressive language—they begin to speak; we comprehend before we speak and read before we write (Myklebust, 1983). Other neurodynamic processes are critical, such as ability to listen. Some children can hear but not listen. Listening is a complex integrative process that involves structuring the auditory field and selecting a specific segment of it, a segment of relevance because of the immediate circumstances confronting the individual; there is an analogous function in vision in which children can see but not look (Myklebust, 1954). Language-learning assumes ability to gain meaning and listening is part of this aspect of cognition.

Some children develop auditory-receptive language well, even normally, but cannot use the spoken word expressively because of childhood expressive aphasia, a form of apraxia. There are other causes of mutism, such as deafness, emotional disturbance, and anarthria, but expressive aphasia should not be overlooked. Expressive aphasics learn to gesture well, have no difficulty in understanding others, and pantomime vociferously. Is expressive aphasia a logical diagnosis for autistic children who do not speak? The designation of expressive aphasia assumes that inner- and receptive-auditory language have been acquired. It is this assumption that is critical, because in autism acquisition of meaning often is limited.

Echolalia

We became intrigued with echolalia some time ago (Myklebust 1954, 1957, 1971). This condition has received wide attention in studies of childhood autism; Schuler and Prizant, 1985) presented a review. It appears mainly in two forms, immediate and delayed. Most authorities agree that echolalia consists of the repetition of what has been said by others. The question is whether this repetition conveys a meaningful message. Although researchers are not always in agreement, studies that provide a basis for judgment are forthcoming. For example, Hermelin and Frith (1971) showed that autistic children can repeat nonsense sentences better than normal children. Fay (1969) indicated that echolalia is language-related but, as in some other studies, the evidence for meaningful communication is slight or only inferential. Frith (1989b) concluded that the language deficit in childhood autism "is a consequence of subtle but far-reaching cognitive dysfunctions" (p. 123). She states further that "we do not need to hypothesize a primary socio-affective impairment in autistic children in order to understand their communication failure" (p. 147). Fine, Bartolucci, Ginsberg, and Szatman (1991), in a controlled study, found that those with autism employ intonation less often for communication and often without indicating expectation that meaning was intended for the hearer. These studies suggest that echolalic behavior is not a means of communication, as in meaningful use of the spoken word.

Perhaps the criterion is whether the child has acquired inner language. If not, he may have no message to convey, in which case the echolalia manifests only a certain integrity of the left brain hemisphere, permitting reception of auditory sequences and their conversion into auditory motor processes so they can be repeated orally without conveying meaning; the integrative meaning system is bypassed. If this is the case, using terms such as aphasia seems irrelevant (A. Damasio & Maurer, 1978; H. Damasio & A. Damasio, 1989); There is a similar condition in reading, sometimes referred to as *word-calling,* in which the child reads words, sentences, and paragraphs correctly but gains little or no meaning from what is read (Myklebust, 1978). Frith and Snowling (1983) studied hyperlexic autistic children and found their comprehension scores to be below their accuracy scores. They suggested that the inability to gain meaning normally is a critical deficit derived from cognitive deficiencies. Attwood, Frith and Hermelin (1988) studied use of interpersonal gesture by autistic children and found that, regardless of the degree of mental retardation, they could imitate gestures but, "unlike Down's syndrome adolescents, and normal preschool children, no autistic adolescent ever used expressive gestures" (p. 241). Use of gestures imitatively, like echolalia or word-calling, does not mean that gestures are being used meaningfully for communication. In a related study, Hermelin and O'Connor (1985) found that children with autism were successful in tests of matching, including form and shape, but when meaning was important to solving the task they were unsuccessful; again we note that imitation (matching) in itself does not necessarily involve meaning. A. Damasio and Maurer (1978) highlighted this observation in stating:

> These are defects that do not derive from impairment of primary linguistic processing and are, accordingly, unrelated to damage to the primary language processing area of the brain. Rather these defects seem to derive from lack of initiative to communicate and from a lack of "orientation" toward stimuli and are suggestive of an underlying impairment in higher motor perceptual, or, more generally, in overall cognitive organization. (p. 779)

Studies of the use of sign-language with autistic children have been reviewed by Layton (1987). Those who gained limited success were those who had some ability in other communication forms, including gestures and vocal speech. Rutter (1971) emphasized that all children with marked deficiencies in auditory comprehension are not autistic. He compared receptive aphasic and autistic children and found that the aphasic children formed play and personal relationships, whereas the autistic children showed pervasive behavioral disturbances. Wing (1971) reported similar findings. In comparison with aphasics, those with autism showed a generalized lack of comprehension, use of gesture, and lack of concept development, to which, she concluded, all else is secondary. Regarding use of nonverbal communication, Mundy, Sigman, Ungerer and Sherman (1986) concluded that

> The data suggest that a disturbance in the development of nonverbal indicating skills is a significant feature of the social skills deficits exhibited by young autistic children. (p. 668)

This emphasis highlights the importance of communication (verbal and nonverbal) but neither the language limitations or lack of social awareness in themselves seem to be primary. The basic involvement seems to be a generalized inability to gain meaning from experience, as discussed by Frith (1989a). It is noteworthy that Baltaxe and Simmons (1983) in a follow-up study of autistic adolescents and adults found that only a small number have a favorable outcome.

NONVERBAL LEARNING DISABILITIES

As indicated previously, learning disabilities are of two major types, verbal and nonverbal. We have less knowledge about the nonverbal type, but we are becoming aware that it is prevalent and sometimes significantly incapacitating. Like the verbal type, this disability can be caused by dysfunctions of the auditory or visual processing systems and may include storage, retrieval or integrative systems. Most investigators agree that these disturbances of learning derive mainly from disorders of the right brain hemisphere (H. Damasio & A. Damasio, 1989; Rourke, 1989). We presented evidence on nonverbal learning disabilities some time ago (Johnson & Myklebust, 1967; Myklebust, 1975, 1981; Myklebust & Boshes, 1969). The realization of the possibility that this type of disability might occur developed from work with many children who presented problems developmentally. From the questions raised by parents and from clinical observations we realized that these disturbances warranted investigation, and that most of them involved learning from everyday experience, behaviors not deliberately taught by parents or teachers. To specify them more concretely, I suggested that these disabilities be designated as disorders of *social perception* (Myklebust, 1975). We use this designation to characterize the child's ability to understand his social environment, particularly his ability to respond appropriately to people and circumstances in his immediate environment. In so doing he must gain meaning from the actions of others, including playmates. Children having nonverbal learning disabilities typically score below average on the performance scale of the Wechsler Test but score average or higher on the verbal scale (Myklebust & Boshes, 1969; Rourke, 1989).

Srull and Weyer (1988) reviewed the progress being made in definition of social perception and its significance. Brewer (1988) referred to this aspect of behavior as "social cognition" and stated,

> Most often the distinction is made in terms of the nature of the object of perception. Ordinary cognition becomes social when the target of interest is a social object, usually another person or group of persons. (p. 1).

Sometimes this process is referred to as *person perception*. For example, Asch (1946) regarded ability to form impressions of others (including their actions) as a basic human capacity that makes social life possible. We know that social cognition is a primary incapacity in autism, and that this aspect of behavior has been a focus of attention for many years (Schopler & Mesibov, 1986). When reviewing the cognitive disturbances found in learning-disabled children, and those related to autism, the question arises as to whether these conditions are similar or identical. Because of the differences in the quality of the social–perceptual functions of these children, it appears unlikely that they are equivalent. The social-cognitive inadequacies of the learning disabled are not pervasive or accompanied by mental retardation; they fall more within a deviance model than a developmental model (Volkmar & Cohen, 1988). These children are not out of contact with others, as illustrated by their wanting to learn to play games. They watch their playmates, indicating that they want to participate, but when they do not understand what is expected of them they are overlooked by the group. They are aware of the game, of the enjoyment being experienced by those at play, but cannot grasp the routines required to participate; they perceive that the play involved is meaningful and they desire to be involved, to gain relationships with others. As autistic children are classified by Wing and Attwood (1987), nonverbal learning-disabled children are not (a) aloof; (b) passive; or (c) active but odd. Most children with autism are pervasively limited in social cognition, which is not true of the learning disabled, whose nonverbal deficits are limited to specific types of social perception, such as way-finding and spatial orientation; these deficits are not pervasive and often are unrecognized diagnostically until high school age or later. Cairns (1986) views the social abilities of autistic children differently. He stated,

> The propensity of autistic children to become attached to inanimate objects would strongly suggest the view that these children are capable of forming some types of social attachments in childhood or later. (p. 27)

But attachment to inanimate objects is not included in social-cognitive function as commonly defined. As Howlin (1986) explained,

> Although descriptions of social competence differ from study to study, there is overall agreement that the essence of social behavior consists of ability to relate to others in a mutually reinforcing and reciprocal fashion and to adapt social skills to the varying demands of interpersonal contexts. (p. 103)

She observed further that "It seems likely that the social abnormality in autism stems from a cognitive deficit that affects fine processing of social and emotional cues" (p. 126). Shah and Wing (1986), in a review of studies of social abilities, suggested that autistic persons cannot normally derive meaning from social experience, including language and emphasized that it is the social impairment that is the hallmark of this pervasive disorder. This may be true but the term *social*, used in this manner, leaves unanswered questions, especially as to whether the social deficits are primary or secondary. Dahl, Cohen, and Provence (1986) clarified the extent of the social limitations in autism when they studied 390 children under 72 months of age—they differed from the other groups.

Fein, Pennington, Markowitz, Braverman, and Waterhouse (1986) focused on the question of how the "hallmark" characteristic of autism might be explained. They concluded "The social/affective deficits in autism are primary and not secondary to deficits in traditionally defined cognitive functions" (p. 209). If the social deficits are primary, what can we infer regarding causation? If we assume that cognitive functions are normal, presumably the inference is that the dysfunction is due to emotional factors, as postulated in the early days of autism. In recent years studies have shown that autism is the result of brain dysfunction. Even the type of insult is being studied successfully (Minshew, 1991; Rourke, 1989).

Facial Agnosia

The inability to recognize faces was identified in adults a number of years ago (Bodamer, 1947; Hecaen & Angelerques, 1962). Benton (1980) described this condition as an "incapacity to identify familiar persons on the basis of visual perception of their faces or, at least, of the more fundamental characteristics of their faces" (p. 177). Although recognized in behavioral neurology and neuropsychology for some time, only recently has this condition been more widely identified. Perception and memory are involved, as is ability to gain meaning; recognition of faces, as well as learning to understand the meaning of facial expressions, is a complex aspect of social–perceptual development (Bruyer, 1986). H. Damasio and A. Damasio (1989) observed,

> Damage within certain sectors of sensory association cortices does affect quality of perception and always within a single modality. Lesions within visual association cortices may impair recognition of the unique identity of faces but allow for recognition of facial expression, nonunique objects, and visual–verbal material. Or they may compromise object recognition and leave face recognition intact, or compromise reading but not object or face recognition. (p. 69)

Benton (1980) stated that there are two major types of facial agnosia: (a) identification of the faces of familiar persons and, (b) discrimination of unfamiliar faces. He also stated that these two disabilities differ neurologically. The ability of autistic children to gain meaning from facial expressions and their ability to distinguish familiar from unfamiliar faces has been the subject of study (Langdell, 1978; Volkmar, Sparrow, Rende, & Cohen, 1989). Langdell showed that autistic children, unlike normal and subnormal children, responded to features of the lower face primarily. He concluded that autistic individuals focused on the mouth area more than the area of the eyes. Some learning-disabled children are deficient in facial recognition but often recognize individuals by the color of their hair, by their clothing, or even by the sound of their voice. There is a difference between autistic and learning-disabled children in the way that facial agnosia is manifested. In autistic children it seems to be more a lack of awareness of the face, not a specific disability, a part of an overall pervasive limitation in ability to gain meaning from experience (Volkmar et al., 1989).

Spatial Agnosia and Way-Finding Disorders

Some learning-disabled children have limitations involving spatial perception. Space has been defined in various ways but scientists are making progress in expanding knowledge of its significance in daily life and in its nature developmentally (Eliot, 1975; Spencer, Blades, & Morsley,

1989). Our concern is why learning-disabled children often manifest limitations in spatial perception, but those with autism usually do not. This observation may be based on too limited a definition of space. Space involves much more, such as learning to use symbolic representations in reading maps, floor plans, and blueprints. In these areas of spatial behavior it appears that some autistic individuals have difficulties. Designations such as spatial knowledge, spatial imagery, spatial thought, distance perception, spatial memory, and environmental cognition are useful when assessing children who have spatial–nonverbal learning disabilities. In studying autistic children, Frith and Hermelin (1969) showed that they function more at the level of *intra*neurosensory processing than at the level of *inter*neurosensory processing as normal children do (Killen, 1975; Myklebust & Morinaga, 1990). The condition of autism seems to alter cognitive functioning so that information is perceived from only one sensory avenue at a time; parallel processing may not be possible. This may explain why those with autism often are competent in specific aspects of spatial perception, as seen in their performance on form boards and block design (spatial-matching tasks).

West, Morris, and Nichol (1985) studied how normal children develop spatial skills, and as shown by Kosslyn (1981), spatial learning involves both auditory and visual imagery. Mental imagery fosters development of spatial knowledge (Cohn, 1985). Gaining such knowledge is not a simple process. Maintaining orientation in space while moving requires ability to process spatial information in relation to oneself as well as in relation to the changing environment (Weatherford, 1985). If this cannot be done, the result is disorientation. The necessary orienting information involves size judgments, patterns of similarity and difference, judgment of distance and speed, identification of landmarks, and other aspects of spatial cognition and memory. Knowledge about spatial learning is expanding (Stiles-Davis, Kritchevsky, & Bellugi, 1988). Spatial knowledge is a specific factor cognitively, separate from other components of cognitive ability. A landmark discussion of spatial agnosia was presented by Jackson (1876).

BRAIN STATUS AND COGNITIVE DYSFUNCTIONS

It has been shown that brain dysfunctions are associated with learning disabilities (Myklebust, 1967; Rourke, 1989). In a matched-pair study of learning-disabled and normal children we found a greater incidence of EEG abnormalities and of neurological disorders in the learning-disabled group (Hughes, 1971; Myklebust & Boshes, 1969). John (1989), using a neurometric EEG system, found differences between normal and learning-disabled children. Deuel (1983) showed that aphasic children who had seizures responded to medication; the aphasia was reduced. Connors (1989) investigated food-related biochemical disorders in learning-disabled hyperactive children. Benson (1983) showed how neuroanatomy provides a foundation for understanding language disorders: spoken, read, and written. Duane (1983) emphasized that neuroanatomical, neurochemical, and brain function studies provide a basis for diagnosis of dyslexia, dysgraphia, and other language disorders.

Brain diseases and brain lesions also are associated with autism. Although not finally determined, there also is growing evidence that hemisphere dominance does not develop normally in autism (Ornitz, 1987). Specific brain disorders have been difficult to ascertain in relation to autism, but we are in a new era insofar as study of the brain is concerned (Denckla & James, 1991). Some investigators are using magnetic resonance imaging (MRI). For example, Gaffney, Tsai, and Michin (1987) concluded that

> in coronal scans the cerebella of autistic patients were proportionately smaller and the fourth ventricles proportionately larger. This suggests that there are morphologic changes in the cerebella of autistic children; such alteration may best be viewed in the MRI coronal plane. (p. 1330).

Courchesne, Hesselink, Jernigson, and Young-Courchesne (1987) investigated the brain status of high-level autistic children and reported,

> Currently the brain imaging technology that yields most anatomical detail is MRI. In particular MRI is much superior to CT technology in imaging the cerebellum and periphery of the brain. (p. 336)

Gillberg, Strattburg and Jacobson (1987), who studied 20 relatively gifted autistic children concluded,

> For our study group, no single examination method would have detected even a third of the signs of abnormal brain function that eventually were disclosed through a combination of careful history taking, review of medical records, physical examination and a host of neurochemical, neuroradiological and neurophysiological assessment methods. (p. 646)

In an enlightening discussion Minshew (1991) observed,

> At the present time, three very different localizations and mechanisms are being proposed for the neurobiology of autism: dysfunction in the cortical mechanisms for selective attention; secondary abnormal ascending projections from the cerebellum and brain stem; dysfunction in information acquisition, i.e., memory; and dysfunction in information processing by association cortex and its distributed network of connections. (p. 778)

The work of H. Damasio and A. Damasio (1989), especially in relation to brain function and acquisition of meaning, seems unusually relevant. They stated,

> Meaning is arrived at by widespread multiregional activation of fragmentary records pertinent to a stimulus, wherever such records may be stored, in a distributed manner, within a large array of sensory and motor structures. A display of the meaning of a stimulus does not exist in a permanent fashion; it is recreated for each and every instantiation. (p. 63)

They concluded further that

> [t]here is an integrative operation capable of bringing together multiple brain activity fragments within a sensory modality and across separate modalities. Without such multiple modality integration, it would not be possible to generate coherent experience. (p. 65)

Rourke's hypothesis also is enlightening. He stated,

> Autistic children who eventually develop language will be shown to have some intrahemispheric (association) white-matter tracts within the left cerebral hemisphere that are intact. . . . Their autistic features would be expected to result from extensive damage to interhemispheric (associational) and/or projection fibre white tracts. (p. 322)

In a similar vein A. Damasio and Maurer (1978), in a discussion of the neurology of childhood autism reported,

> Dysfunction of structures of the neocortex could account for some features of autism . . . the mesocortex is a relay station point for information coming from perceptual neocortex on its way to allocortical structures such as the hippocampus, or to subcortical limbic structures such as the amygdala. (p. 782)

Frith (1989a) added extensively to knowledge regarding the "mind" of autistic children; her conclusions provide a basis for the psychology of autism. She presented observations about the brain pathology and about the intellectual level of these children and concluded, "The key word is rote as opposed to meaningful" (p. 95). She continued,

> In the normal cognitive system there is a built in propensity for coherence over as wide a range of stimuli as possible. It is this drive that results in grand systems of thought, and ultimately in the world's great religions. It is this capacity for coherence that is diminished in autistic children. As a result, their information-processing systems, like their very beings, are characterized by detachment. (p. 100)

Some of her other observations include:

Multiplying numbers is a stereotyped activity, but doing homework is not. (p. 104) The condition of autism does not directly affect input and output processes. (p. 106) With a weakness of central control, but an intact attention mechanism, patterns of attentive behavior would have to be odd rather than impaired. (p. 109) If the ability to achieve central coherence or meaning is extremely limited in autism, then detachment and fragmentation into meaningless activities are inevitable consequences. (p. 117)

CONCLUSIONS

Any one of the learning disabilities can be debilitating and have a severe impact on learning and adjustment. But the impact of autism is far greater, as indicated by Freeman et al. (1991). Their follow-up study of autistic children 12 years after an initial testing showed that only a little more than 20% had progressed. They concluded, "Thus, even though cognitive scores increased or remained relatively stable, patients in all IQ groups still exhibited significant social deficits" (p. 481). Such limited growth developmentally, educationally, and socially is not characteristic of learning-disabled children. As shown by Rourke (1991), with scientific clarification of the various subtypes, verbal and nonverbal, we can assume that new educational remediation programs will evolve, making the future for these children even more hopeful. There also is hope for autistic children because rapid progress is being made in further understanding the full nature of autism.

REFERENCES

Asch, S. (1946). Forming impressions of personality. *Journal of Social Psychology, 41*, 258–290.
Attwood, A., Frith, U., & Hermelin, B. (1988). The understanding and use of interpersonal gestures by autistic and Down's syndrome children. *Journal of Autism and Developmental Disorders, 18*(2), 241–257.
Badian, N. (1983). Dyscalculia and nonverbal disorders of learning. In H. Myklebust (Ed.), *Progress in learning disabilities,* (pp. 235–269). New York: Grune & Stratton.
Baltaxe, C., & Simmons, J. (1983). Communication deficits in the adolescent and adult autistic. *Seminars in Speech and Language, 4*(1), 27–41.
Baltaxe, C., & Simmons, J. (1987). Communication deficits in the adolescent with autism, schizophrenia, and language-learning disabilities. In T. Layton (Ed.), *Language treatment of autistic and developmentally disordered children,* (pp. 155–186). Springfield: Thomas.
Bartak, L., Rutter, M., & Cox, A. (1975). A comparative study of infantile autism and specific developmental receptive disorders. *British Journal of Psychiatry, 1*(126), 127–145.

Benson, F. (1983). The neural basis of spoken and written language. In H. Myklebust (Ed.), *Progress in learning disabilities* (Vol. 5, pp. 3–25). New York: Grune & Stratton.

Benton, A. (1980). The neurophysiology of facial recognition. *American Psychologist, 35*(2), 176–186.

Bodamer (1947).

Brainerd, C. (1987). Sources of working-memory error in children's mental arithmetic. In G. Deloche & X. Seron (Eds.), *Mathematical disorders* (pp. 87–109). Hillsdale, NJ: Erlbaum.

Brewer, M. (1988). *Advances in social cognition* (Vol. 1). Hillsdale, NJ: Erlbaum.

Broca, P. (1864). Deux cas d'aphemic tramatique produite par de la troisieme circonvolution frontale gauche. *Bulletin de la Societe Internationale de Chirurgie, 5,* 51–54.

Bruyer, R. (1986). *The neurophysiology of face perception and facial expression.* Hillsdale, NJ: Erlbaum.

Cairns, R. (1986). Social development: Recent theoretical trends and relevances for autism. In E. Schopler & G. Mesibov (Eds.), *Social behavior and autism* (pp. 15–34). New York: Plenum Press.

Caramazza, A., & McCloskey, M. (1987). Dissociation of calculation processes. In G. Deloche & X. Seron (Eds.), *Mathematical disabilities* (pp. 221–234). Hillsdale, NJ: Erlbaum.

Cohen, D., Paul, R., & Volkmar, F. (1987). Issues in the classification of pervasive developmental disorders and associated conditions. In D. Cohen, A. Donnellan, & R. Paul (Eds.), *Handbook of autism and pervasive developmental disorders* (pp. 20–40). New York: Wiley.

Cohn, R. (1971). Arithmetic and learning disabilities. In H. Myklebust (Ed.), *Progress in learning disabilities* Vol. 2, pp. 322–389). New York: Grune & Stratton.

Cohn, R. (Ed.). (1985). *The development of spatial cognition.* Hillsdale, NJ: Erlbaum.

Coltheart, M., & Funnell, E. (1987). Reading and writing: One lexicon or two? In D. Allport, W. Mackay, W. Prinz, & E. Scheeren (Eds.), *Language perception and production* (pp. 313–339). New York: Academic Press.

Connors, K. (1989). *Feeding the brain.* New York: Plenum Press.

Courchesne, E., Hesselink, J., Jernigson, T., & Young-Courchesne, R. (1987). Abnormal neuroanatomy in a nonretarded person with autism. *Archives of Neurology, 29,* 641–649.

Dahl, E., Cohen, D., & Provence, S. (1986). Clinical and multivariate approaches to the nosology of pervasive developmental disorders. *Journal of American Academy of Child Psychiatry, 25*(2), 170–180.

Damasio, H., & Damasio, A. (1989). *Lesion analysis in neuropsychology.* New York: Oxford University Press.

Damasio, A., & Maurer, R. (1978). A neurological model for childhood autism. *Archives of Neurology, 35,* 777–786.

De Kerckhove, D., & Lunisden, C. (1988). *The alphabet and the brain.* New York: Springer-Verlag.

Deloche, G., & Seron, X. (1987). *Mathematical disabilities.* Hillsdale, NJ: Erlbaum.

Denckla, M., & James, L. (Eds.). (1991). An update on autism: A developmental disorder. *Pediatrics, 87*(5) (Supplement).

Deuel, R. (1983). Aphasia in children. In H. Myklebust (Ed.), *Progress in learning disabilities* (Vol. 4, pp. 29–43). New York: Grune & Stratton.

Duane, D. (1983). Underachievement in written language: Auditory aspects. In H. Myklebust (Ed.), *Progress in learning disabilities* (pp. 177–206). New York: Grune & Stratton.

Eliot, J. (1975). The spatial world of the child. In H. Myklebust (Ed.), *Progress in learning disabilities* (Vol. 3, pp. 49–66). New York: Grune & Stratton.

Fay, W. (1969). On the basis of autistic echolalia. *Journal of Communication Disorders, 2,* 38–47.

Fein, D., Pennington, B., Markowitz, P., Braverman, M., & Waterhouse, L. (1986). Toward a neuropsychological model of infantile autism: Are social deficits primary? *Journal of the American Academy of Child Psychiatry, 25*(2), 198–212.

Fine, J., Bartolucci, G., Ginsberg, G., & Szatman, P. (1991). The use of intonation to communicate in pervasive developmental disorders. *Journal of Child Psychology and Psychiatry, 32*(5), 771–782.

Flynn, J., & Boder, E. (1991). Clinical and electrophysiological correlates of dysphonetic and dyseidetic dyslexia. In J. Stein (Ed.), *Vision and visual dysfunction* (Vol. 13, pp. 121–131). Basingstoke, NY: Macmillan Press Ltd.

Flynn, J., & Deering, W. (1989). Topographic brain mapping and evaluation of dyslexic children. *Psychiatry Research, 29,* 407–408.

Freeman, B., Rahbar, B., Ritvo, E., Bice, T., Yokota, A., & Ritvo, R. (1991). The stability of cognitive and behavioral parameters in autism: A twelve-year prospective study. *Journal of the American Academy of Child and Adolescent Psychiatry, 30*(3), 479–482.

Frith, U. (1989a). *Autism: Explaining the enigma.* London: Blackwell.

Frith, U. (1989b). A new look at language and communication in autism. *British Journal of Disorders of Communication, 24,* 123–150.

Frith, U., & Hermelin, B. (1969). The role of visual and motor cues for normal, subnormal and autistic children. *Journal of Child Psychology and Psychiatry, 60,* 153–163.

Frith, U., & Snowling, M. (1983). Reading for meaning and reading for sound in autistic and dyslexic children. *British Journal of Developmental Psychology, 1,* 329–342.

Gaddes, W. (1980). *Learning disabilities and brain function.* New York: Springer-Verlag.

Gaffney, G., Tsai, L., & Michin, S. (1987). Cerebellar structure in autism. *American Journal of Diseases in Children, 141,* 1330–1332.

Gazzaniga, M., & Smylie, C. (1984). Dissociation of language and cognition. *Brain, 107,* 145–153.

Gillberg, C., Strattburg, S., & Jacobson, G. (1987). Neurobiological findings in 20 relatively gifted children with Kanner-type autism or Asperger syndrome. *Developmental Medicine and Child Neurology, 29,* 641–649.

Golden, G. (1987). Neurological functioning. In D. Cohen, A. Donnellan, & R. Paul (Eds.), *Handbook of autism and pervasive developmental disorders* (pp. 133–147). New York: Wiley.

Grafman, J., & Boller, F. (1987). Cross-cultural approaches to study of calculation processes. In G. Deloche & X. Seron (Eds.), *Mathematical disabilities* (pp. 257–271). Hillsdale, NJ: Erlbaum.

Hartje, W. (1987). The effect of spatial disorders on arithmetical skills. In G. Deloche & X. Seron (Eds.), *Mathematical disabilities* (pp. 121–135). Hillsdale, NJ: Erlbaum.

Haywood, H. (1989). Multidimensional treatment of mental retardation. *Psychology in Mental Retardation and Developmental Disabilities, American Psychological Association, 15,* 1–10.

Hecaen, H., & Angelergues, R. (1962). Agnosia for faces (prosop agnosia). *Archives of Neurology, 7,* 92–100.

Henschen, S. (1925). Clinical and anatomical contributions to brain pathology. *Archives of Neurology and Psychiatry, 13,* 226–249.

Hermelin, B., & Frith, U. (1971). Psychological studies of childhood autism. *Journal of Special Education, 5,* 107–117.

Hermelin, B., & O'Connor, N. (1985). Logico-affective states and nonverbal language. In E. Schopler & G. Mesibov (Eds.), *Communication problems in autism* (pp. 283–309). New York: Plenum Press.

Howlin, P. (1986). An overview of social behavior in autism. In E. Schopler & G. Mesibov (Eds.), *Social behavior in autism* (pp. 103–132). New York: Plenum Press.

Hsu, C. (1988). Correlatives of reading success and failure in a logographic writing system. *Thalamus, 6,* 1–33.

Hughes, J. (1971). Electroencephalography and learning disabilities. In H. Myklebust (Ed.), *Progress in learning disabilities* (Vol. 2, pp. 18–55). New York: Grune & Stratton.

Jackson, H. (1876). Case of large cerebral tumor without optic neuritis and with left hemiplegia and imperception. *Royal London Ophthalmological Hospital Reports, 8,* 434–444.

John, E. (1989). *Neurometric evaluation of brain function in normal and learning disabled children.* Ann Arbor: University of Michigan Press.

Johnson, D., & Myklebust, H. (1967). *Learning disabilities: Educational principles and practices.* New York: Grune & Stratton.

Jones, E., & Aoki, C. (1988). The processing of Japanese kana and kanji characters. In D. de Kerckhove & C. Lunisden (Eds.), *The alphabet and the brain.* New York: Springer-Verlag.

Kass, C., & Myklebust, H. (1969). Learning disability: An educational definition. *Journal of Learning Disabilities, 2*(7), 377–379.

Kawamura, M., Hirayama, K., Hasegama, K., Takahashi, N., & Yamaura, A. (1987). Alexia with agraphia of kanji (Japanese morphograms). *Journal of Neurology, Neurosurgery, and Psychiatry, 50,* 1125–1129.

Killen, J. (1975). A learning systems approach to intervention. In H. Myklebust (Ed.), *Progress in learning disabilities* (Vol. 3, pp. 1–17). New York: Grune & Stratton.

Kirk, U. (1983). *Neuropsychology of language, reading, and spelling.* London: Academic Press.

Kirk, U. (1985). Hemispheric contributions to the development of graphic skills. In C. Best, (Ed.), *Hemisphere function and collaboration in the child* (pp. 193–228). New York: Academic Press.

Kosslyn, S. (1981). The medium and the message in mental imagery: A theory. *Psychological Review, 88,* 46–66.

Langdell, T. (1978). Recognition of faces: An approach to the study of autism. *Journal of Child Psychology and Psychiatry, 19,* 255–268.

Layton, T. (1987). Manual communication. In T. Layton (Ed.), *Language and treatment of autistic and developmentally disordered children* (pp. 189–213). Springfield, IL: Thomas.

Minshew, N. (1991). Indices in neural function in autism: Clinical and biologic implications. *Pediatrics, 87*(5) (Supplement), 774–780.

Morinaga, R. (1981). Learning disabilities: Reading and writing as measured by the letter completion test. [In Japanese]. *Journal of Psychiatria et Neurologia Pediatria Japanica, 20*(2), 41–47.

Mundy, P., Sigman, M., Ungerer, J., & Sherman, T. (1986). Defining the social deficits in autism: The contribution of nonverbal communication measures. *Journal of Child Psychology and Psychiatry, 27*(5), 657–669.

Myklebust, H. (1954). *Auditory disorders in children.* New York: Grune & Stratton.

Myklebust, H. (1957). Babbling and echolalia in language theory. *Journal of Speech and Hearing Disorders, 22*(3), 356–360.

Myklebust, H. (1964). *The psychology of deafness.* New York: Grune & Stratton.

Myklebust, H. (1965). *Development and disorders of written language* (Vol. 1). New York: Grune & Stratton.

Myklebust, H. (1967). Learning disabilities in neurologically disturbed children: Behavioral correlates of brain dysfunction. In J. Zubin & G. Gervis (Eds.), *Psychopathology of mental development* (pp. 298–320). New York: Grune & Stratton.

Myklebust, H. (Ed.). (1968). Learning disabilities: Definition and overview. *Progress in learning disabilities* (Vol. 1, pp. 1–15). New York: Grune & Stratton.

Myklebust, H. (1971). Childhood aphasia: An evolving concept. In L. Travis (Ed.), *Handbook of speech pathology and audiology* (pp. 1181–1202). New York: Appleton-Century-Crofts.

Myklebust, H. (1973). *Development and disorders of written language* (Vol. 2). New York: Grune & Stratton.

Myklebust, H. (Ed.). (1975). Nonverbal learning disabilities: Assessment and intervention. *Progress in learning disabilities* (Vol. 3, pp. 85–121). New York: Grune & Stratton.

Myklebust, H. (Ed.). (1978). Toward a science of dyslexiology. *Progress in learning disabilities* (Vol. 4, pp. 1–39). New York: Grune & Stratton.

Myklebust, H. (1981). *The pupil rating scale revised—screening for learning disabilities.* San Antonio, TX: Psychological Corporation.

Myklebust, H. (Ed.). (1983). Disorders of auditory language. *Progress in learning disabilities* (Vol. 5, pp. 45–77). New York: Grune & Stratton.

Myklebust, H., Bannochie, M., & Killen, J. (1971). Learning disabilities and cognitive processes. In H. Myklebust (Ed.), *Progress in learning disabilities* (Vol. 2, pp. 213–251). New York: Grune & Stratton.

Myklebust, H., & Boshes, B. (1969). *Minimal brain damage in children.* Washington, DC: U.S. Department of Health, Education and Welfare, Health Services and Mental Health Administration.

Myklebust, H., & Morinaga, R. (1990). Approaching definition of learning disabilities, emotional disturbance, autism, and mental retardation. *Thalamus, 7*(1), 1–38.

Ornitz, E. (1987). Neurophysiologic studies of infantile autism. In D. Cohen & A. Donnellan (Eds.), *Handbook of autism and pervasive developmental disorders* (pp. 148–165). New York: Wiley.

Paul, R. (1987). Communication. In D. Cohen, A. Donnellan, & R. Paul (Eds.), *Handbook of autism and pervasive developmental disorders.* New York: Wiley.

Prizant, B., & Schuler, A. (1987). Facilitating communication: Language approaches. In D. Cohen, A. Donnellan, & R. Paul (Eds.), *Handbook of autism and pervasive developmental disorders* (pp. 289–332). New York: Wiley.

Rapin, I. (1991). Autistic children: Diagnosis and clinical features. *Pediatrics, 87*(5) (Supplement), 751–796.

Rourke, B. (1989). *Nonverbal learning disabilities.* New York: Guilford.

Rourke, B. (Ed.). (1991). *Neuropsychological validation of learning disability subtypes.* New York: Guilford.

Rutter, M. (Ed.). (1971). *Infantile autism: Concepts, characteristics and treatment.* London: Longman.

Sasanuma, S. (1981). Kana and kanji processing in Japanese aphasics. *Brain and Language, 2,* 369–383.

Schopler, E., & Mesibov, G. (1986). *Social behavior in autism.* New York: Plenum Press.

Shah, V., & Wing, L. (1986). Cognitive impairments affecting social behavior in autism. In E. Schopler & G. Mesibov (Eds.), *Social behavior in autism* (pp. 153–170). New York: Plenum Press.

Spencer, C., Blades, M., & Morsley, K. (1989). *The child in the physical environment: The development of spatial knowledge and cognition.* New York: Wiley.

Srull, T., & Weyer, R. (1988). *Advances in social cognition* (Vol. 1). Hillsdale, NJ: Erlbaum.

Stevenson, H. (1985). Culture and reading disabilities. *Advances in Developmental and Behavioral Pediatrics, 6,* 177–204.

Stiles-Davis, J., Kritchevsky, M., & Bellugi, U. (1988). *Spatial cognition—brain bases and development.* Hillsdale, NJ: Erlbaum.

Sugishita, M., Iwata, M., Toyokura, Y., Yoshiaka, M., & Yamada, R. (1978). Reading of ideograms and phonograms in Japanese patients after commissurotomy. *Neurologica, 16,* 417–436.

Volkmar, F., & Cohen, D. (1988). Diagnosis of pervasive development disorders. In B. Lahey & A. Kazdin (Eds.), *Advances in clinical child psychology* (Vol. 2, pp. 249–284). New York: Plenum Press.

Volkmar, F., Sparrow, S., Rende, R., & Cohen, D. (1989). Facial perception in autism. *Journal of Child Psychology and Psychiatry, 30*(4), 591–598.

Weatherford, D. (1985). Representing and manipulating spatial information from different environments: Models to neighborhoods. In R. Cohn (Ed.), *The development of spatial recognition* (pp. 41–70). Hillsdale, NJ: Erlbaum.

West, R., Morris, C., & Nichol, G. (1985). Spatial cognition on nonspatial tasks: Finding spatial knowledge when you're not looking for it. In R. Cohn (Ed.), *The development of spatial cognition* (pp. 13–39). Hillsdale, NJ: Erlbaum.

Wing, L. (1971). Perceptual and language development in autistic children: a comparative study. In M. Rutter (Ed.), *Infantile autism: Concepts, characteristics and treatment* (pp. 173–197). London: Longman.

Wing, L., & Attwood, A. (1987). Syndromes of autism and atypical development. In D. Cohen, A. Donnellan, & R. Paul (Eds.), *Handbook of autism and pervasive developmental disorders* (pp. 3–19). New York: Wiley.

Relationship between Autism and Learning Disabilities

ROGER D. COX and GARY B. MESIBOV

INTRODUCTION

Although historically autism and learning disabilities have been independent of one another, changing definitions of these disorders and new conceptions of diagnosis suggest significant overlap (Shea & Mesibov, 1985). Similarities between these groups in learning, attention, communication, and social problems are now recognized, and genetic research (Folstein & Rutter, 1987) has established another connection. In this chapter we explore these similarities by reviewing the history of each diagnostic category and describing overlaps in concepts, learning difficulties, and behaviors.

EARLY CONCEPTUALIZATIONS OF AUTISM

Autism was first described by Kanner (1943), who highlighted two important aspects of this disability: a serious disturbance of social development, and an insistence on sameness (e.g., resisting change). Kanner's early accounts also described communication difficulties, which he in-

ROGER D. COX • Greensboro TEACCH Center, Greensboro, North Carolina 27401. GARY B. MESIBOV • Division TEACCH, Department of Psychiatry, School of Medicine, University of North Carolina at Chapel Hill, Chapel Hill, North Carolina 27599-7180.

Learning and Cognition in Autism, edited by Eric Schopler and Gary B. Mesibov. Plenum Press, New York, 1995.

cluded as part of the social deficit. His rich descriptions of autism included other typical characteristics: sensory disturbances, unusual play and interest in materials, uneven cognitive development, and unusual body use (posturing, body rocking). Although Kanner did not describe sensory disturbances specifically, they figured prominently in the major revisions of the definition by Rutter (1978) and the National Autism Society (Ritvo & Freeman, 1977).

Kanner's descriptions of the autism syndrome were precise and insightful; they are among the best of any clinical syndrome. Kanner appeared fascinated by the social difficulties and communication problems of autism. His writings include poignant examples of these problems, emphasizing their presence from the beginning of life. Kanner viewed autism as different from other childhood psychoses and as the earliest form of adult schizophrenia.

Kanner's contributions were his clear and precise description of an unrecognized syndrome and the distinctions he made between autism and similar diagnostic categories. Following Kanner, autism became a psychiatric diagnosis for severely handicapped children with peculiar communication, limited social relationships, and inappropriate responses to change.

ADJUSTMENTS IN AUTISM DEFINITION

The definition of autism has evolved since Kanner's early reports. Although it has never been specifically related to learning disabilities, several aspects of autism are closely linked to the problems we see in learning-disabled (LD) youngsters. This chapter focuses on the shared attributes of the two disabilities. After ∥ adjustments to ℛₒ A. ∥

 In 1977 the National Society for Children and Adults with Autism (later renamed the Autism Society of America) developed a consensus definition of autism (Ritvo & Freeman, 1977). Autism is a severely incapacitating lifelong developmental disability that typically appears during the first 3 years of life. The symptoms, caused by physical disorders of the brain, include the following:

1. Disturbances in the rate of appearance of physical, social, and language skills.
2. Abnormal responses to sensations. Any one of a combination of functions may be affected: sight, hearing, touch, pain, balance, smell, taste, and the way a child holds his/her body.
3. Speech and language are absent or delayed, whereas specific thinking capacities may be present. Immature rhythms of speech, lim-

ited understanding of ideas, and the use of words without attaching the usual meanings to them are common.

4. Abnormal ways of relating to people, objects, and events. Typically they do not respond appropriately to adults or other children. Objects and toys are not used as normally intended. Autism occurs by itself or in association with other disorders that affect the function of the brain, such as viral infections, metabolic disturbances, and epilepsy. (cf. Ritvo & Freeman, 1977 for the complete text of the definition.)

This definition underscores several fundamental aspects of autism. Similar to Kanner's definition, it suggests that communication and social problems are central to the disability. It places less emphasis than did Kanner, however, on rigid adherence to patterns of behavior, and greater emphasis on abnormal sensory responses. This definition also describes autism as a single, unitary problem and requires that individuals termed autistic have deficits in all of the described areas.

In 1980, the third edition of the *Diagnostic and Statistical Manual of Mental Disorders* (DSM-III) (American Psychiatric Association, 1980) included autism as a Pervasive Developmental Disorder (PDD). This represented a major advance over earlier additions that excluded autism. There were, however, several criticisms of the DSM-III autism definition: The characteristics were too vague; the concept was too inflexible; and the category "Autism, Residual State" was misleading.

Vague and imprecise, the DSM-III definition of autism was difficult to quantify. Several investigators examining the same child came to different diagnostic conclusions. For example, the difficulty in communication was described as "gross deficits in language development." What constitutes a gross deficit was not defined, but rather was left to the clinician's discretion. Disparate interpretations of this and other criteria became common.

Although most researchers acknowledged that autismlike developmental disabilities exist on a continuum with autism, DSM-III presented autism as an absolute. For example, the DSM-III description of the social deficits of autism was a "pervasive lack of responsiveness to other people." Variations in inappropriate social skills were neither described nor acknowledged. The suggestion in DSM-III was that only the most extreme cases were appropriate for a diagnosis of autism.

Another difficulty with the DSM-III definition of autism was the concept of "Autism, Residual State." This implied that the full syndrome of autism had to be present in order to apply this diagnosis. Children who improved after successful interventions or from normal developmental processes were given the Residual State label. This label caused considerable confusion, suggesting that autism was curable, and overlooked the potential for improvement from training or from the natural course of the disability.

DSM-III-R, a revision of DSM-III published in 1987 (APA, 1987), represented a major change in the conceptualization and description of autism. Sixteen specific and definable behavioral characteristics were listed under one of three major categories:

1. Qualitative impairment in reciprocal social interactions
2. Qualitative impairment of verbal and nonverbal communication skills and in imaginative activities
3. Markedly restricted repertoire of activities and interests.

Autism was defined by the presence of at least 8 of the 16 characteristics with at least two items from the social category, and one each from the communication and restricted repertoire of activities categories.

The DSM-III-R approach successfully resolved the major problems raised by DSM-III. Specific and observable, the 16 characteristics were reliably and consistently identified by different observers. The system acknowledged developmental changes in autism and allowed for a continuum of behaviors from mild to severe. Elimination of the Residual State category removed the implication that autism is curable. DSM-III-R also allowed different people to have different manifestations of autism.

Although a marked improvement over its predecessor, the DSM-III-R's approach to autism is not without critics. Major criticisms of the revised diagnostic system included its broad definition of the syndrome, the complexity of the diagnostic process, the lack of empirical support for the 16 criteria, and insufficient information about diagnostic reliability.

Autism is now diagnosed more frequently (Volkmar, Breman, Cohen, & Ciccehetti, 1988). Clinically this is an advantage, because most clients with characteristics similar to autism benefit from the same structured, individualized, education-based programs. A diagnosis of autism increases the likelihood that the client will be eligible for these appropriate services, improving the responsivity of the service-delivery system.

Researchers are less enthusiastic about a broader autism category, arguing that it would create additional difficulties (Van Bourgondien & Mesibov, 1989). Broader diagnostic categories decrease the likelihood that researchers from different centers would be studying similar clients. Questions about neurological and behavioral functioning in a group of autistic people becomes more difficult as their diversity increases. Most researchers argue that the DSM-III-R criteria further inhibited their already difficult search for clues to the causes of this disability.

It has also been suggested that the DSM-III-R system is unwieldy; the criteria are difficult to memorize and cumbersome to use. Faced with a complex checklist of 16 characteristics, most clinicians ignore them when diagnosing the few cases of autism that they typically see.

In addition to being cumbersome, the 16 characteristics of autism in DSM-III-R lack empirical verification. Only one study has examined their validity, finding the criteria "Marked lack of awareness of the existence of feelings of others" and "Persistent preoccupation with parts of objects" the best predictors of the autism diagnosis (Siegel, Vukicevic, Elliott, & Kramer, 1989). This study suggested that the 16 criteria are not equally important; more research on this topic is needed.

The reliability of diagnoses under DSM-III-R is also questionable, due to the complexity of the diagnostic characteristics, lack of specific operational definitions, and absence of reliability data. It remains unclear how frequently trained clinicians make similar diagnostic decisions when evaluating specific children.

EARLY CONCEPTUALIZATIONS OF LEARNING DISABILITIES

Tracing the evolution of the definition of learning disabilities is more difficult than that for autism. It is not even clear who should receive credit for identifying the diagnostic category of learning disabilities. Houck (1984) traced the label to Kirk's (1969) description of children with significant difficulties in learning and behavior that did not result from problems with sensory impairment, mental retardation, emotional disturbance, or environmental deprivation.

Learning disabilities has always been an educational diagnosis and is not specifically reflected in DSM-III or DSM-III-R, although DSM-III-R does have a section of Specific Developmental Disorders that includes the different aspects of learning disabilities. The extensive literature on learning disabilities offers an historical perspective. Since the 1950s there have been five approaches to the diagnosis of children experiencing difficulties with learning: *medical, symptom cluster, potential versus achievement discrepancy,* and *developmental lag.* Each of these has advantages and limitations; they will be reviewed separately in this section.

Medical

One of the earliest medical descriptions of learning disabilities was presented around the turn of the century (Morgan, 1896). Noting learning difficulties among the children he treated, Morgan related them to brain injuries and considered them comparable to strokes for adults. Morgan's assumption was that certain areas of the brain control the specific psychological processes that are involved in the academic skills emphasized in school. This approach was appealing because it suggested that learning disabilities can be defined by a specific set of processes that have clear etiological bases.

Unfortunately the medical approach to defining learning disabilities has not been as productive as anticipated. One problem is that learning disabilities are not as similar to brain damage in adults as had been thought (Hermann, 1959). The more serious problem is that the difficulties of learning-disabled children are more global than the medical theories suggested, making it impossible to relate learning problems to specific areas of the brain.

Symptom Cluster

A second approach to diagnosing learning disabilities was the symptom cluster method. Like the medical approach, this method assumed that learning-disabled children are qualitatively different from normal children and exhibit specific symptoms. Examples of these symptoms include letter reversals and poor spacing of written work. The symptom cluster method identified these qualitative differences and made them the basis of the diagnosis of learning disabilities (Blom & Jones, 1972; Myklebust, 1968). An important advantage of the symptom cluster method was its rapid identification of children without extensive testing, because the unique characteristics of this population are easy to identify. The problem with this technique is that neat patterns do not emerge in large numbers of children. None of the children with learning disabilities have all of these symptoms and many nonhandicapped children show some of them.

Achievement Discrepancy

The third system for diagnosing learning disabilities was the potential versus achievement discrepancy. This approach viewed learning disabilities as interfering with children's ability to achieve their full potential. From this perspective, specific learning disabilities negatively affect academic performance and achievement.

The main advantage of the potential versus achievement concept was its face validity; observations of children with learning disabilities suggested that this was their problem. Another advantage was that it advocated a productive remedial strategy of developing strengths and compensating for deficits. The main problem with this approach is its assumption that potential can be measured and quantified. Even strong proponents of intelligence testing for children do not pretend that these tests adequately evaluate intellectual potential.

Developmental Lag

A fourth theory of learning disabilities was the developmental lag. This approach viewed learning-disabled children as slower in achieving regular milestones than their nonhandicapped peers. For specific learning-disabled children, some milestones are more difficult to achieve than others.

An early advantage of the developmental lag approach was that it was easily quantifiable. One could identify and measure developmental levels effectively. The problem with this approach is that learning disabilities are often more than simply developmental lags. Children with learning disabilities are not only delayed in their development but are qualitatively different from their nonhandicapped peers. The developmental lag hypothesis does not account for these differences.

Each of the five approaches to learning disabilities targets a specific aspect of the problem and has advantages and drawbacks. However, the approach emphasized in this chapter is slightly different from these five. Called the *exclusion approach,* it is the one reflected in the federal guidelines and has been the most influential definition in this country.

EXCLUSION PRINCIPLE

For education classifications such as learning disabilities, the federal guidelines are the equivalent of the DSM diagnosis for mental health conditions. Federal legislation for handicapped children in the 1970s increased professional interest in the diagnosis of learning disabilities and stimulated investigators to develop more precise definitions. In 1977 the Federal Register adopted a definition based on the exclusion principle:

> A disorder in one or more of the basic psychological processes involved in understanding or in using language, spoken or written, which disorder might manifest itself in imperfect ability to listen, think, speak, read, write, spell, or do mathematical calculations, and such disorder may include such conditions as perceptual handicaps, brain injury, minimal brain dysfunction, dyslexia, or developmental problems which are primarily the result of visual, hearing, or motor handicaps, or mental retardation, or emotional disturbance, or of environmental disadvantage. (p. 213) (Federal Register, 1977)

Consistent with the other descriptions of learning disabilities, the exclusion approach focuses on the implications of neurological dysfunctions for the educational progress of an individual. The exclusion approach does not describe this directly. According to this approach the diagnosis of learning disabilities is done indirectly. If one observes learning disabilities, the first priority is to examine other possible causes: visual or hearing difficulties, motor handicaps, mental retardation, or emotional disturbance. In the absence of evidence for any of these, the diagnosis of learning disabilities is then applied.

Although the specific focus of this chapter is on the exclusion definition of learning disabilities, it also invokes concepts from the other historical trends that have been described. These concepts emphasize the heterogeneity of these problems, their manifestations rather than underlying processes, and their possible coexistence with other handicapping conditions. Most definitions identify learning disabilities as a group of disorders manifested by difficulties in the acquisition and use of listening, speaking, reading, writing, reasoning, or mathematical abilities. These disorders are intrinsic to the individuals and presumed to be a result of central nervous system dysfunction.

SIMILARITIES BETWEEN SEVERE LEARNING DISABILITIES AND HIGHER FUNCTIONING AUTISM

There are certain similarities between autism and learning disabilities: They are both organically based developmental disorders, begin early in life, and have a major impact on learning, communication, and social interaction. Both have a strong genetic basis and are associated with other neurological conditions. Closer inspection of these disabilities suggests even more similarities than these general tendencies. Similarities between autism and learning disabilities in social and interpersonal deficits, specific communication problems, cognitive styles, and discrepancies among their learning functions are substantial and significant.

Social and Interpersonal Deficits

Social and interpersonal difficulties characterize children with learning disabilities and those with autism (Baker & Cantwell, 1982; Mesibov, 1986; Schopler & Mesibov, 1986). There is accumulating evidence that children with learning disabilities have lower social status than their normal peers (Bryan, 1978; Siperstein, Bopp, & Bak, 1978). They also struggle with peer relationships, reporting fewer friends or satisfactory social interactions. Current intervention efforts are focusing on these social deficits, attempting to understand them and to help these children adapt more effectively.

Social deficits are a predominant feature of autism. Kanner (1943) coined the term "autism to highlight the social difficulties he observed in these children. Limited and abnormal interpersonal relationships have always been a central feature of the *autism* definition (American Psychiatric Association, 1984; Ritvo & Freeman, 1977; Rutter, 1978). Children with autism have the greatest difficulties with more subtle aspects of social interactions: identifying subtle cues, responding to affective messages, and identifying nonverbal communications.

Communication Deficits

Communication is of major concern for people with learning disabilities. The federal definition of learning disabilities describes an important characteristic as a disorder in language, listening, reading, writing, or spelling (Federal Register, 1977). A more recent consortium of LD advocacy groups described significant problems in the acquisition of listening, speaking, reading, and writing skills as central to this disorder (Hammill, Leigh, McNutt, & Larsen, 1981). Investigators noted numerous communication problems in the LD population: delayed onset of speech (Rutter, 1978), deficits in abstractions, nuances, and inferences (Ricks & Wing, 1976), word-finding problems (Rutherford & Prieto, 1977), and sound-discrimination problems (Johnson & Myklebust, 1964).

Communication problems are also central to the autism deficit and have been described by investigators since the identification of the disability (Kanner, 1943; Schopler & Mesibov, 1985). The most obvious deficit is the inability of approximately half the people with autism to use expressive language functionally. Numerous other examples of peculiar communication development have been noted in autism, such as deficits in understanding and using gestures or facial expressions (Bartak & Rutter, 1976; Ricks & Wing, 1976), difficulty with prosody (Baltaxe & Guthrie, 1987), echolalia (Prizant & Wetherby, 1987) and comprehension problems (Lord, 1985).

Cognitive Disorganization

In children with learning disabilities, disorganization is evident in their poor sequencing skills, impulsivity, distractibility, and problems in carrying out organized plans. Children with autism have similar difficulties; they have trouble with organization, distractibility, sequencing, and generalization. As a result of their difficulties, children with autism depend upon predictable routines, clear directions, and physical boundaries (Mesibov, Hersey, & Schopler, 1994; Schopler, Brehm, Kinsbourne, & Reichler, 1971). This is why a structured teaching approach, providing them with organizational systems, has proven most effective with this group (Bartak & Rutter, 1976; Mesibov, et al., 1994; Schopler, Mesibov, & Baker, 1982).

Discrepancies among Learning Functions

A distinguishing characteristic of learning disabilities and autism is the discrepancy among their learning functions. Uneven patterns of abilities differentiate both conditions from children with mental retardation whose skills generally develop at the same rate. In individuals with learning disabilities or autism, it is possible to observe abilities scattered from severely delayed to superior levels of functioning. Behaviors can be similarly unpredictable across settings.

DIFFERENCES BETWEEN LEARNING DISABILITIES AND AUTISM

Although there are numerous similarities between learning disabilities and autism, there are also significant differences. Many of the differences are in degree of severity and specificity; autism generally produces more severe difficulties and more unique behavior. Differences in the severity and peculiarity of symptoms have been noted in several areas: interpersonal relatedness, communication, cognitive deficits, and behavioral problems.

Although both groups of developmentally handicapped children have social difficulties, most children with learning disabilities are interested in making friends, gaining approval from teachers and parents, sharing ideas, and having experiences with other people. They are often awkward and unskilled in social interactions, but most of them are painfully aware of their problems (Bryan, 1978). LD children and adolescents often miss subtle social cues but their general dress, appearance, and manner are usually consistent with peer-group norms.

Although some children and adolescents with autism share similar social deficits with their LD peers, their problems are usually more severe. Many adolescents with autism have no friends outside of their home and do not even know how to greet another person. Behaviors in public can be obviously odd and peculiar, singling out immediately these young people with autism. They frequently dress quite differently from accepted social norms and are often oblivious to their impact on others.

Learning-disabled children often have language and communication difficulties. Although these can be severely handicapping, especially as they relate to school work, they are relatively minor when compared with communication deficits in autism. LD children and adolescents sometimes have trouble reading, articulating complex emotions, understanding subtle nonverbal communications, and using written language effectively. All of these children, however, can communicate in some way and have a general understanding of what others are saying.

Close to 50% of children with autism have no functional language skills. Their deficits are more severe and handicapping than communication deficits of children with learning disabilities. Children and adolescents with autism also show peculiar linguistic behaviors: echolalia, pronoun reversals, prosodic problems, and excessive reliance on rote phrases. Unlike most children with learning disabilities, people with autism are immediately recognized as different as soon as they begin to communicate.

Behavior problems are also more severe in autistic children than LD children. Many children with learning disabilities have interpersonal difficulties that grow out of their inability to understand social cues and their personal frustration at not having their needs met. Impulsive and unfulfilled, LD children are frequently angry and often involved in fights. Their behavior in the classroom can be inappropriate and disruptive. Teachers normally have more difficulty disciplining these children than their nonhandicapped pupils.

Behavior difficulties in autism are generally more severe and peculiar. The most extreme example is the self-injurious behaviors that sometimes cripple these youngsters. Self-stimulatory behaviors can be troublesome and attract considerable attention. Children with autism are often driven to follow predictable routines, finding change of any kind unsettling and threatening.

CLINICAL IMPLICATIONS OF LEARNING DISABILITIES VERSUS AUTISM DIAGNOSES

Professionals in the educational and mental health/pediatric fields are becoming more aware of the overlap of symptoms between high-functioning autism and certain types of learning disabilities. At present, however, dual diagnoses of autism/LD are seldom considered. As a result, children with characteristics of both disorders may be receiving inappropriate or incomplete educational and psychological services. School psychologists and other educational diagnosticians are much more likely to have received extensive training in diagnosing learning disabilities than in diagnosing and treating autism. The broadening of the learning-disability-diagnostic umbrella so that it includes children with associated social and interpersonal difficulties has not resulted in universally expanded services in social skills training, conflict resolution or communication skills improvement programming.

Although no hard data yet exist, it is highly probable that we are currently overdiagnosing LD cases and underdiagnosing high-functioning autism within our school-aged population in the United States. If so, then high-functioning children with autism are receiving interventions based primarily on uneven cognitive-skill areas or aptitude/performance discrepancy scores, while their social and communication deficits are considered only associated but noncritical features of learning disability.

One reason to suspect that this is happening is the increased number of cases that are referred for autism of young adults who were classified as learning disabled until the onset of puberty placed additional demands for social maturity and the development of more intimate social relationships. In many such cases, a retrospective examination of early history supports the diagnosis of high-functioning autism that included some identifiable learning disability. Similarly, there are also reported cases of adults who are diagnosed as having high-functioning autism even after completion of formal schooling. Typically, social deficits that have led to interpersonal failures or vocational failures due to poor social skillfulness lead clients or family members to seek assistance.

Until better diagnostic instruments can be developed to help educational and psychological diagnosticians distinguish between simple learning disabilities (with related social awkwardness) and high-functioning autism (with related uneven cognitive skills), clients in both diagnostic categories may continue to be inadequately served. A recognition of the interdependence of the diagnostic categories is an important first step in making additional improvements in the identification and treatment of these two disorders.

REFERENCES

American Psychiatric Association (1980). *Diagnostic and statistical manual of mental disorders*, (3rd ed.). Washington, DC: Author.

American Psychiatric Association (1987). *Diagnostic and statistical manual of mental disorders,* (3rd ed., rev.). Washington, DC: Author.

Baker, L., & Cantwell, D. P. (1982). Developmental, social and behavioral characteristics of speech and language disordered children. *Child Psychiatry and Human Development, 12,* 195–206.

Baltaxe, C. A., & Guthrie, D. (1987). The use of primary sentence stress by normal, aphasic, and autistic children. *Journal of Autism and Developmental Disorders, 17,* 255–271.

Bartak, L., & Rutter, M. (1976). Differences between mentally retarded and normal intelligence autistic children. *Journal of Autism and Childhood Schizophrenia, 6,* 109–120.

Blom, G. E., & Jones, A. (1972). Bases of classification of reading disorders. In E. O. Calkins (Ed.), *Reading Forum: A collection of reference papers concerned with reading disability.* NINDS Monograph #11. Bethesda, MD: Dept. of HEW, 1972.

Bryan, T. (1978). Social relations and verbal interactions of learning disabled children. *Journal of Learning Disabilities, 2,* 58–66.

Federal Register. (1977). Rules and regulations for implementing Public Law 94-142, 42. Washington, DC: Government Printing Office.

Folstein, S. E., & Rutter, M. L. (1987). Autism: Familial aggregation and genetic implications. In E. Schopler & G. B. Mesibov (Eds.), *Neurobiological issues in autism* (pp. 83–105). New York: Plenum Press.

Hammill, D. D., Leigh, J. E., McNutt, G., & Larsen, S. C. (1981). A new definition of learning disabilities. *Learning Disabilities Quarterly, 4,* 336–342.

Hermann, K. (1959). *Reading disability: A medical study of word-blindness and related handicaps.* Springfield, IL: Thomas.

Houck, J. H. (1984). Regulation and accreditation: The pros and cons for psychiatric facilities. *Hospital and Community Psychiatry, 35,* 1201–1204.

Johnson, D. J., & Myklebust, H. R. (1964). *Learning disabilities: Educational principles and practices.* New York: Grune & Stratton.

Kanner, L. (1943). Autistic disturbances of affective contact. *Nervous Child, 2,* 217–250.

Kirk, S. A. (1969). Learning disabilities: The view from here. *Progress in parent information, professional growth, and public safety.* San Rafael, CA: Academic Therapy.

Lord, C. (1985). Autism and the comprehension of language. In E. Schopler & G. B. Mesibov (Eds.), *Communication problems in autism* (pp. 257–281). New York: Plenum Press.

Mesibov, G. B. (1986). A cognitive program for teaching social behaviors to verbal autistic adolescents and adults. In E. Schopler & G. B. Mesibov (Eds.), *Social behavior in autism* (pp. 265–303). New York: Plenum Press.

Mesibov, G. B., Schopler, E., & Hearsey, K. A. (1994). Structured teaching. In E. Schopler & G. B. Mesibov (Eds.), *Behavioral issues in autism* (pp. 195–207). New York: Plenum Press.

Morgan, W. P. (1896). A case of congenital word-blindness. *British Medical Journal, 2,* 1978.

Myklebust, H. A. (Ed.). (1968). *Progress in learning disabilities.* New York: Grune & Stratton.

Prizant, B. M., & Wetherby, A. M. (1987). Communication intent: A framework for understanding social-communicative behavior in autism. *Journal of the American Academy of Child and Adolescent Psychiatry, 26,* 472–479.

Ricks, D. M., & Wing, L. (1976). The aetiology of childhood autism: A criticism of the Tinbergens' ethological theory. *Psychological Medicine, 6,* 533–543.

Ritvo, E. R., & Freeman, B. J. (1977). National Society for Autistic Children definition of the syndrome of autism. *Journal of Pediatric Psychology, 2,* 146–148.

Rutherford, R. B., & Prieto, A. G. (1977). An ecological assessment technique for behaviorally disordered and learning disabled children. *Behavioral Disorders, 2,* 169–175.

Rutter, M. (1978). On confusion in the diagnosis of autism. *Journal of Autism and Childhood Schizophrenia, 8,* 137–161.

Schopler, E., Brehm, S., Kinsbourne, M., & Reichler, R. J. (1971). The effect of treatment structure on development in autistic children. *Archives of General Psychiatry, 24,* 415–421.

Schopler, E., & Mesibov, G. B. (Eds.). (1985). *Communication problems in autism.* New York: Plenum Press.

Schopler, E., & Mesibov, G. B. (Eds.). (1986). *Social behavior in autism.* New York: Plenum Press.

Schopler, E., Mesibov, G. B., & Baker, A. (1982). Evaluation of treatment for autistic children and their parents. *Journal of the American Academy of Child Psychiatry, 21,* 262–267.

Shea, V., & Mesibov, G. B. (1985). The relationship of learning disabilities and higher level autism. *Journal of Autism and Developmental Disorders, 15,* 425–435.

Siegel, B., Vukicevic, J., Elliott, G. R., & Kraemer, H. C. (1989). The use of signal detection theory to assess DSM-III-R criteria for autistic disorder. *Journal of the American Academy of Child and Adolescent Psychiatry, 28,* 542–548.

Siperstein, G. N., Bopp, M. J., & Bak, J. J. (1978). Social status of learning disabled children. *Journal of Learning Disabilities, 11,* 98–102.

Van Bourgondien, M. E., & Mesibov, G. B. (1989). Diagnosis and treatment of adolescents and adults with autism. In G. Dawson (Ed.), *Autism: New perspectives on diagnosis, nature, and treatment* (pp. 357–385). New York: Guilford.

Volkmar, F. R., Bregman, J., Cohen, D. J., & Cicchetti, D. V. (1988). DSM-III and DSM-III-R diagnoses of autism. *American Journal of Psychiatry, 145,* 1404–1408.

II

Thinking and Learning

Savant skills

5

Motivating Communication in Children with Autism

LYNN KERN KOEGEL and ROBERT L. KOEGEL

INTRODUCTION

The purpose of this chapter is to discuss *motivation to communicate with others* as a pivotal treatment goal in the habilitation of autism. Once motivation to attempt to communicate with others is improved, a marked melioration occurs not only in language directly, but also in a number of other symptoms of autism (R. Koegel & Frea, 1993; R. Koegel, L. Koegel, & Surratt, 1993). Such attainment of widespread changes is especially important, because individuals diagnosed as having autism exhibit a wide variety of behavioral excesses and deficits when compared to children who are developing typically. These abnormalities usually include qualitative deficits in verbal and nonverbal communication, lack of reciprocal social interaction, and excessive disruptive and self-stimulatory behavior. Other behaviors that may be apparent are flattened, excessive, or otherwise inappropriate affect, self-injurious behavior, a preference for sameness in the environment, and isolated areas of exceptional performance (also termed *savant skills*).

Many behavioral descriptions of autism discuss and treat each of the aforementioned behavioral characteristics as separate entities. However, a

LYNN KERN KOEGEL and ROBERT L. KOEGEL • Autism Research Center, Counseling/Clinical/School Psychology Program, Graduate School of Education, University of California at Santa Barbara, Santa Barbara, California 93106.

Learning and Cognition in Autism, edited by Eric Schopler and Gary B. Mesibov. Plenum Press, New York, 1995.

recent shift in the field emphasizes the interrelationship of these areas (e.g., Crystal, 1987; R. Koegel, Camarata, & L. Koegel, 1994; L. Koegel, Valdez-Menchaca, & R. Koegel, 1993). From this perspective, researchers are discussing motivation as a major factor in autism, affecting communication and many other symptoms including self-stimulation, aggressive behavior, self-injurious behavior, and so on. This has been demonstrated in functional assessments of disruptive behavior that clearly link a social communicative function with various disruptive behaviors such as aggression, self-injury, self-stimulatory behavior, and so on (Carr & Durand, 1985; Durand & Carr, 1987; Durand & Crimmins, 1988; R. Koegel, Camarata, & L. Koegel, in press; L. Koegel, Valdez-Menchaca, & R. Koegel, 1993). Treatment techniques, based on functional assessments of the motivation or the communicative intent of severely disruptive behaviors, can dramatically decrease or successfully replace many disruptive behaviors with appropriate functionally equivalent communicative responses. For example, teaching children to request assistance significantly reduces behaviors such as aggression, tantrums, and self-injury that are being performed in order to escape or avoid a difficult teaching task. Similarly, aggression and other attention-seeking, disruptive behaviors can be reduced by teaching the child to appropriately request attention. This reciprocal pattern is also seen when children are taught to request teacher assistance as a functionally equivalent communicative alternative to certain escape-motivated stereotypic behaviors (Durand & Carr, 1987).

These studies and others demonstrate the significance of motivating children with autism to attempt communication skills that they may perceive as difficult. While typically developing children learn early in life that appropriate vocalizations and verbalizations are desirable to a parent, children with perceptual disabilities or related speech and language impairments may find communication difficult and continue to rely on early patterns of nonverbal communicative behaviors that are relatively mild (e.g., crying and mild tantrums); however, they are likely to develop into more serious behavior problems as the child grows older. Aggression, property destruction, and self-injury are just a few of the more severe problems that can evolve if no appropriate equivalent behaviors are learned early on.

MOTIVATIONAL TREATMENT

A variety of variables have been identified that are important in developing treatments to improve the motivation for social communication. Rapidly growing research data and clinical opinion tend to agree that intervention at a relatively early age is advantageous for improving motivation.

Such intervention can reduce the probability that relatively mild problems will increase in severity, especially if functional communication is a primary goal. However, one difficulty in teaching speech and language to children with autism, as noted previously, is that the children lack motivation to even attempt to learn to communicate. This has been seen already at very young ages in children who actively avoid social situations. Thus, even at very early ages, treatment can be difficult with this population.

To overcome this problem, a number of researchers have developed packages that consist of several highly effective components that have each been shown to be successful in improving motivation (cf. R. Koegel, O'Dell, & L. Koegel, 1987). We will discuss several of the most powerful variables that have been identified and then describe how combining these variables into treatment packages can result in far-reaching developmental gains as the child matures.

Child's Choice of Stimulus Materials Used in Teaching

Many effective motivational treatment techniques discussed in the literature include incorporating *child's choice* of the stimulus items employed during teaching a particular target behavior (R. Koegel, Dyer, & Bell, 1987). For example, a number of studies have shown that for children who already have some verbal ability, social behavior is improved when the child is allowed to determine the content of conversational topics during social interactions. Unfortunately, it is typical for adults who interact with children with disabilities to take almost total control over the conversational topic. If the topic happens to be of interest to the child with autism, the interaction may proceed smoothly for a short time. However, usually the topic will shift to something that is of little or no interest to the child, or may even be aversive to the child if it involves learning difficult new tasks. Under such conditions, the child will typically begin to engage in a variety of inappropriate or disruptive behaviors in order to terminate the interaction. In contrast, if a child with autism is taught to exercise some control over the conversational topic, data show that the interaction proceeds more smoothly, permitting the child to acquire both social and linguistic skills during the course of the interaction (e.g., R. Koegel, Dyer, & Bell, 1987). Treatment procedures for this type of dyadic interaction were described by Koegel, Dyer, and Bell (1987), and consisted of first identifying topics the child enjoys, and then prompting the child to initiate those topics with a conversational partner (a colleague of the therapist). When the partner happened to change the topic to something the child was not interested in, the therapist again prompted the child to initiate another favored topic. This procedure was repeated until the child learned a generalized skill of initiating preferred topics. This then permitted the type of turn-taking that characterizes typically developing individuals' conversational styles.

Extension of this area of research in relation to selection of stimulus items for treatment of other target behaviors, such as vocabulary development, development of an initial lexicon, and more recently, the treatment of phonology, has also been addressed in the literature. These results have shown similar improved patterns of responding with simultaneous reductions in untreated collateral disruptive behaviors when the child's interest is considered, rather than following the adult's agenda (Camarata, L. Koegel, & R. Koegel, 1993; Yoder, Kaiser, & Alpert, 1991; Yoder, Kaiser, Alpert, & Fischer, 1993). Under such conditions, the children appear to be highly motivated to participate in the treatment interaction, and progress on a variety of social and vocabulary treatment targets is enhanced. Likewise, reductions in social-avoidance behavior have been shown to correlate with child-preferred activities and conversational topics. Specifically, decreases in inappropriate pragmatic behaviors such as gaze aversion, closing eyes, hanging head down, turning and moving away, and so on, occurred when the items that were preferred by the child were incorporated into the communicative interactions.

Similar advances while teaching concepts were shown to occur when the child's selection of play items was incorporated into the treatment. For example, if the therapist attempted to teach colors, progress appeared to occur faster if the teaching was accomplished with, for example, colored balls that the child chose to play with, rather than using stimulus materials that the child did not prefer, for example, colored construction paper. It is important to note that incorporation of child's choice into the treatment must be highly individualized. One child may prefer to play with colored balls; another may prefer to select colored candies; and another may prefer to play with construction paper. Typically, it should make little difference to the therapist which of these stimulus items is employed. However, speed of acquisition of the color concept, ease of social interaction, and general ease of treatment were greatly facilitated when the therapist allowed the child to select the stimulus items (Dunlap et al., 1994; Dunlap, Kern-Dunlap, Clark, & Robbins, 1991; Dyer, Dunlap, & Winterling, 1990).

Reinforcing Communicative Attempts

While a child's choice by itself has been shown to be extremely important in improving motivation to communicate, other quite powerful variables have also been identified, especially when used in combination with other techniques. For example, reinforcing even very feeble attempts to communicate has been shown to improve motivation (R. Koegel, O'Dell, & Dunlap, 1988), as long as the attempts are definitely task-oriented, rather than using a more narrowly defined shaping contingency under which only successive approximations to a target verbalization are reinforced. This can be especially important in establishing an initial lexicon. That is, children with autism and related severe disabilities may be so accustomed to failure during initial communicative attempts that they lack the necessary motivation to engage in even very simple communicative interactions. Consider the obvious interactive effect combining child's choice, discussed above, would have with reinforcing attempts. One can imagine how permitting the child to choose the stimuli would raise the probability of the child's attempting a verbal response. Then, immediately rewarding any attempt to communicate, regardless of how distant (phonologically) it is from the adult production, would result in increasing the number of responses and attempts at the targeted phonological, linguistic, or communicative goal. Research in this area suggests that even if the child's initial attempts were far from recognizable speech sounds, as long as they were oriented toward the task and the child was using at least a normal level of voice volume, rewarding such attempts resulted in rapid production of speech use. Such results suggest that the children may have been capable of producing higher quality speech than they initially used, and that their initial failures related more to their lack of motivation than to a motor speech problem.

Interspersing Maintenance Trials

Studies also indicate that motivation and performance can be influenced substantially by manipulating task-sequencing variables (Carr, Newsom, & Binkoff, 1980). For example, interspersing maintenance tasks frequently so that the child experiences a high degree of success throughout the session, rather than solely presenting acquisition (new) tasks was shown to be an important variable influencing motivation (Dunlap, 1984; L. Koegel & R. Koegel, 1986; Neef, Iwata, & Page, 1980). When combined with other variables, task interspersal can be especially powerful. For example, if a therapist presents trials on tasks the child has fully mastered, then intersperses a new acquisition trial (such as a more advanced speech sound, a new vocabulary word, a new reading word, a new language concept, etc.), the child is likely to make at least a feeble attempt to respond, which can then be reinforced immediately by the therapist. Then, before the child's motivation wanes because of repeated presentations of the new and possibly difficult task, the therapist switches back to trials on the previously mastered maintenance tasks. Although the acquisition trial may be very difficult for the child, it appears that the child's confidence level is high and the child is more likely to attempt the task. This is in contrast to sessions in which all of the tasks developed in the child's curriculum consist of new (acquisition) tasks. During such sessions the children may appear highly frustrated and demonstrate increases in disruptive behaviors and decreases in appropriate responding.

Natural Reinforcers That Are Directly Related to the Task

Providing natural, intrinsically reinforcing consequences rather than utilizing any arbitrary reinforcer appears to increase motivation and speed of acquisition. Using a reinforcer that is directly related to the task, such as colored candies, which the child selects, in order to teach colors may help the children to learn that there is a relationship between their own responses and the consequences of their behavior. Thus, the consequences of a response can be directly associated with the specific linguistic form that was emitted. It is important that the consequences that follow the child's verbalizations be natural to the context in which the teaching occurs. Thus, the child's language use results in direct natural consequences, which can be explicitly prompted. This may help the child to associate positive outcomes with his or her own direct efforts, thereby improving motivation in general (cf. Seligman, Maier, & Geer, 1968). Furthermore, using a reinforcer that is inherently related to the response may shorten the delay between the reward and the reinforcer. This would make the reinforcer more powerful and help the child to associate responses with their consequences.

R. Koegel & Williams (1980) discussed the importance of providing a direct response-reinforcer relationship. Here a child with autism was taught to open the lid of a container to obtain a reward inside, as opposed to another trial in which the child was taught to open the lid of an empty container, and then rewarded by an indirectly related food reward. In such cases, the children showed rapid acquisition only when the target behavior was a direct part of the chain leading to the reinforcer (R, Koegel & Williams, 1980; Williams, R. Koegel, & Egel, 1981). This has been replicated in expressive-language teaching with single expressive words or word approximations (R. Koegel, O'Dell, & L. Koegel, 1987) and syntax, such as having the child say "I want" + a desired object (e.g., cookie) whereby the child received the item following the appropriate request (Charlop, Schriebman, & Thibodeau, 1985).

Motivational Treatment Packages

When all these techniques are combined and used in naturalistic-language teaching paradigms for children with autism, the effects are especially powerful (R. Koegel, O'Dell, & L. Koegel, 1987; Laski, Charlop, & Schreibman, 1988). Similarly impressive results occur when such naturalistic-language teaching techniques are used with other populations, such as children who are developing slowly (Hart & Risley, 1980), children with mental retardation (Warren & Kaiser, 1986), or children with specific language impairment (Camarata, 1993; Haley, Camarata, & Nelson, 1994).

Because of these results, there is a growing consensus among researchers and teachers that naturalistic teaching that focuses on motivation is highly desirable in comparison to more traditional discrete trial or analog techniques. Such motivational treatment procedures appear to be especially suited to teaching children in the early stages of language learning, particularly for children who do not verbalize frequently and who are having difficulty learning an initial lexicon. Within this context, there are several linguistic areas that remain to be addressed before communicative competence can be achieved in children with autism. In each case, motivating the child to engage in the communicative act appears to be a critical component in teaching the concepts involved.

For example, communicative competence requires not only an adequate number of utterances, but these utterances need also to represent an adequate variety of communicative functions. The language of children with autism lacks both adequate quantitative *and* qualitative aspects in comparison to typical childrens' language (Wetherby & Prutting, 1984). Although many motivational-teaching procedures have resulted in significant improvements in the quantity of responses, it is important to ensure that the procedures do not merely focus on the child's requests to gain access to desired items. Thus, a logical expansion of these procedures is to increase the child's motivation to engage in a breadth of communicative functions.

These motivational procedures have been proven to increase the child's active participation, initiation, and interest in the language habilitation process. However, this treatment may also make the teacher the primary source of language learning, dependent on manipulating the child's natural environment to provide adequate language-learning opportunities. One study shows that language opportunities only occurred at a low rate if the environment was not manipulated to provide occasions for language use (Peck, 1985). It is also important to remember, however, that in contrast to language-disabled children who often need inordinate amounts of prompting to respond, typically developing children often assume a very active role in the language-learning process, learning from their own self-initiated and self-motivated interactions with a number of sources, including parents, peers, siblings, teachers, and others. More important, many of these learning opportunities are initiated by children actively engaging in reciprocal interactions that directly result in language learning from the environment. Such independent learning skills are evidently emitted infrequently or are nonexistent in language-learning-disabled students, yet potentially represent a very powerful learning device if these children can be taught to access it.

The following section discusses recent preliminary research that focused on expanding the variety of *functions* of language and attempted to address the *outcome* of language use by teaching motivation for a spontaneous, self-initiated social utterance (a deictic question) and transferring motivation for the use of this utterance to nondesired items to expand the children's learning base.

Spontaneous Language and Information Seeking

Lack of motivation to actively use language socially not only conveys extremely poor pragmatic skills, but also results in many missed opportunities to evoke language-learning from the environment. For example, while typically developing children show considerable interest and curiosity in their environment and frequently ask questions to evoke information from adults, children with autism notoriously lack curiosity and information-seeking behavior (Hung, 1977; O'Neill, 1987). For typically developing children, the questions "What," What do," and "Where," appear between 19–28 months and other questions (whose, who, why, and how) appear shortly after, by approximately 31–34 months (Miller, 1981). In contrast, many children with autism lack any question-asking behavior altogether.

While some research has attempted to motivate question use as a functionally equivalent communicative response to replace disruptive attention-seeking and avoidance-driven behavior, the use of interrogative forms for information-seeking purposes has not been investigated thoroughly in the literature relating to autism. Only one study (Hung, 1977) taught the information-seeking questions "What is . . . for?" and "What is/are . . . doing?" to children with autism. The children were taught to ask the questions using a token reinforcement system and praise during 45-minute daily sessions in a classroom setting using common functional objects and events. Eventually, the tokens were faded. None of the children asked spontaneous questions during baseline. Similarly, the rates of spontaneous questions were hardly affected by learning question-asking in the classroom or by following prompting and reinforcement of spontaneous question-asking in nonclassroom settings. Only after token manipulation was introduced did the children's rates of question-asking increase in the generalization setting. Yet, if information seeking is to be taught as an intrinsically reinforcing activity, something akin to curiosity needs to be motivated.

We have recently begun a series of studies for the purpose of extending this line of research by focusing on motivational variables and curiosity so that the children are likely to use strategies that will result in widespread language learning from the environment. This is true because motivating the child to engage in such behaviors is likely to prompt learning language from others. In our initial study, we (Koegel, 1993) taught young children with autism to ask information-seeking questions to adults. In order to improve motivation for using spontaneous speech, in this case the question "What's that?," factors known to influence motivation, as described earlier, were incorporated to attempt to develop intrinsic motivation for curiosity question-asking.

To do this, children were taught to ask "What's that?" to adults. After the question, a highly desired object was pulled out of a bag, labeled, and given to the child. These objects were defined based on a series of videotaped premeasures, and included small toys, candies, and so on. This was done for the purpose of motivating the children to ask the target question. Once the children were producing the target questions at a high rate, items with which the children were unfamiliar were gradually added. Eventually, the bag was faded and the highly desired items were systematically eliminated, so that the children were asking "What's that?" in regard to items with unknown labels. The results of this research demonstrated that in addition to learning the question form, all of the children showed an increase in curiosity and the motivation to ask questions, as well as rapid acquisition of expressive vocabulary labels. Furthermore, all children showed some generalization of the target question to home and/or community settings that were unrelated to the treatment. As a follow-up to this study, we have just completed a parent-intervention program, in which the parents implement the entire training of the target question. Preliminary results related to this study suggest that having the parents teach this target behavior results in more rapid usage of the target question in home and community settings. One reason this increased usage may occur is because the parents have a greater knowledge of the child's preferences, and therefore are able to readily incorporate this variable into the important first-stages teaching.

Interestingly, this research also demonstrated that the children who exhibited behavior problems were significantly less disruptive when they were actively involved in the appropriate communicative interactions they learned in the study. One can speculate as to why the untreated collateral behaviors showed concomitant changes as the motivation to use new linguistic forms and linguistic knowledge improved. Related literature has shown that when children with autism are motivated to initiate activities, rather than having the adults initiate the activity, social-avoidance behavior decreases (R. Koegel, Dyer, & Bell, 1987). Research with other populations also validates this hypothesis that child-initiated goals result in higher performance than those that are adult-initiated. Such interactions, which are similar to the behaviors of typical language learners, may be more rewarding than adult-initiated interactions that do not provide the child with much control.

In summary, serious communication difficulties characterize children with autism and greatly inhibit their ability to function at their maximal potential in integrated community settings. We believe that motivating the children to use self-learning strategies may create an accessible knowledge base and we are currently pursuing this research with a variety of self-initiated strategies.

MOTIVATION AND SOCIAL-COMMUNICATIVE INTERACTIONS IN SCHOOL

Since motivation to interact with others in a social context seems problematic for children with autism, it is not surprising that these children may have difficulties when they begin school. In the next section of this chapter we discuss problems that can occur due to a lack of motivation to interact during initial educational-testing situations and how this information should be used to facilitate school placement, educational goals, and curriculum planning.

Assessment

Traditionally, diagnostic testing has played a major role in classroom placement and educational planning. Since the law in many states only requires reevaluation every 3 years, such testing may have long-term implications for a child's schooling. Therefore, the results of standardized testing of the language ability for children with autism must be accurately interpreted. This task may be more complex than previously assumed because the child's lack of motivation to communicate may play such a critical role during assessment. We have recently completed a research project (L. Koegel, R. Koegel, & Smith, submitted for publication) demonstrating the effect motivation may have on standardized language and intelligence testing. Six pre- and elementary-school-aged children with autism participated in this study. With the exception of two children who attended regular education preschool classes with assistance, all were placed in segregated classrooms for children with moderate to severe intellectual disabilities, based in large part upon their performance during standardized testing situations.

In this research, a variety of standardized language tests and verbal and nonverbal intelligence tests were administered. Two different testing conditions were implemented within the context of a multiple reversal design. During the control condition, the tests were administered as instructed by the test manual, by professionals who were familiar with standardized testing procedures. These professionals had no particular bias with respect to the outcome of the study and many were unaware that another experimental condition was being conducted. Edible and verbal rewards were given for appropriate test-taking behavior.

During the experimental condition, the *motivational* condition, tests also were given by professionals who were experienced test administrators, and often naive to the research hypothesis. However, in this condition, each child was observed in a variety of contexts, and the children's parents were interviewed prior to test administration. The purpose of these preliminary activities was to identify variables that were likely to be problematic from a motivational perspective and might therefore interfere with test taking. Then, based on the outcome of these interviews and observations, individual variables (discussed previously) that were likely to affect each child's motivation were defined and incorporated into the testing procedures. For example, breaks were provided based on the children's attempts to respond to the test items.

The results of this study demonstrated that the children all received considerably higher test scores when the motivational variables were incorporated into the testing situations. While some children showed only relatively small gains in test scores, a few who were untestable scored within the average range during the motivational condition. These improved results were true regardless of the order of conditions of the particular test administered.

This study implies that extreme variability in performance can result when severe motivational problems affect a child and that these variables may need to be considered during educational planning. In such cases, improving motivation during academic teaching may be a more appropriate educational goal, rather than individually attempting to teach academic target behaviors that may actually be well below the child's ability or functioning level.

Results of testing may or may not influence the classroom placement a child receives. However, regardless of classroom placement, this particular problem of communicative and social difficulty and the related inappropriate behaviors that generally accompany it become even more significant in mainstream settings. It can be particularly problematic as the child enters school, and issues of social inclusion in school and community settings gain momentum. For further discussion of these issues see Sailor, Gerry, & Wilson (1991a, 1991b). Integration is now being considered as a primary goal in special-education research. However, mainstreaming and integrating individuals with disabilities by simply placing them together in the same program or setting without systematic programming and support can be counterproductive, resulting in poor social acceptance of the individuals with disabilities, negative rates of social interaction among their peers, poor self-concepts of individuals with disabilities, and a generally negative attitude toward mainstreaming by regular educators (Gresham, 1982). Thus, systematic programming of the motivation for social communicative skills may need to be an integral component of the treatment program if successful school interactions are to be realized.

SUMMARY AND CONCLUSIONS

The present discussion has emphasized the importance of improving motivation to communicate in children with autism, and some of the widespread problems that can result if they lack adequate motivation to learn to communicate with others. Once a child is motivated to use key language structures, it is likely that this language learning will generalize to mainstream settings. To date, most teaching procedures rely heavily on adult initiations. Although such programs are effective in generating short-term language growth, it is neither cost-effective nor efficient for an adult to directly teach the myriad language skills typically seen in language acquisition. Also, children who are not motivated to use language-eliciting strategies, such as asking questions about their environment, remain totally dependent on the adult to establish new language forms. If language is learned by using language, the child needs to be adequately motivated both to respond and to initiate during social interactions. As such, incorporating motivational techniques into the teaching sessions, so that the child becomes more responsive and develops initiations, encourages developmentally therapeutic interactions with the environment. Such interactions are important as one considers life-span needs as the child matures.

ACKNOWLEDGMENTS

Preparation of this manuscript was supported in part by U. S. Department of Education, National Institute on Disability and Rehabilitation Research Cooperative Agreement No. G0087C0234; U. S. Department of Education Research Grant No. H023C30070; and by U. S. Public Health Service Research Grant MH28210 from the National Institute of Mental Health; and by U. S. Department of Education Research Grant No. H023C30070.

REFERENCES

California Association of School Psychologists (1987). Documentation and Recommendations. Millbrae, California.

Camarata, S. (1993). The application of naturalistic conversation training to speech production in children with speech disabilities. *Journal of Applied Behavior Analysis, 26,* 173–182.

Camarata, S., Koegel, L. K., & Koegel, R. L. (1993, November). *Naturalistic treatment for disruptive behavior in autism and other disabilities with speech intelligibility problems.* Speech presented at the American Speech, Language, and Hearing Association. Anaheim, California.

Carr, E. G., & Durand, V. M. (1985). Reducing behavior problems through functional communication training. *Journal of Applied Behavior Analysis, 18,* 111–126.

Carr, E. G., Newsom, C. D., & Binkoff, J. A. (1980). Escape as a factor in the aggressive behavior of two retarded children. *Journal of Applied Behavior Analysis, 18,* 111–126.

Charlop, M. H., Schreibman, L., & Thibodeau, M. G. (1985). Increasing spontaneous verbal responding in autistic children using a time delay procedure. *Journal of Applied Behavior Analysis, 18,* 155–166.

Crystal, D. (1987). Toward a bucket theory of language disability: Taking account of interaction between linguistic levels. *Clinical Linguistics and Phonetics, 1,* 7–21.

Dodge, K. A. (1983). Behavioral antecedents of social status. *Child Development, 54,* 1386–1399.

Dunlap, G. (1984). The influence of task variation and maintenance tasks on the learning and affect of autistic children. *Journal of Experimental Child Psychology, 37,* 41–64.

Dunlap, G., Kern-Dunlap, L., Clarke, S., & Robbins, F. R. (1991). Functional assessment, curricular revision, and severe behavior problems. *Journal of Behavior Analysis, 24,* 387–397.

Dunlap, G., de Perzzel, M., Clarke, S., Wilson, D., Wright, S., White R., & Gomez, A. (1994). Choice making and proactive behavioral support for students with emotional and behavioral challenges. *Journal of Applied Behavioral Analysis, 27*(3), 505–518.

Durand, V. M., & Carr, E. G. (1987). Social influences on "self-stimulatory" behavior: Analysis and treatment application. *Journal of Applied Behavior Analysis, 20,* 119–132.

Durand, V. M., & Crimmins, D. B. (1988). Identifying the variables maintaining self-injurious behavior. *Journal of Autism and Developmental Disorders, 18,* 99–117.

Dyer, K., Dunlap, G., & Winterling, V. (1990). Effects of choice making on the serious problem behaviors of students with severe handicaps. *Journal of Applied Behavior Analysis, 23,* 515–524.

Gresham, F. M. (1982). Misguided mainstreaming: The case for social skills training with handicapped children. *Exceptional Children, 48,* 422–433.

Haley, K. L., Camarata, S. M., & Nelson, K. E. (1994). Social valence in specifically language impaired children during imitation-based and conversation-based language intervention. *Journal of Speech and Hearing Research, 37*(2), 378–388.

Hart, B. M., & Risley, T. R. (1980). In vivo language intervention: Unanticipated general effects. *Journal of Applied Behavior Analysis, 7,* 243–256.

Hung, D. W. (1977). Generalization of "curiosity" questioning behavior in autistic children. *Journal of Behavior Therapy and Experimental Psychiatry, 8,* 237–245.

Hunt, P., Alwell, M., Goetz, L., & Sailor, W. (1990). Generalized effects of conversation skill training. *The Journal of the Association for Persons with Severe Handicaps, 15,* 250–260.

Koegel, L. K., & Koegel, R. L. (1986). The effects of interspersed maintenance tasks on academic performance and motivation in a severe childhood stroke victim. *Journal of Applied Behavior Analysis, 19,* 425–430.

Koegel, L. K., Koegel, R. L., Hurley, C., & Frea, W. D. (1992). Improving social skills and disruptive behavior in children with autism through self-management. *Journal of Applied Behavior Analysis, 25,* 341–353.

Koegel, L. K., Koegel, R. L., & Smith, A. E. (submitted for publication). The influence of motivation and attention in standardized testing of children with autism.

Koegel, L. K. (1993). Teaching children with autism to use a self-initiated strategy to learn expressive vocabulary. Unpublished doctoral dissertation, University of California, Santa Barbara.

Koegel, L. K., Valdez-Menchaca, M., & Koegel, R. L. (1993). Autism: A discussion from a social communication perspective. In. V. Van Hasselt & M. Hersen (Eds.), *Advanced Abnormal Psychology* (pp. 165–187). New York: Plenum Press.

Koegel, R. L., Camarata, S. M., & Koegel, L. K. (1994). Aggression and noncompliance: Behavior modification through naturalistic language remediation. J. L. Matson (Ed.), *Autism in children and adults: Etiology, assessment, and intervention* (pp. 165–180). Pacific Grove, CA: Brooks/Cole.

Koegel, R. L., Dyer, K., & Bell, L. K. (1987). The influence of child-preferred activities on autistic children's social behavior. *Journal of Applied Behavior Analysis, 20,* 243–252.

Koegel, R. L., & Frea, W. D. (1993). Treatment of social behavior in autism through the modification of pivotal pragmatic skills. *Journal of Applied Behavior Analysis, 26,* 369–377.

Koegel, R. L., Koegel, L. K., & Surratt, A. V. (1993). Language intervention and disruptive behavior in preschool children with autism. *Journal of Autism and Developmental Disorders, 22,* 141–153.

Koegel, R. L., & Mentis, M. (1985). Annotation Motivation in childhood autism: Can they or won't they? *Journal of Child Psychology and Psychiatry, 26,* 185–191.

Koegel, R. L., O'Dell, M. C., Dunlap, G. (1988). Producing speech use in nonverbal autistic children by reinforcing attempts. *Journal of Autism and Developmental Disorders, 18,* 525–538.

Koegel, R. L., O'Dell, M. C., & Koegel, L. K. (1987). A natural language teaching paradigm for teaching nonverbal autistic children. *Journal of Autism and Developmental Disorders, 17,* 187–199.

Koegel, R. L., & Williams, J. (1980). Direct vs. indirect response-reinforcer relationships in teaching autistic children. *Journal of Abnormal Child Psychology, 4,* 537–547.

Lambert, N. M. (1981). The clinical validity of the process for assessment of effective student functioning. *Journal of School Psychology, 19,* 323–334.

Laski, K. E., Charlop, M. H., Schreibman, L. (1988). Training parents to use the natural language paradigm to increase their autistic children's speech. *Journal of Applied Behavior Analysis, 21,* 391–400.

Miller, J. (1981). *Assessing language production in children.* Boston, MA: Allyn & Bacon.

Neef, N. A., Iwata, B. A., & Page, T. J. (1980). The effects of interspersal training versus high density reinforcement on spelling acquisition and retention. *Journal of Applied Behavior Analysis, 13,* 153–158.

O'Neill, R. E. (1987). *Environmental interactions of normal children and children with autism.* Unpublished doctoral dissertation, University of California at Santa Barbara.

Peck, C. A. (1985). Increasing opportunities for social control by children with autism and severe handicaps: Effects on student behavior and perceived classroom climate. *Journal of The Association for Persons with Severe Handicaps, 10,* 183–193.

Sailor, W., Gerry, M., & Wilson, W. (1991a). Disability and school integration. In T. Husen & T. N. Postlethwaite (Eds.), *International encyclopedia of education: Research and studies* (2nd suppl.). Oxford, England: Pergamon.

Sailor, W., Gerry, M., & Wilson, W. (1991b). Policy implication of emergent full models for the education of students with severe disabilities. In M. Wang, H. Walberg, & M. Reyonaldo (Eds.), *Handbook of special education* (Vol. 4). Oxford, England: Pergamon.

Seligman, M. E. P., Maier, S. F., & Geer, J. (1968). The alleviation of learned helplessness in the dog. *Journal of Abnormal and Social Psychology, 73,* 256–262.

Turnbull, H. R., III. (1993). *Free appropriate public education: The law and children with disabilities.* Denver, CO: Love.

Warren, S. F., & Kaiser, A. P. (1986). Incidental language teaching: A critical review. *Journal of Speech and Hearing Disorders, 51,* 291–299.

Wetherby, A. M., & Prutting, C. A. (1984). Profiles of communicative and cognitive-social abilities in autistic children. *American Speech-Language-Hearing Association, 27,* 364–377.

Williams, J. A., Koegel, R. L., & Egel, A. L. (1981). Response-reinforcer relationships and improved learning in autistic children. *Journal of Applied Behavior Analysis, 14,* 53–60.

Williams, T. S. (1983). Some issues in the standardized testing of minority students. *Journal of Education, 165,* 192–208.

Yoder, P. J., Kaiser, A. P., & Alpert, C. L. (1991). An exploratory study of the interaction between language teaching methods and characteristics. *Journal of Speech and Hearing Research, 34,* 155–167.

Yoder, P. J., Kaiser, A. P., Alpert, C. L., & Fischer, R. (1993). Following the child's lead when teaching nouns to preschoolers with mental retardation. *Journal of Speech and Hearing Research, 36,* 158–167.

6

The Assessment and Interpretation of Intellectual Abilities in People with Autism

ALAN J. LINCOLN, MARK H. ALLEN,
and ANGELA KILMAN

INTRODUCTION

The purpose of this chapter is to discuss the nature and specificity of intellectual and cognitive abilities in people with autism. The developmental ramifications on intellectual and cognitive development of early brain pathology are initially reviewed, followed by a detailed discussion of specific research findings employing the Wechsler intelligence scales. In addition, the use of the Wechsler scales and the Kaufman Assessment Battery for Children are reviewed with respect to assessing sequential and simultaneous processing abilities in children with autism. Memory functions in persons with autism are reviewed. Practical and clinical considerations for testing children with autism are then summarized. Finally, the conclusion attempts to theoretically integrate the findings of cognitive and intellectual abilities in persons with autism into a neuropsychological developmental model.

Autism is a pervasive, handicapping condition that compromises the social, adaptive, language, and cognitive abilities of individuals with the

ALAN J. LINCOLN and ANGELA KILMAN • Neuropsychology Research Laboratory, Children's Hospital Research Center, and California School of Professional Psychology, San Diego, California 92123. MARK H. ALLEN • Neuropsychology Research Laboratory, Children's Hospital Research Center, San Diego, California 92123.

Learning and Cognition in Autism, edited by Eric Schopler and Gary B. Mesibov. Plenum Press, New York, 1995.

disorder. It is a developmental disorder. Symptoms and atypical developmental patterns are generally observed in infancy. With maturation, symptoms and developmental abilities can vary dramatically from childhood through adulthood. Yet, the mystery that underlies the etiology of autism, or the ways in which such an etiology impacts brain development and functioning are still not well understood. The assessment of cognitive functions has been an important resource in the clinical evaluation of the developmental capabilities of affected individuals. In addition, such assessment has also been used to help identify and understand the ramifications of impaired brain development upon brain functioning.

It is useful to theoretically consider the etiology of the developmental brain impairment in autism as being similar to a developmental brain lesion (Lincoln, et al., 1990). However, in this context the use of the term *lesion* is used in a global, nonspecific manner and only implies that something is wrong with the brain. It is very likely that the developmental brain lesion(s) of autism and the associated effects upon brain functioning impact not only immediate aspects of brain processing (i.e., the ability to rapidly shift attention (Courchesne et al., 1993), or the recognition of contextual probability (Lincoln et al., 1993), but also, and perhaps more important, the learning and developmental sequelae of such processing (Lincoln et al., 1990). Thus, in evaluating the cognitive functions of individuals with autism, one is largely assessing the downstream consequences that the developmental brain lesion(s) had upon early brain processing. In fact, with ongoing maturation it is fully possible that the original developmental brain lesion(s) no longer play a central role in the atypical aspects of brain processing associated with the expressed symptoms of autism. Thus, one may potentially observe the influence of such a lesion in an experimental setting or in some components of tasks utilized to assess cognitive ability. However, by the time the child with autism is of school age, the ripple effects of the developmental brain lesion upon cognitive functions have already played a significant role. By school age, with contemporary methods of cognitive assessment, one can no longer disentangle the processes of cognitive or social functioning directly impaired by the developmental brain lesion(s) from the consequences of such impairment upon previous and new learning, and the development of new cognitive structures. Furthermore, depending on the exact nature of the developmental lesion, the impact upon cognitive, language, and social functioning may differ and result in varying subtypes of the core disorder (Fein et al., 1985).

Therefore, when one attempts to evaluate the cognitive abilities of children, adolescents or adults with autism, one is for all practical purposes evaluating how they have adapted to some primary processing/cognitive deficit(s) and learned to acquire and process information in spite of such primary processing deficit(s). Some types of information-processing demands may be relatively spared and unaffected by either the primary or downstream effects of the lesion. Other types of processing demands may continue to show evidence of impairment or may have depended on impaired processes that have not developed as they should. One might envision these processes as being similar to the building of a brick wall. In parts of the foundation of the brick wall, the bricks may have been placed exactly in the right spots. That part of the wall is built to specification. However, on another part of the wall the foundation is built in a faulty manner. Each row of bricks built upon it is also faulty and does not meet the proper specifications. The completed wall with its portion of truly aligned bricks and its portion of misaligned bricks is not as functional and capable of withstanding the environmental stresses for which it was designed. It is not just the sum total of correctly aligned bricks and poorly aligned bricks, but more important, it is the integration of all the bricks into a complete structure.

There is an important interplay among social, affective, and cognitive components of development. These interdependent components must become integrated in order for development to progress normally. In autism there is poor integration among such components (Hobson, 1989; Kanner, 1943). There is also poor integration of various cognitive functions (Lincoln, Courchesne, Kilman, Elmasian, & Allen, 1988). This is evident in the clinical psychometric assessment of the intellectual and cognitive abilities of people with autism. It is also evident in the experimental assessment of various cognitive and intellectual skills.

ASSESSMENT OF INTELLIGENCE: THE WECHSLER SCALES

David Wechsler considered intelligence to be a global aggregate of abilities that enables an individual "to act purposely, to think rationally and to deal effectively with his or her environment" (Wechsler, 1958, p. 7). Wechsler believed that such abilities could be operationally defined and measured. He also believed that the organization of an individual's intellectual abilities was subsumed in their overall personality makeup. Wechsler devised his measures by operationalizing constructs of several intellectual functions. Such functions included expressive vocabulary, verbal reasoning, abstraction, memory, attention, concentration, visual-motor integration and motor speed. All of the subtests that make up his tests of intelligence include one or more of these various functions. Wechsler believed that any single ability may add relatively little to an individual's overall functioning unless it is well integrated with the other intellectual abilities. He also believed that his tests measured nonintellectual abilities such as motivation or drive.

ASSESSMENT OF AUTISTIC INDIVIDUALS WITH THE WECHSLER SCALES

In the past 16 years there have been several studies that have evaluated the intellectual abilities of people with autism on the Wechsler scales. These studies demonstrate that many individuals with autism have a distinct pattern of intellectual ability (Bartak, Rutter, & Cox, 1975; Freeman, Lucas, Forness, & Rivco, 1985; Lincoln et al., 1988; Lockyer & Rutter, 1970; Ohta, 1987; Rumsey & Hamburger, 1990). Most, but not all, studies report higher Performance IQ than Verbal IQ in samples of persons with autism (See Table 6-1).

Verbal IQ vs. Performance IQ Discrepancy

The Verbal IQ (VIQ) versus the Performance IQ (PIQ) discrepancy is not the best way to assess intellectual strengths and weaknesses. This is because factor analytic studies of the Wechsler measures (WISC-R and WAIS-R) on normal standardization samples are best explained by a three-factor solution, rather than a two-factor (verbal vs. performance) solution (Kaufman, 1990, pp. 234–262 review). The three factors that emerge in factor analytic studies of the Wechsler scales include:

> Factor I (Verbal Comprehension): Information, Vocabulary, Comprehension and Similarities
> Factor II (Perceptual Organization): Picture Completion, Picture Arrangement Block Design, and Object Assembly
> Factor III (Freedom from Distractibility): Arithmetic, Digit Span, and Coding

The means of the subtests that comprise each of these factors is often a better way to evaluate the domain assessed by each individual factor. Subtests within each factor share greater variance than do subtests between different factors. Thus, in obtaining a mean-scaled score from within factor subtests, one is assessing abilities that have a significant amount of their variance in common. In evaluating PIQ or VIQ scores, on the other hand, one is adding together some scores from subtests that may not really

Table 6-1. A Comparison of Verbal and Performance IQ Scores

Study	Sample	Test	VIQ	PIQ
Bartak et al., 1975	Autism, mean age 7 years	WISC	66.6 $N = 9$	96.7 $N = 9$
Dawson, 1983	Autism, mean age 18 years	WAIS/WISC-R	64.1 $N = 10$	80.2 $N = 10$
Freeman et al., 1985	Autism, mean age 8.8 years	WISC-R	90 $N = 21$	105 $N = 21$
Jacobson et al., 1988	Autism, mean age 23	WAIS	83.0 $N = 9$	77.0 $N = 9$
Lincoln et al., 1988 Study 1	Autism, mean age 17.6	WISC-R/WAIS-R	71.0 $N = 33$	83.3 $N = 33$
Lincoln et al., 1988 Study 2	Autism, mean age 10	WISC-R	60.4 $N = 13$	84.1 $N = 13$
Lockyer & Rutter, 1970	Infantile psychosis, mean age 15 years	WAIS/WISC	73.5 $N = 21$	71.4 $N = 27$
Ohta, 1987	Autism, mean age 10 years	WISC	64.9 $N = 16$	85.3 $N = 16$
Rumsey, 1985	Autism, mean age 27 years	WAIS	103 $N = 9$	104 $N = 9$
Rumsey & Hamburger, 1988	Autism, mean age 26.4	WAIS	103.4 $N = 10*$	103.9 $N = 10*$
Szatmari et al., 1990	Autism, mean age 17 years	WISC-R/WAIS-R	84 $N = 17$	81 $N = 17$
Schneider & Asarnow, 1987	Autism, mean age 10.7	WISC-R	80.1 $N = 15$	93.6 $N = 15$

*Same subjects as Rumsey, 1985

share much common variance, and thus, are, in effect, adding apples and oranges.

Factor Solutions of Scale Scores

Table 6-2 shows only those studies from Table 6-1 that reported scaled scores from the Wechsler subtests. This made it possible to calculate the mean-scaled score for each of the three factors (i.e., Verbal Comprehension, Perceptual Organization, and Freedom from Distractibility). Results of the relative mean-scaled scores across all of those studies clearly show that the Verbal Comprehension factor is depressed relative to the Perceptual Organization factor. This finding is consistent with a verbal comprehension deficit in persons with autism compared to their more effective visual-motor and visual-perception abilities. Unfortunately, the Jacobson et al.

Table 6-2. A Comparison of Mean Verbal Comprehension (VC), Perceptual
Organization (PO), and Freedom from Distractibility (FD) Factors Obtained from
Wechsler Subtest Scaled Scores

Study	Sample	Test	VC	PO	FD
Bartak et al., 1975	Autism, mean age 7 years	WISC N = 9	3.6*	10.0	6.8
Dawson, 1983	Autism, mean age 18 years	WAIS/WISC-R N = 10	3.1*	9.8*	*
Freeman et al., 1985	Autism, mean age 8.8 years	WISC-R N = 21	8.4	10.4	8.2
Lincoln et al., 1988 Study 1	Autism, mean age 17.6	WISC-R/WAIS-R N = 33	4.6	8.2	6.1
Lincoln et al., 1988 Study 2	Autism, mean age 10	WISC-R N = 13	2.8	8.0	4.8
Lockyer & Rutter, 1970	Infantile psychosis, mean age 15 years	WAIS/WISC N = 21	4.3	5.9	4.8
Ohta, 1987	Autism, mean age 10 years	WISC N = 16	4.7	7.7	5.7
Rumsey & Hamburger, 1988	Autism, mean age 26.4	WAIS N = 10	9.3	11.1	10.7
Szatmari et al., 1990	Autism, mean age 17 years	WISC-R/WAIS-R N = 17	7.2	7.8	7.4

*One or more subtests omitted.

(1988) and Schneider and Asarnow (1987) studies did not report scaled
scores. Such information would have been useful, because the former
study found higher VIQ and PIQ, whereas the latter found higher PIQ than
VIQ. The Rumsey (1985) study was also not included in Table 6-2, because
the subsequent Rumsey and Hamburger (1990) study reported the IQ
scores from the same subjects.

Lincoln et al. (1988) reported how autistic individuals demonstrate
even more profound differences among selected subtests derived from the
Verbal Comprehension factor (Vocabulary and Comprehension), relative
to selective subtests derived from the Perceptual Organization factor
(Block Design and Object Assembly). Vocabulary and Comprehension
scaled scores were reported as being quite impaired compared to Block
Design and Object Assembly scaled scores in almost all of the subjects with
autism (see Fig. 6-1). Table 6-3 shows how these pairs of subtests compare
across all of the studies shown in Table 6-2. It is clear from Table 6-3 that
the more specific comparison of Vocabulary and Comprehension versus
Block Design and Object Assembly more sensitively demonstrates the
significant unevenness in these individuals verbal and visual-motor cognitive abilities.

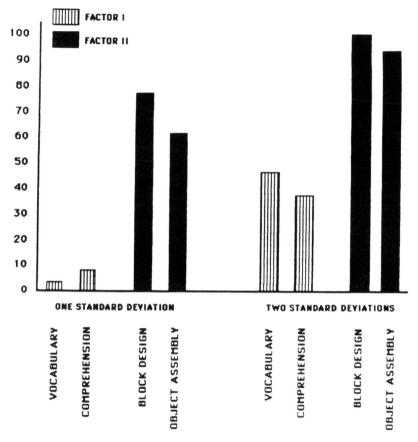

Fig. 6-1. The percent of subjects with mean-age adjusted Wechsler-scaled scores within −1 and −2 standard deviations, respectively. It also shows the factor (Factor I: Verbal Comprehension or Factor II: Perceptual Organization) that these selected subtests have their greatest loading. (From Lincoln et al., 1988, Fig. 2, p. 511.)

Fluid and Crystallized Abilities

It is noteworthy that both Block Design and Object Assembly are good measures of fluid intellectual ability, while Vocabulary and Comprehension are good measures of crystallized ability (Kaufman, 1990, review). Fluid intellectual ability is believed to be innate and not influenced by learning or experience. Crystallized ability is acquired and influenced to a significant degree by environmental experience, learning, and culture.

Table 6-3. A Comparison of the Mean Difference between the Sum of Vocabulary
and Comprehension to the Sum of Block Design and Object Assembly

Study	Sample	Test	V+C	B+O	[(B+O) – (V+C)]/2
Bartak et al., 1975	Autism, mean age 7 years	WISC N = 9	6.8	22.4	7.8
Dawson, 1983	Autism, mean age 18 years	WAIS/WISC-R N = 10	6.4	19.5	6.6
Freeman et al., 1985	Autism, mean age 8.8 years	WISC-R N = 21	14.6	23.0	4.2
Lincoln et al., 1988 Study 1	Autism, mean age 17.6	WISC-R/WAIS-R N = 33	7.4	19.1	5.9
Lincoln et al., 1988 Study 2	Autism, mean age 10	WISC-R N = 13	3.3	19.6	8.2
Lockyer & Rutter, 1970	Infantile psychosis, mean age 15 years	WAIS/WISC N = 21	7.7	15.3	3.8
Ohta, 1987	Autism, mean age 10 years	WISC N = 16	9.5	21.1	5.8
Rumsey & Hamburger, 1990	Autism, mean age 26.4	WAIS N = 10	16.8	26.0	4.6
Szatmari et al., 1990	Autism, mean age 17 years	WISC-R/WAIS-R N = 17	14.4	15.7	.65

Furthermore, the ability to develop intellectual abilities based on environmental experience and learning is dependent on the efficacy of the fluid
intellectual functions. Thus, early poor performance on measures sensitive
to fluid ability may be more predictive of subsequent global intellectual
deficits. The converse, however, may not be true. Adequate fluid ability
may not necessarily facilitate crystallized intellectual functions.

Factor Solutions for Wechsler Scaled Scores in Persons with Autism

Lincoln et al. (1988) described the characteristic pattern of scaled
scores on the Wechsler scales (WAIS-R or WISC-R) obtained from one
sample of 33 persons with autism (see Fig. 6-2), and another sample of 13
children with autism. The similarity of the scaled-score profile was compared to subjects evaluated by Lockyer et al. (1970) and Bartak et al. (1975),
and summarized in Rutter (1978). Figure 6-3 shows that comparison, and
also the different factor structure obtained from a group of autistic individuals. Lincoln et al. (1988) described the first factor that comprised all
of the Wechsler Verbal subtests as being related to their language ability,
and noted the severe verbal comprehension deficit found in these in-

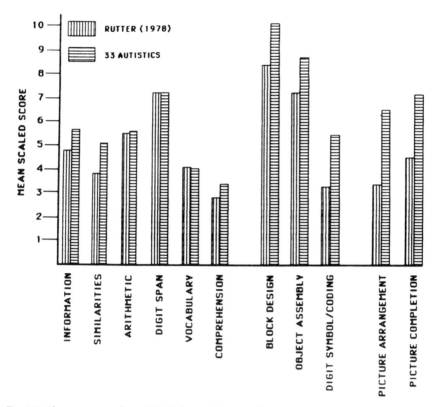

Fig. 6-2. The mean-age adjusted Wechsler-scaled scores for 33 individuals with autism reported by Lincoln et al. and summarized by Rutter (1978). (From Lincoln et al., 1988, Fig. 1, p. 510.)

dividuals. Unlike normal standardization samples, Block Design, Objects Assembly, and Digit Symbol/Coding loaded on a second factor that was attributed to adequate fluid ability and relatively intact visual-spatial and visual-motor integrative skill. It was also suggested that this factor not only had a low verbal loading, but also that it reflected intellectual abilities that did not require the integration of meaningful or context-relevant information. The third factor comprised two subtests, Picture Completion and Picture Arrangement. This factor was more involved in the intellectual appraisal of meaningful and context-relevant information.

As can be seen from Figure 6-3, there is a consistent pattern across all of the studies reported from Table 6-3, in which verbal abilities (Factor I from Lincoln et al., 1988) and the evaluation of meaningful, nonverbal information (Factor III from Lincoln et al., 1988) are relatively depressed compared to the more intact visual-spatial and visual-motor integrative

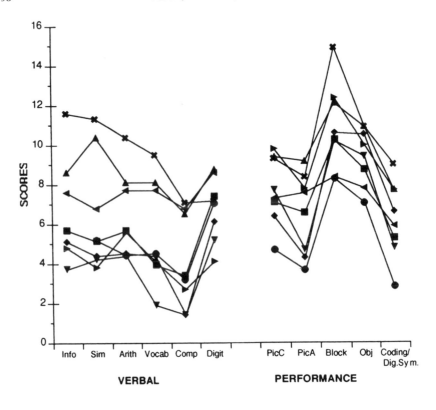

Fig. 6-3. The distribution of Wechsler-scaled scores reported from eight different studies.

abilities related to the appraisal of less meaningful or context-relevant information (Factor III from Lincoln et al., 1988). The relatively lower score consistently found on Digit Symbol/Coding is most likely related to its sensitivity for brain impairment in general (Reitan, 1985).

Specificity of the Pattern of Wechsler-Scaled Scores

Figure 6-4 shows the specificity of the pattern of scaled scores derived from 13 autistic children reported by Lincoln et al. (1988) compared to three other groups of children. As can be seen from the figure, the children with autism from this study demonstrated severe verbal deficits relative to the other three groups. However, their performance on Block Design and Object Assembly was similar to that of the other children.

SEQUENTIAL AND SIMULTANEOUS-PROCESSING ABILITIES

Through the years, there has been increasing emphasis placed upon the specific information-processing distinctions evidenced by high-functioning (nonretarded) autistic individuals, within the context of cerebral hemisphere specialization. The research in this area has provided some support for a hypothesis concerning abnormal hemisphere functioning, which implicates dysfunction of the left cerebral hemisphere (Blackstock, 1978; Prior, 1979; Prior & Bradshaw, 1979; Ricks, 1975; Tanguay, 1976). It has been argued by Hoffman and Prior (1982) that the pattern of cognitive abilities and disabilities shown by high-functioning autistic children may be viewed as reflecting normal ability in tasks presumed to be predominantly mediated by the right hemisphere of the brain (nonverbal, visuospatial, simultaneous, analogic, holistic/gestalt) and severely handicapped performance in tasks presumed to be predominantly mediated by the left hemisphere (language, temporal, analytic, symbolic). One alternative to the content-oriented perspective of the left hemisphere/language abilities versus the right hemisphere/nonverbal visuospatial abilities has been to consider the nature of the cognitive dysfunctions in autism from a process-oriented model (Hoffman & Prior, 1983; Prior & Bradshaw, 1979; Tanguay, 1984). This model considered the effectiveness of processing within a sequential-analytical mode as opposed to a simultaneous-non-analytical mode. These two distinctive types of cognitive activity have long been recognized within the field of psychology and neuropsychology, and over the years have been given a variety of names, such as rational versus intuitive, analytic versus holistic, serial-parallel, and sequential-multiple (Neisser, 1967). As viewed from the perspective of this model, recent

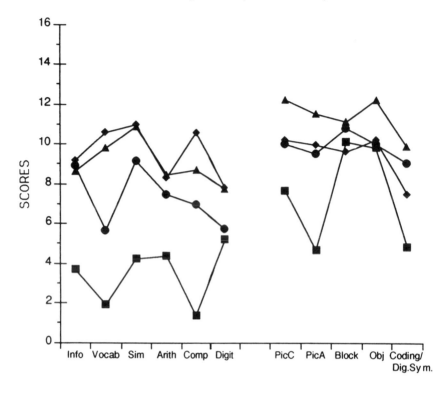

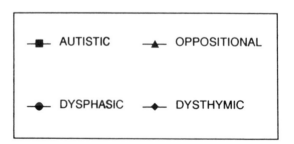

Fig. 6-4. The mean Wechsler-scaled scores for four different childhood disorders: autism, recept-ive dysphasia, oppositional disorder, and dysthymia. (From Lincoln et al., 1988, Table 4, p. 516.)

findings suggested that autistic children may be more impaired in their ability to process temporally ordered information presented in a successive fashion and more effective with processing information that is spatial in nature and presented simultaneously (Hermelin, 1975, 1976; Menyuk, 1978; Tanguay, 1984). In his review, Tanguay (1984) discussed these attributes and furthermore suggested that while autistic persons may demonstrate impairments in both, they should show less impairment in simultaneous- than in sequential-processing skills. Evidence suggests that, similar to autistic individuals, the language difficulties of children with a developmental-receptive language disorder (Dysphasia) without the behavior and social abnormalities of autism may also be a consequence of basic deficits involving sequential-processing ability. They may also demonstrate deficits in processing rapidly occurring sequential information at younger ages (Tallal, 1978; Tallal, Stark, Kallman, & Mellits, 1981). However, unlike adolescents and adults with autism, older adolescents and young adults with developmental dysphasia appear to show deficits in both sequential auditory processing and auditory memory (Lincoln, Dickstein, Courchesne, Tallal, and Elmasian, 1992). Moreover, it is sometimes difficult to differentially diagnose autistic children from severely impaired dysphasic children at young ages. Dysphasic individuals are for these reasons a good control group for studying persons with autism.

   In order to further explore the sequential- and simultaneous-processing capacities of autistic children, Allen, Lincoln, & Kaufman (1991) compared their performance to that of dysphasic children on the Kaufman-Assessment Battery for Children (K-ABC) and selected subtests of the Wechsler Intelligence Scale for Children-Revised (WISC-R). The K-ABC was developed by Kaufman & Kaufman (1983a, 1983b) to include both sequential- and simultaneous-processing scales. Kaufman (1979) had previously suggested an interpretation of the Wechsler tasks from the vantage point of the Luria-Das processing model. He identified Similarities, Picture Completion, Block Design, and Object Assembly as simultaneous processing tasks, and Digit Span, Picture Arrangement, Coding, and Mazes as sequential tasks. Naglieri, Kamphaus, & Kaufman (1983) provided the first empirical basis for this interpretation, and found support for the emergence of factors for the WISC-R resembling Kaufman's sequential and simultaneous dichotomy. For the purpose of their study, Allen et al. (1991) formed the WISC-R-P sequential scale using the subtests Digit Span and Coding, and the Simultaneous Scale using the subtests Picture Completion, Block Design, and Object Assembly, per criteria outlined in Naglieri et al. (1983).

   In line with theoretical expectations (Benton, 1978; Dawson, 1983; Hermelin, 1976; Hoffman & Prior, 1982; Ludlow, 1980; Menyuk, 1978;

Prior & Bradshaw, 1979; Reitan, 1984; Tallal, 1987; Tanguay, 1984) and consistent with previous investigations (Bartak et al., 1975, 1977; Lincoln et al., 1988), Allen et al. (1991) found both autistic and dysphasic children to exhibit similar patterns of uneven intellectual functioning characterized by a relative sequential-processing deficit. In addition, the autistic children displayed a greater degree of overall impairment in their verbal and language skills. In contrast, both groups appeared to be equivalent to each other in their sequential and simultaneous processing abilities (sequential lower than simultaneous) once the level of language impairment was equated between both groups. This finding placed even greater importance upon the disparity between the verbal and nonverbal skills for the autistic children. Moreover, it was those areas of language-based and acquired intellectual skills that appeared to be particularly impaired, thus compromising their evaluation and integrated application of highly verbal and social or context-relevant information. The patterns of mean scores for both autistic and dysphasic children across the sequential- and simultaneous-processing measures are illustrated in Figures 6-5, 6-6 and 6-7.

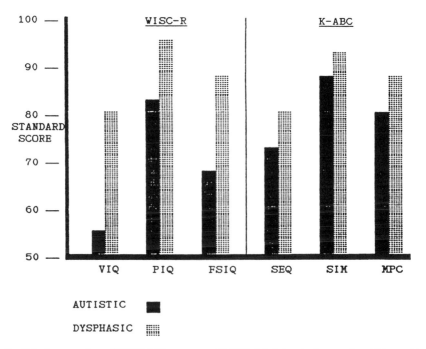

Fig. 6-5. A comparison of WISC-R IQ scores and K-ABC global standard scores for children with autism and receptive dysphasia. (From Allen et al., 1991, Fig. 1, p. 489.)

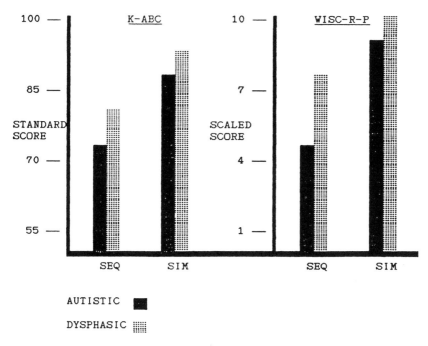

Fig. 6-6. A comparison of sequential and simultaneous processing scale scores derived from K-ABC and WISC-R subtests both for children with autism and receptive dysphasia. (From Allen et al., 1991, Fig. 1, p. 490.)

Although autistic individuals clearly exhibit a greater adeptness for tasks that rely upon processing of information in a simultaneous fashion within the nonverbal and visual-spatial mode, the clinical picture is not always consistent. For example, the findings of the Allen et al. (1991) differed from those of Freeman et al. (1985) in which a group of high-functioning autistic children were found to display no overall differences between sequential and simultaneous scores on the K-ABC (see Fig. 6-8). Where differences in individual cases were found, contrary to their predictions, sequential scores were higher than simultaneous scores. The discrepancy between the studies may be accounted for by the fact that, to begin with, the autistic groups were different. In comparison to the verbally deficient autistic children in the former study, Freeman's subject population had an unusually high mean WISC-R Verbal Scale IQ. The combined results of the two studies suggested a very strong correlation between sequential processing capacities of people with autism and their general level of verbal comprehension skills. This is not surprising, considering the relationship between sequential processing and the develop-

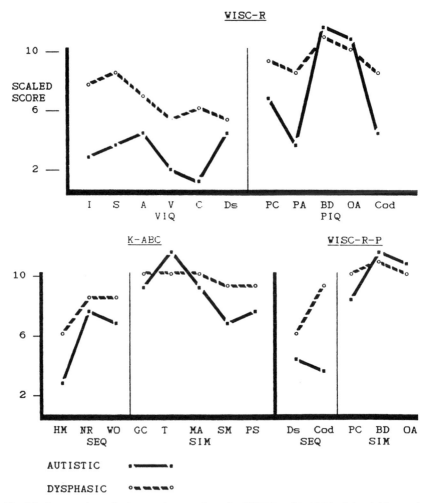

Fig. 6-7. A comparison of subtest scale scores from the WISC-R and K-ABC both for children with autism and receptive dysphasia. (From Allen et al., 1991, Fig. 3, p. 491.)

ment and maintenance of the cognitive-linguistic functions (Reitan, 1984; Tallal, 1987).

Freeman and her colleagues also offered the explanation that the lack of difference in overall processing style may have been an artifact of specific-task demands. They argued that the subtests included on the K-ABC Sequential Processing Scale involve either simple copying of simple visual input (Hand Movements) or rote memory (Number Recall and Word Order), tasks at which high functioning autistic children have been shown

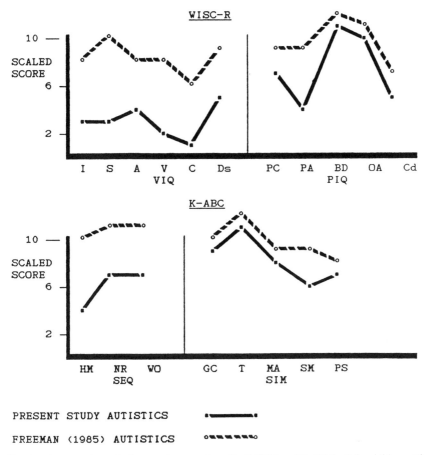

Fig. 6-8. A comparison of subtest scale scores from the WISC-R and K-ABC both for children with autism and receptive dysphasia. This figure also compares the findings of Allen et al. with those reported by Freeman et al. (1985). (From Allen et al., 1991, Fig. 4, p. 497.)

Note: The subtest means for the Freeman autistic group were obtained from Table 3 (p. 360) in Freeman et al. (1985).

to excel (Tanguay, 1984). And yet, as a group, Allen's autistic children demonstrated relative impairment on these particular cognitive abilities.

Intersubtest Variability

As previously emphasized, when viewing a child's broad-range intellectual functioning and profile of cognitive abilities, it is important to consider subtest variability within the global scales. Along these lines, the high-functioning autistic and dysphasic children in the Allen et al. (1991) study displayed similar characteristic patterns of uneven intellectual functioning, along with marked discrepancies between the groups in the severity of impairment they exhibited in their respective levels of verbal intelligence and integration of unique cognitive abilities. Their relative strengths and weaknesses were clearly illustrated in their overall patterns of subtest scores.

Consistent with the findings of Lincoln et al. (1988), these children with autism and dysphasia performed poorly on the Vocabulary and Comprehension subtests of the WISC-R. Both of these subtests are highly dependent upon verbal comprehension, acquired knowledge, and general language requirements (Kaufman, 1975, 1979). In contrast, both groups performed well on the Block Design and Object Assembly subtests of the WISC-R, and Triangles subtest of the K-ABC. These subtests are all highly correlated with visual-motor integration and spatial skills, perceptual organization, recognition without analysis, and simultaneous-processing skills (Kaufman, 1975, 1979; Naglieri et al., 1983). Although children with autism displayed a greater degree of deficit than children with dysphasia, both groups performed poorly on the Coding subtest of the WISC-R, and the Hand Movements, and Spatial Memory subtests of the K-ABC. These subtests all place greater demands for attention, concentration, and sustained effort, as well as a greater degree of visual short-term memory capacity.

The children with autism performed exceedingly poorly on the Picture Arrangement subtest of the WISC-R in comparison to the children with dysphasia. Unlike Block Design, Object Assembly, and Triangles, the Picture Arrangement subtest requires visual processing and evaluation of socially meaningful and context-relevant information. In addition, when compared to the children with dysphasia, children with autism also showed a marked discrepancy between the Triangles and Photo Series subtests of the K-ABC. This difference might be accounted for by the fact that even though both subtests are simultaneous-processing tasks, unlike Triangles, Photo Series demands a greater degree of analysis and processing of contextual information, in addition to having a significant secondary loading on the sequential factor (Kaufman & Kaufman, 1983b). In general, both groups were again found to be most proficient in processing nonverbal, asocial, and noncontextual information while performing best on those visual-spatial tasks that relied on simultaneous processing capabilities, provided immediate visual feedback, and placed modest demands upon visual short-term memory.

The children with autism displayed a significantly greater degree of profile variability on the WISC-R Performance and K-ABC Simultaneous

Processing Scales in comparison to the children with dysphasia. For children with autism, this was due primarily to the marked discrepancies between their significant strengths on the Block Design and Object Assembly subtests and significant weaknesses on the Picture Arrangement and Coding subtests of the WISC-R Performance Scale. In addition, they also demonstrated a marked discrepancy between the Triangles subtest on the one hand, and Photo Series and Spatial Memory subtests of the K-ABC Simultaneous Processing Scale. Therefore, it is the degree of intersubtest variability evidenced on the Performance Scale of the WISC-R and the Simultaneous Scale of the K-ABC that seems to be the most discriminating between these two groups of children.

Since the subtests of Picture Arrangement, Coding, Photo Series, and Spatial Memory all have clear-cut sequential components and secondary loadings on the sequential factor (Kaufman & Kaufman, 1983b; Naglieri et al., 1983), it may be that the autistics' pervasive sequential deficiency lowered both their sequential and simultaneous scores (on the WISC-R as well as the K-ABC), thereby masking their potentially huge advantage in favor of simultaneous processing. The results further suggest that for the children with autism, these particular global scale scores may be measuring isolated abilities that are not well-integrated with their other related cognitive skills rather than measuring a unitary dimension. That is, the unique cognitive profile exhibited by children with autism may be more a matter of isolated strengths and poorly integrated cognitive strengths in the context of a broad range of specific deficits. As Lincoln et al. (1988) described, it may well be that high-functioning autistic children in comparison to dysphasic children are more dependent upon isolated intellectual strengths that may fail to adequately serve them in adapting effectively to their environment.

MEMORY FUNCTIONING

Studies of memory in persons with autism have been conducted on both short- and long-term memory and the interface between memory and language impairments.

A number of studies focused on how children with autism employ short-term memory to process auditory and visual stimuli. Children with autism recall sentences better than nonsentences, as do normal and retarded children matched on mental age (MA). However, the normal control group recall of words in sentences was significantly better than that of the autistic group (Hermelin & Frith, 1971). Furthermore, when compared to control groups, children with autism demonstrated a significant recency effect in their immediate recall of mixed phrases containing part sentences and part nonsentences. Unlike the control groups, who recalled the sentence part of the phrases better than the nonsentences irrespective of position, the autistic group consistently recalled the end of the phrases. They did not use semantic cues to aid their recall, as did the normal control subjects. Based on these results, it was hypothesized that the autistic children, rather than reorganizing auditory stimuli during the input phases, as is the case in normal memory functions, used their memories like an echo. Clearly, clinical descriptions of autistic children illustrate their tendency to repeat phrases that have been said and to use echolalic speech.

In a more recent study investigating the recency effect, defined as *echoic memory capacity*, Boucher (1978) found that autistic and normal children matched on chronological age and digit span had comparable echoic memory capacities for words when immediately recalled. Although the autistic group did not demonstrate supranormal capacity, their echoic memory was identified as a peak ability. Furthermore, as a group, the autistic children had greater difficulty recalling earlier presented words than did the normal children. This result occurred because of language deficits and lack of semantic coding, and these impairments were not compensated for by more efficient acoustic coding.

In processing visual stimuli, autistic children demonstrated the recency effect, as well as good short-term memories (Hermelin & O'Connor, 1975). In a study that controlled for acquisition, autistic, normal, and retarded children matched on MA were compared on a two-choice visual discrimination task in which three delay intervals were used (Prior & Chen, 1976). Autistic children did not demonstrate a short-term memory impairment as compared to the other groups. With increasing delays, all groups showed loses in retention. On a serial memory task, in which interference was manipulated, autistic, normal, and retarded children all learned the task at the same rate (Prior & Chen, 1976). Overall, no specific memory impairments were found in the autistic group.

In order to determine whether high-functioning autistic subjects utilize the meaningfulness of visually presented stimuli in a visual recognition task, they were compared with normal control subjects matched on chronological age and sex (Ameli et al., 1988). In this study, the subjects were presented with a nonmatching-to-sample task incorporating both pictures and nonsense shapes, with and without 1-minute delays. The subjects' task was to recognize the new stimulus, which they had not seen before, from among stimuli which had just been previously presented. The results indicated that the autistic group performed significantly more poorly than the control group. However, they utilized semantic cues in assisting their visual memory, as did the normal subjects. The subjects with autism performed better when using meaningful stimuli than with meaningless stimuli, and the authors reasoned that this occurred because in the nonsense-stimuli condition, the autistic subjects could only use their visual memory without any semantic cues (i.e., object name). In order to perform well on this task, the ability to use cognitive processes in a flexible manner is required to encode the stimuli. These authors suggest that further research is needed to determine the relationship between inflexible cognitive approach to encoding and memory processes in autism.

Lincoln et al. (1992) found short-term auditory memory to be normal in adolescents and young adults with autism. In their study, autistic, dysphasic, and normal controls were compared for their ability to remember tone series of varying lengths (one to seven tones). The autistic subjects recalled series of tones as well as controls and significantly better than dysphasic subjects. Furthermore, autistic subjects showed normal patterns of primacy and recency effects, whereas dysphasic subjects showed abnormal recency memory.

Long-term memory, or retention over time, is another area of memory functioning in autism that has been explored. Boucher & Warrington (1976) compared autistic children with chronological age-matched normal children and retarded children matched on verbal and nonverbal ability on a number of tasks measuring retention. The test stimuli used in all of the tasks were written words, spoken words, and pictures. Boucher and Warrington found a number of significant results. Autistic children demonstrated impaired retention on a recall task with a filled-retention interval. Furthermore, on a forced-recognition task, autistic subjects were impaired as compared to control groups, and this deficit was not related to weak language ability. On this task, in particular, the performance of the autistic subjects was quite variable and the authors suggested that only some autistic children have difficulties with recognition. Similarly, Boucher and Warrington demonstrated that poor language ability does not account for impaired recall. Autistic subjects were also found to make use of semantic cues, as was found by Ameli et al. (1988), as well as acoustic and graphemic cues. Retention in cued recall was normal and associative learning was not impaired.

In another experiment of long-term memory, autistic subjects showed impaired ability to recall activities in which they had recently participated, as compared to normal chronological-age matched and retarded-age and verbal- and nonverbal-ability matched controls (Boucher, 1981). It was felt that on this task, comprehension and encoding was adequate, as was expressive language ability. The author suggested that these result support the hypothesis that language abnormalities in autism may be partly due to difficulties remembering appropriate things to say. It was also postulated that people with autism have difficulty deliberately evoking memories.

Finally, the effects of memory impairments on the communicative abilities of autistic children have been studied (Boucher & Lewis, 1989).

These authors felt that specific memory difficulties might contribute to some of the underlying causes of language difficulties seen in autism. In their first experiment, it was found that autistic children were impaired in their ability to follow spoken or visually demonstrated directions as compared to learning-impaired retarded subjects. Difficulty in carrying out instructions results because autistic subjects are impaired in their ability to remember the instructions, particularly if they are distracted. It was found that the autistic group could use written instructions in order to make up for their difficulty in remembering. Rather than being required to follow spoken directions, written or pictorial instructions could be used by persons with autism.

In a second experiment, autistic subjects' ability to remember previously asked questions was impaired and thus questions were repeated. This difficulty was overcome by the use of picture cards, so that the children could remember what they had been asked by looking at the picture. The third experiment tested memory for recent events using open questions and questions designed to facilitate cued recall. As expected, the autistic subjects were impaired in their ability to respond to open questions. They performed better when the questions offered cues to the past activities. In all three experiments, alternative methods helped the autistic individuals to circumvent their memory impairments.

As can be seen from this review, memory functions in autism are fairly unimpaired. Autistic children have adequate immediate recall of auditory and visually presented stimuli. Their short-term and serial-memory memories seem relatively intact. Cued recall and associative learning is normal. There is disagreement, however, whether semantic cues are used to aid memory, and this is an area that needs further research. Areas in which autistic children show impairments are recall and recognition after filled-retention intervals. Their ability to remember recent events is also impaired, as is their ability to follow directions and ask questions without repetition. Further research could focus on developing methods to help autistic individuals bypass their memory impairments, as was done in the Boucher & Lewis (1989) study, as well as investigating encoding and retrieval strategies.

PRACTICAL CONSIDERATIONS FOR THE ASSESSMENT OF INTELLECTUAL AND COGNITIVE ABILITIES

1. Any item a child can pass during formal psychometric assessment is probably a real sample of their ability. However, the opposite is not true. If children are not successful, one cannot be sure whether they lacked the

skill to complete the task or whether they lacked the motivation, a concept of what was being asked, or attention to the task.

2. It has been demonstrated that there is generally good predictability and stability for intelligence and developmental quotients for autistic children between preschool and school ages (Lord & Schopler, 1989; Shah & Holmes, 1985). Shah & Holmes (1985) reported good agreement between the Performance IQ of WISC-R and the Leiter International Performance Scale in a group of autistic children between 8 and 14 years of age. However, Lord & Schopler (1989) noted exceptions to their general findings of test stability that included the following:

1. Individual autistic children showed substantial changes over time in test scores.
2. Large increases were found between early Bayley Scale, Mental Developmental scores, and subsequent school age IQ scores.
3. Different tests utilized at different times of assessment generally yielded lower stability coefficients.

Lincoln et al. (1988) reported a very stable pattern of Wechsler (WISC-R and WAIS-R) subtest variability in one autistic individual over a 10 year period.

3. It may be best to appreciate the advice of Alfred Binet in recognizing that during standardized assessment one is obtaining a current rough index of ability. One should carefully distinguish between poor performance on a cognitive or intellectual test and poor cognitive or intellectual ability. Test performance is a sample of skills that we associate with cognitive or intellectual functioning. One should closely examine the children's functioning in contexts where their motivation and attention may be much higher. For example, a 5-year-old boy with autism could not comprehend the simple matching concepts at the two-year level necessary to perform the Leiter International Performance Scale, but could boot an Apple IIe computer, select software to run, and play an interactive computer game. Thus, the examiner needs to obtain a history of the child's adaptive functioning. This may be partially accomplished through a structured interview or as part of a thorough intake history.

4. Presently there are very few clinical methods of assessment that actually measure learning. This is certainly true for the most frequently used methods that assess intelligence or other cognitive abilities. Most standardized tests of intelligence or cognitive ability measure more static functions, that is, *what* has been learned as opposed to *how* easily or the manner in which something was learned. There are presently no studies evaluating the methodology of dynamic assessment or learning potential (Feurerstein et al., 1987; Feurerstein et al., 1986) on autistic individuals.

Learning-potential theory and methodology attempt to assess the gain in performance on intellectual or cognitive tasks after abilities or strategies and skills associated with such tasks have been taught, rehearsed, and practiced. Because people with autism frequently lack the skills necessary for effective adaptive functioning in specific contexts, it may be more accurate to utilize assessment techniques that incorporate both the more static intellectual/cognitive measurements, *and* the ability to gain from training.

CONCLUSIONS

According to the Luria–Das model and information-processing approach to intellectual functioning (Das, Kirby, & Jarman, 1979), cognition is divided into three interdependent functional systems (Blocks I, II, and III) that are not localized in narrow areas of the brain, but take place through the interaction of brain structures that work in concert (Luria, 1966, 1973). Block I includes the functions of arousal and attention. Block II functions include coding, memory, sequential, and simultaneous processes. Block III includes the higher order executive functions.

Deficits in the Block I system, which regulates mental activity, would be in line with research that views autism as involving dysfunctions in a variety of subcortical structures (Dawson & Lewy, 1989a, 1989b; Jacobson et al., 1988), such as the reticular formation (Ornitz, 1974, 1978; Ornitz & Ritvo, 1968), which could lead to a disorder of sensory modulation, or of the cerebellum, which could lead to impairment in the ability to rapidly shift attention and ultimately engage in joint attention (Courchesne et al., 1993).

Block II functions involving memory and simultaneous processing appear to be relatively intact in persons with autism. Sequential processing is relatively impaired, particularly in younger autistic individuals. This processing deficit may further compromise the ability of the autistic child to evaluate stimulus probability (Lincoln et al., 1993) and appropriately generate hypotheses that would modify their expectations. In an infant such a deficit would be devastating, insofar as their ability to learn from the early repetitive social interactions that form the basis of early communication would be compromised.

Block III executive functions involving representational capacity, inferential ability, verbal reasoning, hypothesis generation, and context recognition are impaired in autistic individuals to varying degrees (Rumsey, 1985; Lincoln et al., 1988). These abilities are crucial and necessary for daily functioning (Regan & Kilman, 1979), and also encompass significant portions of intellectual behavior measured by standardized tests of intelligence. There is not a good developmental model for the development of Block III functions. However, it is reasonable to conclude that the development of Block III functions depends upon the information and learning derived from Block I and II functions. The Block III system, for example, is believed to interact extensively with the reticular formation in discriminating between relevant and irrelevant information for the purpose of allocating attention (Crosson, 1985). Thus, the significant language and cognitive deficits observed by school age in children with autism must reflect, in part, the faulty development of Block III functions due to developmentally aberrant Block I, arousal, and attentional mechanisms, and also aberrant Block II, sequential mechanisms. Deficits in the proper allocation of attention, coupled with sequential processing deficits may lead to a lack of smooth integration between Blocks I, II, and III. Furthermore, the subsequent developmental consequences due to that lack of integration may grossly impede developmental processes necessary for normal intellectual functioning.

Finally, the finding that children with autism exhibit sequential processing deficits is consistent with prior research, and compatible with the emphasis that cerebral specialization theorists have placed on the verbal components of left hemisphere dysfunction and on their relationship to sequential processing deficits in general (Bogen, 1969; Gazzaniga, 1975; Kaufman, 1979; Lezak, 1983). Although specific localization of cerebral dysfunction cannot necessarily be directly inferred from the present results, the striking patterns of cognitive strengths and weaknesses exhibited by the autistic children provide one more piece of supportive evidence for a specific cognitive impairment involving functions for which the left hemisphere/frontal-temporal regions are thought to be specialized (Blackstock, 1978; Cohen, 1976; Das, Kirby, & Jarman, 1979; Dawson, 1983; Luria, 1973; Prior & Bradshaw, 1979; Tanguay, 1976). However, this does not imply that there is anatomical or physiological maldevelopment of these regions *per se*, but only that some cognitive functions normally subserved by these regions are abnormal.

ACKNOWLEDGMENTS

This chapter was supported by a NINCDS grant 1-R01-N28614-01 awarded to Alan Lincoln. We also appreciate the support of the Neuropsychology Research Laboratory at Children's Hospital, the San Diego Regional Center and the San Diego Unified School District.

REFERENCES

Allen, M. H., Lincoln, A. J., and Kaufman, A. S. (1991). Sequential and simultaneous processing abilities of high functioning autistic and language impaired children. *Journal of Autism and Developmental Disorders, 21*(4), 483–502.

Ameli, R., Courchesne, E., Lincoln, A., Kaufman, A., & Grillon, C. (1988). Visual memory processes in high-functioning individuals with autism. *Journal of Autism and Developmental Disorders, 18*, 601–615.

American Psychiatric Association. (1987). Diagnostic and statistical manual of mental disorders (3rd ed., rev.). Washington, DC: Author.

Bartak, L., Rutter, M., & Cox, A. (1975). A comparative study of infantile autism and specific developmental receptive language disorders. *British Journal of Psychiatry, 126*, 127–145.

Bartak, L., Rutter, M., & Cox, A. (1977). A comparative study of infantile autism and specific developmental receptive language disorders: III. Discriminant function analysis. *Journal of Autism and Childhood Schizophrenia, 7*(4), 383–396.

Benton, A. L. (1978). The cognitive functioning of children with developmental dysphasia. In M. A. Wyke (Ed.), *Developmental dysphasia* (pp. 43–62). New York: Academic Press.

Blackstock, E. G. (1978). Cerebral asymmetry and the development of early infantile autism. *Journal of Autism and Childhood Schizophrenia, 8*, 339–353.

Bogen, J. E. (1969). The other side of the brain (Parts I, II, and III). *Bulletin of the Los Angeles Neurological Society, 34*, 73–105, 135–162, 191–203.

Boucher, J. (1978). Echoic memory capacity in autistic children. *Journal of Child Psychology and Psychiatry, 19*, 161–166.

Boucher, J. (1981). Memory for recent events in autistic children. *Journal of Autism and Developmental Disorders, 11*, 293–302.

Boucher, J., & Lewis, V. (1989). Memory impairments and communication in relatively able autistic children. *Journal of Child Psychology and Psychiatry, 30*, 99–122.

Boucher, J., & Warrington, E. K. (1976). Memory deficits in early infantile autism: Some similarities to the amnesic syndrome. *British Journal of Psychology, 67*, 73–87.

Cohen, D. J., Caparulo, B., & Shawitz, B. (1976). Primary childhood aphasia and childhood autism. *Journal of the American Academy of Child Psychiatry, 15*, 604–645.

Courchesne, F., Townsend, J., Akshoomoff, N., Yeung-Courchesne, R., Press, G., Murakemi, J., Lincoln, A. J., James, H., Saitoh, O., Haas, R., & Schreibman, L. (1993). A new finding in autism: Impairment in shifting attention. In S. H. Broman and J. Grafman (Eds.), *Atypical cognitive deficits in developmental disorders: Implications to brain functions* (pp. 107–137).

Crosson, B. (1985). Subcortical functions in language: A working model. *Brain and Language, 25*, 257–292.

Das, J. P., Kirby, J., & Jarman, R. F. (1975). Simultaneous and successive synthesis: An alternative model for cognitive abilities. *Psychological Bulletin, 32*, 37–103.

Das, J. P., Kirby, J., & Jarman, R. F. (1979). *Successive and simultaneous cognitive processes.* New York: Academic Press.

Dawson, G. (1983). Lateralized brain function in autism: Evidence from the Halstead–Reitan neuropsychological battery. *Journal of Autism and Developmental Disorders, 13*, 369–386.

Dawson, G., & Lewy, A. (1989a). Reciprocal subcortical-cortical influences in autism: The role of attentional mechanisms. In G. Dawson (Ed.), *Autism: Nature, Diagnosis and Treatment* (pp. 144–173). New York: Guilford Press.

Dawson, G., & Lewy, A. (1989b). Arousal, attention and the socioemotional impairments of individuals with autism. In G. Dawson (Ed.), *Autism: Nature, Diagnosis and Treatment* (pp. 49–74). New York: Guilford Press.

Fein, D., Waterhouse, L., Lucci, D., & Snyder, D. (1985). Cognitive subtypes in developmentally disabled children: A pilot study. *Journal of Autism and Developmental Disorders, 15*(1), 77–95.

Feurerstein, R., Rand, Y., Jensen, M. R., Kaniel, S., & Tzuriel, D. (1987). Prerequisites for assessment of learning potential: The LPAD model. In C. S. Lidz (Ed.), *Dynamic Assessment: An Interactional Approach to Evaluating Learning Potential* (pp. 35–51). New York: Guilford Press.

Feurerstein, R., Rand, Y., Jemsem, M., Kaniel, S., Tzuriel, D., Shachar, N. D., & Mintzker, Y. (1986). Learning potential assessment. *Assessment of Exceptional Children, 2*(2-3), 85–106.

Freeman, B. J., Lucas, J. C., Forness, S. R., Ritvo, E. R. (1985). Cognitive processing of high-functioning autistic children: Comparing the K-ABC and the WISC-R. *Journal of Psychoeducational Assessment, 4*, 357–362.

Gazzaniga, M. S. (1975). Recent research on hemispheric lateralization of the human brain: Review of the split-brain. *UCLA Educator, 17*, 9–12.

Hermelin, B. (1976). Coding and the sense modalities. In L. Wing (Ed.), *Early childhood autism: Clinical, educational and social aspects* (pp. 135–168). Elmsford, NY: Pergamon Press.

Hermelin, B., & O'Connor, N. (1975). The recall of digits by normal, deaf and autistic children. *British Journal of Psychology, 66*, 203–209.

Hermelin, B., & Frith, U. (1971). Psychological studies of childhood autism: Can autistic children make sense of what they see and hear *Journal of Special Education, 5*, 107–117.

Hobson, P. (1989). Beyond cognition: A theory of autism. In G. Dawson (Ed.), *Autism: Nature, Diagnosis and Treatment* (pp. 22–48). New York: Guilford Press.

Hoffman, W. L., & Prior, M. R. (1982). Neuropsychological dimensions of autism in children: A test of the hemispheric dysfunction hypothesis. *Journal of Clinical Neuropsychology, 4*, 27–41.

Jocobson, R., Le Couteur, A., & Rutter, M. (1988). Selective subcortical abnormalities in autism. *Psychological Medicine, 18*, 39–48.

Kanner, L. (1943). Autistic disturbances of affective contact. *Nervous Child, 2*, 217–250.

Kaufman, A. S. (1975). Factor analysis if the WISC-R at eleven age levels between 6 ½ and 16 ½ years. *Journal of Consulting and Clinical Psychology, 43*, 135–147.

Kaufman, A. S. (1979). *Intelligent testing with the WISC-R*. New York: Wiley-Interscience.

Kaufman, A. S., & Kaufman, N. L. (1983a). *Kaufman Assessment Battery for Children: Administration and Scoring Manual*. Circle Pines, MN: American Guidance Service.

Kaufman, A. S., & Kaufman, N. L. (1983b). *Kaufman Assessment Battery for Children: Interpretive Manual*. Circle Pines, MN: American Guidance Service.

Kaufman, A. (1990). Assessing adolescent and adult intelligence. Boston: Allyn and Bacon.

Lezak, M. D. (1983). *Neuropsychological assessment* (2nd ed.). New York: Oxford University Press.

Lincoln, A. J., Courchesne, E., & Elmasian, R. (1990). Considerations for the study of event-related brain potentials and developmental psychopathology. In A. Rothenberger (Ed.), *Brain and Behavior in Child Psyciatry* (pp. 17–33). New York: Springer-Verlag.

Lincoln, A. J., Courchesne, E., Harms, L., & Allen, M. (1993). ERP abnormalities in autistic children associated with context evaluation and decision making: Part 1. *Journal of Autism and Developmental Disorders, 23*(1), 37–58.

Lincoln, A. J., Courchesne, E., Kilman, B. A., Elmasian, R., & Allen, M. H. (1988). A study of intellectual abilities in people with autism. *Journal of Autism and Developmental Disorders, 18*(4), 505–524.

Lincoln, A. J., Dickstein, P., Courchesne, E., Elmasian, R., & Tallal, P. (1992). Auditory processing abilities in non-retarded adolescents and young adults with developmental language disorder and autism. *Brain and Language, 43,* 613–622.

Lockyer, L., & Rutter, M. (1970). A 5- to 15-year follow-up study of infantile psychosis: IV. Patterns of cognitive ability. *British Journal of Social and Clinical Psychology, 9,* 152–163.

Lord, C., & Schopler, E. (1989). The role of age at assessment, developmental level, and test in the stability in intelligence scores in young autistic children. *Journal of Autism and Developmental Disorders, 19*(4), 483–499.

Ludlow, C. L. (1980). Children's language disorders: Recent research advances. *Annals of Neurology, 7,* 497–507.

Luria, A. R. (1966). *Higher cortical functions in man.* New York: Basic Books.

Luria, A. R. (1973). *The working brain: An introduction to neuropsychology.* New York: Basic Books.

Menyuk, P. (1978). Linguistic problems in children with developmental dysphasia. In M. Wyke (Ed.), *Developmental dysphasia* (pp. 135–158). London: Academic Press.

Naglieri, J. A., & Das, J. P. (1988). Planning-arousal-simultaneous-successive (PASS): A model for assessment. *Journal of School Psychology, 26,* 35–48.

Naglieri, J. A., Kamphaus, R. W., & Kaufman, A. S. (1983). The Luria-Das successive-simultaneous model applied to the WISC-R data. *Journal of Psychoeducational Assessment, 1,* 25–34.

Neisser, U. (1967). *Cognitive Psychology.* New York: Appleton-Century-Crafts.

Ohta, M. (1987). Cognitive disorders of infantile autism: A study employing the WISC, spatial relationship, conceptualization and gesture imitations. *Journal of Autism and Developmental Disorders, 17*(1), 45–62.

Ornitz, E. M. (1974). The modulation of sensory input and motor output in autistic children. *Journal of Autism and Childhood Schizophreniz, 4,* 197–215.

Ornitz, E. M. (1978). Neurophysiologic studies. In M. Rutter & E. Schopler (Eds.), *Autism: A reappraisal of concepts and treatment* (pp. 117–139). New York: Plenum Press.

Ornitz, E. M., & Ritvo, E. R. (1968). Perceptual inconstancy in early infantile autism. *Archives of General Psychiatry, 18,* 76–98.

Prior, M. R., & Bradshaw, J. L. (1979). Hemispheric functioning in autistic children. *Cortex, 15,* 73–81.

Prior, M. R., & Chen, C. S. (1976). Short-term and serial memory in autistic, retarded, and normal children. *Journal of Autism and Childhood Schizophrenia, 6,* 121–131.

Regan, J., & Kilman, B. Application of anthropological linguistic theory to the study of autistic children's discourse. In G. D. Haydu (Ed.), *Experience Forms: Their Cultural and Individual Places and Function* (pp. 61–93). The Hague, Netherlands: Mouton.

Reitan, R. M. (1984). *Aphasia and sensory-perceptual deficits in children.* Tucson, AZ: Neuropsychological Press.

Reitan, R. (1985). Relationships between measures of brain function and geberal intelligence. *Journal of Clinical Psychology, 41,* 245–253.

Ricks, D. M. (1975). Vocal communication in pre-verbal normal and autistic children. In N. O'Connor (Ed.), *Language, cognitive deficits and retardation.* London: Butterworths.

Rumsey, J. (1985). Conceptual problem-solving in high verbal, nonretarded autistic men. *Journal of Autism and Developmental Disorders, 15*(1), 23–36.

Rumsey, J., & Hamburger, S. (1990). Neuropsychological divergence in high-level autism and severe dyslexia. *Journal of Autism and Developmental Disorders, 20*(2), 155–168.

Rutter, M. (1978). Language disorder and infantile autism. In M. Rutter & E. Schopler (Eds.), *Autism: A reappraisal of concepts and treatment* (pp. 247–264). New York: Plenum Press.

Schneider, P., & Asarnow, R. F. (1987). A comparison of cognitive/neuropsychological impairments of nonretarded autistic and schizophrenic children. *Journal of Abnormal Child Psychology, 15*(1), 29–45.

Shah, A., & Holmes, N. (1985). Brief report: The use of the Leiter International Performance Scale with autistic children. *Journal of Autism and Developmental Disorders, 15*(2), 195–203.

Szatmari, P., Tuff, L., Finlayson, A., & Bartolucci, G. (1990). Asperger's syndrome and autism: Neurocognitive aspects. *Journal of the American Academy of Child and Adolescent Psychiatry, 29*(1), 130–136.

Tallal, P. (1978). An experimental investigation of the role of auditory temporal processing in normal and disordered language development. In A. Caramazza & E. B. Zurif (Eds.), *Language acquisition and language breakdown: Parallels and divergencies.* Baltimore: Johns Hopkins University Press.

Tallal, P. (1987). Neuropsychological foundations of specific developmental disorders of speech and language: Implications for theories of hemisphere specialization. In J. O. Cavenar (Ed.), *Psychiatry,* Vol. 3 (section 67, 1–15). New York: Basic Books.

Tallal, P., & Piercy, M. (1978). Defects of auditory perception in children with developmental dysphasia. In M. A. Wyke (Ed.), *Developmental dysphasia.* London: Academic Press.

Tallal, P., Starks, R., Kallman, C., & Mellits, D. (1981). A re-examination of some non-verbal perceptual abilities of language impaired and normal children as a function of age and sensory modality. *Journal of Speech and Hearing Research, 24,* 351–357.

Tanguay, P. E. (1976). Clinical and electrophysiological research. In E. R. Ritvo (Ed.), *Autism: Diagnosis, current research and management* (pp. 75–84). New York: Spectrum.

Tanguay, P. E. (1984). Toward a new classification of serious psychopathology in children. *Journal of American Academy of Child Psychiatry, 23,* 373–384.

Wechsler, D. (1958). *The measurement and appraisal of adult intelligence* (p. 7). Baltimore: Williams and Wilkins.

A Fresh Look at Categorization Abilities in Persons with Autism

LAURA G. KLINGER and GERALDINE DAWSON

INTRODUCTION

The significance of what people said to me, when it sank in as more than just words, was always taken to apply only to that particular moment or situation. Thus, when I once received a serious lecture about writing graffiti on Parliament House during a class trip, I agreed that I'd never do this again and then, ten minutes later, was caught outside writing different graffiti on the school wall. To me, I was not ignoring what I had been told, nor was I trying to be funny; I had not done exactly the same thing as I had done before. My behavior puzzled others, but theirs puzzled me too. It was not so much that I had no regard for their rules as that I couldn't keep up with the many rules for each specific situation. (written by Donna Williams, an autistic adult, 1992, p. 69)

Categorization is a mental process that allows individuals to integrate new information with previous experiences. This process does not usually occur through the memorization of specific rules, but rather it typically involves an abstraction of information during learning. Without this ability, individuals would be overwhelmed by the complexity of their environment, being unable to make inferences based on past experience. In

LAURA G. KLINGER • Department of Psychology, University of Alabama, Tuscaloosa, Alabama 35487. GERALDINE DAWSON • Department of Psychology, University of Washington, Seattle, Washington 98195.

Learning and Cognition in Autism, edited by Eric Schopler and Gary B. Mesibov. Plenum Press, New York, 1995.

the quote above, Donna Williams, a woman with autism, eloquently de-scribes her difficulty learning and applying new information to her current situations. Rather than abstracting knowledge across many situations and generalizing this information to new situations, Ms. Williams describes a process of trying to learn a new set of rules for every unique situation. An impairment in category learning may explain some of the be-haviors observed in persons with autism. For example, the development of repetitive and ritualized behaviors, difficulties understanding new situa-tions, and impairments in generalization from one situation to another may all be caused by underlying category-learning impairments. Each of these characteristics is briefly reviewed.

Since Kanner's (1943) original description of the syndrome of autism, a defining characteristic of persons with autism has been a tendency to engage in repetitive, routinized behaviors. These repetitive behaviors in-clude stereotyped body movements, self-injurious behaviors, ritualistic use of objects, and preoccupation with a particular topic of interest (Amer-ican Psychiatric Association, 1987). In her autobiography, Donna Williams (1992) described herself as engaging in repetitive behaviors as a means of coping with new situations: "The constant change of things never seemed to give me any chance to prepare myself for them. Because of this I found pleasure and comfort in doing the same thing over and over again." (p. 44) We suggest that this tendency to engage in repetitive behaviors, especially when faced with changes in routine, is an adaptive-coping mechanism persons with autism engage in because they have difficulty categorizing new information. Usually categorization abilities provide individuals with an understanding of their environment and thereby produce in them feelings of control over their environments. If persons with autism have category impairments, they may engage in repetitive behaviors as a means of achieving some sense of control.

Ferrara and Hill (1980) reported that children with autism displayed more withdrawn behaviors when placed in unpredictable, novel situa-tions. In contrast, they found that children with autism engaged in more play behaviors when placed in a situation where social and nonsocial events were predictable. Dawson and colleagues (Dawson & Lewy, 1989a, 1989b, Klinger & Dawson, 1992) proposed that the specific social impair-ments displayed by individuals with autism result from an inability to process social information because of its novel, unpredictable nature. They found that children with autism tend to be more socially responsive and show a higher level of social ability when placed in a highly predictable social situation (Dawson & Adams, 1984; Dawson & Galpert, 1990; Klinger & Dawson, 1992; Klinger, Dawson, & Lewy, 1993). The process of cate-gorization allows individuals to make inferences about new situations based on past experience. Without this ability to make inferences, new situations become highly unpredictable and confusing. Thus, we propose that difficulties in categorization may explain the research demonstrating an impaired functioning in novel, unpredictable environments.

In addition to having difficulty processing information in novel, unpredictable environments, children with autism display an impaired ability to generalize previously learned information to new situations. Lovaas, Koegel, & Schreibman (1979) suggested that impaired generalization abilities result from "stimulus overselectivity," characterized by a tendency to attend to idiosyncratic, irrelevant cues during learning. For example, Rincover and Koegel (1975) taught children with autism to touch their noses upon request and then examined whether this skill generalized to a new experimenter in another environment. They reported that 40% of the children with autism were unable to generalize this simple behavior. Upon further examination, it was apparent that the children had learned the task in response to an idiosyncratic cue (e.g., the experimenter's hand movement) rather than the relevant verbal cue. This tendency to attend to idiosyncratic cues during learning suggests that persons with autism may categorize on the basis of partial information. This narrow form of categorization may produce impairments in the ability to make inferences about new situations based on past experience.

Taken together, repetitive behaviors, difficulties in understanding novel, unpredictable information, and impaired generalization skills are all suggestive of an underlying impairment in the formation of conceptual categories during learning. Other researchers (Tager-Flusberg, 1985a, 1985b; Ungerer & Sigman, 1987) hypothesized that persons with autism may have a specific impairment in category learning, but they have not found evidence supporting this claim. In general, previous research in this area suggests that children with autism demonstrate categorization skills commensurate with their mental age. In this chapter we present evidence suggesting that although children with autism *can* categorize information, they do not use the same mental *processes* of categorization as persons without autism.

We believe that this focus on the *processes* by which individuals with autism construct their world is critical for understanding the syndrome of autism. Too often, research has only asked *whether* persons with autism are capable of certain abilities and has ignored the more critical issue of *how* such an ability is achieved. A child with normal development and a child with autism may perform similarly on certain tests of cognitive functioning, but the two children may have achieved this skill through very different mental processes. The distinction between achievement abilities on a task and the processes used to accomplish that task was made by Werner

(1937) and, more recently, by Cicchetti and Pogge-Hesse (1982). They argued that similar levels of achievement do not necessarily reflect similar mental processes by which they are achieved.

Given our emphasis on the processes involved in categorization, we first briefly review some of the current theories regarding how normally developing individuals categorize information. Next, we elaborate on our discussion of past research examining categorization abilities in persons with autism. We then present hypotheses suggesting that certain processes of categorization are intact, whereas other types are impaired in persons with autism. Finally, we present some preliminary data supporting these hypotheses.

CATEGORIZATION IN NORMAL DEVELOPMENT

Categories are rarely explicitly taught; rather, children somehow abstract category information from experience. The ability to form categories allows human beings to identify something they have never seen before. Once a child learns a concept, he or she can categorize a novel object as either belonging or not belonging to the category and can make inferences about the object based on previous experience with category members.

Several theories have been proposed to explain the process by which human beings are able to abstract information and form conceptual categories. Researchers initially believed that categories are defined by necessary and sufficient criteria. For example, all objects with four equal sides that are joined by 90-degree angles are squares. These "classical" theorists argued that a definition could be provided for each category (see Smith and Medin, 1981, for a review of classical theories). Classical theories have been criticized for failing to explain natural categories, most of which cannot be defined by a list of necessary and sufficient rules. For example, there is no list of necessary and sufficient criteria that defines the category "dog." Dogs can be many different sizes and colors; some don't have tails, and some don't bark. Classical theories also cannot account for the existence of category members that are more "typical" than other members (Rosch, Mervis, Gray, Johnson, & Boyes-Braem, 1976). For example, a robin is a more typical instance of a bird than is an ostrich. If classical theorists were correct, both a robin and an ostrich would be equally representative of the category "bird."

New theories were developed to account for typicality effects in which some category members are more typical than others. Some researchers have proposed that human beings store individual examples in memory and then compare new objects to previously stored examples (Medin and

Schaffer, 1978). Other researchers have suggested an abstraction process whereby a single best example (a prototype) is abstracted from experience with different category members and stored in memory. Posner and Keele (1968, 1970) argued that a prototype is created by forming a central tendency of a particular category. This central tendency is an average of all previously experienced category members.

By storing summary images (prototypes) in memory, adults do not need to memorize all instances of a category in order to effectively use that category (Rosch, 1978). Individuals who have formed a prototypic representation of "dogness" can identify any such animal as a dog, even one that they have never seen before. Posner and colleagues (Posner, Goldsmith, & Welton, 1967; Posner & Keele, 1968; 1970) were among the first researchers to examine prototype formation in adults. In this study, they created four prototypes: dot patterns depicting a diamond, an "M", an "F", and a random arrangement (Posner et al., 1967). Subjects were shown distortions of these dot patterns and asked to categorize previously seen distortions, novel distortions, and the prototypes. Results showed that adults were more accurate in categorizing previously seen distortions and prototype figures than new distortions. Following a 1-week delay, there was a tendency for subjects to forget the previously seen distortions, but they continued to recall the prototypes (Posner & Keele, 1970). These results suggest that adults do indeed form central representations, or prototypes, during category learning.

Recent studies have reported similar prototype-formation abilities among infants (Husaim & Cohen, 1981; Strauss, 1979; Younger & Gotleib, 1988). Using an infant habituation paradigm, Younger (1990) presented 10-and 13-month-old infants with a series of schematic drawings of animals that varied on dimensions such as width of tail, width between the ears, length of legs, and length of neck. Following this familiarization period, infants received two test trials. During the first test trial, infants were shown two novel animals, the average prototype animal (an average of all the features they had previously seen), and an animal composed of familiar features seen during the familiarization trials but in a novel combination. Both groups of children looked at the prototype significantly less often than would have occurred by chance, indicating that they viewed the prototype as the more familiar animal. In other words, infants responded as if the prototype were more familiar than an animal composed of familiar features! During the second test trial, neither group of infants discriminated between one of the same animals they had seen during the familiarization trials and a novel animal composed of familiar features. Thus, infants did not appear to "remember" individual animals they had seen during the familiarization trials. Similar results have been found in infant studies using facial features (Strauss, 1979) and dot patterns (Bomba & Siqueland, 1983). Walton and Bower (1993) recently demonstrated the existence of facial-prototype learning in infants who were 8 to 78 hours old. These results suggest that by 10 months of age, and perhaps within a few hours of birth, infants do not learn categories by memorizing specific examples; rather, they learn by forming prototypic mental representations of category examples. There have been several studies examining categorization abilities in persons with autism, and these studies are reviewed in the next section. None of these studies, however, examines the abstraction of prototypes in individuals with autism.

CATEGORIZATION IN AUTISM

Noach (1974) was one of the first researchers to examine conceptual abilities in persons with autism. She proposed that individuals with autism display

> instances of compulsive concreteness in thought and action. Their overall intellectual functioning, their perception, and their language, in particular, seem to reflect a disturbance in the capacity for concept formation. (p. 100)

Based on Vygotsky's (1962) developmental stages of concept formation, Noach examined autistic children's ability to group objects by the categories of height and size while ignoring other categories such as color. Noach reported that the children with autism were at significantly lower concept-formation levels than children with normal development. That is, children with autism displayed some concrete-grouping abilities, but did not display more abstract-grouping abilities. In contrast, all of the normally developing children displayed abstract-grouping abilities.

Based on her findings, Noach hypothesized that individuals with autism may be unable to abstract meaning from experiences. However, Noach did not include a comparison group of nonautistic, developmentally delayed children in her research. Thus, her findings may be a result of mental retardation, rather than being specific to the syndrome of autism.

This apparent difficulty in abstracting meaning from experience shown by persons with autism does not appear to be caused by rote-memory deficits. Hermelin and O'Connor (1970) found that in comparison to children with normal and delayed development, children with autism did not memorize words by grouping them into conceptual categories (e.g., grouping all of the color words together and all of the food words together, etc.). However, they could remember at least as many randomly arranged words as did children with normal and retarded development. Similarly, Minshew, Goldstein, Muenz, and Payton (1992) reported that while individuals with autism could remember as many words as control subjects on the California Verbal Learning Test, they did not use organizing strategies such as categorizing items into fruits, spices, clothing, and tools. These studies suggest that persons with autism do not have rote-memory impairments. However, they do not appear to aid memory by grouping information into categories. In contrast, normally developing children tend to use category-grouping strategies to improve memory.

Categorization abilities have also been measured in numerous studies of neuropsychological functioning in persons with autism. A standard neuropsychological assessment instrument, the Wisconsin Card Sorting Task (WCST), is a measure of both rule-based categorization and set-shifting abilities. The WCST consists of picture cards depicting one to four shapes in one of four colors. Cards can be sorted according to one of three categories (color, shape, or number). Subjects first learn to categorize the cards according to a simple rule (e.g., sorting by color). This initial rule is changed to a new rule (e.g., sorting by shape) after subjects have mastered the initial rule. Thus, subjects are required to learn the initial rule and then flexibly alter their strategy (or set) when a new rule is introduced. Results using this paradigm have been equivocal; several studies have found no differences between individuals with autism and control subjects (Minshew et al., 1992; Schneider & Asarnow, 1987), whereas other studies have found significant deficits on this task among subjects with autism (Prior & Hoffman, 1990; Rumsey & Hamburger, 1988, 1990). Since this task confounds set-changing and categorization abilities, it has not been possible to use the WCST to determine which skill underlies the impairments observed in individuals with autism. However, this neuropsychological research is consistent with the notion that some persons with autism have categorization impairments.

Only three studies have directly compared categorization abilities in children with autism to categorization abilities in children with mental retardation and children with normal development (Tager-Flusberg, 1985a, 1985b; Ungerer and Sigman, 1987). Tager-Flusberg (1985a,b) used two different methodologies to examine categorization abilities in children with autism, mental retardation, and normal development, who were matched on receptive-language age. She first used a matching-to-sample task (Tager-Flusberg, 1985a) in which children were shown a target picture (e.g., an armchair) and then asked to choose a picture that matched the target (e.g., a rocking chair vs. a sedan car). She then used a sorting task (Tager-Flusberg, 1985b) in which children were asked to sort pictures by category. For example, she asked children to choose all the pictures of a boat from a stack containing three typical members (sailboat, tugboat, canoe), three peripheral members (submarine, barge, raft), three related pictures (light buoy, anchor, watermelon wedge), and three unrelated pictures (kite, leaf, arrow). For both tasks, there were no differences between the three groups of children. In both of these studies, children in all three groups were more accurate in sorting typical category members than peripheral members. Tager-Flusberg suggested that children with autism do develop representational abilities, but may have specific difficulties using their cognitive abilities and representations in a flexible manner.

Ungerer and Sigman (1987) found that preschool-aged children with autism could sort objects into categories on the basis of perceptual (e.g., color and shape) and functional (e.g., furniture, fruit, vehicles, etc.) domains. Children with autism and children with mental retardation were matched on age, mental age, and IQ score. A group of normally developing children was matched to the children with autism by chronological age. Categorization was inferred if children sequentially touched objects belonging to the same category. There were no significant differences among the three groups in the percentage of same-category object contacts for the perceptual or functional tasks. Interestingly, receptive-language ability was correlated with categorization ability for both the mentally retarded and normally developing groups, but was not related to categorization ability in the autistic group. Based on these findings, Ungerer and Sigman argued that the delayed language development in autism cannot be attributed to categorization impairments. They suggested that categorization ability is not specifically impaired in autism and that instead, specific impairments, such as in the use of verbal and gestural symbols, may account for the children's inability to learn social rules and categories.

In summary, previous categorization studies have not found compelling evidence of specific categorization impairments in children with autism. These studies have documented that children with autism are able to form concepts (e.g., color, shapes, function) and can categorize new objects based on these concepts. Researchers have viewed this evidence as an indication that children with autism do have underlying representational abilities. Thus, investigators have moved away from theories suggesting a deficit in basic representational abilities, and have begun to explore whether individuals with autism have specific impairments in *meta*representational abilities. For instance, Baron-Cohen and colleagues (Baron-Cohen, 1989; Baron-Cohen, Leslie, & Frith, 1985, 1986) proposed that individuals with autism are impaired in their ability to understand that people can have beliefs, desires, and intentions different from their own. They further suggest that this "theory-of-mind" deficit reflects an underlying impairment in metarepresentation.

Reexamining the Question of Categorization in Autism

From the review provided above, it is tempting to conclude that persons with autism simply do not have difficulty categorizing their worlds. Indeed, that is the conclusion of many investigators (Tager-Flusberg, 1985a, 1985b; Ungerer & Sigman, 1987). We believe that this conclusion is premature. Our clinical observations compel us to look again at this question.* We observed that many persons with autism attempt in vain to construct strict, rule-based categorizations, and that, like the adult with autism quoted at the beginning of this chapter, this inflexible manner of categorizing the world often creates problems for them. We began to question whether persons with autism categorize incoming information much like the classical categorization theorists originally proposed. We believe that they may not form abstract, prototypic mental representations of the world, that is, representations that allow new instances of a category to be easily assimilated. Instead, they may utilize a concrete, rigid, rule-based approach to understanding the world around them. Support for these hypotheses would suggest that individuals with autism have a basic representational impairment in concept formation that underlies problems understanding novelty, the inability to generalize information, and impaired metarepresentational abilities.

Several studies have provided evidence for the hypothesis that persons with autism do, in fact, use rule-based strategies during learning. Hermelin and O'Connor (1986) reported that autistic individuals with savant abilities are able to infer and apply rules necessary to calculate past and present calendar dates. In a cognitive-shifting task similar to the WCST, Berger et al. (1993) found that individuals with autism were able to infer the correct category rule during the acquisition stage of learning. That is, prior to being asked to change set (or change the rule they were using), individuals with autism did not show any impaired rule-based category learning.

---

*For example, a father recently related his frustration in trying to teach his adolescent autistic son not to interact with "strangers." The difficulty was that his son kept insisting on a set of necessary and sufficient criteria that he could use to determine whether a given person should be classified as a "stranger." His son asked whether the woman behind the grocery checkout stand was a stranger, and whether he should respond if someone at the bus stop said, "Hello," and so on. His father quickly discovered that such criteria were impossible to define.

In the next section, we present a study examining rule-based and prototype categorization abilities in persons with autism.

PROCESSES UNDERLYING CATEGORIZATION IN AUTISM

We recently completed a study examining rule-based and prototype-category learning in children with autism, Down's syndrome, and normal development. Twelve children with autism, 12 children with Down's syndrome, and 12 children with normal development participated. Children in each group were individually matched on receptive-language age as measured by the Peabody Picture Vocabulary Test-Revised.

Rule-Based Categorization

Using stimuli similar to those developed for infant research (Younger, 1990), children were presented with a series of familiarization trials in which they observed schematic drawings of animals that varied on feature dimensions such as width of tail, width between the ears, length of legs, and length of neck. In the rule-based conditions, each of these animals possessed a unique feature that determined category membership (e.g., a long neck). In the explicit-rule condition, children were told the defining feature. In the implicit-rule condition, children were required to infer the rule themselves. During the test trials, children were shown two novel animals that differed only on the defining feature (e.g., one animal had a short neck and the other animal had a long neck). Children were asked to touch the animal that belonged with the animals seen in the familiarization trials.

All three groups of children chose the stimuli that followed the explicit rule at above-chance levels (where chance performance equals 50% correct). Thus, all groups of children demonstrated the ability to categorize using a classical or rule-based learning strategy when the rule was explicitly told to them. Specifically, children with autism were accurate 83% of the time, children with Down's syndrome, 97% of the time, and children with normal development, 86% of the time. Although the children with Down's syndrome appeared to be more accurate than children in the other two groups, this difference was not statistically significant. That is, all three groups of children's performances were statistically equal on the explicit-rule task.

Similarly, all three groups of children chose the stimuli that followed the implicit rule significantly more often than by chance. Thus, children across all three diagnostic groups could infer and apply a rule that defined category membership. Specifically, children with autism were accurate 80% of the time, children with Down's syndrome, 75% of the time, and children with normal development, 86% of the time. Again, all three groups of children were statistically equal on the implicit-rule task. These data are displayed in Figure 7-1.

Prototype-Based Categorization

In the prototype condition, children were again presented with a series of schematic drawings of animals. During the familiarization trials, children were exposed to multiple members of a single animal category. The category members differed on several feature dimensions (e.g., length of neck, length of legs, etc.). In contrast to the rule-based conditions, no single feature or combination of features determined category membership. During one test trial, children were shown two novel animals, the average prototype animal (an animal composed of the average of each of the features they had seen during the familiarization trials) and an animal

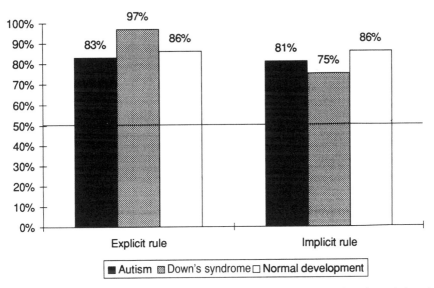

Fig. 7-1. Percent of children correctly following the rule in the explicit and implicit rule-based category learning conditions.

composed of features seen during the familiarization trials, but in a novel combination. As predicted by previous research, children with normal development chose the average prototype significantly more often than the novel animal composed of previously seen features. Specifically, they chose the average prototype 79% of the time, which was significantly greater than by chance. In contrast to the normally developing children, neither the children with autism nor the children with Down's syndrome differentiated between the average prototype and the animal composed of previously seen features. Children with autism chose the prototype 54% of the time, and children with Down's syndrome, 42% of the time. These data suggest that, in contrast to the normally developing children, neither the children with autism nor the children with Down's syndrome formed prototypic mental representations during category learning.

During another test trial, children were shown an animal that was identical to one of the animals they had seen during the familiarization trials and an animal composed of features seen during the familiarization trials but in a novel combination. None of the normally developing children chose the familiar animal significantly more often than the novel animal composed of previously seen features. That is, normally developing children did not appear to be memorizing individual examples during category learning. Similarly, children with autism and Down's syndrome did not perform as if they remembered the familiar animal. These data are displayed in Figure 7-2.

Our data suggest that children with autism and Down's syndrome are capable of categorizing information if a concrete rule can be used to determine category membership. However, in the absence of a concrete rule, children with autism *and* children with Down's syndrome appear to have difficulty categorizing information. Our data suggest that both groups may have a specific impairment in their ability to form an abstract summary representation, a prototype. That is, in situations without a concrete rule, both groups of children may be unable to examine incoming information and relate this information to previously experienced information. Taken together, these data suggest that children with autism and children with Down's syndrome process information in a more restricted manner than children without developmental disabilities.

These results cannot be explained by an inability to understand task demands or an inability to categorize in general. Children with autism and those with Down's syndrome did demonstrate category learning when exposed to categories defined by a concrete rule, even when they were required to infer the rule. Thus, category-learning impairments were specific to the prototype-categorization condition, the condition in which a rule-based process could not be applied.

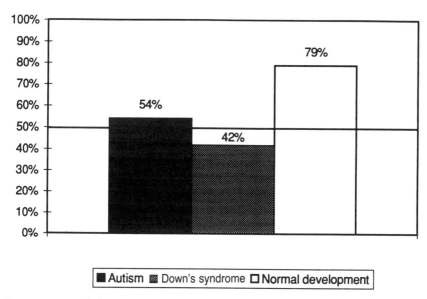

Fig. 7-2. Percent of children correctly choosing the prototype in the prototype category learning condition.

Success on the average-prototype conditions was not correlated with children's receptive-language age. This finding, along with the fact that children were individually matched on receptive-language age, suggests that the deficits in autism and Down's syndrome may not simply be a function of retardation or receptive-language age. If the ability to form categories using a prototype strategy was a function of mental age, we would have expected the normally developing children matched on receptive-language mental age to also show difficulties employing this type of strategy. Instead, the normally developing children successfully categorized information using a prototype-based categorization strategy.

Thus, children with autism appear to be able to form categories using rule-based strategies, but to be unable to form categories using abstraction-based prototype strategies. Individuals with Down's syndrome also may suffer from such an impairment. Thus, this type of impairment may be common to individuals with various types of retardation rather than being specific to autism. Other interpretations are possible, however; we explore these alternatives in the next section.

A FRESH LOOK AT CATEGORIZATION ABILITIES IN AUTISM

Our research suggests that we need to take a fresh look at categorization abilities in autism. Persons with autism do, in fact, appear to have difficulty forming abstract, prototypic mental representations of their world. Recent research on the normal development of categorization abilities suggests that prototypes are fundamental to the way in which information is stored, even by infants just hours old. Furthermore, early social and linguistic skills, such as the classification of facial expressions and speech, appear to depend fundamentally on the formation of perceptual prototypes (Kuhl, 1991). Thus, a deficit in prototype formation would represent a very basic and early developing kind of processing impairment. This kind of deficit would help to explain the autistic person's inflexibility and obsessive need for sameness. Moreover, this deficit may also shed light on the autistic person's difficulty in processing speech and social stimuli. Previously, we have argued that processing of social stimuli may be particularly difficult for persons with autism because social stimuli are inherently unpredictable, changing, and complex (Dawson & Lewy, 1989a; Klinger & Dawson, 1992). In other words, unlike many nonsocial stimuli, social stimuli defy any attempt to classify them in a rule-based manner. Reliance on a rule-based strategy, therefore, would theoretically result in particular difficulty in categorizing social stimuli. It would obviously be interesting to examine the formation of prototypes utilizing social information, such as facial expressions, in persons with autism.

Our research also suggests, however, that a difficulty in prototype formation may not be unique to individuals with autism. Our sample of individuals with mental retardation also showed impairments in this area. Further research is needed to determine whether the nature of the deficit shown by persons with autism and persons with mental retardation is the same. We suspect that these two groups will be found to differ in the nature of their processing impairments. Research by Zeaman and House (1979) has shown that adults with mental retardation are slow at learning a discrimination task, such as the one used in this study. However, once they have mastered the task, their accuracy is equivalent to nonretarded individuals. Thus, it is possible that persons with mental retardation would benefit from a longer stimulus-exposure period or more familiarization trials. The key question here is whether individuals with autism also would benefit from increased processing time. Again, the focus is on the process of learning rather than the final achievement.

Given the good rote memory skills commonly seen in individuals with autism, it is unlikely that difficulty in retrieving information from memory leads to impaired category learning. However, impairments in category abstraction may be suggestive of an underlying encoding problem, particularly in the area of attention. It may be that unless there is a concrete rule, children with autism and children with Down's syndrome focus on a single, idiosyncratic feature of the stimulus rather than encoding all the features of the whole figure. This hypothesis is supported by the "overselectivity" findings reported by Lovaas et al. (1979). Additionally, Berger et al. (1993) reported that persons with autism focused their attention on a single feature to learn a rule-based category, and could not shift their attention to focus on another feature when a new rule was introduced. This attentional hypothesis could be tested by examining eye-tracking during category learning, or alternatively, by examining whether prototype formation is enhanced by cueing children to look at specific features.

CONCLUSIONS

A new perspective can be gained by focusing not on the question of whether persons with autism can categorize information (they can), but how they do so. We believe that this change of focus from achievement of a skill to the process by which the achievement is made would benefit much of the research on the cognitive and social deficits that underlie this syndrome. If future research provides further support for an impairment in prototype formation during category learning in autism, we will need to examine whether this impairment explains other deficits common to the syndrome of autism, for instance deficits in joint attention (Mundy, Sigman, Ungerer, & Sherman, 1986), symbolic play (Riguet, Taylor, Benaroya, & Klein, 1981), theory-of-mind (Baron-Cohen, Leslie, & Frith, 1985), and executive function (see Ozonoff, Chapter 11, in this volume).

ACKNOWLEDGMENTS

This chapter is based on a doctoral dissertation submitted by the first author as partial fulfillment of the requirements for the Ph.D. in psychology at the University of Washington. We wish to thank the Washington Association for Retarded Citizens for funds provided to Laura Grofer Klinger and Geraldine Dawson to study categorization in children with autism and Down's syndrome. We gratefully acknowledge the children and their parents in Seattle, Washington, and Fayetteville, Arkansas, who participated in the study described in this chapter. We also wish to thank

Mark Klinger, Melanie Cotter, and Natalie Hill for their critical comments on earlier drafts of this manuscript.

REFERENCES

American Psychiatric Association (1987). *Diagnostic and statistical manual of mental disorders* (3d ed., rev.). Washington, DC: Author.

Baron-Cohen, S. (1989). The autistic child's theory of mind: A case of specific developmental delay. *Journal of Child Psychology and Psychiatry, 30*, 285–297.

Baron-Cohen, S., Leslie, A., & Frith, U. (1985). Does the autistic child have a "theory of mind"? *Cognition, 21*, 37–46.

Baron-Cohen, S., Leslie, A. M., & Frith, U. (1986). Mechanical, behavioural and intentional understanding of picture stories in autistic children. *British Journal of Developmental Psychology, 4*, 113–125.

Berger, H., van Spaendonck, K., Horstink, M., Buytenhuijs, E., Lammers, P., & Cools, A. (1993). Cognitive shifting as a predictor of progress in social understanding in high-functioning adolescents with autism: A prospective study. *Journal of Autism and Developmental Disorders, 23*, 341–359.

Bomba, P. C., & Siqueland, E. R. (1983). The nature and structure of infant form categories. *Journal of Experimental Child Psychology, 35*, 294–328.

Cicchetti, D., & Pogge-Hesse, P. (1982). Possible contributions of the study of organically retarded persons in developmental theory. In E. Zigler & D. Balla (Eds.), *Mental retardation: The developmental-difference controversy* (pp. 277–318). Hillsdale, NJ: Erlbaum.

Dawson, G., & Adams, A. (1984). Imitation and social responsiveness in autistic children. *Journal of Abnormal Child Psychology, 12*, 209–226.

Dawson, G., & Galpert, L. (1990). Mothers' use of imitative play for facilitating social responsiveness and toy play in young autistic children. *Development and Psychopathology, 2*, 151–162.

Dawson, G., & Lewy, A. (1989a). Arousal, attention, and the socioemotional impairments of individuals with autism. In G. Dawson (Ed.), *Autism: Nature, diagnosis, and treatment* (pp. 49–74). New York: Guilford.

Dawson, G., & Lewy, A. (1989b). Reciprocal subcortical-cortical influences in autism: The role of attentional mechanisms. In G. Dawson (Ed.), *Autism: Nature, diagnosis, and treatment* (pp. 144–173). New York: Guilford.

Ferrara, C., & Hill, S. (1980). The responsiveness of autistic children to the predictability of social and nonsocial toys. *Journal of Autism and Developmental Disorders, 10*, 51–57.

Hermelin, B., & O'Connor, N. (1970). *Psychological experiments with autistic children*. Oxford: Pergamon Press.

Hermelin, B., & O'Connor, N. (1986). Idiot savant calendrical calculators: Rules and regularities. *Psychological Medicine, 16*, 885–893.

Husaim, J., & Cohen, L. (1981). Infant learning of ill-defined categories. *Merrill-Palmer Quarterly, 27*, 443–456.

Kanner, L. (1943). Autistic disturbances of affective contact. *Nervous Child, 2*, 217–250.

Klinger, L. G., & Dawson, G. (1992). Facilitating early social and communicative development in children with autism. In S. F. Warren & J. Reichle (Eds.), *Causes and effects in communication and language intervention* (pp. 157–186). Baltimore, MD: Brookes.

Klinger, L. G., Dawson, G., & Lewy, A. (1993, March). *Facilitating social interaction in children with autism*. Paper presented at the Meeting of the Society for Research in Child Development, New Orleans, LA.

Kuhl, P. K. (1991). Human adults and human infants show a "perceptual magnet effect" for the prototypes of speech categories, monkeys do not. *Perception and Psychophysics, 50*, 93–107.

Lovaas, O. I., Koegel, R. L., & Schreibman, L. (1979). Stimulus overselectivity in autism: A review of research. *Psychological Bulletin, 6*, 1236–1254.

Medin, D., & Schaffer, M. (1978). Context theory of classification learning. *Psychological Review, 85*, 207–238.

Minshew, N. J., Goldstein, G., Muenz, L. R., Payton, J. B. (1992). Neuropsychological functioning in non-mentally retarded autistic individuals. *Journal of Clinical and Experimental Neuropsychology, 14*, 749–761.

Mundy, P., Sigman, M., Ungerer, J. A., & Sherman, T. (1986). Defining the social deficits of autism: The contribution of nonverbal communication measures. *Journal of Child Psychology and Psychiatry, 27*, 657–669.

Noach, M. (1974). Concept formation in the speaking autistic child. *International Journal of Mental Health, 3*, 100–109.

Ozonoff, S. (1995). Executive function impairments in autism. In E. Schopler and G. Mesibov (Eds.), *Learning and cognition in autism* (pp. 199–220). New York: Plenum Press.

Posner, M. I., Goldsmith, R., & Welton, K. E. (1967). Perceived distance and the classification of distorted patterns. *Journal of Experimental Psychology, 73*, 28–38.

Posner, M. I., & Keele, S. W. (1968). On the genesis of abstract ideas. *Journal of Experimental Psychology, 77*, 353–363.

Posner, M. I., & Keele, S. W. (1970). Retention of abstract ideas. *Journal of Experimental Psychology, 83*, 304–308.

Prior, M., & Hoffman, W. (1990). Brief report: Neuropsychological testing of autistic children through an exploration with frontal lobe tests. *Journal of Autism and Developmental Disorders, 20*, 581–590.

Riguet, C. B., Taylor, N. D., Benaroya, S., & Klein, L. S. (1981). Symbolic play in autistic, Down's, and normal children of equivalent mental age. *Journal of Autism and Developmental Disorders, 11*, 439–448.

Rincover, A., & Koegel, R. L. (1975). Setting generality and stimulus control in autistic children. *Journal of Applied Behavioral Analysis, 8*, 235–246.

Rosch, E. (1978). Principles of categorization. In E. Rosch (Ed.), *Cognition and categorization* (pp. 27–48). Hillsdale, NJ: Erlbaum.

Rosch, E., Mervis, C., Gray, W., Johnson, D., & Boyes-Braem, P. (1976). Basic objects in natural categories. *Cognitive Psychology, 8*, 382–439.

Rumsey, J., & Hamburger, S. (1988). Neuropsychological findings in high-functioning men with infantile autism, residual state. *Journal of Clinical and Experimental Neuropsychology, 10*, 201–221.

Rumsey, J., & Hamburger, S. (1990). Neuropsychological divergence of high-level autism and severe dyslexia. *Journal of Autism and Developmental Disorders, 20*, 155–168.

Schneider, S. G., & Asarnow, R. F. (1987). A comparison of cognitive/neuropsychological impairments of nonrelated autistic and schizophrenic children. *Journal of Abnormal Child Psychology, 15*, 29–46.

Smith, E. E., & Medin, D. L. (1981). *Categories and concepts*. Cambridge, MA: Harvard University Press.

Strauss, M. S. (1979). Abstraction of prototypical information by adults and 10-month-old infants. *Journal of Experimental Psychology: Human Learning and Memory, 5*, 616–632.

Tager-Flusberg, H. (1985a). Basic level and superordinate level categorization in autistic, mentally retarded, and normal children. *Journal of Experimental Child Psychology, 40,* 450–469.

Tager-Flusberg, H. (1985b). The conceptual basis for referential word meaning in children with autism. *Child Development, 56,* 1167–1178.

Ungerer, J., & Sigman, M. (1987). Categorization skills and receptive language development in autistic children. *Journal of Autism and Developmental Disorders, 17,* 3–16.

Vygotsky, L. (1962). *Thought and language.* Cambridge, MA: MIT Press.

Walton, G. E., & Bower, T. G. R. (1993, March). *Newborns' formation of prototypical faces.* Paper presented at the Meeting of the Society for Research in Child Development, New Orleans, LA.

Werner, H. (1937). Process and achievement: A basic problem of education and developmental psychology. *Harvard Educational Review, 7,* 353–368.

Williams, D. (1992). *Nobody nowhere.* New York: Time Books.

Younger, B. (1990). Infant categorization: Memory for category-level and specific item information. *Journal of Experimental Child Psychology, 50,* 131–155.

Younger, B., & Gotleib, S. (1988). Development of categorization skills: Changes in the nature or structure of infant form categories? *Developmental Psychology, 24,* 611–619.

Zeaman, D., & House, B. J. (1979). A review of attention theory. In N. R. Ellis (Ed.), *Handbook of mental deficiency research, psychological theory, and research* (2nd ed., pp. 63–120). Hillsdale, NJ: Erlbaum.

8

How People with Autism Think

TEMPLE GRANDIN

INTRODUCTION

I am a high-functioning person with autism. I operate a successful live-stock-equipment design business and I hold a teaching position at Colorado State University. During the last 7 years I have published and lectured on my experiences with autism. I provide a unique perspective by combining scientific knowledge with my own experiences.

This chapter is divided into five sections: Autism Subtypes, Visual Thinking, Implications of Visual Thinking, Emotions and Empathy, and Sensory Problems and Attention. The first section discusses possible subtypes of autism and how they relate to sensory processing and cognitive sensory and concreteness-of-thinking continuum of autism subtypes. In the second section, I describe my visual methods of thinking, and in the third section I discuss the implications of visual thinking on educational methods, abstract thought, and cognition. In the fourth section, my experiences with empathy and emotion are described. In the last section, I describe where I fall on the continuum of autism and how autism subtypes may affect the efficacy of educational and therapeutic methods.

TEMPLE GRANDIN • Department of Animal Science, Colorado State University, Fort Collins, Colorado 80523.

Learning and Cognition in Autism, edited by Eric Schopler and Gary B. Mesibov. Plenum Press, New York, 1995.

AUTISM SUBTYPES

Autism is a heterogeneous disorder with many subtypes, ranging from genius level to very low functioning with mental retardation. Autism diagnosis is further clouded by neurological disorders that produce autistic symptoms such as Fragile X, undiagnosed PKU, tuberous sclerosis, neurofibromatosis, Rhett Syndrome, very high fevers at a young age, or damage to the fetus caused by drug or alcohol abuse. Most of my discussion is limited to types of autism that are not caused by the aforementioned conditions.

Some types of autism are characterized by true problems with concreteness and rigidity of thinking, and in another type individuals may appear retarded due to problems with sensory processing. The rigid thinking described by Kanner (1943) and the theory-of-mind problems described by Frith (1989) may be at one end of an autistic continuum. Autistic persons in this group have true abnormalities in their thinking patterns, which are described in detail in other chapters of this book.

At the other end of the spectrum is Sands and Ratey's (1986) concept of noise confusion and hyperarousal as being the basis of autism. Which is correct? Both are probably correct because each research group was studying a different population. It is like the blind men describing the proverbial elephant. Sands and Ratey (1986) studied an institutionalized adult population of low-functioning individuals. Most research on cognitive processes has been on less severely afflicted individuals who are able to cooperate during testing.

At conferences, I have talked to hundreds of parents and have seen a pattern of autistic subtypes. Autism in which genetics is most likely to be one of the primary causes may be divided into two broad categories that merge together in a continuum. At one end of the spectrum, there are the Kanner/Asperger types described by Kanner (1943) and Asperger (1944), and at the other end of the spectrum are the so-called "low-functioning" types. I prefer to use the term regressive/epileptic. In Figure 8-1, I illustrate a single continuum that encompasses both concreteness and rigidity of thinking and sensory-processing problems. There may be several continuua for autism, such as sensory processing, movement disorders, concreteness of thinking, visual thinking, and other cognitive characteristics. This discussion is limited to rigidity of thinking and sensory-processing dysfunction.

The Kanner/Asperger types have rigid, concrete thinking patterns and definite problems with certain types of cognitive processing. The thinking patterns of classical Kanner-types are beautifully described by Hart (1989).

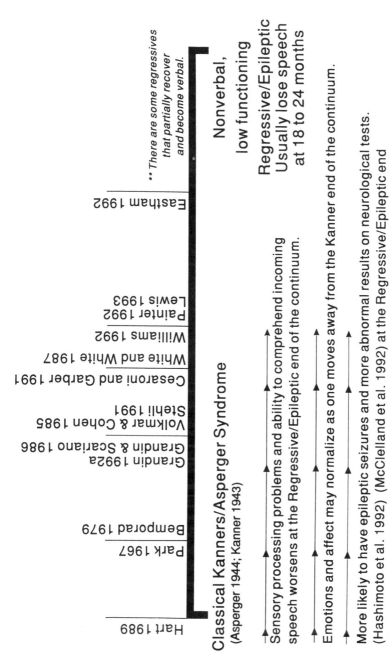

Fig. 8-1. Autistic continuum: Position of people described in published literature on the continuum.

The regressive/epileptics usually have a period of normal development for 18 to 24 months and then lose the power of speech. However,
there are some individuals at this end of the continuum who have no
period of normal language development. Kurita, Kita, and Miyake, (1992)
stated that people with autism who lose their speech tend to have lower
mental development. Persons who lose speech at a later age may be even
more severely impaired (Volkmar & Cohen, 1989). Gedye (1991) spec-
ulated that some symptoms of autism may be caused by frontal lobe
seizures, and that these seizures are difficult to detect on a standard EEG
test (Gedye, 1989).

In the chapter I wrote for *High-Functioning Individuals with Autism*
(Grandin, 1992a), I described problems with sensory hypersensitivity.
Low-IQ scores in the regressive-epileptic group may be partially due to
sensory jumbling and mixing. It is likely that this group has much more
severe sensory difficulties than the oversensitivities that I had to sound
and touch (Grandin, 1992a, Grandin & Scariano, 1986). Most Kanner/As-
perger types, such as myself, can attend to simultaneous visual and auditory input. As one moves away from the Kanner/Asperger end of the
spectrum, sensations from the eyes and ears may mix together (Cesaroni
& Garber, 1991; Joliffe, Lakesdown, & Robinson, 1992; Painter, 1992; Williams, 1992). Cesaroni and Garber (1991) described mixing and confusing
sensory input from different sensory modalities. One autistic man stated
that touching the lower part of his face caused a soundlike sensation. He
also reported that sounds came through as color and he theorized that
some stimuli act as "triggers" that disorganize processing, similar to epi-
leptic seizures triggered by a flashing light.

Donna Williams (a woman with autism) explained to me that she has
problems determining where her body boundary is. The tendency of nonverbal, severely impaired people with autism to constantly touch or tap
themselves and objects in the environment may be an attempt to stabilize
the boundaries of their own body and other objects. Joliffe wrote that there
were no clear boundaries to anything and that she could understand
things better through her fingers (Joliffe et al., 1992). Donna Williams,
Therese Joliffe, and the cases described by Cesaroni and Garber (1991) may
be midway on the autism continuum.

Lewis (1993) described her son, who may also be midway on the
continuum. He does not have the rigid thinking of a typical Kanner type
and he understands the give and take of conversations. Her son has self-
stimulatory behaviors in every sensory modality that indicate serious sensory-processing problems.

Brain autopsies indicate that the different subtypes have a similar
pattern of immature development of the cerebellum and limbic system

(Bauman, 1991). Bauman studied both Kanner types and regressive types (Bauman, 1993, personal communication). Although the basic pattern of abnormality is the same for both types, there may be slight variations in the pattern, which could account for more severe sensory-processing problems at the regressive end of the spectrum, and more severe concreteness-of-thinking problems at the Kanner end of the spectrum (Bauman, 1993, personal communication). Cerebellar abnormalities could possibly explain sensory oversensitivity, and brain stem abnormalities may explain sensory jumbling and mixing.

Research with cats and rats indicating that the cerebellum modulates sensory input (Chambers, 1947; Courchesne, Young-Courchesne, Press, Hesselink, & Jernigan, 1988; Crispino & Bullock, 1984; Murakami, 1989) revealed that high-functioning autistic individuals have abnormalities of the cerebellar vermis and smaller cerebellar hemispheres. MRI scans indicated that my own cerebellum is 20% smaller than normal, and a computer genius with classical Kanners had a cerebellum that was 30% undersized.

McClelland, Eyre, Watson, C. Sherrard, & E. Sherrard, 1992) found that lower functioning people with autism have slower electrical transmission through the brain stem compared to higher functioning autistics. Autistics with lower IQs also tend to have small, undersized brain stems (Hashimoto et al., 1992). In the next sections, I describe how rigidity and concreteness of thinking affect learning in people on the Kanner end of the continuum and how sensory-processing problems inhibit learning and language at the other end of the spectrum. An example of a thinking problem in Kanner-type autism is the lack of common sense and ability to generalize. One mother told me that it was impossible to teach her autistic son the meaning of money, even though he had a genius IQ and could program computers. At the other end of the continuum, sensory jumbling and mixing may interfere with learning because the autistic child has difficulty understanding his teachers and how to make proper responses.

VISUAL THINKING

I am a visual thinker, and visual thinking and perspective drawing is often evident at an early age in high-functioning Kanner-type children (Park, 1992). At conferences I have been given drawings in perspective drawn by 7- and 9-year-old autistic children. I have discussed thinking patterns with many highly verbal people with autism. Most of them are visual thinkers, although there are a few who may not be. Virtually everybody near the Kanner end of the spectrum uses visual modes of thought.

The few nonvisual thinkers have very severe sensory-jumbling problems and occupy a midpoint position between the two ends of the autistic spectrum.

In previous publications (Grandin, 1984, 1992a; Grandin & Scariano, 1986), I discussed visual thinking in detail, but I have had some more recent insights. Language and words are alien ways of thinking for me. All my thoughts are like playing different tapes in the videocassette recorder in my imagination. Before I researched other people's thinking methods, I assumed that everybody thought in pictures.

At conferences and during business trips I have asked hundreds of people to allow me to conduct a little test regarding the way they access information from memory. I asked them to access their memories of church steeples or cats. When I access my own memory, I see many different "videos" of specific cats or churches I have seen. Many people reported that they saw a visual image. Further questioning indicated that in most people, the image was very vague and generalized compared to the vivid cat and church "videos" that I imagined. They had a sort of generic, generalized outline of a church steeple or a cat. Like me, most parents of autistic children, artists, and engineers had a strong series of visual images, whereas school administrators and many speech therapists had poor visualization skills. Some brilliant people had no visual thought at all. They accessed their cat concept as auditory or written language. My cat or church steeple concept is based on a series of "videos" of different cats or churches I have experienced. To obtain a good concept of cats or churches, I need to experience many different ones to fill up my "video" library. There is no generalized cat concept. I can manipulate the cat or church "videos." I can put snow on the roof of the church and imagine what it would be like during different seasons. Park (1992) reported that when her autistic daughter painted a picture, her eye acted like a camera.

My mind works like the computer programs that are used to make high-tech special effects in movies. I can take many different bits and pieces and combine them into new images. I use this method when I design equipment in my livestock equipment-design business. The more bits and pieces I have in my "video library," the better I can design equipment. I have videos of many things, such as metal posts, sheet metal, bearings, cattle, motors, gates, and so on. To create a new design, I pull the bits out of memory and combine them into a new piece of equipment. Over the years, I have become better and better at designing equipment because I have a bigger library of "videos." I have a great urge to see and actually operate all kinds of equipment to add more data to my memory. After the machine is designed, I can run simulations under many different conditions and rotate the machine in my head. I don't need computers with fancy graphics programs, because I have a sophisticated drawing and graphics computer in my head. In my imagination I can duplicate the functions of the most sophisticated, computerized virtual-reality systems. However, my mind works slowly. When I draw a detailed three-dimensional drawing, it takes several hours. Attempts to draw rapid sketches result in very crude drawings.

Visualization of Nonvisual Information

I have no language-based memory. When I hear the word *over* by itself, I visualize a childhood memory of a dog jumping over a fence. To store material that I have read, I either read it off a page I have photographed in my memory or I translate the written material into visual images. To retrieve the information, I have to replay the "video." This method of thinking is slower. It takes time to replay the "video" in my imagination. In computer language my memory is like a CD-ROM disc.

Other autistic people have described visual thinking methods for tasks that many people do sequentially. An autistic computer programmer stated that he visualized the overall pattern of the program tree and then he filled in the code on each branch. A composer with autism told me he made "sound" pictures. It appears that his thought processes are similar to mine. He uses bits and pieces of other music to make new compositions. In both of these cases, and my own, a hazy gestalt is visualized and details are added in a nonsequential manner.

I use this same method when I review the scientific literature and do troubleshooting work for meat plants. It is a nonsequential process, which is like trying to figure out what the picture is on a jigsaw puzzle when only a third of the pieces are put together. A piece is put at one corner, then another corner, and then a clump of pieces are put together in the middle. At a certain point, the picture becomes obvious. When I review scientific literature, I look for new patterns. I write the essential findings or "bottom line" of each journal article on a slip of paper. I then pin papers containing related information next to each other on a bulletin board. Patterns will form between unrelated articles. As I become more experienced and obtain a bigger and bigger library of research information in my mind, the physical bulletin board is no longer needed.

Language

If I had to learn a foreign language, I would have to learn it by reading. When I was in Mexico and Iceland, I started to pick up a few nouns from signs. I have to see the word in print and convert it to a picture in order to store it. The TEACCH program utilizes visual methods for organization of the classroom and educational activities (Mesibov, Schopler, & Hearsey, 1994). In Iceland I visited a classroom where TEACCH methods were being used. Labels were attached to various objects in the room. When I recall the Icelandic word for computer, *tolva*, I immediately see the Apple computer in that classroom with a label taped to it. After I see a word and store it in memory, I can then pick it up in a conversation. The best program for teaching me a foreign language would be careful reading and translation of airline magazine articles that are written in both languages. I would also want to use American movies with foreign subtitles. The phrases on the subtitles could then be associated with the pictures on the film and stored in my memory. I could then use these phrases to communicate. This style of learning may explain why some autistic children use phrases from television commercials in an appropriate manner. During my last trip to Mexico I found that I could pick up the meaning of Spanish words from television commercials. It was much easier to learn from commercials compared to the regular programs. My early attempts to speak Spanish consisted of nouns and simple phrases.

Park (1967) reported that her autistic daughter learned nouns first. Nouns are easy because they can be associated with pictures. Words with no concrete meaning such as *put* or *on* have to be seen in writing in order to be heard or remembered. Park further described how inappropriate words were used. Her daughter said "Dick" to mean *painting*. This occurred because she saw a picture of Dick painting in a book. Pronoun reversal problems may occur because she thinks her name is *you* instead of *I*. Hart (1989) beautifully summarized autistic thinking in a single sentence: "Ted's thought processes aren't logical, they are associational." Visual thinking may explain some theory-of-mind problems described by Frith (1989). Visual associations may explain why one child says "French toast" when he is happy. French toast became associated with happiness because sometime in the past the child had a very happy, pleasant time while eating French toast. Therefore, when he visualizes French toast in his mind, he becomes happy.

IMPLICATIONS OF VISUAL THINKING

Never burden a visual thinker with long strings of verbal information. If verbal directions contain more than three steps, I have to write them down. If an autistic child can read, it is best to provide written instructions that he or she can refer to. Boucher and Lewis (1989) found that written instructions were superior compared to verbal instructions or demonstration of a task. Some highly verbal autistic persons such as myself can learn reading more easily with old-fashioned phonics (Grandin, 1992a). A visual picture should be paired to each phonetic sound. For nonverbal children with more severe sensory-processing problems, plastic magnetic letters that the child can feel are often helpful. Eastham (1990) taught her nonverbal son to read by holding his hand and tracing his fingers over sandpaper letters. The phonetic sound for each letter was spoken while with his fingers he felt the shape of the letter.

Singing can also facilitate learning. I learned the alphabet by singing it. When I had to recall a specific letter, I had to sing the alphabet song from the beginning until I reached the letter I wanted. I had to start at the beginning of my alphabet singing "video" in my imagination. When I sang the alphabet, I visualized the front porch of our house, because one of the first times I successfully sang the entire alphabet song, I was standing on the porch.

Certain subjects in school were easy because I could convert the material to visual images, and other subjects, such as algebra, were almost impossible. I cannot hold one piece of information in my mind while I manipulate the next step in the sequence. I also mix up the steps because I have many dyslexic traits, such as mixing up similar-sounding words like *over* or *other*. To learn math procedures I have to write down each step.

Williams (1992) had similar difficulties. She had to write down every step. If one little step is left out, the autistic mind can't go to the next step. She needed a visual image written on paper. Written language is often easier for autistic individuals to learn. Word processors and typewriters should be made available to young, autistic children. Typing is often easier than writing because many people with autism have highly illegible writing due to motor-control problems. In my own case, I can express myself better in writing when I want to describe my emotions. For mute, lower functioning children with no ability to hear, speech and language should be introduced through visual methods (Allen & Rapin, 1993). Some of these children may learn to speak after they have learned to read.

Abstract Thought

All abstract thought has to be converted to pictures in order for me to understand. I visualized the Lord's Prayer. "The power and the glory" were high-tension electric wires and a blazing sun. The word *trespass* I visualized as a "no trespassing" sign on a tree (Grandin, 1992a). I visualize concepts such as justice or truth as pictures of the scales of justice, or a courtroom, and placing my hand on a Bible and taking an oath. When I was in boarding school, I knew I would have to learn to live on my own. It was impossible for my purely visual mind to comprehend this concept without a physical way of thinking about it. I found a little door that went out on the roof and I would actually walk through it to help me think about learning to be on my own. It was not enough to think about it, I needed to actually walk through the little door. Thirty years ago, I wrote the following in my diary:

March 20, 1964

It was windy that night. I looked up at that door that goes out on the roof. I knew if I went through I'd be going one step beyond where I should go. I walked up to the door, I stood in front of it, I looked out the window in the door, out onto the roof on a cold and windy night. I knew I should not open it. I turned the latches. I could feel the wind trying to push it open. I still stood waiting, watching, wondering if I should open the door—I opened it slowly.

April 2, 1964

I think I have answered part of the question. The door goes one step beyond authority. After I went through the door and closed it behind me, authority was on the other side. The door looked different closed from the other side. I could see back through the window back into the house. I stood on the roof looking at the door. That door leads somewhere I don't know. Maybe everybody has to go through that door. There is a time when one must be on his own—then he takes a step beyond authority. In the house looking at the door, I don't know what lies behind that door.

Park and Younderian (1974) also reported the use of visual symbols, such as doors, to describe abstract concepts. Today I look at these diary entries and they seem almost silly. My reliance on concrete door symbols was greatly reduced after I started taking low doses of Tofranil (imipramine) to control my anxiety (Grandin, 1992a; Grandin & Scariano, 1986). When the panic attacks and constant feeling of stage fright subsided, it was easier to think more slowly and logically. Today the new antidepressant Anafranil (clomipramine) is recommended (Gordon, State, Nelson, Hamburger & Rapport, 1993; McDougal et al., 1992). Taking medication has also reduced my tendency to perseverate on one topic, and it has enabled me to cope with unexpected changes in my schedule.

Over the years I have accumulated so much information in my memory that I no longer need concrete door symbols. To understand interactions with people, I compare them to something I have read or experienced. Asperger (1944) stated that normal children learn social skills instinctively. In autistic people, the intellect is used to learn social skills. Jim, a 27-year-old graduate student, stated that people with autism lack the basic instincts that make communication a natural process (Cesaroni & Garber, 1991). For example, in my equipment-design business, an argument between myself and one of my clients is similar to something I have read about the United States and Europe fighting over trading rights. Over the years I have accumulated vast amounts of information from newspapers and books.

I am like Data, the android man, on "Star Trek, the Next Generation." As he accumulates more information, he has a greater understanding of social relationships. I am a scientist who has to learn the strange ways of an alien culture. Jim Sinclair, a man with autism, stated that he needed an orientation manual for extraterrestrials (Mesibov, 1992). When I encounter a new social situation, I have to scan my memory and look for previous experiences that were similar. I also have, in my memory, information on the social consequences of different methods of response. I then make a purely logical decision on how to respond. As I accumulate more memories, I become more and more skilled at predicting how other people will act in a particular situation. I have learned from experience that certain behaviors make people mad. Sometimes my logical decisions are wrong because they are based on insufficient data.

At the age of 46, I have a vast data bank and I am able to logically determine which people have good intentions and which have bad intentions. When I was younger I was dismayed to discover that some people had very bad intentions. This is something all people with autism have to learn. In business dealings I am now very good at figuring out a person's intentions.

Cognitive Differences

Visual thinking is a true difference in cognitive function. New research findings indicate that verbal thought and visual thinking work via different brain systems. (Farah, 1989; Zeki, 1992). Studies of patients with brain damage indicate that one system can be damaged, while another system may be normal. The brain is designed with modular systems. These systems may work together or separately to perform different tasks. For example, people with certain types of brain damage can recognize objects with straight edges, but they cannot recognize objects with irregular edges. The brain module that recognizes irregular shapes has been damaged (Weiss, 1989). In autism, the systems that process visual-spatial problems are intact. There is a possibility that these systems may be expanded to compensate for deficits in language. The nervous system has remarkable plasticity; one part can take over and compensate for deficits in language, and another part can take over and compensate for a damaged part (Huttenlocher, 1984). Even though I think visually, I have difficulty recognizing faces. It is also interesting that an autistic woman named Jessie (Park, 1992) and I can both draw fabulous buildings and objects, but we draw very poorly realistic-looking people. Possibly, one visual subsystem works much better than another. Problems with face recognition and drawing of people are probably not related to avoidance of eye contact. Study of normal adults with brain damage from accidents or strokes indicates that face recognition may reside in a separate brain subsystem (Bishop, 1993).

Visual thinking is also associated with being intellectually gifted (Ramo & Rosenberg, 1993). Albert Einstein was a visual thinker who failed his high school language requirement and relied on visual methods of study (Holton, 1971–1972). His theory of relativity was based on visual imagery of moving boxcars and riding on light beams. Einstein's family history included a high incidence of autism, dyslexia, food allergies, high intellectual aptitude, and musical talent, and he himself had many autistic traits. An astute reader can find evidence of them in Einstein and Einstein (1987). Other great scientists, such as Leonardo da Vinci, Faraday, and Maxwell, were visual thinkers (West, 1991).

Intellectual giftedness is common in the family histories of many persons with autism. My grandfather on my mother's side invented the automobile pilot for airplanes, and my mother was an honor's student. One of my sisters is dyslexic and is brilliant in the art of decorating houses. My great grandfather on my father's side was a pioneer who started the largest corporate wheat farm in the world.

Mild autistic traits often show up in parents, siblings, and other relatives (Landa et al., 1992; Narayan, Moyes, & Wolff, 1990). Some of these traits include intellectual giftedness, shyness, learning disabilities, depression, anxiety, panic attacks, Tourette's syndrome and alcoholism (Narayan et al., 1990; Sverd, 1991). There may be an advantage if a person has a few of these traits, such as creativity or high intelligence, but too many of these traits may cause problems (Clark, 1993). I hypothesize that emotions may get more normal as the subtype moves away from classical Kanner's.

EMOTIONS AND EMPATHY

I definitely have emotions, and I was very angry when Happé (1991) implied that I was not able to express emotion. When I was a child and other kids teased me, it really hurt and I became upset. I derive great emotional satisfaction from my career of designing livestock equipment. When a facility I designed pleases a client, I am happy. Jack, a piano tuner with autism, also stated that pleasing other people is important (Dewey, 1991). If one of my projects fails to work or a client criticizes me unfairly, I become depressed and upset. Jack has similar sensitivities to criticism. He stated, "If I was successful (referring to music composition) I might get some very caustic reviews and I would be crushed because of the way I feel about criticism" (Dewey, 1991, p. 203). I receive great emotional satisfaction by doing something that is of value to society. My work on livestock systems has resulted in improvements in animal treatment all over the United States. It makes me feel good to help other people with autism and their parents. It is also very pleasurable for me to use my visualization skill to figure out a design problem. Exercising my cerebral cortex on an interesting design problem is fun. I have observed that my nonautistic engineering friends also find intellectual use of the brain a very pleasurable activity. Many engineers and scientists value intellect more than emotion.

When important people in my life die, I become very sad, and I often cry during sad movies. If I see someone abusing animals it makes me angry or upset. There are a few areas where my emotions may be different. I am not easily shocked or horrified. If I see something nasty, it may make me angry or sad, but it does not shock me. Another difference is that I use logic and intellect to guide my decisions rather than emotions. I have developed a reputation in the livestock industry for being objective. I can provide an objective evaluation of another scientist's work even if I hate him or her as a person. I have observed that most people have a hard time doing this. I can set my dislike for the person aside and look at his or her scientific work without letting my dislike affect my judgment.

I have learned by interviewing other people that when they think about past traumatic experiences they sometimes become overwhelmed with emotion. When I think about past traumatic experiences, I seldom become upset. The only exceptions are the deaths of my aunt and Tom Rohrer, manager of the local Swift plant, who helped get my career started. I will sometimes cry when I think about their deaths, but I am not overwhelmed. When I experience strong emotion it is powerful while I am actually experiencing it, but it does not become deeply imprinted in my brain. I have no subconscious or repressed memories. I can access all memories and there are no repressed memories due to emotional content that would impede access.

I am successful in designing livestock systems because I can imagine myself as an animal, with an animal's body shape and senses. I am able to visualize myself as an animal going through one of my systems. This "video" is complete with touch, sound, visual and olfactory sensations. I can play this "video" from two perspectives. The perspective is either me watching the animal, or me inside the animal's head looking out through its eyes. Many systems used in meat plants are designed poorly because the engineers never thought about what the equipment would feel like when it contacted the animal's body. I can imagine how the animal will feel, and set my own emotions aside. I can imagine realistically what the animal would feel because I do not allow my own emotions to cloud the picture.

When I handle cattle in one of my handling systems and the animals remain calm and do not feel pain or discomfort, I have good emotional feelings. If they become agitated or excited, I get upset. Recently, I designed a new restraining chute for holding cattle during kosher slaughter. It is operated with hydraulics. After some practice, I learned to gently ease the animal's body and head into position so that the rabbi could perform kosher slaughter. When the cattle remained calm I felt peaceful. Operating the device gently is an act of kindness and a person has to really love the cattle in order to operate it humanely. Most people who love animals have such a negative emotional reaction to being in a slaughter plant that their emotions interfere with really empathizing with the cattle. As I operated the chute, I concentrated on holding the animals gently and I was very careful not to squeeze them too hard. I wanted to make them as comfortable as possible during the last moments of life. It was like being a hospice worker. When I think about this experience, by replaying it on the "video" in my imagination, I feel good.

Many people in the autism field are somewhat perplexed about Donna Williams's (1992) book, with its poetic, dreamlike descriptions of an abusive family and living on the streets. When I talked to her on the telephone, she sounded completely normal with lots of affect. She did not have the flat monotone of a classical Kanner autistic. Possibly, her type of autism has a more normal mind trapped in a totally dysfunctional sensory system.

SENSORY PROBLEMS AND ATTENTION

In lower functioning (epileptic/regressive) autistics, the poor performance on IQ tests may be partially due to sensory jumbling and mixing caused by miniepileptic seizures between poorly myelinated neurons. McClelland et al. (1992) believe that people with autism have a myelinization defect, which could account for abnormal brain stem-evoked potentials in older autistic children and epileptics. Possibly, poor myelinization could also account for mixing of sensory input and "blankouts" when autistic persons become excited.

Gillberg and Schaumann (1983) reported on a case of Childhood Absence Epilepsy (CAE, Petit mal) and autistic symptoms. The subjects' EEG normalized and autistic behaviors disappeared after taking the epilepsy drug Zarontin (ethosuximide). Parents of autistic children report that vitamin B_6 and magnesium work best in children who lost speech at 18–24 months. Possibly, it is acting as a natural antiseizure substance. Miniepileptic seizures may cause speech to fade in and out like a distant radio station. One autistic man described how another person's voice faded in and out and that his ears played tricks on him (G. White & M. White, 1987).

Therapy Methods and Subtypes

A teaching program that was successful for me may be terrible for a child with more severe sensory-jumbling and mixing problems. In my book (Grandin & Scariano, 1986) I described how my speech therapist held my chin and forced eye contact. Doing this jerked me out of my world of daydreaming and stereotypical behavior. Intrusive methods may cause further withdrawal in children with more severe sensory-processing difficulties. In a letter, an autistic man wrote me that when somebody looked him in the eye, his mind went blank and his thoughts stopped; it was like a twilight state.

Donna Williams also told me that forced eye contact would cause her brain to shut down. As Donna further described, "their words became a mumble jumble, their voices a pattern of sounds" (Painter, 1992). Donna Williams may be an important bridge of understanding between the Kanner-type autism and so-called lower functioning autism. Her sensory problems are much more severe than mine, or the sensory problems described in Stehli (1991) and Cesaroni and Garber (1991). Talks with hundreds of parents and over 50 verbal autistic people indicate that no other verbal person has described such severe sensory impairments.

Donna explained to me how she can use only one sensory channel at a time. When Donna listens to a friend talk, she is unable to perceive a cat jumping on her lap. If she fully directs her attention to the cat, speech perception is blocked. Visual perception was not fully blocked because she perceived a black shape on her lap. Possibly, the cat was being perceived by one cortical subsystem of the visual cortex. It is well documented that visual perceptions are formed by merging of three cortical subsystems that register, motion, form, and color (Zeki, 1992).

She also told me that she hated the suggestion in my book (Grandin & Scariano, 1986) that teachers should enunciate with lots of intonation. If she listens to intonation, she is not able to hear the words.

Maggie Karen, a psychologist in Hawaii, found that lower functioning children need a quiet environment with a minimum of distracting stimuli. Low-functioning children often respond better to a quiet voice or a whisper, which does not overload their senses. In order to hear words, they need a pause between each word. Karen also found that they could not look at something and talk at the same time. Due to slow sensory processing, they needed to be given more time to respond.

Mesibov et al. (1994) also reported that minimizing distractions assists the learning process. I like lots of visual stimulation, such as bright colors. High-functioning Kanner types may be attracted to visual stimulation that would overload the brain of a low-functioning child. Park (1992) described her daughter's use of vivid colors in her art. Colors and stimulation that are attractive to me may be painful and overpowering to a child with more severe sensory-processing problems. G. White and M. White (1987) and McKean (1993) described how bright colors "hurt" their eyes. Differences in the severity of sensory-processing problems may explain why one autistic child is attracted to the sound of a toilet flushing and another child screams when hearing it.

Sensory integration methods, such as the application of pressure (Ayres, 1979; Grandin, 1992b; King, 1989; Zisserman, L., 1992), are helpful for all autistic subtypes. A sensory-integration method of rubbing her skin with brushes helped to integrate Donna's senses. Sensory processing improved when she was calm and concentrated on one sensory channel.

Attention-Shift Problems

The odd social behavior and rigid thinking patterns of a classical Kanner autistic are probably due to true abnormalities in thinking and cognition, but the problems Donna Williams has may be mainly due to faulty sensory processing and extreme attention-shifting problems. I hypothesize that emotions and thinking gradually become more normal as one progresses away from the Kanner/Asperger end of the spectrum. Donna Williams's book (1992) does not have the rigid, concrete style of classical Kanner autism. On Figure 8-1 she is placed halfway along the autistic continuum between Kanner/Asperger and Regressive/Epileptic. Donna would never make the type of cognitive mistakes Hart (1989) described in relating that his autistic son put wet clothes away in the dresser when the dryer was broken.

On a radio show, Donna described how her brain can switch back and forth between hearing and seeing without warning. Courchesne (1991) hypothesized that difficulties in shifting attention make it difficult to follow complex social interactions. People with autism may be using a different selective attention mechanism than normal people (Ciesielski, Courchesne, & Elmasian, 1990). Their research has shown that people with autism take much longer to shift between visual and auditory stimuli. Attention shifting may explain some socially inappropriate behavior. Donna explained that it is difficult to look for social rules in her memory at the moment an event is occurring. In some cases, perseveration may be an extreme dysfunction of attention shifting. In her book, Donna describes sewing button holes all over a fur coat (Williams, 1992). She could not stop the response. Afterward, she knew it was wrong.

SUMMARY

➤ Autism is a heterogeneous disorder with subtypes along a continuum ranging from highly verbal classical Kanner's syndrome, to nonverbal regressive/epileptic types with poor receptive speech. The major impairment in Kanner-type autism may be a true deficit in cognition that causes rigid concrete-thought processes. On the low-functioning regressive/epileptic end of the autism continuum, the major deficit may be a totally dysfunctional sensory system where hearing and vision inputs jumble and mix together. The child is nonverbal because he may be unable to make sense from jumbled input. ➤

Most verbal people with autism are visual thinkers. All my thoughts are played as "video tapes" in my imagination. I have no language-based thought. To remember words such as *over*, I visualize a childhood memory of a dog jumping over a fence. When I encounter a new social situation I have to scan my "video tape" library of experiences and find a similar situation for comparison. I then make a logical decision based on previous experiences.

Slightly intrusive educational methods such as forced eye contact worked well for me to jerk me out of my world of daydreaming. However, these intrusive methods may cause a child with severe sensory impairment to withdraw due to sensory overload. I liked colorful visual stimulation, but children with severe sensory jumbling and mixing may make more educational progress if they are taught in a neutral-colored, quiet environment in which the teacher speaks softly and slowly. In conclusion, intrusive, stimulating educational and therapeutic methods that were effective for me may be detrimental to a child with very severe sensory-processing problems.

REFERENCES

Allen, D. A., & Rapin, I. (1993). Autistic children are also dysphasic. In H. Naruse & E. M. Ornitz (Eds.), *Neurobiology of autism.* New York: Elsevier.

Asperger, H. (1944). Dic Autistischen Psychopathen im Kindersaltr, *Archive für Psychiatier Und Neruenkrankhieten, 117* 76–136. Translated by U. Frith, *Autism and Asperger syndrome.* Cambridge University Press, 37–92.

Ayers, J. A. (1979). *Sensory integration and the child.* Western Psychology Service, Los Angeles, CA.

Bauman, M. L. (1991). Microscopic neuroanatomic abnormalities in autism. *Pediatrics, 78.* (supplement no. 1), 791–796.

Bemporad, M. L. (1979). Adult recollections of a formerly autistic child. *Journal of Autism and Developmental Disorders, 9,* 179–197.

Bishop, J. E., (1993, September). One man's accident is shedding new light on human perception. *The Wall Street Journal,* pp. 1,6.

Boucher, J., & Lewis, V. (1989). Memory impairments and communication in relatively able autistic children. *Journal of Child Psychology and Psychiatry, 30,* 99–122.

Cesaroni, L., & Garber, M. (1991). Exploring the experience of autism through first hand accounts. *Journal of Autism and Development Disorders, 21,* 303–312.

Chambers, W. W. (1947). Electrical stimulation of the interior cerebellum of the cat. *American Journal of Anatomy, 80,* 55–93.

Ciesielski, K. T., Courchesne, E., & Elmasian, R. (1990). Effects of focused, selective attention tasks on event-related potentials in autistic and normal individuals. *Electroenceph Photography and Clinical Neurophysiology, 75,* 207–220.

Clark, R. P. M. (1993). A theory of general impairment of gene expression manifesting as autism. *Individual Differences, 14,* 465–482.

Courchesne, E. (1991). A new model of brain and behavior development in infantile autism. *Proceedings of the Autism Society of America, 25.*

Courchesne, E., Yeung-Courchesne R., Press, G. A., Hesselink, J. R., & Jernigan, T. L. (1988). Hypoplasia of cerebellar vernal lobules VI and VII in autism. *New England Journal of Medicine, 318,* 1349–1354.

Crispino, L., & Bullock, T. M. (1984). Cerebellum mediates modality specific modulation of sensory responses of midbrain and forebrain of rats. *Proceedings of the National Academy of Science (USA), 81,* 2917–2929.

Dewey, M. (1991). Living with Asperger's syndrome. In U. Frithe (Ed.), *Autism and Asperger Syndrome* (pp. 184–206). Cambridge, UK; Cambridge University Press.

Eastham, M. (1990). *Silent words, forever friends.* Ontario, Canada: Oliver Pate.

Einstein, A., & Einstein, M. W. (1987). *The collected papers of Albert Einstein* (A. Beck & P. Havens, Trans.). Princeton, NJ: Princeton University Press.

Farah, M. J., (1989). The neural basis of mental imagery. *Trends in Neuroscience, 12,* 395–399.

Frith, U. (1989). A new look at language and communication in autism. *British Journal of Disorders and Communication, 24,* 123–150.

Gedye, A. (1989). Episodic rage and aggression attributed to frontal lobe seizures. *Journal of Mental Deficiency Research, 33*, 369–379.

Gedye, A. (1991). Frontal lobe seizures in autism. *Medical Hypothesis, 34*, 174–182.

Gillberg, C., & Schaumann, H. (1983). Epilepsy presenting as infantile autism: Two cases studies. *Neuropediatrics, 14*, 206–212.

Gordon, C. T., State, R. C., Nelson, J. E., Hamburger, S. D., & Rapport, J. L. (1993). A double-blind comparison of Clomipramine, desipramine and placebo in the treatment of autistic disorder. *Archives of General Psychiatry, 50*, 441–447.

Grandin, T. (1984). My experiences as an autistic child and review of related literature. *Journal of Orthomolecular Psychiatry, 13*, 144–174.

Grandin, T. (1992a). An inside view of autism. In E. Schopler and G. B. Mesibov (Eds.), *High functioning individuals with autism.* (pp. 105–126). New York: Plenum Press.

Grandin, T. (1992b). Calming effects of deep touch pressure in patients with autistic disorders, college students and animals. *Journal of Child and Adolescent Psychopharmacology, 2*, 63–70.

Grandin, T., & Scariano, M. (1986). *Emergence: Labeled autistic.* Navato, CA: Arena Press.

Happé, F. G. (1991). The autobiographical writings of three Asperger's syndrome adults— Problems of interpretation and implications for theory. In V. Frith (Ed.), *Autism and Asperger syndrome* Cambridge: Cambridge University Press.

Hart, C. (1989). *Without Reason,* New York: Harper & Row.

Hashimoto, T., Tayama, M., Miyazaki, M., Sakurama, N., Yoshimoto, Tsutomu, Murakawa, K., & Kurodo, Y. (1992). Reduced brain stem size in children with autism. *Brain and Development, 14*, 94–97.

Holton, G. (1971–1972). On trying to understand scientific genius. *American Scholar, 41*, 102.

Huttenlocher, P. R. (1984). Synaptic elimination in the cerebral cortex. *American Journal of Mental Deficiency, 88*, 488–496.

Joliffe, T., Lakesdown, R., & Robinson, C. (1992). Autism, a personal account. *Communication, 26* (3), 12–19.

Kanner, L. (1943). Autistic disturbances of affective contact. *Nervous Child, 2*, 217–250.

King, L. (1989, July 19–22). Facilitating neurodevelopment. *Proceedings of the Autism Society of America* (pp. 117–120). Seattle, WA.

Kurita, H., Kita, M., & Miyake, Y. (1992). A comparative study of development and symptoms among disintegrative psychosis and infantile autism with and without speech loss. *Journal of Autism and Developmental Disorders, 22*, 175–188.

Landa, R., Piven, J., Wzorek, M. M., Gayle, J. O., Chase, G. A., & Folstein, S. E. (1992). Social language use in parents of autistic individuals. *Psychological Medicine, 22*, 245–254.

Lewis, L. (1993). [Letter to the Editor]. *The Maap,* Crown Point, IN. pp. 3–4.

McClelland, D. G., Eyre, D., Watson, G. J., Sherrard, C., & Sherrard, E. (1992). Central conduction time in autism. *British Journal of Psychiatry, 160*, 659–663.

McDougal, C. J., Price, L. H., Volkmar, F. R., Goodman, W. K., O'Brien, D. W., Nielson, J., Bregman, J., & Cohen, D. J. (1992). Clomipramine in autism: Preliminary evidence of efficacy. *Journal of the American Academy of Child and Adolescent Psychiatry, 31*, 746–750.

McKean, T. A. (1993). *An alternate look at autistic perceptions.* International Conference on Autism Proceedings, Future Education Inc., Arlington, Texas.

Mesibov, G. (1992). Treatment issues with high functioning adolescents and adults with autism. In E. Schopler & G. B. Mesibov (Eds.), *High-functioning individuals with autism* (pp. 143–155). New York: Plenum Press.

Mesibov, G. B., Schopler, E., & Hearsey, K. (1994). Structured teaching. In E. Schopler & G. B. Mesibov (Eds.), *Assessment and Treatment of Behavior Problems in Autism.* New York: Plenum Press.

Murakami, J. W. (1989). Reduced cerebellar hemisphere size and its relationship to vernal hypoplasia in autism. *Archives of Neurology, 46,* 689–694.

Narayan, S., Moyes, B., & Wolff, S. (1990). Family characteristics of autistic children: A further report. *Journal of Autism and Developmental Disorders, 20,* 523–535.

Painter, K. (1992, November 11). Autistic and writing close the gulf. *USA Today,* Section D, p. 1.

Park, C. C. (1967). *The siege.* Boston, MA: Little, Brown.

Park, C. (1992). Autism into art: A handicap transfigured. In E. Schopler & G. B. Mesibov (Eds.), *High-functioning individuals with autism* (pp. 250–259). New York: Plenum Press.

Park, C., & Youderian, P. (1974). Light and number: Ordering principles in the world of an autistic child. *Journal of Autism and Childhood Schizophrenia, 4,* 313–323.

Ramo, J. C., & Rosbenberg, D. (1993, June 28). The puzzle of genius. *Newsweek,* pp. 46–51.

Sands, S., & Ratey, J. J. (1986). The concept of noise. *Psychiatry, 49,* 290–297.

Stehli, A. (1991). *Sound of a miracle.* New York: NY: Doubleday.

Sverd, J. (1991). Tourette's syndrome and autistic disorder: A significant relationship. *American Journal of medical Genetics, 39,* 173–179.

Volkmar, R. R., & Cohen, D. J. (1989). Disintegrative disorder or "late onset": Autism. *Journal of Child Psychiatry, 30,* 717–724.

Volkmar, R. R., & Cohen, D. J. (1985). The experience of infantile autism: A first person account by Tony W. *Journal of Autism and Developmental Disorders, 15,* 47–54.

Weiss, R. (1989, November 11). Why a man may mistake his wife for a cat. *Science News,* p. 309.

West, T. G. (1991). *In the mind's eye: Visual thinkers, gifted people with learning difficulties, computer images and the ironies of creativity.* Buffalo, NY: Prometheus Books.

White, G. B., & White, M. S. (1987). Autism from the inside. *Medical Hypothesis, 24,* 223–229.

Williams, D. (1992). *Nobody nowhere.* New York: Time Books.

Zeki, S. (1992, September). The visual image in the mind and brain. *Scientific American,* pp. 69–76.

Zisserman, L. (1992). The effects of deep pressure on self-stimulating behaviours in a child with autism and other disabilities. *American Journal of Occupational Therapy, 46,* 547–551.

III

Social Cognition

9

Social and Cognitive Understanding in High-Functioning Children with Autism

MARIAN D. SIGMAN, NURIT YIRMIYA, and LISA CAPPS

INTRODUCTION

One of the central concerns of our research program has been to identify the abilities and disabilities of autistic individuals. The purpose of this research is to determine the extent to which problems exist generally for autistic individuals in cognitive understanding of both people and objects, or more specifically, in social understanding. A second issue is whether the social unrelatedness observed in many autistic children stems primarily from a lack of interest in others or from a failure to understand others. These are difficult questions to address, and we have only partial answers. This chapter summarizes very briefly our conclusions based on our studies of 70 young children with autism and then discusses in detail the findings from a much smaller group of older, high-functioning children with autism.

Because cognitive and social understanding and social relatedness become increasingly interwoven with development, we chose to begin our research with a series of studies of young autistic children, ranging in age

MARIAN D. SIGMAN • Neuropsychiatric Institute and Hospital, University of California at Los Angeles, Los Angeles, California 90024-1759. NURIT YIRMIYA • Department of Psychology, Hebrew University of Jerusalem, Mount Scopus, Jerusalem, Israel 91905. LISA CAPPS • Department of Psychology, University of California at Los Angeles, Los Angeles, California 90024.

Learning and Cognition in Autism, edited by Eric Schopler and Gary B. Mesibov. Plenum Press, New York, 1995.

from 3 to 5 years. One aim of these studies was to determine what young autistic children are capable of knowing, whether it be about the social or inanimate world. The results of our studies suggested that autistic children are fairly competent at solving problems that do not have to do with people (Sigman & Ungerer, 1984). At the very least, they are no less competent than nonautistic children with mental retardation who are functioning at the same developmental level. At the same time, these autistic children seem to perform remarkably poorly when any kind of social awareness is required of them.

The kinds of tasks that were relatively easy for the autistic children included object permanence, tool use, and sorting of objects into categories (Sigman & Ungerer, 1984; Ungerer & Sigman, 1987). While the autistic children did not perform these tasks as well as normal children of the same chronological age, they were just as skillful as normal children of the same mental age. On the other hand, they were much less able or willing to imitate a gesture made by another or to involve themselves in imaginary play, particularly when this play involved directing actions outward to a doll or another person or representing the actions of an imaginary person.

Imitation and symbolic play might be considered more cognitively complex than object permanence and categorization, so the difficulty might be attributable to the higher cognitive demands of these activities rather than to their social demands. This is exactly the claim made by Alan Leslie (1987) when he described play as involving metarepresentational skills. In Leslie's formulation, social-pretend play requires that the child be able to represent the partner's informational relation to her or his actions and expressions (see Happé & Frith, Chap. 10, this volume for a more extensive discussion). On the other hand, both imitation and play (even solitary play) also involve social and, often, emotional transactions or representations. Therefore, the difficulty for autistic children could be in the higher affective and social demand of these activities. These conjectures led us to investigate the social and emotional reactions of young autistic children.

Our research on social and affective interactions suggested to us that the autistic children had the most difficulty when they were required to integrate cognition with social activity. To our surprise, we observed far more social interaction and responsiveness than we had anticipated when the children merely had to respond to an initiating adult (Mundy, Sigman, Ungerer, & Sherman, 1986; Sigman, Mundy, Sherman, & Ungerer, 1986). From reading the literature, we had imagined that young autistic children would rebuff social initiations and gaze away during dyadic interactions. Instead, the young autistic children were responsive and would even attempt, at times, to initiate social involvement, although they were generally more passive than the control children (Kasari, Sigman, & Yirmiya, 1993). Their affective expressions were mostly like those of the other children (Yirmiya, Kasari, Sigman, & Mundy, 1989), although they did combine looking and smiling at others somewhat less frequently (Kasari, Sigman, Mundy, & Yirmiya, 1990).

The area in which they were most startling deviant was any form of social responsiveness that involves the beginnings of social knowledge (Mundy, et al., 1986; Sigman et al., 1986). The young normal infant begins in the second half-year of life to look at others for information in situations that are ambiguous or confusing. Although it is not clear what the infant imagines about the other person's attitudes or knowledge, this behavior has to be the beginning of an awareness that the facial expressions and gaze patterns of others can be read. The individual continues throughout life to check the gaze and facial expressions of others in all kinds of situations to get some clue as to what might be in their minds. For us, this behavior is a precursor to "theory of mind" in that the child who does not have the opportunity to learn from others' faces has to work particularly hard to construct an awareness of other's feelings and thoughts.

Early social referencing and joint attention seem to involve emotional as well as cognitive factors. Infants look up at others' faces not only for information but also to share emotional experiences. These glances at the face of another person when an interesting event has occurred or when the infant has been successful at mastery are often accompanied by smiling. Autistic children, when they do glance at others, smile less in these situations than normal and mentally retarded children (Kasari et al., 1990). Normal infants also stop what they are doing and stare fixedly at an individual who shows strong negative emotions of fear or distress. Young autistic children may not even glance at individuals showing distress or fear in some situations and, if they do, they do not seem very interested (Sigman et al., 1992). Because we see cognition and emotion as inextricably intertwined even in early infant social development and we have identified deficits in development that normally occurs between 9–14 months, it seems logical that the social comprehension of the autistic child is deviant because of problems in both the emotional and cognitive domains.

The major problem in studying both infants and very young autistic children is that it is so difficult to know what they are thinking and feeling. One has to construct ingenious experimental paradigms to reveal their concepts, and it is often challenging to know just why they responded as they did. For this reason, it seemed worthwhile to address the same questions in a study with older children, preferably those with greater verbal ability.

In contrast to most individuals with autism who are intellectually impaired, about 5–30% of all individuals with autism function intellectually within the near average to above average range (DeMyer, 1979). Kanner (1943) appears to have been the first to describe these higher functioning individuals with autism. Two of the 11 children in the original group were portrayed in their young adulthood as functioning well within society, based on their social adaptive skills and their ability to maintain a regular job (Kanner, Rodriquez, & Ashenden, 1972). When Kanner et al. extended their follow-up study by adding 96 individuals who were diagnosed by them as autistic prior to 1953, 13 high-functioning individuals with autism, including the aforementioned 2 individuals, were identified. These individuals were found to be "mingling, working, and maintaining themselves in society" (p. 31). Indeed, they had paid employment such as working as a bank teller, a laboratory technician, an accountant, a busboy, and a truck-loading supervisor. Eight were living by themselves, and 11 even drove cars. Yet, forming meaningful relationships continued to be a major area of difficulty, because many of these individuals lacked any motivation or capacity for such endeavors.

This information suggested that individuals with autism but without retardation would be an ideal group for studying cognitive abilities and emotional awareness in that we could use verbal tasks and ask about emotional experiences. We hypothesized that the high-functioning autistic group would show less social understanding and empathy and less awareness of their own emotions than a control group of normal children. On the other hand, we did not expect any differences in the cognitive skills of the two groups, because we had not found any problems specific to autism in knowledge of object permanence, sensorimotor abilities, or categorization skills in the group of young autistic children.

The purpose of this chapter is to describe the results of our research program with a group of high-functioning children. The chapter is divided into two sections, one on social understanding and the other on cognitive abilities. The chapter concludes with a discussion of the implications of our findings for prevalent theoretical conceptualizations of autism.

SAMPLE DESCRIPTION

The sample of high-functioning children with autism consisted of 18 children between the ages of 9 years, 3 months and 16 years, 10 months. Their full-scale intelligence quotient (IQ) scores as measured by the WISC-R were within the range of 75 to 136. These children were recruited from the UCLA Center for Research on Childhood Psychoses and from clinicians in the area. Inclusion criteria for the high-functioning children with autism entailed a DSM-III (American Psychiatric Association, 1980) diagnosis of infantile autism or infantile autism, residual state, and an absence of any additional major diagnoses such as seizure disorder or depression. Eleven of the 18 children received diagnoses of infantile autism, while the remaining 7 children received diagnoses of infantile autism, residual state. The diagnosis of infantile autism, residual state, implies that at one time the individual exhibited behavior that met the criteria for infantile autism, but that the current clinical picture does not meet the full criteria for the diagnosis of infantile autism. However, these individuals continued to experience major difficulties in social relationships and vocational life. In this chapter, all results are presented for the group of 18 high-functioning children with autism as a whole.

The control sample included 14 normally developing children between the ages of 9 years, 3 months and 14 years, 6 months. Their full-scale IQ scores as measured by the WISC-R were within the range of 82 to 128. The normally developing children were recruited from three regular schools. These children were matched on a one-to-one basis with the high-functioning children with autism, based on sex, chronological age, and full-scale IQ score. *Post hoc* comparisons revealed that the groups also were not statistically different in regard to mental age, Verbal IQ, Performance IQ, and Social-Economic Status as measured by the Hollingshead Index (1957).

SOCIAL UNDERSTANDING

Several tasks of social understanding were administered. These included measures of the ability to speak about one's emotional experiences, to identify correctly the emotions shown by another child, to take the emotional perspective of this child, and to respond empathetically to the other child's emotions.

The Ability to Describe Emotion-Eliciting Experiences

The subjects' ability to speak about their own emotions was evaluated by presenting them with a list of seven emotional labels (*proud, happy, embarrassed, satisfied, angry, sad,* and *afraid*) counterbalanced for order across children. It seemed important to ascertain that the high-functioning children with autism had a basic understanding of the emotional terms before asking them about the emotions of others. The subjects were asked to tell the experimenter about a time when they felt each emotion. Most of the high-functioning children with autism and the normally developing children were able to describe roughly appropriate experiences relating to the emotional labels. Four children in each group had some difficulties with one or two emotional labels. Thus, at a fundamental level, these autistic children seemed as able as the normal children to link an emotion with an appropriate event. There were some group difference when the nature of the responses was investigated more precisely. Based on previous theoretical conceptualizations and empirical work with normally developing children (Seidner, Stipek, & Feshbach, 1986), we decided to examine closely the responses that the children gave to four of the aforementioned emotion labels, namely *happy, sad, proud,* and *embarrassed* (Capps, Yirmiya, & Sigman, 1992). Whereas happiness and sadness are conceptualized as simple emotions, pride and embarrassment are more complex because they entail higher level social understanding about cause and consequence. For example, pride is differentiated from happiness in that it encompasses some personal responsibility and controllability. One may be happy after being given a model airplane, yet proud after assembling it by oneself. Similarly, embarrassment is differentiated from sadness on the basis of locus (internal in embarrassment vs. external in sadness) and controllability (predominantly present in embarrassment vs. predominantly absent in sadness).

Although they were somewhat slow in responding, the high-functioning children with autism did surprisingly well on all emotional labels, a finding also reported by Van Lacker, Cornelius, and Needleman (1991). In describing feeling happy, 82% of the high-functioning children with autism and 79% of the normally developing children described external and uncontrollable events. Similarly, when describing feeling proud, 71% of the high-functioning children with autism and 86% of the normally developing children gave examples of internal and controllable events, thus distinguishing well between the two emotions. While they were fairly capable of describing experiences of pride and happiness, the high-functioning children with autism required more time to offer responses and needed more prompts.

Other meaningful differences between the two groups emerged. Some of these may have occurred because of differences in experience rather than in ability. When describing experiences relating to feeling happy, most children referred to receiving a wished-for gift or doing something enjoyable. Some of the high-functioning children with autism mentioned food, a reference not made by the normally developing children. Additionally, the high-functioning children with autism never talked about birthdays and birthday parties, a common theme of the normally developing children. Four high-functioning children with autism gave the same example for both *happy* and *proud*, whereas all of the normally developing children described different examples for the two emotional labels. In addition, two high-functioning children with autism offered two examples for *proud* that were somewhat less appropriate. One child responded, "proud of a dog" and another said, "somebody gave me gold and silver."

Regarding sadness and embarrassment, the normally developing children distinguished the two emotions correctly based on locus with mostly internal embarrassing events and external-uncontrollable sad events. The high-functioning children with autism, however, reported many external-uncontrollable events for embarrassment as well as for sadness. For example, in relating experiences of feeling embarrassed, the high-functioning children with autism offered many more examples of "being teased" and "feeling afraid and stupid," thus communicating something about their own idiosyncratic experiences. In contrast, the normally developing children offered much lighter experiences indicating mistakes and errors rather than enduring personal characteristics. In describing experiences of sadness both groups mentioned themes of loss. Yet, the high-functioning children with autism again offered themes of being hurt or teased.

Parental Reports of Emotional Expressiveness

Parental reports of their children's emotions supported the impression given by the high-functioning children with autism that they had more experiences that made them feel hurt and sad than normal children (Capps, Kasari, Yirmiya & Sigman, 1993). The parents of both groups of children were asked to report how often during the past 2 weeks their children showed behaviors indicative of the following emotions: *interest, joy, sadness, anger, fear, shame,* and *guilt.* Each emotion was considered separately and rated in relation to a variety of specific behavioral manifestations of emotion: *actions, facial affect, body posture/gait, tone of voice/vocalization,* and *verbal expression.* Ratings were given on a scale of 1 to 10. Parents of high-functioning autistic children reported that their children showed more frequent expressions of sadness, fear, anger, shame, and guilt and less frequent expressions of joy than the parents of normal children. While joy was more frequently reported than sadness in both groups, the discrepancy between joy and sadness was significantly greater within the normal sample.

The Ability to Identify the Affects of Others Correctly

The high-functioning autistic children's ability to label the affect of others was fairly good but still significantly less accurate than that of the control children, a finding also reported for autistic and normal adults by Macdonald et al. (1989) and Ozonoff, Pennington, & Rogers (1990). One of our measures involved presenting the children with eight photographs, each depicting a child expressing an emotion (Capps et al., 1992). Some pictures offered contextual cues, such as a boy who just walked out of a restroom, with a big sign on the door that read "Girls." The two groups offered similar responses both in describing the emotions of each child and the motives for these emotions. Yet, on several occasions, the high-functioning children with autism offered less apt responses such as "shy," "scornful," and "itchy" in response to a photograph of a boy shaking his fist, to which most of the normally developing children offered labels such as "angry" or "happy." The task also seemed more difficult for the high-functioning autistic children in that they required more time and more prompts to respond than the normally developing children.

Empathy and the Ability to Take the Affective Perspective of Another

Another measure consisted of five 2-minute videotaped segments displaying a child feeling either *sad, happy, angry, afraid,* or *proud* (Yirmiya, Sigman, Kasari, & Mundy, 1992). For example, the segment designed for sadness displayed a boy looking for his lost dog. These segments were carefully designed based on common experiences described by children (Feshbach, 1982). Children were asked what the protagonist was feeling (label task) and what they were feeling (empathy task) after each one of the five segments. In addition, following the empathy task they were asked to explain why they felt the emotion that they reported for themselves (affective perspective-taking task). The label and empathy data were collected at least a week apart to avoid the possibility of perseveration and were counterbalanced for order. The videotapes were shown during both sessions.

Empathy is a complex process that involves both cognitive and affective components (Eisenberg, Fabes, Schaller, & Miller, 1989; Feshback, 1982; Hoffman, 1984). It stems from the apprehension of an emotional state experienced by another, and involves a congruent emotional state of the self with the other. According to Feshbach's (1982) conceptualization of empathy, three components are involved in the process of responding with empathy. These three components are (a) the ability to recognize and discriminate among affective states of others; (b) the ability to assume the perspective and role of another person; and (c) an emotional response. The measures of *labeling, affective-perspective taking,* and *empathy* were used to tap each of these components. The overall scores on the three empathy-related measures were compared with a MANOVA and there was a significant group effect. Follow-up analyses of variance (ANOVAs) showed significant group effects on all three empathy-related scores. The high-functioning children with autism performed significantly less well than the normally developing children on labeling of emotion, empathy, and cognitive mediation (see Fig. 9-1).

Individual Differences

The impression that we had in watching the tapes was that these tasks were not so simple for the high-functioning children with autism. This

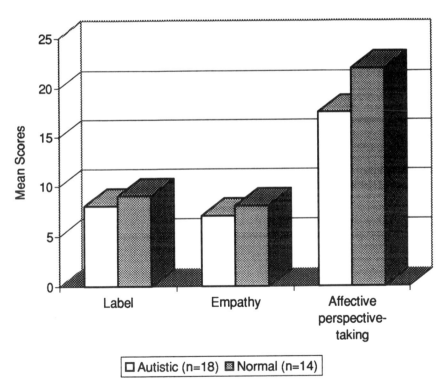

Fig. 9-1. Mean scores on labeling, empathy, and affective perspective-taking by the children in each group.

impression was supported by data showing that the autistic children took longer to answer the questions and required more prompts than the normally developing children. Moreover, the high-functioning children with autism appeared to be using their cognitive skills to figure out the right response, as if they were "solving math problems," according to one viewer. In order to test the possibility that the high-functioning autistic children were using cognitive strategies to understand and empathize with the feelings of others more than the normally developing children, correlations were calculated between IQ and the three empathy-related scores. More intelligent autistic children were better able to label the affect of others and were more empathetic than less intelligent autistic children. There was no association between social understanding and empathy with IQ within the normal sample and the correlations were significantly different for the two groups. Thus, our impression that the high-functioning autistic children were relying on their cognitive skills to understand the emotions of others was supported by these data.

Emotional Expressions of the Subjects Attending to the Tapes

Other evidence also supported the impression that this kind of social understanding was effortful for the high-functioning children with autism. Since the subjects' faces were videotaped as they watched the taped vignettes, we were able to code the affect that they themselves showed in response to these tapes (Capps et al., 1993). The sample was somewhat different from that described earlier because we found that, with group matching, we could code the facial expressions of 16 autistic and 19 normally developing children, thereby enlarging the sample somewhat. Subjects' facial expressions were coded second by second, using the following scale: *very positive, slightly positive, neutral, slightly negative, very negative* and *concentration*. Only the first administration of the vignettes was coded and the anger episode was not included because the data were obscured for a sizeable number of subjects.

The high-functioning children with autism showed much more concentration during the presentation of these vignettes than the normally developing children, supporting our clinical impressions (see Fig. 9-2). Moreover, the high-functioning children with autism also showed more positive affect. In order to understand this more fully, we went back to the videotapes and selected two 5-second periods within each vignette where the most important information was conveyed. For example, in the happy episode, the boy who is given a bike only learns about it at the very end.

In a similar vein, it becomes clear that a boy will win a race (engendering pride) at a certain point in the vignette. The question we wished to address was whether the high-functioning autistic children displayed appropriate affect at the points in the vignette that would most strongly elicit emotion. The answer was that, for the most part, they did. They showed more positive affect than negative affect and more concentration than negative affect while watching happy scenes. They showed more concentration than positive and negative emotion while watching both happy and unhappy scenes. Thus, they did confine their positive affect mostly to the happy scenes but used concentration for both sets of hedonically toned vignettes.

There are several reasons why these findings about emotional expression in the high-functioning children with autism are interesting. First, these observations contrast startingly with those made of the young au-

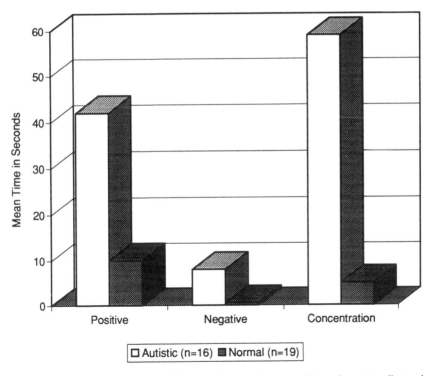

Fig. 9-2. Mean time in seconds that children in each group showed positive and negative affect and concentration.

tistic children we also studied (and described in the Introduction), who showed almost no attention to and interest in an adult showing emotion. Thus, these high-functioning, older children seem to have developed interest in others' affect, albeit much later than one would expect in normally developing children. It is not clear whether low-functioning autistic children also develop this interest as they grow older; this is a question that we are currently investigating. Second, the high-functioning children with autism were markedly more expressive than the normally developing children. We think that this is due to the fact that normal children learn certain display rules; it is forbidden for most 12-year-olds to show much emotional expression in front of an adult or a videocamera. Thus, the high-functioning children with autism naively display feelings that their peer group tends to hide. While this is endearing to adults, it is likely to have fatal consequences for social interactions with peers.

Finally, it is of considerable interest that in viewing these videotaped vignettes, the high-functioning children with autism showed appropriate emotional responsiveness that they were not always able to put into words. It should be said that there was a correlation between the amount of positive affect shown by the children and their score on the empathy task, so that more responsive children were more empathic. However, the correlation was not so large as to account for all the variance ($r = .56$), so that some high-functioning autistic children must have shown appropriate emotional expressiveness even when they could not own the feeling, at least in words. This suggests that it may be very useful to combine observations of facial expression with verbal responses when studying the reactions of high-functioning children and adults in social situations.

COGNITIVE ABILITIES

We chose to study how the high-functioning children with autism performed on three Piagetian tasks: *perceptual perspective taking, conservation,* and *seriation*. These tasks were chosen because traditionally they have been conceptualized as measuring cognitive abilities. However, perceptual perspective taking involves taking someone else's viewpoint and as such may be conceptualized as involving social understanding as well. At the time that the study was designed in 1985, we hypothesized that the two groups of children would not differ in their abilities on any of these tasks. These hypotheses were based on our own previous findings discussed earlier in this chapter, as well as studies by others that reported no difficulties in the perspective-taking abilities of the autistic children.

Perceptual Perspective-Taking Ability

As it turned out, the findings did not confirm our hypotheses. The perceptual-perspective task involved two rotating turntables (wooden lazy Susans) with various displays on them (Yirmiya, Sigman, & Zacks, 1994). The first turntable displayed three objects: a small toy owl, a small cup on a saucer, and a small plastic apple. The second turntable included 10 objects: a miniature doll, an airplane, a car, and several miniature animals, such as a lion and a cow. Children were asked to turn the rotating tables around so that they would be able to see them from where they were in the same way that the experimenter now saw them from where she stood. This procedure was repeated three times for each of the two turntables: with the experimenter standing across from the child, to his or her left, and to the right.

The high-functioning autistic children as a group were less able to take the perceptual perspective of the experimenter than the normally developing children. Among the autistic children, 7 children made a total of 31 errors, of which 20 errors involved the turning of the turntable to its original position (i.e., the perspective that the child had seen initially). In contrast, only 3 normally developing children made 1 error each.

Conservation Abilities

There were also group differences on the conservation task (Yirmiya et al., 1992). The conservation task (Goldschmidt & Bentler, 1968), involved six tasks adapted from Piaget (1967): *conservation of two-dimensional space; number; substance; continuous quantity; weight;* and *discontinuous quantity.* Children were initially presented with two identical substances. After agreeing that the two substances were the same (e.g., two Play-Doh balls), one substance was changed (one play-doh ball was rolled into the shape of a hot dog). Children were asked whether the two were still the same or not, and the reasons for their answer. One point was assigned for each correct response so that the highest possible score was 12.

Results indicated that 9 of the 18 high-functioning children with autism did not understand conservation. Five children with autism received a score of zero because they did not pass any of the items. The remaining 4 autistic children received scores of 2, 4, 6, and 10, respectively. In contrast, most of the normally developing children displayed perfect understanding of conservation. Comparison of the 9 high-functioning children with autism who displayed perfect understanding of conservation with the 9 high-functioning children with autism who displayed less-than-perfect understanding of conservation revealed that the former group also had significantly higher IQs and empathy scores than the latter group.

Ability to Seriate

The only task in which there was no group difference was the seriation task (Yirmiya et al., 1994). The version used was designed by Kingma (1984) and included *single seriation for length, multiple seriation for length and color, single seriation for weight, multiple seriation for weight and color, single seriation for size,* and *multiple seriation for size and color.* The children were asked to place the objects, which were small wooden shapes, in order. The tasks were administered in the aforementioned order.

There were no significant differences between the groups in their ability to seriate. Examination of the number of children who erred within each group revealed that 10 high-functioning autistic children and 10 normally developing children made errors on one or more of the six seriation tasks. However, an examination of the time required to complete the tasks revealed that the normally developing children were significantly faster than the high-functioning children with autism on these problems.

GENERAL DISCUSSION

The results of this study of high-functioning children with autism confirmed some of our findings with younger, retarded children with autism and disconfirmed others. As with the younger children, the high-functioning autistic children tended to have the most difficulty when they were required to use social understanding, concepts that depend heavily on the integration of affective responsiveness and cognitive skills. Looking at the pattern of strengths and weaknesses that they displayed, one could not state that they suffered solely from a cognitive deficit or solely from affective impairment. Thus, in contrast to theories that attribute autism only to a cognitive deficit, we continue to view the impairments of autism as also involving an affective, social component.

At the same time, some of the results were surprising. The high-functioning children with autism were somewhat more skillful in describing their own emotional states, in identifying the emotions of others accurately, and in empathizing with others both with affective expressions and with words than we had anticipated. We think that the evidence exists here to credit these children's motivation and intelligence as the route to their social understanding. They work so hard at these tasks that we can forget how automatically the normally developing child responds to them. If asked about a time that they felt happy, normal children do not think for a long time, come up with a scripted answer, or look at the interrogator as if to ask whether they got the right answer. But this is the response pattern shown by most of the high-functioning autistic children. Although the abilities of the high-functioning autistic children in this domain were somewhat surprising, this is because we did not imagine when we started the study how hard the children would work with their good intelligence to solve problems that were hardly problems for the normally developing children.

Moreover, we know from some other data that these autistic children's social understanding does not carry them very far. Their parents gave them much lower scores on the Socialization Scale of the Vineland Adaptive Behavior Scales, although their Communication and Daily Living Scores were appropriate for their ages (Yirmiya, Capps, & Sigman, 1993). Moreover, the high-functioning children with autism saw themselves much more negatively in all ways when they compare themselves to other children. No wonder that the parents reported that the children with autism show more negative affect in their daily lives. The flow of human interaction is too swift for the slow processing of social cues required by the autistic children. Moreover, their social understanding is fragmented and fragile, so that the higher metarepresentational abilities and emotional sensitivity required in complex social situations are often beyond them.

The biggest surprise in these findings was the relatively poor performance of the high-functioning autistic children on the cognitive tasks. We did not confirm the results of other investigators that autistic children would be as capable of perceptual perspective taking as normally developing children. This is congruent with our findings on joint attention in young autistic children or other researchers' findings on deficits in "theory of mind." We would not expect children who could not share attention with others or understand the minds of others to be able to take their perspective too well. The results of our studies may have contrasted with the findings from other studies because we used somewhat more difficult situations. This is an area in need of replication and clarification.

The difficulties with conservation were totally unanticipated by us in planning our study. It is difficult to see conservation skills as involving social understanding, although at least one researcher has claimed that metarepresentational abilities are crucial for knowledge of conservation (Pratt, 1988). If the difficulties with conservation hold up to replication, these deficits may be related to the problems in executive function described by several researchers (see Ozonoff, Chap. 11). Conservation may require the kind of ability to switch sets and plan as tapped by the Wisconsin Card Sort and the Tower of Hanoi. These findings of a deficit in conservation among these very intelligent autistic children remind us that cognitive and planning problems continue to bedevil high-functioning adults with autism.

In summary, we see our research as supporting the notion that the autistic child suffers from a deficit in a *hot theory of mind*. This term, coined by Leslie Brothers (in press) to acknowledge the affective component in social understanding, seems to us more apt that the rather cold description of the development of social understanding suggested by some who espouse the "theory of mind." In our view, the only children who achieve metarepresentation and social comprehension without recourse to the nearly automatic emotional understanding that most normal people possess are autistic children. Moreover, the evidence from the study detailed in this chapter is that logical construction of social understanding does not work very well for autistic children, despite their courageous and diligent efforts.

ACKNOWLEDGMENTS

This research was supported by NINDS Grant NS25243. We are grateful to Michael Espinosa for assistance with data analysis, and to Margie Greenwald for administering our research program.

REFERENCES

American Psychiatric Association. (1980). *Diagnostic and statistical manual of mental disorders* (3rd ed.). Washington, DC: Author.

Brothers, L. (in press). Neurophysiology of the perception of intentions by primates. In M. Gazzaniga (Ed.), *The cognitive neurosciences* Boston, MA: MIT Press.

Capps, L., Kasari, C., Yirmiya, N., & Sigman, M. (1993). Parental perception of emotional expressiveness in children with autism. *Journal of Consulting and Clinical Psychology, 61,* 475–484.

Capps, L., Yirmiya, N., & Sigman, M. (1992). Understanding of simple and complex emotions in nonretarded children with autism. *Journal of Child Psychology and Psychiatry, 33,* 1169–1182.

DeMyer, M. D. (Ed.). (1979). *Parents and children in autism.* Washington, DC: Winston.

Eisenberg, N., Fabes, R. A., Schaller, M., & Miller, P. A. (1989). Sympathy and personal distress: Development, gender differences, and interrelations of indexes. In N. Eisenberg (Ed.), *Empathy and related emotional responses* (pp. 107–126). San Francisco: Jossey-Bass.

Feshbach, N. D. (1982). Sex differences in empathy and social behavior in children. In N. Eisenberg (Ed.), *The development of prosocial behavior* (pp. 315–338). New York: Academic Press.

Goldschmid, M. L., & Bentler, P. M. (1968). *Concept Assessment Kit—Conservation.* San Diego: Educational & Industrial Testing Service.

Happé, F., & Frith, U. (in press). Theory of mind in autism. In E. Schopler, & G. B. Mesibov (Eds.), *Learning and cognition in autism.* New York: Plenum Press.

Hoffman, M. L. (1984). Interaction of affect and cognition in empathy. In C. E. Izard, J. Kagan, & R. B. Zajonc (Eds.), *Emotions, cognition, and behavior* (pp. 103–131). New York: Cambridge University Press.

Hollingshead, A. B. (1957). *Two-factor index of social position.* Unpublished manuscript, Yale University, New Haven, CT.

Kanner, L. (1943). Autistic disturbances of affective contact. *Nervous Child, 2,* 217–250.

Kanner, L., Rodriguez, A., & Ashenden, B. (1972). How far can autistic children go in matters of social adaptation? *Journal of Autism and Childhood Schizophrenia, 2,* 9–33.

Kasari, C., Sigman, M., Mundy, P., & Yirmiya, N. (1990). Affective sharing in the context of joint attention interactions of normal, autistic, and mentally retarded children. *Journal of Autism and Developmental Disorders, 20,* 87–100.

Kasari, C., Sigman, M., & Yirmiya, N. (1993). Focused and social attention in interactions with familiar and unfamiliar adults: A comparison of autistic, mentally retarded and normal children. *Development and Psychopathology, 5,* 401–412.

Kingma, J. 91984). The influence of task variations in seriation research: Adding irrelevant cues to the stimulus material. *Journal of Genetic Psychology, 144,* 241–253.

Leslie, A. M. (1987). Pretense and representation: The origins of "theory of mind." *Psychological Review, 94,* 412–426.

Macdonald, H., Rutter, M., Howlin, P., Rios, P., Le Couteur, A., Evered, C., & Folstein, S. (1989). Recognition and expression of emotional cues by autistic and normal adults. *Journal of Child Psychology and Psychiatry, 30,* 865–877.

Mundy, P., Sigman, M., Ungerer, J. A., & Sherman, T. (1986). Defining the social deficits in autism: The contribution of nonverbal communication measures. *Journal of Child Psychology and Psychiatry, 27,* 657–669.

Ozonoff, S., Pennington, B. F., & Rogers, S. J. (1990). Are there emotion perception deficits in young autistic children? *Journal of Child Psychology and Psychiatry, 31,* 343–361.

Piaget, J. (Ed.). (1967) *The psychology of intelligence.* London: Routledge & Kegan Paul.

Pratt, C. (1988). The child's conception of the conservation task. *British Journal of Developmental Psychology, 6,* 157–167.

Seidner, L. B., Stipek, D. J., & Feshbach, N. D. (1986). A developmental analysis of elementary school-aged children's concepts of pride and embarrassment. *Child Development, 59,* 367–377.

Sigman, M., Kasari, C., Kwon, J. H., & Yirmiya, N. (1992). Responses to the negative emotions of others in autistic, mentally retarded, and normal children. *Child Development, 63,* 796–807.

Sigman, M., Mundy, P., Sherman, T., & Ungerer, J. A. (1986). Social interactions of autistic, mentally retarded, and normal children with their caregivers. *Journal of Child Psychology and Psychiatry, 27,* 647–669.

Sigman, M., & Ungerer, J. A. (1984). Cognitive and language skills in autistic, mentally retarded, and normal children. *Developmental Psychology, 20,* 293–302.

Ungerer, J. A., & Sigman, M. (1987). Categorization skills and language development in autistic children. *Journal of Autism and Developmental Disorders, 17,* 3–16.

Van Lacker, D., Cornelius, C., & Needleman, R. (1991). Comprehension of verbal terms for emotions in normal, autistic, and schizophrenic children. *Developmental Neuropsychology, 7,* 1–18.

Yirmiya, N., Capps, L., & Sigman, M. (1993, March). *Adaptive behavior and emotional understanding in nonretarded autistic children.* Paper presented at the Society for Research in Child Development, New Orleans, LA.

Yirmiya, N., Kasari, C., Sigman, M., & Mundy, P. (1989). Facial expressions of affect in autistic, mentally retarded, and normal children. *Journal of Child Psychology and Psychiatry, 30,* 725–735.

Yirmiya, N., Sigman, M. D., Kasari, C., & Mundy, P. (1992). Empathy and cognition in high-functioning children with autism. *Child Development, 63,* 150–160.

Yirmiya, N., Sigman, M., & Zacks, D. (1994). Perceptual perspective taking and seriation abilities in high-functioning children with autism. *Developmental Psychology, 6,* 263–272.

10

Theory of Mind in Autism

FRANCESCA HAPPÉ and UTA FRITH

INTRODUCTION

Human beings are essentially social creatures. In what does this social ability lie? In the ability to love, to feel sympathy, to make friendships? Or, is it in the ability to cheat, deceive, and outsmart opponents? In fact it is these unpleasant abilities that reveal the extent of human social understanding. These abilities demonstrate our special human ability to think about thoughts, and hence to "out-think" one another. It is this ability to attribute mental states to oneself and others that is captured by the phrase "theory of mind." Of course, a theory of mind also has positive effects; it allows us to empathize, to communicate, and to imagine others' hopes and dreams.

It has been suggested that theory of mind—the capacity to "mind-read"—is precisely the ability that autistic people lack (Baron-Cohen, Leslie, & Frith, 1985). A whole new experimental approach has arisen from this claim, and an exciting theoretical debate about the nature of the ability in normal and abnormal development is now in progress (Astington, Harris, & Olson, 1988; Baron-Cohen, Tager-Flusberg, & Cohen, 1993; Wellman, 1990; Whiten, 1991; Perner, 1991). In this chapter we examine what led to the claim in the first place, how the theory was tested, and what it has contributed to the understanding of autism. But first, how is it possible

FRANCESCA HAPPÉ and UTA FRITH • Cognitive Development Unit, Medical Research Council, London WC1H 0BT, United Kingdom.

Learning and Cognition in Autism, edited by Eric Schopler and Gary B. Mesibov. Plenum Press, New York, 1995.

that a single cognitive deficit, such as difficulty in mind-reading, can actually *explain* a biologically based condition such as autism?

ADDRESSING CAUSES AT DIFFERENT LEVELS

Different types of answers can be given to the question, "What causes autism?" None of these answers is *the* answer, since each is appropriate for a different sense of the question. In order to find the right answer for the question in any one context, we need to think about our reasons for asking. One can think about the distinction between the different senses of a question in terms of different *levels of explanation.*

In the study of developmental disorders, three levels in particular are useful: the biological, the cognitive, and the behavioral (Frith, Morton, & Leslie, 1991). It is important to keep these levels separate, because each has a different role in our understanding of autism. So, for example, to inform the search for prevention or cure for a disorder, it may be appropriate to look at the biological nature of the problem, whereas to inform management and teaching it may be more important to consider the behavioral description of the problem.

Keeping distinct these three levels of explanation helps in thinking about a number of issues to do with autism. So, for example, people often ask whether autism is part of a normal continuum: Are we all "a bit autistic?" The answer to this question is different at the different levels of explanation. At the *behavioral* level the answer may be "yes"—at least in some respects; the autistic person may *behave* much like the very shy normal person in some situations, and everyone shows some stereotypies (e.g., finger-tapping). At the *cognitive* level we suggest that the answer is "no." Here, in terms of cognitive processes and mechanisms, autistic individuals may be qualitatively different from nonautistic people. Very different *reasons* may underlie apparently similar behavior by the autistic and the normal person; just think of an autistic adult and a normal rebellious teenager, both of whom may dress inappropriately for social situations. So, the autistic child's social difficulties have a quite different cause (at the cognitive level) from those of the normal shy person, although the behaviors produced (avoiding people, social anxiety, inappropriate eye contact) may be very similar.

At the *biological* level, too, we suggest that people with autism are almost certainly different from people who do not suffer from autism. Autism is caused by a problem at the biological level—something in the anatomical structure or physiological functioning of the brain, which is abnormal.

THE PUZZLE OF THE TRIAD

If several symptoms co-occur reliably, the most parsimonious explanation is that they are caused by the same underlying deficit. Impairments in socialization, communication, and imagination cohere (Wing & Gould, 1979). Could a single cognitive deficit underlie these three diverse features of autism?

The triad of impairments in socialization, communication, and imagination has formed the background for recent psychological research into autism. It defines the problem to be solved and the picture to be explained. A minimum requirement for psychological theories of autism, then, is to explain the co-occurrence of these three deficits.

THE THEORY-OF-MIND HYPOTHESIS

Pretense as the Key

According to Leslie (1987, 1988) pretense is the key to cracking this puzzle. The autistic child's failure to show pretend play is striking (Wulff, 1985). By pretend play, we mean symbolic play (Baron-Cohen, 1987), in which one object is used to represent another object, or when imaginary objects are involved (e.g., a child playing with an imaginary pet, drinking imaginary tea, or using a spoon as an imaginary microphone). Children who are neglected may show an unwillingness to communicate, but non-autistic children in such situations appear to embrace the world of imagination as a vital refuge (e.g., the case of "Paul" in Bettelheim, 1955). Mentally handicapped children without autism (Beeghly, Weiss-Perry, & Cicchetti, 1989; Wing, Gould, Yeates, & Brierley, 1977), as well as congenitally blind children (Fraiberg, 1977; Rogers & Pulchalski, 1984), show mental age (MA)-appropriate imaginative play. The autistic child's imagination handicap is rarely the feature that worries parents or teachers. And yet it should be, for the development of pretense in the normal child demonstrates the emergence of a startling new cognitive capacity, on which are built many of the child's most important abilities.

Pretense is an extraordinarily complex behavior to emerge so early in development. During the second year of life, just as the child is learning, for example, what a telephone is, that bananas are good to eat, and the names for these things, a mother may suddenly pick up a banana and hold it to her ear saying, "Look, Mummy's on the telephone!." This is no way to teach the child about bananas and telephones. The child should be upset, confused; instead he or she is delighted. Around 18 months of age

the normal child can understand and indulge in pretend play (Fein, 1981).
How is this possible without wrecking the child's encyclopedic world
knowledge?

Representing Pretense

Leslie (1987, 1988) suggested that in order to prevent *representational
abuse*—the interference of pretense with real knowledge—the child must
possess two types of representation. Pretense is, for Leslie, good evidence
that the 2-year-old has not only *primary representations* of things as they
really are in the world (with a premium on accuracy and veridicality), but
also *metarepresentations* that are used to capture pretending (and are not
checked against the real world for accuracy). Pylyshyn (1978, p. 593)
defined *metarepresentational ability* as the "ability to represent the representational relation itself." Since then, however, the term has been used
in rather different ways by different writers (e.g., Perner, 1991). In Leslie's
(1988) terminology a metarepresentation is a three-place relation, containing four elements:

Agent—Informational Relation—Anchor—"Expression"

In a specific example this might have the following content:

e.g., Mother—Pretends—of this banana—"It is a telephone."

The expression element is placed in quotation marks to indicate that it is
kept separate (technically, decoupled) from reality (as represented in primary representations).

Representing Mental States

The absence of early make believe in autistic children led Leslie to
hypothesize that autistic individuals are impaired in their ability to form
metarepresentations. This would be a circular argument, except that Leslie
pointed out that metarepresentations are necessary for more than just
pretense—they are vital for representing other informational relations or
propositional attitudes, such as thinking, hoping, intending, wishing and
believing. In fact, the properties of logical opacity that apply to mental
states have a parallel in the pretend play of young children (Table 10-1).
So just as to understand mother's pretend action a child must rep-

Table 10-1. Logical Isomorphism between the Properties of
Mental States and the Types of Pretend Play

Logical properties of propositional attitudes	Types of pretend play
1. *Referential opacity* e.g., Just because John knows the Queen lives in the palace, doesn't mean he knows that Elizabeth Windsor lives there.	*Object substitution* e.g., pretending a banana is a telephone
2. *Nonentailment of truth* e.g., Just because John believes it is raining, doesn't mean it really is.	*Attribution of properties* e.g., pretending the doll's face is dirty
3. *Nonentailment of existence* e.g., Just because John thinks Santa Claus exists, doesn't mean he does.	*Imaginary objects* e.g., pretending there is tea in the empty cup

Adapted from Leslie (1988).

resent her informational relation to an expression kept separate from reality (or, technically, decoupled), so also to understand someone else's beliefs the child must use the same four-element metarepresentation. Here the informational relation will be not "pretends" but "believes";

e.g., Someone (stupid!)—believes—of this banana—"It is a telephone."

This hypothesis generated a testable prediction, then, about the social handicap in autism. If autistic children do not show pretense because they lack metarepresentations, then they should also be incapable of understanding mental states, since this, too, requires metarepresentation.

While it is clear that autistic children show social impairments, proving that they lack understanding of mental states requires a precise test. Research into the nature of the social deficit in autism has therefore been greatly helped by recent work on the normal development of social competence, and specifically on the development of the child's so-called "theory of mind."

TESTING THE HYPOTHESIS

Understanding a False Belief

Research into theory of mind began with nonhuman primates. Premack and Woodruff (1978) tested chimpanzees' ability to deceive a "nasty" keeper in order to keep a reward for themselves. They hoped to be able to show in this way that the chimpanzee had what they termed a "theory of mind"—the ability to impute independent mental states to self and others and to use these mental states to predict and explain behavior. Although their methodology made it hard to interpret the results in terms of anything other than learning the means to a behavioral end, the discussion of their work gave rise to a consensus of opinion as to what would be a sound test of theory of mind. Dennett (1978) pointed out that only understanding and predicting a character's behavior based on a *false* belief could show theory of mind conclusively; otherwise the real state of affairs (or the subject's own convictions) could be appealed to without the need to postulate mental states at all. Such a strict test of the ability to represent mental states was exactly what was needed to test Leslie's metarepresentational theory of autism. However, it was first necessary to know at what age such ability develops in normal children. Only the failure of autistic subjects of a mental age in excess of this age would provide good support for Leslie's theory.

Wimmer and Perner (1983) took up Dennet's suggestion, and tested normal children on what has become a classic false belief task; Maxi has a chocolate and puts it in his box before he goes out to play. While he is out, his mother comes in and moves Maxi's chocolate from the box to the cupboard. Then Maxi comes back in from playing. Question: Where will Maxi look for his chocolate/think his chocolate is? Here, and in a number of replications (Leslie & Frith, 1988; Moore, Pure, & Furrow, 1990; Moses & Flavell, 1990; Perner, Frith, Leslie, & Leekam, 1989; Perner, Leekam, & Wimmer, 1987), it was found that while 4-year-olds correctly predicted that Maxi would expect the chocolate to be in the box where he left it, most 3-year-olds said that he would look where the chocolate really was, that is, they took no account of his false belief.

The 3-year-old's difficulty with false belief is now fairly well established (for a recent review of this rapidly growing area, see Astington & Gopnik, 1991). In another task, the child himself is the holder of a belief that is revealed to be false. In the "smarties task" (Perner et al., 1987), the child is asked to guess what a closed smartie tube (the recognizable package of a well-known British candy, like M&Ms) contains. The child having answered "sweets" or "smarties," the tube is opened to show the real contents, a pencil. The lid is then replaced and the child is asked, "When you first saw this box, before we took off the lid, what did you think was inside?" In this task 3-year-olds do not seem to recall their false belief but answer instead "a pencil" (Gopnik & Astington, 1988; Wimmer & Hartl, 1991). The same pattern emerges if the child is asked what another child, who has not seen inside the tube, will say when asked what is inside; 3-year-olds expect a true belief while 4-year-olds recognize the false expectation ("smarties").

Equipped, then, with a good test of the ability to represent mental states, Baron-Cohen et al. (1985) explored the prediction that autistic children lack a theory of mind. They tested 20 autistic children with MAs well over 4 years (mean nonverbal MA 9:3, verbal mental age [VMA] 5:5) on a variation of the "Maxi" story, the Sally-Ann task (see Fig. 10-1), and found that 80% (16/20) of these children failed to appreciate Sally's false belief. In contrast, 86% of Down's syndrome children (12/14) of rather lower mental age (nonverbal 5:11, VMA 2:11) succeeded on the task. The success of the mentally handicapped controls was particularly important, suggesting that problems in mind-reading are specific to autism, and not simply due to developmental delay.

FURTHER EXPERIMENTAL EVIDENCE

Autistic subjects' failure on false belief tasks has now been replicated in a number of studies, using real people instead of toys, using a "think" question rather than a "look" question, and using a control group of specifically language-impaired children to rule out a language-deficit explanation (Leslie & Frith, 1988; Perner et al. 1989). Autistic children fail not only the Sally-Ann and "smarties" false belief tasks (Perner et al. 1989), but also other tasks tapping the ability to mind-read, such as picture-sequencing tasks involving mental states (Baron-Cohen et al., 1986). Table 10-2 lists the major studies relevant to this area.

ARGUMENTS AND ARTIFACTS

The finding that most autistic children fail theory-of-mind tasks was met with much the same barrage of methodological criticism that was launched on behalf of normal 3-year-olds, who also fail false belief tasks. Researchers have suggested that autistic failure is due to pragmatic difficulties with the "look" question (Eisenmajer & Prior, 1991), to perceptual salience of the real location (Hughes & Russell, 1993; Russell, Mauthner, Sharpe, & Tidswell, 1991), or to lack of motivation to deceive (De Gelder, 1987). Most such criticisms do not address the finding that autistic children fail a whole array of false belief tasks, with very different controls and methodologies. For example, in a recent study by Sodian and Frith (1992) autistic children's ability to keep a sweet from a puppet competitor by deception and by sabotage was examined. By contrasting these two conditions, it was possible to rule out lack of motivation or failure to comprehend the instructions. The only difference between the two conditions was that deception (lying or pointing to the empty location) manip-

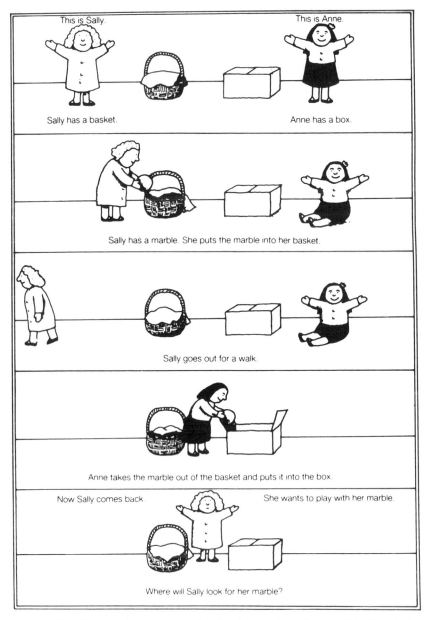

Fig. 10-1. The Sally-Ann task, a test of "mind-reading." (Reproduced from U. Frith, 1989, *Autism: Explaining the Enigma*, Oxford: Blackwell. With kind permission of the artist, Axel Scheffler.)

Table 10-2. Studies Relevant to Theory of Mind in Autism to Date

Date	Authors	Relevant results
1985	Baron-Cohen, Leslie, & Frith	Most autistic subjects fail a first-order false belief task (Sally-Ann).
1986	Baron-Cohen, Leslie, & Frith	Autistic children show selective problems sequencing "intentional" story pictures.
1987	Dawson & Fernald	Autistic children are impaired in "conceptual perspective taking"; they cannot choose gifts appropriate for different people.
1988	Harris & Muncer	Autistic children find "false" desires as difficult as false beliefs.
1988	Leslie & Frith	Autistic children understand seeing but not knowing or believing (even tested with real actors, not puppets).
1988	Riviere & Castellanos	Autistic children fail Sally-Ann task.
1989	Baron-Cohen (a)	Even those autistic children who pass first-order false belief tasks, fail a second-order false belief task.
1989	Baron-Cohen (b)	Autistic children fail to distinguish mental vs. physical entities, appearance vs. reality, and the mental functions of the brain.
1989*	Oswald & Ollendick	Autistic children are not significantly worse than mentally handicapped controls on picture sequencing or Sally-Ann tasks, but worse on a "Hide the penny" game.
1989	Perner, Frith, Leslie, & Leekam	Autistic children fail the "smarties" test of false belief, cannot infer knowledge from perceptual access, and fail to communicate preferentially information unknown to hearer. Controls were specific language-impaired children.
1990	Nunez & Riviere	Autistic children fail Sally-Ann task.
1990*	Prior, Dahlstrom, & Squires	Autistic children are only significantly different on Sally-Ann task, not on "smarties," Sally-Ann with people, or picture-sequencing.
1990	Reed & Peterson	Autistic children fail both ignorance and false belief questions (Sally-Ann).
1991*	Tan & Harris	Autistic children recall correctly their own past, unfulfilled desires.
1991	Baron-Cohen (a)	Autistic children show specific deficits in understanding only those emotions caused by false beliefs.
1991	Eisenmajer & Prior	Most autistic children fail a Sally-Ann task; half of those who fail, pass if question includes "look first" wording.

(continued)

Table 10-2. Continued

Date	Authors	Relevant results
1991	Leekam & Perner	Autistic children fail Sally-Ann task but pass "false" photo task.
1991	Ozonoff, Pennington, & Rogers	High-functioning autistic children are impaired on Sally-Ann, mental vs. physical, appearance/reality, second-order false belief, and mental function of brain tasks. No worse, however, at picture sequencing of intentional stories.
1991	Ozonoff, Rogers, & Pennington	High-functioning autistic, but not "Asperger's syndrome" subjects, show second-order false belief impairments.
1991	Russell et al.	Autistic children fail the "windows" test of deception.
1992*	Bowler	A group of "Asperger's syndrome" subjects does as well on second-order false belief as do normal controls.
1992	Charman & Baron-Cohen	Autistic children fail Sally-Ann task but pass a "false" line-drawing task.
1992	Leslie & Thaiss	Autistic subjects fail Sally-Ann task but pass "false" photo task.
1992	Sodian & Frith	Autistic children can sabotage but not deceive a competitor, and cannot attribute a false belief.

* = surprising success on mind-reading tasks

ulated the competitor's beliefs, while sabotage (locking the box where the sweet was) simply manipulated his behavior. The children also had to refrain from misleading or obstructing a co-operator who helped the child. In this experiment the autistic children proved surprisingly competent at sabotage, but largely incapable of deception. Such well-designed experiments would appear to render untenable explanations of autistic failure in terms of methodological artifacts.

Several of the marked findings (e.g., Tan & Harris, 1991) in Table 10-2, showing surprising success on mind-reading tasks, come from studies showing that autistic people can understand desires. However, it may be that desires (as distinct from, e.g., intentions) can be understood in a more primitive way, which does not require representation of a propositional attitude (i.e., metarepresentation). It may be possible to represent desire using primary representation only, as a sort of tropism, a tendency to act in a certain way toward the desired object.

Tests and Competence

In several studies the theory-of-mind deficit explanation of autism is criticized on the basis of findings that not all subjects fail such tests (Ozonoff, Pennington, & Rogers, 1991) and it has become vital to know what this test success actually signifies. There is an almost universal tendency to equate test performance with underlying cognitive ability, and while researchers are often keen to show that there are many reasons for failing a test, they rarely stop to consider that there may be quite as many ways of passing it. Preliminary data from attempts to train mind-reading make clear that success on one test may have few implications for social understanding in general. Swettenham (1992) trained autistic subjects who failed the Sally-Ann test on a computer-displayed version of this task. Although the autistic children could be taught the correct answer for this task over a small number of training sessions, and were also correct when tested on the standard Sally-Ann task, training did not generalize to other tests of false belief (e.g., the "smarties" task). By contrast, Down's syndrome children and normal 3-year-olds who initially failed the Sally-Ann task, showed generalized success on other tasks after training.

Assuming social competence from theory-of-mind task performance might have dangerous practical consequences. One can imagine forensic implications—theory-of-mind tests might be used to try to prove the cognizance and responsibility of an autistic person who committed a violent crime. In the provision of special education, able autistic people who pass theory-of-mind tests might therefore have their true social handicap glossed over, and be inappropriately placed in mainstream schools.

FINE-CUTS TECHNIQUE

The power of the "mind-blindness" theory of autism is that it makes predictions that are both specific and far-reaching enough to fit the clinical picture of autism (Frith, 1989a). In particular it can explain not only the handicaps of autism, but also the preservation of some functions. It predicts that any skill requiring only primary representations should be unimpaired in autism, thus allowing for the islets of ability, good rote memory, savant abilities, and above-average IQ seen in some autistic people. Other theories have to meet this challenge.

By contrast, any emotional or motivational explanation of autism would seem to predict too blanket a degree of social disinterest. Many autistic people actually do show MA-appropriate attachment in infancy (Shapiro, Sherman, Calamari, & Koch, 1987; Sigman & Ungerer, 1984), and later in life may show preferences for, and even "crushes" on, certain people (e.g., Tantam, 1991). What is striking is the lack of understanding of the two-way nature of relationships. The mind-blindness (i.e., a lack of mind-reading) explanation of autism has allowed researchers to make clear cuts in what appeared to be very similar behaviors—cutting nature at the joints according to a precise theory about the underlying cognitive "bone structure" (Frith, 1991). For example, Attwood, Frith, and Hermelin (1988) found that the autistic child's well-known absence of gestures actually applied only to those gestures that normally influence *mental states* (e.g., expressions of consolation, embarrassment, and goodwill), whereas autistic children showed as many gestures that manipulate *behavior* (e.g., signals to come, be quiet, or go away) as did mentally handicapped controls. Similarly, Baron-Cohen (1989c) found that autistic subjects were impaired in their use and understanding of pointing for the sake of sharing attention (protodeclarative pointing), but not of pointing in order to get a desired object (protoimperative pointing). Other fine cuts have been made between, for example, of understanding seeing versus knowing (Perner et al., 1989), and recognizing happiness versus surprise (Baron-Cohen, 1991a). Such distinctions in the smooth continuum of everyday behaviors would appear to be hard to derive from or explain by theories of primary emotional deficits in autism or motivational problems.

Are Autistic Individuals like 3-Year-Olds?

Autistic children and normal 3-year-olds make the same errors on tests of false belief. Yet, 3-year-olds are not autistic, and mentally handicapped adults who have a mental age of 3 years do not necessarily show Wing's triad of impairments. This puzzle may be explained by recalling that task performance is only a distant measure of underlying competence. So, any one task can be passed or failed for a number of different reasons— this is the distinction between the levels of cognition and of behavior.

Any single task, X, can only be a distant probe and an impure measure of an underlying cognitive component, and will generally demand the intact functioning of a number of different cognitive mechanisms. A subject who fails task X may do so because of a fault in any one of these mechanisms. The only way to understand which mechanism at the cognitive level is at fault, is to give a number of tasks that tap separately the different mechanisms required for succeeding on task X. This is the rationale behind the "fine-cuts" methodology discussed previously. If autistic subjects pass tasks that appear to require all the cognitive mechanisms *except* mind-reading, then we can be more confident that their failure on false belief tasks is due to an inability to represent mental states.

The method of making fine-cuts has given researchers insight into the differences between autistic subjects and 3-year-olds. For example, Leekam and Perner (1991) demonstrated that the autistic child does not have a problem with representing *all* representations—using a "false photograph" task devised by Zaitchik (1990). Zaitchik's task resembles the Maxi or Sally-Ann false belief tasks in every detail, with one crucial exception. Instead of a story character's belief becoming out-of-date after an object is moved to another place (in his or her absence), a polaroid photograph becomes an out-of-date representation. A photo is taken of the object at place 1, placed face down on the table while the object is moved to place 2, and the child is then asked, "In the photo, where is the object?" Normal 3-year-old children found this task as hard as the standard false belief task, from which Zaitchik concluded that the change from 3–4 years of age involves a growing understanding of representation *in general*. This finding has since been replicated (Leekam & Perner, 1991; Leslie & Thaiss, 1992), and shown also with drawings (Charman & Baron-Cohen, 1992), thus dismissing doubts that the 3-years-olds were hampered by a lack of experience with cameras. In all three studies, autistic children who failed the false belief task were able to pass the photograph test.

The difference between autistic people and 3-year-old children has been explored further by Roth and Leslie (1991). They found that in a speaker–listener scenario in which a lie was told, different patterns of performance were found in three groups of subjects. Normal 5-year-olds recognized the intention to deceive, whereas 3-year-olds attributed a mistaken belief to the speaker. By contrast, autistic children did not consider the speaker's mental state at all.

From all these studies it seems, then, that autistic children and normal 3-year-olds fail false belief tasks for different reasons; only autistic children have a *specific* problem with *mental* representations.

PUZZLES THAT REMAIN

Of course, the mind-blindness theory of autism cannot explain everything, and many puzzles still remain in this fascinating disorder.

The Talented Minority

A particular challenge to the metarepresentation theory of autism stems directly from the data that support it. It has been found that a minority of autistic children in any study will pass false belief tasks (in the Baron-Cohen et al. 1985 study, 20% of autistic subjects passed). How can a lack of metarepresentations and hence of mind-reading explain the autistic handicap if some equally handicapped autistic people appear to possess a theory of mind? Two types of answers can be suggested to this problem: delay and compensatory strategy.

Baron-Cohen (1989a) suggested that autistic people are merely grossly delayed in their acquisition of a theory of mind, and that it is therefore no surprise that a few autistic people should manage to pass these tests eventually. It has been a consistent finding that those who pass tend to be the more verbally able and older children. Frith, Morton, and Leslie (1991) found that of 42 autistic subjects tested on false belief tasks, those who passed were (with only one exception) over 11.5 years old and of a MA over 5.5 years. It must be remembered, however, that many equally advanced autistic children fail. Age and verbal ability may be necessary but they are not sufficient to ensure success on theory-of-mind tasks. Therefore it is not the case, as has been suggested (Eisnmajer & Prior, 1991), that failure is simply due to lack of verbal ability. The age and ability of the children tested do, however, seem to be at the root of the slightly different proportions of subjects found to pass in different studies (Frith et al., 1991).

The hypothesis that autism is characterized by a developmental delay in acquiring the ability to mind-read could be disproved by the existence of a clearly autistic child who passes all available tests of theory of mind *at the normal age.* No such child has yet been found.

Another way of explaining the success of a minority of autistic people on false belief tasks is to suggest that they learn to pass these tests using a non-theory-of-mind strategy. In this case, the passers' superior IQ and age are taken as signs that they have managed to "hack out" a solution to the puzzle thanks only to experience, and using generalized problem-solving skills (Frith et al., 1991). This possibility has not been investigated experimentally, although it does make some testable predictions about the abilities of those autistic people who pass theory-of-mind tasks. For example, it might be expected that ability to pass theory-of-mind tasks would be related to some measure of general problem-solving skill in autistic but not control groups. Recent work by Riviere and colleagues supports this idea. Riviere and Castellanos (1988) found that good theory-of-mind performance was highly correlated with success on a test of operational thinking in autistic subjects. No correlation was found between performance on these two tasks in normal 3- to 5-year-olds (Nunez & Riviere, 1990).

Subgroups in the Autistic Spectrum

At the beginning of this chapter we suggested that thinking about a developmental disorder at the cognitive level enables us to identify clear categories where surface behavior cannot. The mind-blindness hypothesis is a particularly good theoretical instrument for this job, since it allows one to move from a continuum of social, communicative, and imaginative handicaps in behavior, to a discrete ability that subjects may either lack or possess. It may therefore be possible to go from quantitative differences in surface behaviors to qualitative differences in cognitive deficits. This may help in the making of principled distinctions between some apparently similar disorders (e.g., autism, schizoid personality disorder, Asperger's syndrome, semantic-pragmatic disorder). This approach would be suitable for discovering whether subgroups can be distinguished not only in terms of severity of handicap, but also in terms of subtle but clear qualitative differences in underlying cognitive capacities (Happé, 1991). Such distinctions would have significant implications for prognosis, education, and management.

Non-Triad Features

There are other unsolved questions. For example, can a mind-blindness theory of autism explain the nonsocial handicaps in autism? What theory can shed light on features such as insistence on sameness, stereotypies, savant skills, and self-injurious behavior? It is part of the excitement and frustration of research that there are always further questions to ask, and other theories to be developed.

Precursors

When Leslie (1987) proposed a metarepresentational deficit in autism, he took as his starting point the glaring lack of pretend play. This raised the possibility that the disorder would only reveal itself in the second year of life and not before. Contrary to much popular belief, evidence for the clear manifestation of autism in the first year is indeed hard to come by (Frith, 1989a; Johnson, Siddons, Frith, & Morton, 1992).

Mundy and Sigman (1989) argued that older autistic children do not show joint-attention behaviors, which develop prior to pretense in the normal child, proving that autism results from a deficit other than (and earlier than) an inability to metarepresent. However, this argument rests on the assumption that the emergence of pretense marks the emergence of metarepresentation. This, as Leslie and Happé (1989) argued, is unlikely. While pretense is an early sign that metarepresentations must be available to the child, even earlier ostensive communication behaviors such as joint attention may also signal the emergence of the ability to represent mental states (Baron-Cohen, 1991b). After all, these behaviors convey the intention to communicate something. Leslie and Happé discuss the possible mechanism that allows the young child to differentiate pretend and real acts, and related this to the larger distinction between ostensive and nonostensive behavior. Sperber and Wilson (1986) suggest that ostensive behavior is marked by two properties: it is attention-grabbing, and yet is irrelevant in itself, thus forcing the observer to recognize the actor's intended meaning. Pretense and joint-attention behaviors fulfill these criteria, and Leslie and Happé suggested that the infant may be hard-wired to perceive such exaggerated behaviors as signs of intention or goal-directedness, in much the same way as the infant perceives physical causality in certain patterns of movement (Leslie & Keeble, 1987).

Hobson (1986a, 1986b, 1989), on the basis of experiments on emotion recognition, suggested that autistic children's lack of a theory of mind is a result of a more basic, *primary emotional deficit* in interpersonal relations. For him, the autistic child's problems are not caused by an inability to form metarepresentations, although this may be an important secondary consequence. A primary emotional deficit would lead to the child's not receiving the necessary social experiences in infancy and childhood to develop the cognitive structures for social understanding. The problem with Hobson's theory is that it is hard either to prove or disprove, because the crux of the matter lies in causal priorities. Most symptoms of autism (e.g., failure to recognize emotional expressions) could, in themselves, be explained by either a cognitive or affective primary deficit, and can be seen as either springing directly from such a deficit or developing as a secondary consequence. The arguments on both sides have been discussed by Hobson (1990) and Leslie and Frith (1990). The affect-cognition debate continues and, although such argument is healthy, data that would settle the question are not yet available. Perhaps the only kind of evidence that would satisfy both parties would have to be gained from longitudinal case studies, starting soon after birth.

PRACTICAL IMPLICATIONS OF THE MIND-BLINDNESS THEORY

Could the capacity to understand mental states be the single cognitive component at fault in autism? The ability to mind-read may be of such evolutionary importance that it is performed by a special, innately determined part of the brain. Could it be that the symptoms of autism follow from the lack of such a module? Certainly an inability to form metarepresentations and the consequent inability to reflect on the mental states of self and others would have far-reaching effects on behavior. The triad of impairments seen in autism could well be due to such an inability to mind-read (Frith et al., 1991): The inability to pretend generated the model; the social impairment would follow from the lack of a theory of mind; and the characteristic communicative impairments would follow from an inability to represent intentions, or recognize utterances as interpretations of the speaker's thoughts (Frith, 1989b).

The mind-blindness theory seems to explain the triad, but does it have practical implications for the care and education of people with autism? Can we use this theory to "get inside the mind" of a person with autism?

> Imagine yourself alone in a foreign land. As you step off the bus, the local people crowd toward you, gesticulating and shouting. Their words sound like animal cries. Their gestures mean nothing to you. Your first instinct might be to fight, to push these intruders away from you; to fly, to run away from their incomprehensible demands; or to freeze, to try to ignore the chaos around you. (Happé, 1994, p. 49)

The world of the person with autism may be rather like this. If autistic people lack the ability to "think about thoughts," their own as well as others', then they are like strangers in a foreign land, because the world we inhabit is a social world. The most important element in our surroundings is human. We make sense of behavior in terms of mental states. Without such a theory of mind, the social world must be a terrifying, unpredictable place. No wonder the autistic child often fights against it, or withdraws from it physically or mentally.

What is the practical value of this insight? Much of the autistic person's strange behavior can be better understood if we remember that he or she cannot mind-read in the way most of us do. Take for example the autistic girl who had a tantrum every time she was told she was going swimming, until someone thought to say, "We're going swimming—*and we're coming back!*" Without an understanding of the intentions behind speech, communication breaks down; as for the autistic child who in response to the request, "Can you pass the salt?" replied in all earnestness; "Yes." Understanding the autistic child's mind-blindness can also help parents, who often have to face apparently unkind behavior from their children. A child who enjoys making people cry may seem cruel, but without insight into mental states, provoking tears may be as rewarding and more interesting than prompting a smile.

At present there is no cure for autism, just as there is no cure for many types of actual blindness. We would not try to bully a blind person into seeing, or insist that if only they tried harder they would be able to see. In the same way, perhaps, we should accept the fundamental handicap underlying the autistic person's social difficulties. For the mind-blind person, just as for the actually blind, a more constructive approach may be to adapt the world to their needs while teaching compensatory skills. Blind people can be encouraged to use their other senses to help compensate for their very real handicap in one domain. Similarly, people with autism have skills and talents (such as good or even exceptional memory for facts) that can be developed and used to bolster existing deficits. Concentrating on assets, with a realistic awareness of deficits, may be more kind than wishing away handicaps that really exist. Once a real handicap is acknowledged, positive and concrete steps can be taken. To help a blind person we might arrange a room in a set order, tell them explicitly about what we see, and give them the opportunity to acquaint themselves with the geography of each new place. In the same way, for the mind-blind person with autism, we can help by introducing some degree of regularity in the social world, by telling them explicitly about aspects of social interaction that they would otherwise not notice, and by teaching them coping strategies for each new situation, situation by situation.

The mind-blindness explanation of autism suggests that when interacting with autistic people we must restrain our ingrained habit of assuming mind-reading ability in others. At the same time, we should use our own special human capacities of social understanding, communication, and imagination in order to gain a better understanding of autism. Only in this way can we begin to help the autistic person to a better understanding of the invisible world of mental states.

REFERENCES

Astington, J. W., & Gopnik, A. (1991). Theoretical explanations of children's understanding of the mind. *British Journal of Developmental Psychology, 9,* 7–31.

Astington, J. W., Harris, P. L., & Olson, D. R. (Eds.) (1988). *Developing Theories of Mind.* Cambridge, UK: Cambridge University Press.

Attwood, A. H., Frith, U., & Hermelin, B. (1988). The understanding and use of interpersonal gestures by autistic and Down's syndrome children. *Journal of Autism and Developmental Disorders, 18,* 241–257.

Baron-Cohen, S. (1989a). The autistic child's theory of mind: A case of specific developmental delay. *Journal of Child Psychology and Psychiatry, 30,* 285–297.

Baron-Cohen, S. (1989b). Are autistic children behaviourists? An examination of their mental–physical and appearance–reality distinctions. *Journal of Autism and Developmental Disorders, 19,* 579–600.

Baron-Cohen, S. (1989c). Perceptual role taking and protodeclarative pointing in autism. *British Journal of Developmental Psychology, 7,* 113–127.

Baron-Cohen, S. (1991a). Do people with autism understand what causes emotion? *Child Development, 62,* 385–395.

Baron-Cohen, S. (1991b) Precursors to a theory of mind: Understanding attention in others. In A. Whiten (Ed.), *Natural Theories of Mind* (pp. 233–251). Oxford: Blackwell.

Baron-Cohen, S., Leslie, A. M., & Frith, U. (1985). Does the autistic child have a "theory of mind"? *Cognition, 21,* 37–46.

Baron-Cohen, S., Leslie, A. M., & Frith, U. (1986). Mechanical, behavioural and intentional understanding of picture stories in autistic children. *British Journal of Developmental Psychology, 4,* 113–125.

Baron-Cohen, S., Tager-Flusberg, H., & Cohen, D. J. (Eds.), (1993). *Understanding other minds: Perspectives from autism.* Oxford, UK: Oxford University Press.

Beeghly, M., Weiss-Perry, B., & Cichetti, D. (1989). Affective and structural analysis of symbolic play in children with Down's syndrome. *International Journal of Behavioural Development, 12,* 257–277.

Bettelheim, B. (1955). *Truants from life: The rehabilitation of emotionally disturbed children.* New York: Free Press.

Bowler, D. M. (1992). Theory of mind in Asperger's syndrome. *Journal of Child Psychology and Psychiatry, 33,* 877–893.

Charman, T., & Baron-Cohen, S. (1992). Understanding drawings and beliefs: A further test of the metarepresentation theory of autism. *Journal of Child Psychology and Psychiatry, 33,* 1105–1112.

Dawson, G., & Fernald, M. (1987). Perspective-taking ability and its relationship to the social behavior of autistic children. *Journal of Autism and Developmental Disorders, 17,* 487–498.

DeGelder, B. (1987). On not having a theory of mind. *Cognition, 27,* 285–290.

Dennett, D. C. (1978). Beliefs about beliefs. *The Behaviorial and Brain Sciences, 4,* 568–570.

Eisenmajer, R., & Prior, M. (1991). Cognitive linguistic correlates of "theory of mind" ability in autistic children. *British Journal of Developmental Psychology, 9,* 351–364.

Fein, G. G. (1981). Pretend play: An integrative review. *Cognitive Development, 52,* 1095–1118.

Fraiberg, S. (1977). *Insights from the blind.* New York: Basic Books.

Frith, U. (1989a). *Autism: Explaining the enigma.* Oxford: Blackwell.

Frith, U. (1989b). A new look at language and communication in autism. *British Journal of Disorders of Communication, 24,* 123–150.

Frith, U. (1991). Cognitive development and cognitive deficit. *The Psychologist, 5,* 13–19.

Frith, U., Morton, J., & Leslie, A. M. (1991). The cognitive basis of a biological disorder: Autism. *Trends in Neuroscience, 14,* 433–438.

Gopnik, A., & Astington, J. (1988). Children's understanding of representational change and its relation to the understanding of false belief and the appearance/reality distinction. *Child Development, 59,* 26–37.

Happé, F. G. E. (1991). The autobiographical writings of three Asperger syndrome adults: Problems of interpretation and implications for theory. In U. Frith (Ed.), *Autism and Asperger syndrome* (pp. 207–242). Cambridge: Cambridge University Press.

Happé, F. (1994). *Autism: An introduction to psychological theory.* London: UCL Press.

Harris, P. L., & Muncer, A. (1988). *Autistic children's understanding of beliefs and desires.* Paper presented at the meeting of the Developmental section of the British Psychological Society, Coleg Harlech, Wales.

Hobson, R. P. (1986a). The autistic child's appraisal of expressions of emotion. *Journal of Child Psychology and Psychiatry, 27,* 321–342.

Hobson, R. P. (1986b). The autistic child's appraisal of expressions of emotion: A further study. *Journal of Child Psychology and Psychiatry, 27,* 671–680.

Hobson, R. P. (1989). Beyond cognition: A theory of autism. In G. Dawson (Ed.), *Autism: Nature, diagnosis and treatment* (pp. 22–48). New York: Guildford.

Hobson, R. P. (1990). On acquiring knowledge about people, and the capacity to pretend: A response to Leslie. *Psychological Review, 97,* 114–121.

Hughes, C. H., & Russell, J. (1993). Autistic children's difficulty with mental disengagement from an object: Its implications for theories of autism. *Developmental Psychology, 29,* 498–510.

Johnson, M. H., Siddons, F., Frith, U., & Morton, J. (1992). Can autism be predicted on the basis of infant screening tests? *Developmental Medicine and Child Neurology, 34,* 316–320.

Leekam, S., & Perner, J. (1991). Does the autistic child have a metarepresentational deficit? *Cognition, 40,* 203–218.

Leslie, A. M. (1987). Pretence and representation: The origins of "theory of mind." *Psychological Review, 94,* 412–426.

Leslie, A. M. (1988). Some implications of pretence for mechanisms underlying the child's theory of mind. In J. W. Astington, P. L. Harris, & D. R. Olson (Eds.), *Developing Theories of Mind* (pp. 19–46). New York: Cambridge University Press.

Leslie, A. M., & Frith, U. (1988). Autistic children's understanding of seeing, knowing, and believing. *British Journal of Developmental Psychology, 6,* 315–324.

Leslie, A. M., & Frith, U. (1990). Prospects for a cognitive neuropsychology of autism: Hobson's choice. *Psychological Review, 97,* 122–131.

Leslie, A. M., & Happé, F. (1989). Autism and ostensive communication: The relevance of metarepresentation. *Development and Psychopathology, 1,* 205–212.

Leslie, A. M., & Keeble, S. (1987). Do 6-month-old infants perceive causality? *Cognition, 25,* 265–288.

Leslie, A. M., & Thaiss, L. (1992). Domain specificity in conceptual development: Evidence from autism. *Cognition, 43,* 225–251.

Moore, C., Pure, K., & Furrow, D. (1990). Children's understanding of the modal expression of speaker certainty and uncertainty and its relation to the development of a representational theory of mind. *Child Development, 61,* 722–730.

Moses, L. J., & Flavell, J. H. (1990). Inferring false beliefs from actions and reactions. *Child Development, 61,* 929–945.

Mundy, P., & Sigman, M. (1989). The theoretical implications of joint attention deficits in autism. *Development and Psychopathology, 1,* 173–183.

Nunez, M., & Riviere, A. (1990, August). *Theory of mind and other cognitive developments.* Poster presented at IV European Conference of Developmental Psychology, Stirling, Scotland.

Oswald, D. P., & Ollendick, T. (1989). Role taking and social competence in autism and mental retardation. *Journal of Autism and Developmental Disorders, 19,* 119–128.

Ozonoff, S., Pennington, B. F., & Rogers, S. J. (1991). Executive function deficits in high-functioning autistic children: Relationship to theory of mind. *Journal of Child Psychology and Psychiatry, 32,* 1081–1106.

Ozonoff, S., Rogers, S. J., & Pennington, B. F. (1991). Asperger's syndrome: Evidence of an empirical distinction from high-functioning autism. *Journal of Child Psychology and Psychiatry, 32,* 1107–1122.

Perner, J. (1991). *Understanding the representational mind.* Cambridge, MA: MIT Press.

Perner, J., Frith, U., Leslie, A. M., & Leekam, S. R. (1989). Exploration of the autistic child's theory of mind: Knowledge, belief, and communication. *Child Development, 60,* 689–700.

Perner, J., Leekam, S. R., & Wimmer, H. (1987). Three-year-olds' difficulty with false belief: The case for a conceptual deficit. *British Journal of Developmental Psychology, 5,* 125–137.

Perner, J., & Wimmer, H. (1985). "John *thinks* that Mary thinks that . . . " Attribution of second-order beliefs by 5–10 year old children. *Journal of Experimental Child Psychology, 39,* 437–471.

Premack, D., & Woodruff, G. (1978). Does the chimpanzee have a theory of mind? *The Behavioural and Brain Sciences, 4,* 515–526.

Prior, M. R., Dahlstrom, B., & Squires, T. L. (1990). Autistic children's knowledge of thinking and feeling states in other people. *Journal of Child Psychology and Psychiatry, 31,* 587–601.

Pylyshyn, Z. W. (1978). When is attribution of beliefs justified? *The Behavioural and Brain Sciences, 1,* 592–593.

Reed, T., & Peterson, C. (1990). A comparison study of autistic subjects' performance at two levels of visual and cognitive perspective taking. *Journal of Autism and Developmental Disorders, 20,* 555–568.

Riviere, A., & Castellanos, J. L. (1988). *Autismo y teoria de la mente [Autism and theory of mind].* Paper presented at IV Congreso Nacional de AETAPI, Cadiz, Spain.

Rogers, S. J., & Pulchalski, C. B. (1984). Development of symbolic play in visually impaired infants. *Papers in Early Childhood Special Education, 3,* 57–64.

Roth, D., & Leslie, A. M. (1991). The recognition of attitude conveyed by utterance: A study of pre-school and autistic children. *British Journal of Developmental Psychology, 9,* 315–330.

Russell, J., Mauthner, N., Sharpe, S., & Tidswell,.T. (1991). The "windows" task as a measure of strategic deception in preschoolers and autistic subjects. *British Journal of Developmental Psychology, 9,* 331–349.

Shapiro, T. D., Sherman, M., Calamari, G., & Koch, D. (1987). Attachment in autism and other developmental disorders. *Journal of the Academy of Child and Adolescent Psychiatry, 26,* 480–484.

Sigman, M., & Ungerer, J. A. (1984). Attachment behaviours in autistic children. *Journal of Autism and Developmental Disorders, 14,* 231–244.

Sodian, B., & Frith, U. (1992). Deception and sabotage in autistic, retarded, and normal children. *Journal of Child Psychology and Psychiatry, 33,* 591–605.

Sperber, D., & Wilson, D. (1986). *Relevance: Communication and cognition.* Oxford: Blackwell.

Tan, J., & Harris, P. (1991). Autistic children understand seeing and wanting. *Development and Psychopathology, 3,* 163–174.

Tantam, D. J. H. (1991). Asperger's syndrome in adulthood. In U. Frith (Ed.), *Autism and Asperger syndrome* (pp. 147–183). Cambridge: Cambridge University Press.

Wellman, M. M. (1990). *The child's theory of mind.* Cambridge, MA: MIT Press.

Whiten, A. (Ed.). (1991). *Natural theories of mind: Evolution, development, and simulation of every day mind reading.* Oxford, UK: Blackwell.

Wimmer, H., & Hartl, M. (1991). Against the Cartesian view on mind: Young children's difficulty with own false beliefs. *British Journal of Developmental Psychology, 9,* 125–138.

Wimmer, H., & Perner, J. (1983). Beliefs about beliefs: Representation and the constraining function of wrong beliefs in young children's understanding of deception. *Cognition, 13,* 103–128.

Wing, L., & Gould, J. (1979). Severe impairments of social interaction and associated abnormalities in children: Epidemiology and classification. *Journal of Autism and Developmental Disorders, 9,* 11–29.

Wing, L., Gould, J., Yeates, S. R., & Brierley, L. M. (1977). Symbolic play in severely mentally retarded and autistic children. *Journal of Child Psychology and Psychiatry, 18,* 167–178.

Wulff, S. B. (1985). The symbolic and object play of children with autism: A review. *Journal of Autism and Developmental Disorders, 15,* 139–148.

Zaitchik, D. (1990). When representations conflict with reality: The preschoolers' problem with false belief and "false" photographs. *Cognition, 35,* 41–68.

Executive Functions in Autism

SALLY OZONOFF

INTRODUCTION

Although autism has been relatively well described at the symptom level (American Psychiatric Association, 1987; Rapin, 1991; Rutter, 1978a; Rutter & Schopler, 1987), the nature of the underlying processes responsible for the behavioral manifestations of the disorder is not yet clear. As Rutter (1988) emphasized, a thorough understanding of any developmental psychopathology requires a shift from descriptive accounts and statistical approaches to a focus on causal processes and underlying psychobiologic mechanisms. Unfortunately, in the field of autism, there remains a large gap between our ability to recognize and diagnose the disorder and our understanding of the impairments underlying it. Identification of so-called "primary deficits" is critical for the eventual understanding of the neural substrate of the disorder. It will also likely have implications for early diagnosis, treatment, and educational remediation (Frith, 1988).

This chapter presents one potential candidate for a primary deficit of autism: executive function. First, executive function abilities are described. Behavioral similarities between patients demonstrating executive function deficits and people with autism are highlighted, followed by a review of the empirical evidence of executive function deficits in autism. A model is

SALLY OZONOFF • Department of Psychology, University of Utah, Salt Lake City, Utah 84112.

Learning and Cognition in Autism, edited by Eric Schopler and Gary B. Mesibov. Plenum Press, New York, 1995.

then presented that may be useful in explaining a variety of symptoms associated with the disorder. Finally, educational and treatment implications are discussed.

IDENTIFYING PRIMARY DEFICITS OF AUTISM

Over the past several decades, many theories have been put forth regarding the nature of the primary deficit(s) underlying autism. Candidates have included impairments in sensory modulation (Ornitz, 1985), arousal and attention (Dawson & Lewy, 1989), affective and interpersonal relatedness (Hobson, 1989), and language (Rutter, 1978b). In the last 5 years, research has focused on a deficit in "theory of mind," or the ability to infer the mental states of others, as potentially primary to autism, capable of explaining the social and communicative disabilities of the syndrome (Baron-Cohen, 1988). Empirical support for this hypothesis was provided by a series of studies demonstrating that retarded autistic children were unable to correctly predict the beliefs of others, whereas controls of lower mental age were able to do so with facility (Baron-Cohen, 1989; Baron-Cohen, Leslie, & Frith, 1985, 1986; Perner, Frith, Leslie, & Leekam, 1989). Several recent investigators found, however, that some nonretarded, verbal autistic children and adolescents are capable of passing theory-of-mind tasks, performing as well as controls (Bowler, 1992; Eisenmajer & Prior, 1991; Ozonoff, Rogers, & Pennington, 1991b). Since we would expect that the fundamental underlying deficit of autism would be present among individuals of all mental ages, these results appear to undermine the explanatory power of the theory-of-mind hypothesis.

If theory-of-mind deficits are not primary to autism, what are other candidates for central deficits? Recent research has suggested that executive functions may be uniquely impaired in autistic individuals. It has been proposed that deficits in this domain may underlie many symptoms of the disorder (Harris, 1993; Ozonoff, Pennington, & Rogers, 1991a; Russell, Mauthner, Sharpe, & Tidswell, 1991).

EXECUTIVE FUNCTIONS AND AUTISM

Definition of Executive Function

Executive function is the cognitive construct used to describe behaviors thought to be mediated by the frontal lobes (Duncan, 1986). It has been defined as the ability to maintain an appropriate problem-solving set for attainment of a future goal (Luria, 1966). Executive function behaviors include planning, impulse control, inhibition of prepotent but incorrect responses, set maintenance, organized search, and flexibility of thought and action. What all executive function behaviors appear to share is the ability to disengage from the immediate environment or external context and guide behavior instead by mental models or internal representations (e.g., plans, goals or scripts; Dennis, 1991).

Executive function deficits are frequently seen in individuals who have sustained damage to the frontal lobes. The deficits incurred have been richly described by Luria (1966) and, more recently, by Duncan (1986) and Stuss and Benson (1986); they include repetitive, aimless movements or speech; difficulty inhibiting familiar or obvious responses; inappropriate repetition of previous thoughts or actions; and diminished capacity for planning. Stuss (1987, cited in Mateer & Williams, 1991) described several additional information-processing deficits resulting from frontal lobe pathology, including a tendency to focus on one aspect of information, difficulty relating or integrating isolated details, problems managing simultaneous or multiple sources of information, and impaired ability to act on or apply knowledge in a meaningful manner.

Some features of autism are reminiscent of the executive function deficits that follow frontal injury. The behavior of autistic people often appears rigid and inflexible; many children with autism become distressed over trivial changes in the environment and insist on following routines in precise detail. They are often very perseverative, focusing on one narrow interest or repetitively engaging in one stereotyped behavior. They may be impulsive, having trouble delaying or inhibiting responses. Some individuals with autism possess a large store of information, but seem to have trouble applying or using this knowledge meaningfully. Finally, autistic people often seem narrowly focused on details and have difficulty "seeing the big picture." Thus, there appear to be similarities between autism and executive function deficits at the descriptive, behavioral level. What empirical evidence is there of a relationship between the two?

Studies of Executive Function in Autistic Individuals

Prior to the era of formal empirical investigations of executive functioning in autism, a few case reports were published that described what we would now call executive function deficits. The first was published shortly after Kanner's (1943) original description of the autistic syndrome. Scheerer, Rothmann, and Goldstein (1945) described the clinical features and assessment results of an autistic adolescent. The authors attributed the boy's cognitive, social, and academic difficulties to "an impairment of abstract attitude" (p. 27). This interpretation is relevant to executive functioning in that these authors, particularly Goldstein, were neuropsychologists who considered the frontal lobes to be the substrate for abstract thought. Although not explicitly stated as such, the explanation put forth in this early monograph may represent the first frontal theory of autism.

A second case study examined executive function abilities in a high-functioning autistic adult (Steel, Gorman, & Flexman, 1984). While the subject performed in the average to superior range on spatial and non-verbal analytic measures, and was only mildly impaired on tests of memory and language, he demonstrated severe deficits on measures of executive function, including the Wisconsin Card Sorting Test (WCST) and the Porteus Mazes. He made many perseverative responses and his problem-solving strategies were rigid and inflexible.

The first controlled studies of executive functions in autistic adults were undertaken by Rumsey and her colleagues (Rumsey, 1985; Rumsey & Hamburger, 1988, 1990). Rumsey (1985) found that the WCST performance of a group of nonretarded, verbal men with autism (residual state) was significantly more perseverative than that of the sex-, age-, and IQ-matched control group. In a second study utilizing a more comprehensive neuropsychological test battery, Rumsey and Hamburger (1988) again found executive function deficits in a group of high-functioning autistic men. Performance on the WCST was again deficient relative to controls, this time in terms of number of categories achieved, as was the ability to complete a planned-search task. These relatively severe impairments were specific to the executive function domain, whereas other neuropsychological abilities were only mildly affected or entirely unaffected. Very similar results were found when the executive function skills of high-functioning autistic men were compared with those of severely dyslexic individuals (Rumsey & Hamburger, 1990).

Thus, several studies have documented executive function deficits in autistic adults. Until recently, this domain had not been studied in children and adolescents with autism. Prior and Hoffman (1990) were the first to do so. They administered several measures of executive function to autistic children with abilities in the borderline-to-normal range of intelligence. The children with autism performed significantly less well than both mental-age and chronological-age controls on the WCST and a maze test, demonstrating deficits in planning and in the use of feedback to flexibly shift problem-solving strategies. The authors noted that the autistic subjects, but not the controls, had difficulty learning from mistakes; they "perseverated with maladaptive strategies, made the same mistakes repeatedly, and seemed unable to conceive of a strategy to overcome their difficulties" (p. 588). The autistic group performed as well as the control group on a design-copying measure (Rey Complex Figure Test). However, the authors noted that the autistic subjects' approach to the copying task was often more disorganized than that of the controls; the autistic children also tended to focus on details, rather than on the overall figure, in copying the design.

A recent study examined a broad range of neuropsychological processes, including executive functions, to explore which deficits might be specific and universal to autism, and thus potentially primary to the disorder. Ozonoff et al. (1991a) compared a group of nonretarded, verbal autistic children and adolescents to a clinical control group matched on Verbal IQ, age, sex, and socioeconomic status. A comprehensive test battery was administered that included measures of executive function, theory of mind, emotion perception, verbal memory, and spatial abilities. Executive function deficits proved to be the most widespread and universal impairment among the autistic sample, whereas theory of mind deficits were found only in subjects of lower verbal mental age (Ozonoff et al., 1991b). In addition, an executive function measure, the Tower of Hanoi (to be described in detail), was best able to discriminate between the groups and correctly predict group membership. Performance on this test classified 80% of the subjects in each group correctly. Theory-of-mind variables, on the other hand, misclassified 35% of the autistic sample, while other neuropsychological variables (e.g., memory, emotion perception, spatial abilities) predicted group membership at no better than chance level.

The classification power of the executive function measure was unexpected, because the control group contained children who might also have had executive function difficulties. The control sample was a heterogenous clinical group whose diagnoses included dyslexia, other learning disabilities, mild mental retardation, and Attention Deficit Hyperactivity Disorder (ADHD). Of most interest is the subset (25%) of the control sample meeting criteria for ADHD, a disorder in which executive function deficits are known to play a role (Chelune, Ferguson, Koon, & Dickey, 1986). It was surprising that even in relation to children whom we might suspect would also demonstrate executive function difficulties, the nonretarded sample of children with autism was still strikingly impaired.

Finally, a recent investigation examined executive functioning in very young autistic children (McEvoy, Rogers, & Pennington, 1992). Several tests thought to measure executive function were drawn from the nonhuman primate and human infant literature. These included a Piagetian A-not-B task, a delayed response task, a spatial reversal task, and an alternation task. In each of these measures, a mental representation (e.g., a plan, schema or response set) must be held on-line to successfully complete the task. For example, in the spatial reversal task, a shield is lowered to block vision and an object is hidden in one of two identical wells; when the screen is lifted, the subject is allowed to search for the object. The side of hiding remains the same until the subject has successfully located the object for four consecutive trials (indicating that a response set has been formed). The side of hiding is then changed to the other well. Successful performance requires formation of a response set (or mental representation) of where the object was hidden, as well as flexibility in shifting response set when a strategy is no longer correct. This type of measure is considered a classic test of frontal function in nonhuman primates and human infants (Diamond & Goldman-Rakic, 1986).

These tests were administered to autistic children between the ages of 3 and 7, developmentally delayed nonautistic controls matched on nonverbal ability, and normally developing children matched on verbal ability. Verbal and nonverbal mental age of subjects ranged from 10 to 40 months. While floor and ceiling effects complicated the interpretation of results on several tasks, significant group differences were found on the spatial reversal measure, the most appropriate task for the mental age range of the subjects. The autistic children had difficulty shifting set when necessary and made significantly more perseverative errors than children in either control group. Interestingly, a significant relationship was found between executive function and joint attention behavior in this study, suggesting that the ability to shift cognitive set may be important to the ability to share attention with another person.

Although the tasks used in the study of McEvoy et al. (1992) differed somewhat in form and content from executive function measures used with older children and adults (e.g., the WCST), similar deficits appeared to underlie performance across the tasks. That is, in both the developmentally simpler spatial reversal task and the more cognitively advanced WCST, autistic individuals are more likely to persist in using a previously reinforced strategy, even when that strategy is no longer successful.

This series of studies provides empirical support for the existence of executive function deficits in autistic individuals across a wide range of chronological and mental ages. This suggests that executive function impairment may be a central deficit of autism. If this is the case, how are difficulties in this domain related to other symptoms of the disorder? Might there be a common process that underlies multiple symptoms of autism, a mechanism that helps account for the diversity of behavioral manifestations of the disorder? These questions are explored in the following section.

TOWARD A UNIFYING MODEL OF AUTISM: PREFRONTAL DYSFUNCTION?

As outlined previously, executive function is the construct used to describe cognitive abilities mediated by the frontal lobes. Frontal cortex is important to skills other than executive function, however. The frontal lobes, particularly prefrontal cortical regions, also appear to be intimately involved in the regulation of social behavior, emotional reactions (Stuss & Benson, 1986, chap. 8), and social discourse (Dennis, 1991). Frontal patients often demonstrate lack of insight, social isolation, shallow or flat affect, and lack of appreciation of social rules (Damasio & Van Hoesen, 1983; Stuss & Benson, 1986). In attempts at social discourse, individuals with frontal damage often insert irrelevant material; for example, in answering a simple question, they might launch into a lengthy monologue filled with unrelated material (Duncan, 1986). Recent studies demonstrated that childhood frontal lobe damage produces a severely impaired ability to understand others' viewpoints and to demonstrate appropriate empathic reactions (Gratten, Bloomer, Archambault, & Eslinger, 1990; Grattan & Eslinger, 1992; Price, Daffner, Stowe, & Mesulam, 1990).

Autistic individuals bear similarities to frontal patients in the nature of their social behavior and discourse abilities, just as they share the cognitive executive function deficits described previously. Social impairment is a primary feature of the autistic syndrome. Even the most high-functioning autistic people demonstrate difficulties understanding social conventions, reading the emotional expressions and taking the perspectives of others, and understanding the rules of interpersonal interaction (Cesaroni & Garber, 1991; Dewey & Everard, 1974; Yirmiya, Sigman, Kasari, & Mundy, 1992). Deficits in pragmatic aspects of communication (e.g., the use of language in a social context) and discourse abilities are also prominent. Autistic people frequently engage in lengthy monologues, showing little appreciation of the needs and interests of the listener. They often have difficulty organizing their communication so that it is readily followed by others. For example, they may fail to supply important information that the listener needs to follow the narrative. They may include irrelevant details, recite factual information without integrating or relating the elements in a meaningful manner, and express incomplete thoughts.

Goldman-Rakic (1987) proposed a theory of prefrontal function that encompasses both cognitive and social–emotional domains of functioning and thus, is helpful in understanding possible mechanisms underlying the behavior of both frontal patients and autistic individuals. She has hypothesized that the function of prefrontal cortex is to guide behavior by mental representations or "inner models of reality" (p. 378). Different areas of prefrontal cortex are hypothesized to access representations in different domains, holding them "on-line" (p. 381) to guide future behavior. Dorso-lateral cortex is thought to guide behavior using visuospatial representa-tions, whereas orbital cortex appears to guide behavior using representa-tions of affective and social information (Goldman-Rakic, 1987). When prefrontal damage disrupts this system and individuals are not able to use internal representations to guide behavior, a dependence on external en-vironmental cues results (Goldman-Rakic, 1987; Lhermitte, 1986).

Since frontal cortex is central·to the regulation of both executive func-tion and emotional behavior, and autistic individuals manifest difficulties in both domains, it may be that disturbed frontal processes are the un-derlying mechanisms capable of explaining both cognitive and social symptoms of autism. Just such a connection between frontal impairment and the symptoms of autism has been drawn by several authors (Damasio & Maurer, 1978; Gedye, 1991; Reichler & Lee, 1987). As Damasio and Maurer (1978) described,

> near-normal autistic individuals strikingly resemble patients with some types of frontal lobe defects. They share a similar lack of initiative, a similar concreteness in thought and language, an inability to focus atten-tion, shallowness of affect, and lack of empathy. (p. 782)

Can this analogy be extended to help explain the deficits autistic children display on experimental tasks?

Relationship of Prefrontal Dysfunction to Symptoms

Executive Functions

As previously suggested, prefrontal dysfunction might result in the type of deficits demonstrated in empirical studies of executive functions in autism (McEvoy et al., 1992; Ozonoff et al., 1991a; Prior & Hoffmann, 1990). The importance of using internal representations to guide future behavior is nicely illustrated by examining the performance demands of the Tower of Hanoi, a measure of planning capacity (Borys, Spitz, & Dorans, 1982). In this task, a board with three vertical pegs and three circular disks of different sizes is placed before the subject. A "goal state" configuration is displayed in front of the experimenter, while the subject's disks are dis-tributed among different pegs. The subject is instructed to move his or her disks to build a tower that matches the goal state. In doing so, the subject must not place a larger disk on top of a smaller disk and must achieve the goal state in the fewest moves possible. This task requires the ability to plan ahead and predict future consequences of each disk transfer. Selection of the next move cannot be made solely upon the present arrangement of the disks or the immediate effects of the transfer, but must also take into account future hypothetical intermediate configurations. Ozonoff et al. (1991a) found that autistic subjects performed significantly less well on this task than did controls.

Goldman-Rakic (1987) used similar reasoning to explain deficits in inhibition and cognitive flexibility. Impaired in the ability to access and hold mental representations on-line, autistic children might instead rely on cues in the external environment to guide their behavior; this would result in difficulty inhibiting prepotent but incorrect responses. Perseveration would occur when a subject was unable to use mental representations to override the strong tendency to repeat a previously reinforced response. Again, behavior would be controlled by external stimuli present at the time of response (e.g., reinforcement), rather than by an internal representation (e.g., a sorting rule that runs contrary to previous reinforcement).

Theory of Mind

Similarly, social deficits typical of autism might also ensue from an impaired ability to hold a representation on-line. To demonstrate an empathic reaction and fully appreciate the thoughts and feelings of others, internal representations of these mental states must be used to guide responses. Lacking this, autistic children might fall back on cues in the environment. To fully illustrate how this difficulty might affect social abilities, the performance of autistic subjects on a prototypical theory-of-mind task is described.

The M&Ms's (or Smarties) False Belief Task is a classic theory-of-mind measure first used with autistic children by Perner et al. (1989). Subjects are shown a box of M&M's and asked what it contains. After they respond "M&M's," the box is opened to reveal that it actually contains a pencil. Subjects are then asked to predict what the next child who sees the box will think it contains. Perner and associates (1989) found that autistic children were impaired on this task relative to mental age controls. The explanation of failure made by the authors was that children with autism suffer from a deficiency in the ability to attribute mental states to others.

However, prefrontal dysfunction and consequent difficulty guiding behavior by mental representation could also explain this pattern of deficit. Impaired in the ability to use an internal representation, autistic children solve this problem using the best data they have available, that is, what *they* know and have just seen is in the box. Thus, their behavior is driven by a prepotent cue in the environment. In effect, what appears to be an inability to take another's perspective may actually be a failure to disengage from the external context and use an internal representation (e.g., someone else's belief) to solve the problem.

Just such an analysis of the root of theory-of-mind impairment has also been made by Russell and Jarrold (1992). In an ingenious experiment, the capacity of children with autism to strategically deceive an experimenter was examined. In the first part of the experiment, a competitive game was played in which the subject was taught to point to one of two boxes to tell the experimenter where to look for a piece of candy; if the subject pointed to the empty box, the experimenter would be deceived into looking in the incorrect location and the child would get to keep the candy. Subjects were able to see the contents of the boxes, while the experimenter could not. Control subjects with Down's syndrome easily learned to point to the empty box and win the candy. Autistic children, on the other hand, continued to point to the box with the chocolate in it over many trials, even though by doing so, they failed to obtain the candy.

In the second part of the investigation, autistic subjects were reexamined to see if they would continue to fail the task when there was no competitor present in the game and thus no need for strategic deception. This time, all subjects needed to do to win the candy was point to the empty box. Again, while controls learned to do this, autistic subjects persisted in indicating the baited box and losing the candy over many trials.

Russell and Jarrold (1992) concluded that what made this task difficult was not the deception component, but the requirement that subjects ignore a prepotent perceptual cue. What at first glance appeared to be a theory-of-mind impairment, stemming from an inability to predict the beliefs and intentions of others, instead appeared to be due to an inability to mentally disengage from a salient cue in the environment and respond on the basis of an internal representation (in this case, the rule, "point to the empty box to win the candy").

Emotion Perception

Several studies suggested that autistic children are impaired at processing emotional cues (Hobson, 1986; Ozonoff et al., 1991a; Sigman, Ungerer, Mundy, & Sherman, 1987). Ozonoff and colleagues (1991a) found that autistic children not only performed less well than controls on an emotion matching task, but also were significantly more likely than controls to make incorrect matches that were similar to the target emotion in perceptual features (e.g., mistakenly matching a picture of surprise with a picture of fear, both of which share the perceptual feature of an open mouth). These results are consistent with a deficit in the ability to hold the schema of a prototypical affective expression on-line. Lacking this, their responses are instead driven by the external stimuli, that is, how these particular faces look; thus, they are "captured" by a prepotent, but irrelevant, dimension, the perceptual pattern of the faces.

Imitation

Similarly, this underlying impairment may account for imitation deficits found in children with autism (Jones & Prior, 1985; Ohta, 1987; Rogers & Pennington, 1991). Imitating another person's body movements once they have finished performing them requires holding a representation of these movements on-line to imitate. In fact, just such an explanation was put forth by Hammes and Langdell (1981) in accounting for imitation deficits; they hypothesized that autistic children lacked the ability to form "mental images" to guide their imitation behavior.

Spatial Reasoning

In a similar vein, Shah and Frith (1983) pointed out that autistic children do poorly on spatial tasks "that can only be solved with reference to and manipulation of internal visual representations" (p. 618). They contended that autistic children perform well on spatial tasks only as long as external stimuli are present to guide their behavior (such as in the Block Design subtest of the Wechsler Intelligence Scales).

Pretend Play

Harris (1993) also hypothesized that autism involves a "deficiency in internal relative to external contextual control" (p. 238). He presents an elegant framework for understanding the pretend-play deficits of autism as extensions of this primary difficulty. The ability to pretend, he argued, requires disengaging from environmental cues and the schema normally elicited by them. Detachment from the external context allows an internal, nonliteral transformation of environmental cues (i.e., a pretend-play schema) to drive the child's behavior, rather than the demands of "reality."

Thus, Harris (1993) hypothesized that the fundamental difficulty responsible for the pretend-play deficits of autism is neither deficient symbolic capacity (Ricks & Wing, 1975) nor deficient perspective-taking ability (Baron-Cohen, 1987), as previously hypothesized, but executive function deficits.

Other Early-Appearing Autistic Symptoms

In theorizing about potential mechanisms underlying the symptoms of autism, researchers have long struggled to account for the signs of the disorder that first become apparent in infancy, such as joint attention. Several candidates for primary deficits (e.g., language, theory of mind, symbolic capacity) have been criticized because they do not precede the earliest appearing symptoms of autism in the course of normal development (Ozonoff, Pennington, & Rogers, 1990). For example, it is difficult to invoke deficient perspective-taking capacity to explain joint attention deficits, because impaired joint attention is present before the cognitive functions responsible for theory of mind emerge (Mundy & Sigman, 1989).

The ability to guide behavior by internal representations begins developing in infancy (Diamond & Goldman-Rakic, 1985), however, at approximately the same time that early autistic symptoms become apparent (e.g., abnormalities in joint attention, gaze, eye contact, and referential pointing; Adrien et al., 1991; Gillberg et al., 1990). Therefore, it may provide a theoretically more satisfying explanation for the mechanism underlying autism than other models put forth previously.

Returning to the example of joint attention, the coordination of two mental sets or mental perspectives, that of the self and that of the other, is required. A deficit in the ability to access an internal representation of the other person's attentional set might lead to joint attention impairment. Some support for this hypothesis is provided by the study of McEvoy et al. (1992) described previously, which found that executive function and joint attention abilities were significantly correlated. It has also been hypothesized that frontal lobe maturation is responsible for the development of joint attention and early referential communication (e.g., manual pointing) in the first year of life (Butterworth & Grover, 1988).

Related Neurological Findings

The potential role of executive function deficits (and underlying prefrontal dysfunction) to symptoms of autism has been outlined. What neurological evidence exists to support this hypothesis? Unfortunately, there is little information available to answer this question, because only a few investigations have directly examined the frontal region of the brain in autistic individuals. Piven, Berthier, Starkstein, Nehme, Pearlson, & Folstein (1990) recently reported evidence of abnormal neuronal migration in the frontal lobes of three autistic subjects; however, these individuals made up only one-fifth of their sample, so the generalizability of the findings is unclear.

The most consistently documented findings of neurological investigations have been abnormalities in the limbic system and cerebellum (Bauman & Kemper, 1988). Courchesne and colleagues found that two areas of the cerebellum, vermal lobules VI and VII, were significantly smaller than controls in 78% of their autistic sample (Courchesne, Yeung-Courchesne, Press, Hesselink, & Jernigan, 1988). Frontal lobe dysfunction may be consistent with these findings, however. First, the frontal lobes, limbic system, and cerebellum are richly connected to each other (Heath, Dempsey, & Fontana, 1980), so abnormalities in one could change the functioning of the others by disrupting the normal information flow between the neural centers.

Second, cerebellar abnormalities may not be central to autism, but may instead be the most easily detectable manifestation of more widespread central nervous system damage. Although little is known about the role of the cerebellum in learning and behavior, it is not typically associated with the types of social and cognitive deficits seen in autism. Thus, it has been suggested that cerebellar abnormalities may not be critically important to producing the behavioral symptoms of the disorder, but instead, may be neurological markers that reflect the timing of damage to forebrain regions during neuronal development (Gaffney, Kuperman, Tsai, & Minchin, 1989; Gaffney, Tsai, Kuperman, & Minchin, 1987). Forebrain abnormalities may co-occur with cerebellar anomalies, but be more subtle and difficult to detect.

It may be that the imaging techniques necessary to detect prefrontal differences have only recently become available. Most neurological studies of autism have used imaging techniques (e.g., CT and MRI) best suited for examining major structural anomalies. Such gross morphological abnormalities, however, do not appear to be present in most autistic individuals (Rumsey et al., 1988); instead, the neuropathology of autism may involve more subtle differences in brain cytoarchitecture or neural connections. Imaging techniques that examine the structure of the brain may not be sensitive enough to detect such abnormalities. If this is the case, then our failure to find evidence of prefrontal abnormalities in autism may simply reflect the limitations of current technology.

In fact, in one of the few imaging studies of autism examining brain *function* (rather than structure), Horwitz, Rumsey, Grady, and Rapoport (1988) found significantly lower correlations between frontal and parietal regions on positron emission tomographic (PET) scans of their autistic sample. Correlated brain activity among neural centers is thought to reflect integrated processing of information; reduced functional associations on PET scans thus may indicate less integrated functioning between the brain regions. Since the frontal lobes play an inhibitory role in the brain and one function of the parietal lobes is integration of sensory input from the environment, an imbalance in frontal–parietal interactions might result in excessive control of behavior by external stimuli. Thus, the data of Horwitz et al. (1988) provides some indirect neurological support for the theory put forth in this chapter.

Limitations of the Prefrontal Dysfunction Hypothesis

There are a few difficulties with a prefrontal theory of autism, however. First, why do children with early frontal lesions not appear autistic (Price et al., 1990)? While the literature reviewed previously points out many similarities between frontal patients and individuals with autism, it is clear that no one confuses the two or mistakes one for the other. Prefrontal dysfunction may be a necessary, but not a sufficient, criterion for the development of autism; perhaps other cognitive deficits, or neurological dysfunction, must also be present to produce the full-blown syndrome. A similar suggestion has been made by Prior and Hoffmann (1990), who hypothesized that both frontal and subcortical abnormalities may be necessary to account for all the processing difficulties of autism.

Second, there are some abilities that are not impaired in autistic children, but that a deficit in using mental representations to guide behavior would predict to be impaired. For example, the performance of young autistic subjects on object permanence tasks does not differ from that of mental-age controls (Morgan, Cutrer, Coplin, & Rodrigue, 1989), although successful performance would appear to rely on the ability to access an internal representation of the absent object.

In addition, it has recently been demonstrated that autistic children are not impaired on "false photograph" tasks (Leslie & Thaiss, 1992). In these tasks, a situation is photographed (e.g., a cat sitting on a table) and then the situation is changed (e.g., the cat is moved to the bed). The photograph is then turned over so it is not visible to the subject. When autistic children are asked to predict where the cat is sitting in the photograph, they are able to do so, although the situation depicted in the photograph differs from the present arrangement of the environment. A strict application of the hypothesis outlined above would predict failure on this task, because autistic children would be expected to use external context, rather than a mental representation, to guide their response.

However, autism probably does not involve an absolute inability to disengage from the external environment or guide behavior by internal representations. Instead, there is more likely a dynamic interplay of several factors, including the salience and familiarity of the external cues, the nature and complexity of the mental representations, and the number of competing response alternatives (Welsh, Pennington, & Groisser, 1991) that determine how well autistic individuals guide behavior by mental representations. If the mental set in question is novel or highly abstract (e.g., a false belief, as in theory-of-mind tasks), it may be more difficult for autistic children to hold on-line, resulting in reliance on external cues. However, if the mental representation being accessed is an overlearned or highly familiar one, the autistic child may be able to guide behavior with internal models.

Returning to the false photograph task, autistic children may have had sufficient experience with photographs to know that the situations they depict do not change. The mental representation of the photograph's contents would thus be fairly concrete, relative to the abstractness of a false belief, and perhaps easier to hold on-line for guidance of future responses. Thus, a number of factors may be important in determining whether individuals with autism can use internal models, rather than external context, to guide behavior. This theory awaits future investigation and further refinement.

A final difficulty with a strict prefrontal account of autism is that frontal lobe cognitive dysfunction is not specific to autism. Research has shown that children with attention deficit disorder (Chelune et al., 1986), conduct disorder (Lueger & Gill, 1990), and early-treated phenylketonuria (Welsh, Pennington, Ozonoff, Rouse, & McCabe, 1990) manifest executive function impairment as well. Clearly, further research is needed to understand how executive function deficits might be related to autism in a way that differentiates it from other disorders. It is possible that a more fine-grained analysis of executive function behaviors might help answer this question. The term *executive function* is often used in a nonspecific fashion, including a wide variety of behaviors under its umbrella (e.g., planning, organization, sustained attention, self-monitoring, impulse control, cognitive flexibility). It is not unreasonable to hypothesize that only a subset of these abilities are deficient in autism. Perhaps the profile of executive function strengths and weaknesses might distinguish autism from other disorders demonstrating executive function impairment; for example, autistic children may be most deficient in flexibility and planning, whereas children with attentional disorders may have most difficulty with sustained attention and impulse control. Research to further explore this question is currently underway in our laboratory at the University of Utah.

IMPLICATIONS FOR TREATMENT AND EDUCATIONAL REMEDIATION

If further research supports the hypothesis that prefrontal dysfunction underlies some symptoms of autism, then the focus of treatment and classroom management might shift slightly to reflect this view. An early focus of treatment would be to educate those who work with autistic individuals about the impact of executive function deficits on a wide range of abilities. At first glance, executive function abilities may appear to be under more voluntary control than other cognitive skills; deficits in this domain may be more likely to be mistaken for intentional misbehavior or lack of motivation than other symptoms of autism. As Mateer and Williams (1991) pointed out, executive function problems require recognition, understanding, and patience on the part of those who work with these children, perhaps more so than other types of learning difficulties.

Remediation efforts might then highlight the development of specific executive function skills. For example, to aid in planning, children could be taught to break tasks into steps, develop a hierarchy of increasingly complex subgoals, and sequence activities to accomplish the superordinate goal. To combat deficits in knowledge consolidation and application, teachers and parents could help autistic students identify the main idea in new information, draw associations between new information and already-acquired knowledge, and "see the big picture," rather than focus on details. While teachers and parents would likely need to provide a great deal of organizational assistance at the outset, the ultimate goal of these techniques would be the development of independent study and living skills. Other helpful suggestions for the educational remediation of executive function deficits are described in Mateer and Williams (1991).

SUMMARY

This chapter focused on particular psychobiological mechanisms that might underlie the symptoms of autism, suggesting that executive function deficits, and more generally, prefrontal dysfunction, might be viable candidates for the underlying impairment of the disorder. This theory is not new, having been previously proposed by several authors who high-lighted the behavioral similarities between frontal patients and autistic individuals (Damasio & Maurer, 1978; Gedye, 1991; Reichler & Lee, 1987). However, the prefrontal dysfunction hypothesis of autism is far from fully explored. This chapter outlined the results of recent investigations of ex-ecutive functions in autism and highlighted the utility of the model for explaining a variety of symptoms associated with the disorder. Given the paucity of direct neurological evidence of frontal dysfunction in autistic individuals and the lack of specificity of executive function deficits to autism, further refinement of the model is clearly necessary. It is hoped that this chapter will stimulate further interest in the prefrontal dysfunc-tion hypothesis within the autism research community and eventually contribute to a more complete understanding of the complexities of the disorder.

ACKNOWLEDGMENTS

I am very grateful to Bruce Pennington, Professor, University of Denver, for his helpful comments on an earlier version of this manuscript.

REFERENCES

Adrien, J. L., Faure, M., Perrot, A., Hameury, L., Garreau, B., Barthelemy, C., & Sauvage, D. (1991). Autism and family home movies: Preliminary findings. *Journal of Autism and Developmental Disorders, 21,* 43–49.

American Psychiatric Association. (1987). *Diagnostic and statistical manual of mental disorders* (3rd ed., rev.). Washington, DC: Author.

Baron-Cohen, S. (1987). Autism and symbolic play. *British Journal of Developmental Psychology, 5,* 139–148.

Baron-Cohen, S. (1988). Social and pragmatic deficits in autism: Cognitive or affective? *Journal of Autism and Developmental Disorders, 18,* 379–402.

Baron-Cohen, S. (1989). Are autistic children behaviorists? An examination of their mental–physical and appearance–reality distinctions. *Journal of Autism and Developmental Disorders, 19,* 579–600.

Baron-Cohen, S., Leslie, A. M., & Frith, U. (1985). Does the autistic child have a "theory of mind"? *Cognition, 21,* 37–46.

Baron-Cohen, S., Leslie, A. M., & Frith, U. (1986). Mechanical, behavioral, and intentional understanding of picture stories in autistic children. *British Journal of Developmental Psychology, 4,* 113–125.

Bauman, M., & Kemper, T. L. (1988). Limbic and cerebellar abnormalities: Consistent findings in infantile autism. *Journal of Neuropathology and Experimental Neurology, 47,* 369.

Borys, S. V., Spitz, H. H., & Dorans, B. A. (1982). Tower of Hanoi performance of retarded young adults and nonretarded children as a function of solution length and goal state. *Journal of Experimental Child Psychology, 33,* 87–110.

Bowler, D. (1992). Theory of mind in Asperger's syndrome. *Journal of Child Psychology and Psychiatry, 33,* 877–893.

Butterworth, G., & Grover, L. (1988). The origins of referential communication in infancy. In L. Weiskrantz (Ed.), *Thought without language* (pp. 5–24). Oxford: Clarendon Press.

Cesaroni, L., & Garber, M. (1991). Exploring the experience of autism through firsthand accounts. *Journal of Autism and Developmental Disorders, 21,* 303–313.

Chelune, G. J., Ferguson, W., Koon, R., & Dickey, T. O. (1986). Frontal lobe disinhibition in attention deficit disorder. *Child Psychiatry and Human Development, 16,* 221–234.

Courchesne, E., Yeung-Courchesne, R., Press, G. A., Hesselink, J. R., & Jernigan, T. L. (1988). Hypoplasia of cerebellar vermal lobules VI and VII in autism. *New England Journal of Medicine, 318,* 1349–1354.

Damasio, A. R., & Maurer, R. G. (1978). A neurological model for childhood autism. *Archives of Neurology, 35,* 777–786.

Damasio, A. R., & Van Hoesen, G. W. (1983). Emotional disturbances associated with focal lesions of the limbic frontal lobe. In K. M. Heilman & P. Satz (Eds.), *The neuropsychology of human emotion.* (pp. 85–110). New York: Guilford.

Dawson, G., & Lewy, A. (1989). Arousal, attention and the socioeconomic impairments of individuals with autism. In G. Dawson (Ed.), *Autism: Nature, diagnosis and treatment* (pp. 49–74). New York: Guilford.

Dennis, M. (1991). Frontal lobe function in childhood and adolescence: A heuristic for assessing attention regulation, executive control, and the intentional states important for social discourse. *Developmental Neuropsychology, 7,* 327–358.

Dewey, P., & Everard, P. (1974). The near-normal autistic adolescent. *Journal of Autism and Childhood Schizophrenia, 4,* 348–356.

Diamond, A., & Goldman-Rakic, P. S. (1985, April). *Evidence that maturation of frontal cortex of the brain underlies behavioral changes during the first year of life: The A-not-B task.* Paper presented at the biennial meeting of the Society for Research in Child Development, Toronto, Canada.

Diamond, A., & Goldman-Rakic, P. S. (1986). Comparative development in human infants and infant rhesus monkeys on cognitive functions that depend on prefrontal cortex. *Society of Neuroscience Abstracts, 12,* 742.

Duncan, J. (1986). Disorganization of behavior after frontal lobe damage. *Cognitive Neuropsychology, 3,* 271–290.

Eisenmajer, R., & Prior, M. (1991). Cognitive linguistic correlates of theory of mind ability in autistic children. *British Journal of Developmental Psychology, 9,* 351–364.

Frith, U. (1988). Autism: Possible clues to the underlying pathology: Psychological facts. In L. Wing (Ed.), *Aspects of autism: Biological research* (19–30). New York: American Psychiatric Press.

Gaffney, G. R., Kuperman, S., Tsai, L. Y., & Minchin, S. (1989). Forebrain structure in autism. *Journal of the American Academy of Child and Adolescent Psychiatry, 28,* 534–537.

Gaffney, G. R., Tsai, L. Y., Kuperman, S., & Minchin, S. (1987). Cerebellar structure in autism. *American Journal of Diseases of Children, 141,* 1330–1332.

Gedye, A. (1991). Frontal lobe seizures in autism. *Medical Hypotheses, 34,* 174–182.

Gillberg, C., Ehlers, S., Schaumann, H., Jakobsson, G., Dahlgren, S. O., Lindblom, R., Bagenholm, A., Tjuus, T., & Blidner, E. (1990). Autism under age 3 years: A clinical study of 28 cases referred for autistic symptoms in infancy. *Journal of Child Psychology and Psychiatry, 31,* 921–934.

Goldman-Rakic, P. S. (1987). Circuitry of primate prefrontal cortex and regulation of behavior by representational memory. In V. B. Mountcastle, F. Plum, & S. R. Geiger (Eds.), *Handbook of physiology: The nervous system.* (pp. 373–417). Bethesda, MD: American Physiological Society.

Grattan, L. M., Bloomer, R., Archambault, F. X., & Eslinger, P. J. (1990). Cognitive and neural underpinnings of empathy. *The Clinical Neuropsychologist, 4,* 279.

Grattan, L. M., & Eslinger, P. J. (1992). Long-term psychosocial consequences of childhood frontal lobe lesion in patient DT. *Brain and Cognition, 20,* 185–195.

Hammes, J. G. W., & Langdell, T. (1981). Precursors of symbol formation and childhood autism. *Journal of Autism and Developmental Disorders, 11,* 331–346.

Harris, P. L. (1993). Pretending and planning. In S. Baron-Cohen, H. Tager-Flusberg, & D. Cohen (Eds.), *Understanding other minds: Perspectives from autism* (pp. 228–246). New York: Oxford University Press.

Heath, R. G., Dempsey, C. W., & Fontana, C. J. (1980). Feedback loop between cerebellum and septal-hippocampal sites; Its role in emotion and epilepsy. *Biological Psychiatry, 15,* 541–556.

Hobson, R. P. (1986). The autistic child's appraisal of expressions of emotion. *Journal of Child Psychology and Psychiatry, 27,* 321–342.

Hobson, R. P. (1989). Beyond cognition: A theory of autism. In G. Dawson (Ed.), *Autism: Nature, diagnosis and treatment* (pp. 22–48). New York: Guilford.

Horwitz, B., Rumsey, J. M., Grady, C. L., & Rapoport, S. I. (1988). The cerebral metabolic landscape in autism: Intercorrelations of regional glucose utilization. *Archives of Neurology, 45,* 749–755.

Jones, V., & Prior, M. (1985). motor imitation abilities and neurological signs in autistic children. *Journal of Autism and Developmental Disorders, 15,* 37–46.

Kanner, L. (1943). Autistic disturbances of affective content. *Nervous Child, 2,* 217–250.

Leslie, A., & Thaiss, L. (1992). Domain specificity in conceptual development: Neuropsychological evidence from autism. *Cognition, 43,* 225–251.

Lhermitte, F. (1986). Human autonomy and the frontal lobes, Part II: Patient behavior in complex and social situations: The "environmental dependency syndrome." *Annals of Neurology, 19,* 335–343.

Lueger, R. J., & Gill, K. J. (1990). Frontal lobe cognitive dysfunction in conduct disorder adolescents. *Journal of Clinical Psychology, 46,* 696–706.

Luria, A. R. (1966). *The higher cortical functions in man.* New York: Basic Books.

Mateer, C. A., & Williams, D. (1991). Effects of frontal lobe injury in childhood. *Developmental Neuropsychology, 7,* 359–376.

McEvoy, R. E., Rogers, S. J., & Pennington, B. F. (1992). *Executive function and social communication deficits in young autistic children.* Manuscript submitted for publication.

Morgan, S. B., Cutrer, P. S., Coplin, J. W., & Rodrigue, J. R. (1989). Do autistic children differ from retarded and normal children in Piagetian sensorimotor functioning? *Journal of Child Psychology and Psychiatry, 30,* 857–864.

Mundy, P., & Sigman, M. (1989). The theoretical implications of joint attention deficits in autism. *Development and Psychopathology, 1,* 173–183.

Ohta, M. (1987). Cognitive disorders of infantile autism: A study employing the WISC, spatial relationships, conceptualization, and gesture imitation. *Journal of Autism and Developmental Disorders, 17,* 45–62.

Ornitz, E. M. (1985). Neurophysiology of infantile autism. *Journal of the American Academy of Child Psychiatry, 24,* 251–262.

Ozonoff, S., Rogers, S. J., & Pennington, B. F., Rogers, S. J. (1990). Are there emotion perception deficits in young autistic children? *Journal of Child Psychology and Psychiatry, 31,* 343–361.

Ozonoff, S., Pennington, B. F., & Rogers, S. J. (1991a). Executive function deficits in high-functioning autistic individuals: Relationship to theory of mind. *Journal of Child Psychology and Psychiatry, 32,* 1081–1105.

Ozonoff, S., Rogers, S. J., & Pennington, B. F. (1991b). Asperger's syndrome: Evidence of an empirical distinction from high-functioning autism. *Journal of Child Psychology and Psychiatry, 32,* 1107–1122.

Perner, J., Frith, U., Leslie, A. M., & Leekam, S. R. (1989). Exploration of the autistic child's theory of mind: Knowledge, belief, and communication. *Child Development, 60,* 689–700.

Piven, J., Berthier, M. L., Starkstein, S. E., Nehme, E., Pearlson, G., & Folstein, S. (1990). Magnetic resonance imaging evidence for a defect of cerebral cortical development in autism. *American Journal of Psychiatry, 147,* 734–739.

Price, B. H., Daffner, K. R., Stowe, R. M., & Mesulam, M. M. (1990). The compartmental learning disabilities of early frontal lobe damage. *Brain, 113,* 1383–1393.

Prior, M., & Hoffman, W. (1990). Neuropsychological testing of autistic children through an exploration with frontal lobe tests. *Journal of Autism and Developmental Disorders, 20,* 581–590.

Rapin, I. (1991). Autistic children: Diagnosis and clinical features. *Pediatrics, 87* (Supplement), 751–760.

Reichler, R. J., & Lee, E. M. C. (1987). Overview of biomedical issues in autism. In E. Schopler & G. B. Mesibov (Eds.), *Neurobiological issues in autism* (pp. 14–41). New York: Plenum Press.

Ricks, D. M., & Wing, L. (1975). Language, communication, and the use of symbols in normal and autistic children. *Journal of Autism and Child Schizophrenia, 5,* 191–220.

Rogers, S. J., & Pennington, B. F. (1991). A theoretical approach to the deficits in infantile autism. *Development and Psychopathology, 3,* 137–162.

Rumsey, J. M. (1985). Conceptual problem-solving in highly verbal, nonretarded autistic men. *Journal of Autism and Developmental Disorders, 15,* 23–36.

Rumsey, J. M., Creasey, H., Stepanek, J. S., Dorwart, R., Patronas, N., Hamburger, S. D., & Duara, R. (1988). Hemispheric asymmetries, fourth ventricular size, and cerebellar morphology in autism. *Journal of Autism and Developmental Disorders, 18,* 127–137.

Rumsey, J. M., & Hamburger, S. D. (1988). Neuropsychological findings in high-functioning autistic men with infantile autism, residual state. *Journal of Clinical and Experimental Neuropsychology, 10,* 201–221.

Rumsey, J. M., & Hamburger, S. D. (1990). Neuropsychological divergence of high-level autism and severe dyslexia. *Journal of Autism and Developmental Disorders, 20,* 155–168.

Russell, J., & Jarrold, C. (1992). *The role of the object in deception and false belief tasks.* Manuscript submitted for publication.

Russell, J., Mauthner, N., Sharpe, S., & Tidswell, T. (1991). The "windows task" as a measure of a strategic deception in preschoolers and autistic subjects. *British Journal of Developmental Psychology, 9,* 331–349.

Rutter, M. (1978a). Diagnosis and definition of childhood autism. *Journal of Autism and Developmental Disorders, 8,* 139–161.

Rutter, M. (1978b). Language disorder and infantile autism. In M. Rutter & E. Schopler (Eds.), *Autism: A reappraisal of concepts and treatment* (pp. 85–104). New York: Plenum Press.

Rutter, M. (1988). Epidemiological approaches to developmental psychopathology. *Archives of General Psychiatry, 45,* 486–495.

Rutter, M., & Schopler, E. (1987). Autism and pervasive developmental disorders: Concepts and diagnostic issues. *Journal of Autism and Developmental Disorders, 17,* 159–186.

Scheerer, M., Rothmann, E., & Goldstein, K. (1945). A case of "idiot savant": An experimental study of personality organization. *Psychological Monographs, 58,* 1–63.

Shah, A., & Frith, U. (1983). An islet of ability in autistic children: A research note. *Journal of Child Psychology and Psychiatry, 24,* 613–620.

Sigman, M., Ungerer, J. A., Mundy, P., & Sherman, T. (1987). Cognition in autistic children.

In D. J. Cohen, A. M. Donnellan, & R. Paul (Eds.), *Handbook of autism and pervasive developmental disorders* (pp. 103–120). New York: Wiley.

Steel, J. G., Gorman, R., & Flexman, J. E. (1984). Neuropsychiatric testing in an autistic mathematical idiot savant: Evidence for nonverbal abstract capacity. *Journal of the American Academy of Child Psychiatry, 23,* 704–707.

Stuss, D. T., & Benson, D. F. (1986). *The frontal lobes.* New York: Raven Press.

Welsh, M. C., Pennington, B. F., & Groisser, D. B. (1991). A normative-developmental study of executive function: A window on prefrontal function in children. *Developmental Neuropsychology, 7,* 131–149.

Welsh, M. C., Pennington, B. F., Ozonoff, S., Rouse, B., & McCabe, E. R. B. (1990). Neuropsychology of early-treated PKU: Specific executive function deficits. *Child Development, 61,* 1697–1713.

Yirmiya, N., Sigman, M. D., Kasari, C., & Mundy, P. (1992). Empathy and cognition in high-functioning children with autism. *Child Development, 63,* 150–160.

12

Facilitating Social Inclusion
Examples from Peer Intervention Programs

CATHERINE LORD

INTRODUCTION

Autism is a developmental disorder defined by a particular constellation of deficits in social and communication skills and by limited and unusual interests and behaviors. Although the social handicap is gradually gaining acceptance as one of the primary, if not the primary deficit underlying autism, social deficits also arise out of problems in other areas (e.g., poor receptive language, unusual sensory interests) and from the marked limitations in social experience that characterize autistic children and adolescents. Social handicaps secondary to experience may be more modifiable in the long run than those that are direct manifestations of more basic biological abnormalities in development. To the degree that we can modify experience, we may be able to make changes in the social motivation and behaviors of autistic children and adolescents.

This is the same assumption offered to support the need for intensive early intervention programs. Yet, as children enter later childhood and adolescence, spontaneous positive interaction with peers requires somewhat different skills than do interactions with adults and other children in more formal settings. There are numerous well-designed social skills programs intended for children and adolescents with learning and/or behav-

CATHERINE LORD • Department of Psychiatry University of Chicago Hospital, Chicago, Illinois, 60637.

Learning and Cognition in Autism, edited by Eric Schopler and Gary B. Mesibov. Plenum Press, New York, 1995.

ior difficulties. However, the goals of these programs comprise skills for which autistic children do not have the prerequisites. Frequently the focus is on getting children to use skills they already possess (Dodge, Pettit, McClaskey & Brown, 1986), when autistic children really may not have the target behaviors in their repertoire.

The purpose of this chapter is to describe several different models for promoting positive social experiences with peers for children and adolescents with autism. Each of these programs involves the creation of a context in which autistic students regularly interact with nonhandicapped students of the same age, and in some cases, with children who have other behavior difficulties or other autistic children as well. The chapter attempts to provide a practical guide to designing such social experiences either within the school day or by building on educational resources. Descriptions are provided of several peer interventions in which I, along with colleagues, have been involved over the last 15 years. Although many of these social experiences arose out of research projects, on the whole, few data are available concerning their efficacy. In part, this is because we often studied changes in one aspect of behavior (e.g., social initiative), only to find later that changes in other domains seemed much more salient (e.g., changes in affect). Research documenting the efficacy of these programs has also been limited by our impatience. That is, often, having heard of a new strategy, we were unwilling to hold to planned baselines or techniques that were obviously only partially effective for the sake of documenting their effectiveness. Thus, what is offered here, rather than a scholarly review, is descriptive, clinical information for practitioners interested in providing supervised peer experiences for children and adolescents with autism. Programs by Mesibov (1986) and Strain (1983), developed about the same time as our first social groups, had very important effects on our strategies, and since that time, we have also been influenced by programs by Wohlberg and Schuler (1992), Williams (1989) and Magill (1987).

Following a discussion of general principles, two programs are discussed: (a) a peer tutor program for autistic children in elementary and middle schools; and (b) an after-school and evening weekly-social-group program for autistic children from about age 10 up through adolescence and young adulthood. In addition, a summer daycamp organized on the same principles as the after-school social group, is discussed briefly throughout the description of the weekly social groups.

PRINCIPLES UNDERLYING PEER INTERVENTION

Although the two types of interventions discussed are quite different in their structure, they share five principles.

1. *Peer intervention must be conducted in a positive environment in which interactions with age-mates are pleasurable.* Simply placing autistic children near other children is not sufficient. Organizing activities that require interaction (e.g., sharing, taking turns) is also not sufficient if there is no attention to how to make the experience pleasant for all the students. With nonautistic students, we often assume that making a boring task social will make it more pleasurable. However, for a student with autism, this may make already-difficult social encounters even more difficult. Because social experiences may not be intrinsically motivating for children with autism, and because interacting with an autistic child does not always offer the same social benefits as ordinary friendships for nonautistic children, a deliberate effort must be made to design interesting activities, use novel materials, and monitor the length of the sessions to ensure that they remain positive for all concerned. The foremost goal of these sessions is for autistic children's interactions with peers to become a predictable, positive experience.

2. *Peers are supported in their interactions with the autistic children and adults, but are not directed how to behave.* Because the objective of the intervention is to have *spontaneous peer interaction*, the role of the adult is that of the "producer/director" of a play rather than as an active participant. Having an adult present whom the autistic participants trust and to whom they will respond, if necessary, is critical. However, the adult affects the students primarily through the other children or through environmental manipulation, not through direct interaction with the autistic group members.

Nonautistic participants are given some orientation and suggestions before they participate in an intervention. Depending on their age and situation (if they are from the same school as the autistic children), peers are given general information about autism as a problem that affects how children talk and play or interact with others. This information is given in a simple, matter-of-fact manner, and questions are answered in the same way.

Peers are then typically given a number of standard guidelines, adapted from the original modeling paradigm of Strain (Strain, Kerr, & Raglund, 1979). These suggestions are depicted in Table 12-1. The intention is to keep guidelines simple and to let the peers decide how they will behave.

3. *The temporal and physical structure of the group is deliberately varied around the needs of the group members.*

a. *Follow a standard schedule* for at least the first few sessions. Once the group has become established, then the schedule can be varied. Post the schedule at the beginning, if necessary, using pictures as well as words to describe the different components.

Table 12-1. Suggestions to Peer Tutors and Volunteers

1. If you see a group member who is alone, go to him or her. Do not stay with *old* friends.
2. Be persistent; don't give up if the student with autism does not respond right away.
3. Join his or her activity.
   a) Put yourself in the same space as your partner (if he or she sits, you sit). Stay close to him or her.
   b) Find some of the same materials for yourself.
   c) Do what he or she is doing.
   d) Modify what you are both doing gradually to be something you would like to do.
   e) Using simple language, tell the autistic child/adult what you are doing while you are doing it.
   f) Praise the student anytime he or she works to create an interaction; notice even small actions.
4. Ignore unusual behaviors unless they seem dangerous.
5. If anything worries you, call an adult.

b. *Carefully structure space for different activities* with a particular eye to keeping group members in close proximity to each other when they are expected to interact. Use furniture, dividers, and markings (e.g., for the "game area") to identify where they are supposed to be.

c. *Provide themes for each session* that can be built on during interaction. These can range in sophistication from very simple concepts (everyone wearing their favorite color or something to total their favorite number: e.g., two shoes) to sophisticated topics (current events, countries in Europe), and everything in between (game shows, Olympics, holidays). Participants should be told about themes in advance so that they can bring something related to them (e.g., an item of clothing, an object) to the sessions and, if possible, practice communicating about them at home. Older children and adolescents may be quite interested in helping to select the themes for their groups.

d. *Activities should be designed around a shared objective that requires cooperation or, at least, attention to others.* This objective may be accompanied by having truly interactive activities (e.g., building something) or by having a group endpoint for an essentially individual activity (e.g., creating a museum to display everyone's artwork) or by working in teams that accumulate points (so that the score can be manipulated to ensure no hurt feelings).

e. *Activities should not require understanding or production of complex language or skilled fine/gross motor behaviors.* Because many autistic individuals have deficits in these areas, activities that do not emphasize skill are necessary. However, often it is possible to create activities that leave room for creativity (e.g., mosaics) and real skill (e.g., silly relays) without requiring them.

f. *Activities should be relatively brief.* Depending on the age of the group members, activities should range from 5- to 30-minutes long. If in doubt, shorter is better. A good activity can always be extended at the last minute, but activities that are scheduled for too long a time may result in behavior problems or lengthy transitions if there is nothing else planned.

g. *Develop group rituals.* Select favorite activities and do them frequently, with minor variations. These could include snacks, standard rituals from school (e.g., saying hello or goodbye), telling a favorite joke each week (Van Bourgondien & Mesibov, 1987), and playing get-to-know-you games (e.g., social bingo). Even for older adolescents and adults, these rituals can be very helpful, particularly as they are mastered by the autistic participants who can then teach them to new group members.

4. *Sessions must occur with sufficient frequency so that group rapport develops.* The difficulty here is often the participation of nonhandicapped peers who have other demands on their time. However, our experience is that it is better to schedule a group to meet frequently for a short period of time (3–4 days a week for 15 minutes for 2 weeks for peer tutors in school or once a week for 10 weeks for social groups) than to have less frequent sessions spaced further apart, such as every 2 weeks. Once a social program is well-established and most of the autistic members are familiar with it, then there is more room for variation. However, new members still may benefit from a "loading dose" of relatively frequent sessions in order to get started (this also holds true for new organizers of groups).

5. *Autistic students must comprise less than half of the group.* The exception here is peer-pairs (to be discussed) that consist of an autistic student and a peer tutor. However, in creating any group greater than two, a general strategy of recruiting at least one extra nonhandicapped student works best. This is because there are some nonautistic students (about 10–20% in our experience) who, for a variety of reasons, require as much help in a peer situation as the autistic children or adolescents. If nonautistic children with other handicaps or disabilities are used as "tutors" or volunteers in social groups, the proportion of nonautistic volunteers may even need to be a bit higher. Most children, even those with learning disabilities or nonautistic psychiatric problems, function very well in such groups, but it is worthwhile being prepared for one or two children who need more attention and who function more like the autistic students in terms of their demands on others' time rather than as volunteers. Overall, the role of the adult is to create the environment and then be available from the sidelines.

For this to happen, there has to be a sufficient number of socially competent children.

6. *Set specific goals for each autistic student in the intervention and evaluate progress after a specified time.* After several sessions, it is important to be sufficiently aware of each student's skills and needs, so that a small number of individual goals can be specified. These goals may range from general behaviors (e.g., recording the time Charlie voluntarily stays near [within 3 feet] other students during joke-telling) or be more specific (e.g., Charlie will learn to tell a simple joke during joke-telling time). Goals should reflect parents' and teachers' everyday priorities as well as those that arise within the group. Having a written list of individual goals can be helpful in planning activities that address skills for individual students. These principles apply to both the in-school and after-school programs described later.

PEER TUTOR/BUDDIES PROGRAM

The peer tutor program was originally started in the St. Paul Public Schools autism program with J. Michael Hopkins and Linda Bream, and has since been implemented in several other school districts (Lord, 1984; Lord & Hopkins, 1986). The goal of the program is to give autistic elementary and middle school students an opportunity to play with agemates in a natural, but sheltered environment. It has been carried out with a range of autistic students, from those with profound mental handicaps to highly verbal, high-functioning children. Over the course of various programs, we also attempted to study several practical questions concerning the most appropriate age of the playmate, the most useful instructions, and the most effective number of sessions.

Recruiting/Selecting Peers

Each autistic student is assigned a nonhandicapped child to be his/her "buddy" for 2–3 weeks. Buddies are children of the same sex as the autistic child, selected by regular classroom teachers because they can afford to miss 10–15 minutes of class three or four times a week for several weeks, and who are not extraordinarily shy or troubled. In general, children who are described by their teachers as outgoing, energetic, and flexible are most comfortable in this role; however, if the teacher presents the program to the class in an enthusiastic way, we have found that almost all children who participated as buddies reported that they enjoyed the experience (and seemed to do so).

The program is most effective when a regular classroom teacher agrees to support it strongly and to encourage students to participate. The teacher needs to understand that although exceptions arise, sessions must be frequent and predictable for the autistic child. We have found that buddies of approximately the same age (particularly not much younger) are most effective (Lord & Hopkins, 1986). However, we also found that the number of children who found being a buddy difficult in this situation was much higher for children under ages 8 or 9 (Lord, 1984). Thus, we would generally recommend recruiting children 9 or 10 years of age and older, even for younger autistic children. Though a 10-year-old nonhandicapped child playing with an autistic 5-year-old does not usually engage in completely egalitarian play, the 10-year-old's behavior is sufficiently different from an adult's to provide a good "child" model. In fact, even when a 10-year-old nonhandicapped child plays with an autistic 10-year-old, his/her contribution to the interactions is not usually truly equal. It is worth noting that there are tremendous individual differences in younger, nonhandicapped children's skill and interest in participation in such a program. We have worked with some five-year-olds who have been outstanding buddies, although most have not. The variability among nonhandicapped children in coping with and enjoying the role of buddy or tutor is much smaller after age 8 years.

Preparation of Peers

A variation of Strain's peer training (Strain, et al., 1979) is employed with the buddies before the sessions begin. A teacher works with each new buddy individually for about 20 minutes, explaining the purpose of the program (to help children who want to play with other children, but don't quite know how), and explaining that some autistic children do not know how to talk very well yet and so need extra help by being shown how to do things. They are given the guidelines in Table 12-1. We also use Strain's technique for practicing with the new buddies in learning how to get an autistic child's attention (with the teacher play-acting the part of the autistic child who will be the partner and doing some of the things that the autistic child might do). The children are then introduced to each other; a photograph of the nonhandicapped child is posed in the autistic child's classroom, and after the autistic child returns to class, the peer is asked if he/she has any questions.

After the first week, the buddies are often brought into the classroom(s) of the autistic children as a group for a special visit. At the end of all of the sessions, nonhandicapped children are given a snack with their buddies and a certificate.

In several research projects, using techniques adapted from Strain (1983) and Odom, Hoyson, Jamiesen, and Strain (1985), we showed, as did other researchers before us, that teaching the nonhandicapped children behavioral techniques to get the autistic children's attention and to instruct the autistic children what to do next, resulted in high levels of interaction very quickly (Lord, 1984). When nonhandicapped children were trained only to follow the guidelines in Table 12-1, the frequency of interaction increased more gradually than when the peers were taught more behavioral techniques. However, the end result, after about a week of sessions without behavioral training, was the same in terms of the frequency of interaction and the responsiveness of the autistic child to his or her playmate.

On the other hand, when the behavior of the nonhandicapped children was less intrusive, autistic children were more likely to make some overtures themselves, rather than being completely passive recipients of their partners' initiations. Nonhandicapped children who had had formal behavioral training behaved much more like adults than like children playing with each other. Generalization of the autistic children's new behaviors to new buddies who had not had the training, and to other situations, was not as good as when the peers behaved more naturally.

It is most important to design the program to fit the needs of the individual child. Thus, there may be situations, particularly with autistic children who are rather passive and who have limited play and communication skills, when it is advantageous to use the very effective behavioral techniques developed by researchers such as Strain and Odom (Strain et al., 1979; Odom & Strain, 1984). Often, however, with a little more time and by following the guidelines listed in Table 12-1 and creating a physical and task-oriented structure as described previously, nonhandicapped children can develop their own child-oriented ways of approaching and interacting with autistic children. In the long run, more natural interventions may produce better generalization and a more natural kind of interaction than the use of more explicit behavioral techniques (Lord, 1984).

Scheduling

In the peer/tutor program, dyads met three or four times a week for 10–20 minutes at the same time of day in the same place. In many cases, this schedule was supplemented by other activities with the whole class.

For example, the autistic child may already be included in his or her buddy's class for physical education and reading, plus having recess and lunch with his or her class. A reverse-mainstreaming program might also exist, with students from the buddy's class coming to a special education class for art or music. Such opportunities are important in giving both partners a chance to generalize the skills they learn in dyads.

We generally schedule the same dyad to play together for 2 weeks at a time. If the buddies are very keen to maintain the relationship, giving them a break of a few weeks or a month and then letting them complete another 2-week session or assigning them a more structured role as a "lunch buddy" or "playground buddy" may be helpful. Our experience is that nonhandicapped children are less energetic and enthusiastic if they are expected to participate in sessions at this intensity level every day for more than 2 weeks (even by the end of the first week, if they are not given a fixed endpoint). The energy level of the children is very important.

Sessions can occur at various times of the day, depending on the class schedule, but should follow a predictable schedule for each pair. Often teachers prefer to have sessions at the end of the day, just preceding lunch or following recess, because this minimizes class disruption. One of the critical factors in creating a supportive environment is creating a space that is large enough that the children feel comfortable, but small enough so that it is very difficult for them to avoid each other. We generally did this by marking off an area of about 8 by 10 feet, either with masking tape on the floor or by moving furniture to create natural dividers. The supervising adult sat outside the area in the same room, and engaged in paperwork so that the children did not feel watched, but so that they did know someone was available to intervene if necessary. The role of the adult is to help the children during transitions from one activity to another and to ensure that the children stay within the designated area. The adult is also available if a child becomes distressed or very fixed on a particular activity. Having the space organized and identified with the program helps the children settle into the activities and feel more comfortable. It also makes it possible to measure improvement, especially for the younger, nonverbal autistic children, by computing the average distance (e.g., by number of masking tape boxes on the floor) between the autistic child and his or her buddy during free times.

Activities

A format similar to the expanded schedule for the social groups (to be described) is followed (Dewey, Lord, & Magill, 1988; Lord, 1991; Lord &

Magill, 1988). Sessions always start with the supervising adult asking the children to build or make something (e.g., different kinds of blocks, Legos™, floor puzzles) together for about 5 minutes. Different toys are provided each day during this session. After this, children are given materials to carry out routine "scripts," such as serving food at McDonald's, going grocery shopping with a real or pretend cash register and shopping baskets, being in the hospital (with surgical clothes, crutches and a Resusci-Annie doll) or in a rock group (with appropriate clothes and musical instruments). A large mirror is brought out during this time so that the children can see themselves dressed up.

After 5–10 minutes, depending on the level of the autistic child and the interest of the pair in these activities, these materials are removed and a standard set of toys for free play are made available. Toys are rotated through the sessions so that not all toys are put out together. The children are then allowed to do as they wish until the end of the session. This routine is followed fairly rigidly for the first three or four sessions, until the children are familiar with the schedule, and then followed more generally throughout the following weeks.

Once the children understand the routine and are comfortable, some aspects can be varied; for example, how long they have access to materials for construction or imaginative play may be shortened or lengthened, depending on the children's level of interest and the events of that particular day. On the whole, the adult's goal is to stay outside the interaction, but if the children get "stuck" in an activity (e.g., after throwing a ball back and forth for several minutes, they begin to get bored), the adult first tries to get the nonhandicapped child to think of other things they can do with the ball, and if this does not work, then suggests something new they can do.

These kinds of activities and materials were selected because our research showed that, in general, the pairs seemed most calm and comfortable during structured, construction-type activities, and showed the highest level of positive interaction during imaginative play (Dewey et al., 1988). In addition, if given a choice, both autistic and nonhandicapped children selected imaginative play over other kinds of activities. The particular nature of the materials obviously will vary according to the interests and levels of the autistic children. The purpose remains the same: to give the autistic children the opportunity to use a range of materials, and to give both children in each pair an environmental "frame" through structuring of time and place and objects, within which they can enjoy each other's company without being bored or worried about what will happen next (Lord & Schopler, 1993; Lord, Schopler, & Bristol, 1993).

Toys to be used should not be the same as those usually available to the children in their regular classes. Often, the most successful toys are those that do not require much fine motor coordination, that have high interest and some novel characteristic that can be used jointly by two children (a brightly colored, large, light beach ball; a tube the children can crawl through and push each other in; very large, decorated cardboard blocks, floor puzzles, a McDonald's set of food and containers; very large coloring books and special markers; air hockey, Happy Hippo). It is important that the toys be appealing to the nonhandicapped children, even if they are at a simpler cognitive level than toys with which they usually play. Nonhandicapped children are usually quite happy to play with toys intended for children of much younger ages for brief periods of time, as long as a variety of different activities are available throughout each session and across sessions, and it is clear that no one will judge them negatively for doing so.

Final Comments

Obviously, it is possible to adapt the model above in many ways for different children and situations. This model has been used not only in full-day school programs, but also with children enrolled in aftercare. The latter programs had the real advantage of giving the autistic children an opportunity to play more intensively than they typically could have (because of the special space restrictions, lack of distraction, and structured tasks that we designed) with the peers, in a situation where relationships begun in the structured, supervised setting of the peer/playmate program could be followed up in the daily activities of the after-school group.

We have also used a modified version of the peer/tutor strategy during the summer daycamps in order to give the autistic children a chance to get to know a few of the other campers more intimately. Having children play together in dyads once or twice a day during a full-day daycamp provides a more structured, quieter opportunity for peer interaction each day, in addition to the activities that typically involve larger groups or less structure. Another modification has been to use two normally developing peers to play with one autistic child, particularly one who is difficult to engage or to keep in sustained interaction. This generally works best when at least one of the nonhandicapped children is very assertive and committed to the interaction, and when the nonhandicapped children are *not* best friends, but children who can concentrate on working together to play with the autistic child, rather than being distracted by each other. With younger autistic children and younger nonhandicapped children, we have also experimented with using a similar approach to that described previously, but having the adult lead the interaction or at least be physically more involved in the activity. In this case as well, having two or even three nonhandicapped children assigned together as buddies for an autistic child seems to be more enjoyable for the nonhandicapped children and results in more interaction for the autistic child than pairs composed of one autistic and one nonhandicapped child. This last model may be appropriate for younger children with autism who are fully included in regular or noncategorical special education preschool classes, and who, even though they are physically near other children all day, often have very little sustained interaction with them (Wohlfberg & Schuler, 1992).

INTEGRATED SOCIAL GROUPS/DAYCAMPS

The overall structure of the after-school integrated social groups and daycamps follows much the same guidelines discussed earlier. Goals are similar; length, number and kind of activities obviously vary with the age of the children and the type of program. We have offered after-school and evening social groups for children as young as 10-years-old up through adulthood. Two-week daycamps have been run successfully for children from about age 7 or 8 up to adults as well (with age spans of 3 or 4 years within each group except for the adults). To date, these groups have included only relatively high-functioning autistic children and adolescents with some verbal skills. Many of these strategies would work with less verbal or nonverbal students, but activities and staff/student ratios would need to be altered.

Recruiting Nonhandicapped Peers

One of the greatest challenges in running integrated social programs is the recruitment of nonhandicapped children and adolescents. We have been most successful in attempting to recruit nonhandicapped participants from agencies and organized programs, such as Boy Scouts, Girl Guides, church groups, and school clubs, although we do also include individual volunteers. We ask the organized groups to make a commitment that the same children will come to social groups three times a month for a total of about 10 sessions. Larger agencies are easier to work with because they can contribute more volunteers over a longer period of time (e.g., six volunteers for the first 10 weeks, then six others for the second 10 weeks, and so on to fill out the school year). It has generally been worth the extra effort to persist through the bureaucratic procedures required by larger agencies in order to have access to their members for after-school and evening groups. For the summer social groups and daycamps, we have generally been successful recruiting past participants of after-school and evening programs and siblings of the autistic children (attending either the group that their brother or sister attends or a different one).

Finding the best agency from which to recruit volunteers depends a great deal on luck. It is important that the organization be fairly large because, in most cases, a social group for children or adolescents within a particular age range needs at least six to nine nonhandicapped participants, and not everyone wants to volunteer. We have insisted that children within the larger organization (e.g., Boy Scouts) not be forced to come if they do not wish to do so.

It is helpful to find two different sources of volunteers, so that the nonhandicapped children do not all know each other, and so there is a fall-back if an activity occurs that requires all of the volunteers from a particular group (e.g., Boy Scout Jamboree) to miss a session. We have been very surprised at the variability among different agencies in their interest in participating in our groups. In one city, we were able to work out a very positive relationship with the Boy Scouts, in which boys from different troops came to social groups over many years, and even deliberately created activities outside the group and invited the children with autism to join them. In another city, the officials running the Boy Scouts had no interest in a program such as this. Other sources have been intramural athletic teams, fraternities (for young adults), service and honors clubs from middle schools and high schools, and Boys and Girls Clubs sponsored by social services. The critical feature seems to be finding one, or preferably two adult leaders within an organization who are interested in the project and sufficiently organized to help the children with whom they work become involved. Once these adults are identified, they often know other people who can also be helpful. The secret is to be persistent and not to give up, because such individuals do exist; it is a matter of finding them. When selecting children/adolescents out of a larger organization to attend the social group, we generally request that children do not come with their "best friends," but with one or two other children they like. From the start, we stress that the hour or two of social group is not time for them to spend with each other, but with the autistic group members; they may be together with friends sometimes, but the goal is always to interact with the group members with autism.

It has generally been a positive experience to include children and adolescents with equivalent intellectual skills to the autistic children but who have other sorts of severe social difficulties (e.g., paired with high-functioning autistic adolescents have been other teenagers with early onset schizophrenia, mixed conduct-emotional and learning disabilities; paired with lower functioning autistic adolescents have been nonautistic mentally handicapped youngsters.) Having more participants within a smaller age group helps with the group cohesiveness. The nonautistic adolescents often respond very quickly and more overtly to the positive atmosphere and structure offered by the groups than do the autistic adolescents, thought they sometimes introduce other problems (e.g., dealing with adolescent sexual relationships) that are relatively rare in the autistic group members. This can be helpful in widening the organizers' focus on autism. In considering recruitment of normally developing peers, children with nonautistic difficulties need to be counted with the autistic participants (and so require additional nonhandicapped "matches").

Preparation of Peers

Orientations for volunteers should be low-key and simple. Leaders of the organizations from which the volunteers are typically recruited have been given a one or two page handout before the groups begin; it explains what the groups are like and what we are trying to accomplish. In some cases, slide or video presentations are made for group leaders. For the children and adolescents, the emphasis is on practical suggestions for how to behave and cope with behaviors of the participants with autism, which volunteers may not understand. The focus is on our goal of positive interaction, rather than on what is wrong with our group members. Older children and adolescent volunteers are typically asked to come to the first group about 15 minutes early in order to be shown around and to discuss the group rules, depicted in Table 12-1. For younger children, a visit to the site of the daycamp or social group with the organization from which they have been recruited is arranged. At this time, goals and rules are discussed.

We use the term *autism* with the volunteers, but in a matter-of-fact way, with reference to the volunteers' job of helping children and other teenagers who do not know how to make friends or play learn how to do these things. Group members' questions about general issues are answered as directly as possible; queries about individual participants, except for practical questions about how to respond to a certain behavior, are not encouraged. On the other hand, an effort is made to support and praise all group members, volunteers, and participants with autism or other difficulties, for their group efforts and participation.

Scheduling

It is very important, at least at the start, that a group meets frequently enough that the children form a routine that they can anticipate for the next meeting. One schedule that has worked well for the adolescents has been to meet three times a month for approximately a school term (September–December) and then take a break of a month or two around holidays and exams. A new group is then formed after the holidays, comprising new volunteers (previous volunteers may return if they wish, but are under no obligation to do so) for the next set of sessions (February–May). In some situations, meeting with this frequency may not be possible. It then seems important to meet frequently (once every 2 weeks) for the first few sessions, and then convert to once a month. Groups that meet once a month may provide a social outlet for the autistic youngsters, but do not accomplish the same goal of regular, positive social contact as those that meet more frequently.

When groups are just starting, sessions are initially kept quite short: usually about an hour. This allows time for four 15-minute activities. Even this amount of time can be quite exhausting for some autistic youngsters, because it comprises fairly constant interaction. As the group members become more relaxed and better able to come up with more spontaneous activities during free time, then the time may be increased up to 90 minutes, particularly for the older teenagers. It is better to start with shorter sessions and increase the time, than to have students upset because they are overwhelmed.

On the other hand, summer daycamps were run for "full-days" (9:30 to 2:30) and half-days (9 to 12; 1 to 4) quite successfully, initially to our surprise. During the daycamps, the pace is slower; activities, especially meals and sports, are a bit longer; free times are interspersed throughout the day and there are field trips. The fact that the daycamp is the primary activity of the participants during this time, in contrast to after-school groups in which the members had been in school or at work all day, may also make a difference.

Activities

For evening and after-school social groups, activities follow a predictable pattern, except during outings, which are arranged about once a month, or every four sessions. A typical schedule for a group is depicted in Table 12-2. As described earlier, each meeting has a theme, with an activity specified in advance and for which students are asked to bring

Table 12-2. Example of Schedule for After School
or Evening Social Group

3:15–3:30	Students arrive; play with partners in quiet activities
3:30–3:45	Social skills activities
3:45–4:05	Large group activity related to theme
4:05–4:20	Snack
4:20–4:30	Free play

something (e.g., an item of clothing, a kind of food, a newspaper clipping) related to the theme.

Groups always begin with a quiet period in which furniture and activities are set up to facilitate play in dyads or groups of three and four. With the younger children, partners (mixed pairs of autistic and non-handicapped children, or one autistic, one behavior-disordered and two nonhandicapped children) are directed to specific activities that have been selected beforehand on the basis of the autistic child's interests and abilities. Students are told that they need to have a "partner" and to stay with the same partner until large group activities begin. With the youngest students, stickers are used (e.g., all the "tigers" play in the "tiger corner") to indicate partners and play areas. Activities during this time include board games, ping-pong, bowling, floor puzzles, play with Fisher Price sets, air hockey, preparation of materials for that day's group activity or computer games that require two people. Students are also encouraged to show their partners whatever they brought relevant to the theme and to talk about what they will be doing during the large group.

Playing with partners is followed by our most formal attempt at "social skills" training for about 10–20 minutes, depending on the age of the group members. These techniques were developed by Mesibov (1986) for the TEACCH adult social groups. A specific social skill is identified that relates in some way to the theme (e.g., introducing someone, joining a conversation, choosing topics of conversation, sharing). Autistic and behavior-disordered students are again placed in pairs with non-handicapped volunteers. The pairs are asked to practice the social skill as it should be done and also to come up with an example of how it should not be done. Depending on the complexity of the social skill and the experience of the volunteers and the autistic participants in the group, sometimes "scripts" are used to get the pairs started. That is, if the skill is asking for help in a store, a three- or four-sentence script of one way to do so might be distributed to each pair. After the pairs have practiced the "right way" and the "wrong way" to carry out the assigned task, each pair presents either their wrong way or their right way to the entire group.

Sometimes these presentations are videotaped and watched and discussed.

The sophistication of the social skills selected as goals varies widely depending on the age and needs of the participants. We have practiced everything from job interviews and phone calls to acquaintances or strangers, to sharing food or greeting a family member. How much the skills can be developed spontaneously and how much they are dependent on the scripts also varies widely. On the whole, if the pace of this activity is appropriate and the goals are clear (particularly to the nonhandicapped volunteers), the students enjoy acting out the social situations, especially doing things the wrong way. Specific social skills are selected from the goals developed for each student in conjunction with parents and teachers.

After "social skills," typically there is a large group activity that lasts from 15 to 30 minutes. This often consists of some sort of craft or series of group games around the theme. For example, one group of teenagers used various countries and cultures as their theme over the course of several sessions. Crafts were selected to go with each country. Games, such as pin the city on a map, bingo in which group members had to ask each other questions about the theme (e.g., Have you ever been to Mexico? Do you like tacos?) in order to fill in the bingo card, and relays (e.g., a modified version of a hat dance), were organized around each country.

Sometimes the large group activity may consist of planning or preparing or purchasing materials for the following week. As members of a particular group get to know each other and become accustomed to the group situation, the goal is to give the group increasing independence to plan and prepare their own activities.

After the large group activity, there is always a snack. Although it sounds obvious, this is a very important part of the group. Eating with someone is a familiar activity for all the participants, and there is an inherent theme and script to this activity that makes it less demanding than others for many of the group members. Good food is an almost universal motivator and source of shared enjoyment. In this atmosphere, the students are required to sit together and, in an informal way, are pressed to interact.

After the snack, students are given free time to use any of the materials available with whomever they wish. During this time, volunteers are encouraged to continue to be available for the autistic students, but autistic students are not required to interact if they do not wish to do so.

Activities for daycamps follow much the same sequence as the afternoon or evening social groups within each 2-hour period, with the exception of regular opportunities for sports (e.g., swimming every day; playing outside in a playground or at a park) available twice a day. That is, each day begins with play between partners, includes some kind of social skills activity (usually once a day), followed by a large group activity, snack, swimming or outdoor activities, either before or after the snack, and then free time. For the full-day daycamp, after lunch and more free time, the sequence begins again with activities intended for small groups or dyads, then another large group or social skills activity, followed by a snack and some time outdoors and free time. In the daycamps, the group as a whole is frequently divided into smaller "teams" consisting of a total of 6–8 autistic and nonautistic students and 2 or 3 counselors who remain together consistently through the daycamp. These teams stay together for about half of the activities and snacktimes, but are not required to be together during lunch or free time. This allows the possibility of setting up centers in which one group is doing one activity while another group does something else.

CONCLUSIONS

All of these activities have included an open-door policy for family members and friends. Parents are welcome to watch the group at any time and often join in the group toward the end of snack-time and during the last free time. Siblings are welcome to come with participants throughout all the activities, at their autistic brothers or sisters' invitation. For many of the autistic students, this group is the first time that they are participating in something which they can invite their siblings to and which the siblings are interested in visiting (particularly if the food is good and the activities look interesting). Several times we have run summer daycamps in which autistic students brought their siblings along as regular members. One of the positive offshoots of these groups with younger students has been the opportunity for the parents of the autistic youngsters to get to meet each other in an informal way as they come and go from group activities.

A final point is that it is very important to plan interesting, age-appropriate activities, in which all the students will want to participate. This does not mean that the activities have to be difficult or use expensive materials, but planning and creativity are essential in order to keep the interest of all the students. Because students with autism are less able and less comfortable entertaining themselves in socially appropriate ways, it is important that activities are available to give them a framework in which to build beginning social relationships. Such a framework requires time and planning on the part of group organizers.

Overall, our goal continues to be one of providing positive opportunities for students with autism to interact, and enjoy interacting, with other youngsters. We hope that these experiences lead them to increasing independence and flexibility in social situations and to more positive expectations about social situations and their own ability to participate and enjoy these situations. Clearly, there are many different ways to accomplish such a goal. The strategies presented here are intended to be a start that schools, families, and communities can build on in unique ways to match the needs of their students.

ACKNOWLEDGMENTS

Programs described in this paper represent the work and ideas of many individuals including J. Michael Hopkins, Linda Bream, Joyce Magill, Deborah Dewey, Sharon Storoschuk, Debra Combs, Pamela DiLavore, Marquita Fair, and Allison Houlik. This paper is dedicated to the memory of Kim Sipes.

REFERENCES

Dewey, D., Lord, C., & Magill, J. (1988). Qualitative assessment of the effect of play materials in dyadic peer interactions of children with autism. *Canadian Journal of Psychology, 42,* 242–260.

Dodge, K. A., Pettit, G. S., McClaskey, C. L., & Brown, M. M. (1986). Social competence in children. *Monographs of the Society for Research in Child Development, 51.*

Lord, C. (1984). The development of peer relations in children with autism. In F. J. Morrison, C. Lord, & D. P. Keating (Eds.), *Advances in applied developmental psychology* (pp. 165–229). New York: Academic Press.

Lord, C. (1991). A cognitive-behavioral model for the treatment of social-communicative deficits in adolescents with autism. In R. J. McMahon & R. D. Peters (Eds.), *Behavior disorders of adolescence* (pp. 155–174). New York: Plenum Press.

Lord, C., & Hopkins, J. M. (1986). The social behaviour of autistic children with younger and same-age nonhandicapped peers. *Journal of Autism and Developmental Disorders, 16,* 249–262.

Lord, C., & Magill, J. (1988). Methodological and theoretical issues in studying peer-directed behaviour and autism. In G. Dawson (Ed.), *Autism: Nature, diagnosis and treatment* (pp. 326–35). New York: Guilford.

Lord, C., & Schopler, E. (1993). TEACCH services for preschool children. In S. L. Harris & J. S. Handelman (Eds.), *Preschool education programs for children with autism* (pp. 87–106). Austin, TX: Pro-Ed.

Lord, C., Schopler, E., & Bristol, M. (1993). Early intervention for children with autism and related developmental disorders. In E. Schopler & G. Mesibov (Eds.), *Preschool issues in autism* (pp. 199–219). New York: Plenum Press.

Magill, J. (1987). *The nature of social deficits of children with autism.* Unpublished doctoral dissertation, University of Alberta, Canada.

Mesibov, G. B. (1986). A cognitive program for teaching social behaviors to verbal autistic adolescents and adults. In E. Schopler & G. Mesibov (Eds.), *Social behavior in autism* (pp. 265–281). New York: Plenum Press.

Mesibov, G., & Stephens, J. (1990). Perceptions of popularity among a group of high-functioning adults with autism. *Journal of Autism and Developmental Disorders, 20,* 33–43.

Odom, S. L., & Hoyson, M., Jamieson, B., & Strain, P. S. (1985). Increasing handicapped preschoolers' peer social interactions: Cross-setting and component analysis. *Journal of Applied Behavior Analysis, 18,* 3–16.

Odom, S. L., & Strain, P. S. (1984). Peer mediated approaches to promoting children's social interaction: A review. *American Journal of Orthopsychiatry, 54,* 544–557.

Ousley, O. Y., & Mesibov, G. B. (1991). Sexual attitudes and knowledge of high-functioning adolescents and adults with autism. *Journal of Autism and Developmental Disorders, 21,* 471–482.

Strain, P. S. (1983). Identification of social skill curriculum targets for severely handicapped children in mainstream preschools. *Applied Research in Mental Retardation, 4,* 369–382.

Strain, P. S., & Kerr, M. M., & Ragland, E. U. (1979). Effects of peer-mediated social initiations and promoting/reinforcement procedures on the social behavior of autistic children. *Journal of Autism and Developmental Disorders, 9,* 41–54.

Van Bourgondien, M. E., & Mesibov, G. B. (1987). Humor in high functioning autistic adults. *Journal of Autism and Developmental Disorders, 17,* 417–424.

Williams, T. (1989). A social skills group for autistic children. *Journal of Autism and Developmental Disorders, 19,* 143–155.

Wohlfberg, P., & Schuler, A. (1992). *Integrated play groups: Resource manual.* San Francisco, CA: San Francisco State University.

IV

Education and Treatment

13

Structured Teaching in the TEACCH System

ERIC SCHOPLER, GARY B. MESIBOV,
and KATHY HEARSEY

INTRODUCTION

The positive outcome of structured special education for youngsters with autism has long been recognized. Already in the late 18th century, Itard (1962) had reported his well-known case study of educating Victor, a boy who was considered autistic. Learning from living with him, Itard reported the importance of daily routines and the use of visual information, as well as the written word, for developing the boy's language skills. More recently, Fischer and Glanville (1970), Halpern (1970), and Graziano (1970) examined the use of structured teaching. Although the studies differed in methodology, diagnosis of children, and composition of educational program, the usefulness of structured teaching persisted.

The reader may wonder why, in light of this much research evidence, consistent use of structured teaching for autism was so slow to develop. A review of the early history suggests an important distinction between professionals who pursued the empirical evidence available and those who preferred other educational interventions. The former included growing numbers who worked with autistic children and formulated their

ERIC SCHOPLER, GARY B. MESIBOV, and KATHY HEARSEY • Division TEACCH, Department of Psychiatry, School of Medicine, University of North Carolina at Chapel Hill, Chapel Hill, North Carolina 27599-7180.

Learning and Cognition in Autism, edited by Eric Schopler and Gary B. Mesibov. Plenum Press, New York, 1995.

research on the basis of that experience, whereas the latter group included mostly professionals with a primary commitment to a theoretical system like psychoanalysis (Bettelheim, 1967), nondirective therapy (Axline, 1947), and other ideological systems.

Among the first empiricists to compare systematically the effect of structure on development in autistic children (Schopler, Brehm, Kinsbourne, & Reichler, 1971), we found that autistic children did better in a structured than in an unstructured teaching situation, and that within their variations in response, children at earlier levels of development needed structure more than children at more advanced levels of functioning. Our study was replicated and expanded to a comparison of three types of educational program by Bartak (1978). He compared three programs: a first emphasizing free play, a second combining permissiveness with some special education techniques, and a third emphasizing skills development. Of these three programs, the third and most structured class was most effective.

During the two decades following our structure study, we have evolved increasingly precise teaching strategies based on the learning problems most common to autism and related pervasive developmental disorders. Moreover, this structured teaching is one of the major principles guiding our TEACCH system, discussed in several volumes of this series.

In this chapter we review autism characteristics for which structured teaching serves as an environmental accommodation, and also how this relates to some of the guiding principles for our TEACCH system. It serves as an expansion of Mesibov, Schopler, & Hearsey (1994), which focuses on structured teaching as an intervention. We describe the four major components of structured teaching, including physical organization, schedules, individual work systems, and learning task organization. We also review the individualized developmental levels for which each component can be adjusted.

AUTISM CHARACTERISTICS

The three most recent volumes of the *Diagnostic and Statistical Manual of Mental Disorders* (DSM-III, 1980; DSM-III-R, 1987; and DSM-IV, 1994) vary in their precise definitions of autism, but all three agree that it is a syndrome involving impairment in social interaction and communication, and restricted interests or activities. These same three features defining autism also include a number of cognitive characteristics not identified in the defining criteria, but perhaps more important for optimum educational intervention with autism.

Current research on the social deficit in autism has generated data showing that people with autism have greater difficulty understanding social and emotional information than control groups. This sociocognitive deficit has been described in part as the children's lack of a "theory of mind" (Baron-Cohen, Leslie, & Frith, 1985; Frith, 1989). This theoretical concept has been operationalized as an impairment in shared meaning for communicative intent and reciprocal interactions. These include problems with functions such as joint social attention; social attachment; shared understanding; taking turns; maintaining conversational topics; and interpreting social cues such as tone or rhythm of voice, facial expression, and gestures (Sigman, 1994). It is not hard to imagine the array of behavior problems produced by such social deficits, especially in a school classroom.

Some of the cognitive-perceptual difficulties in autism include problems of comprehension, poor verbal expression, attention deficit, abstraction difficulties, disorganization, poor memory for nonspecial interests, deficits in auditory processing, problems with generalizing information, and difficulty with change. On the other hand, relative patterns of cognitive strengths have been identified in the special interests, rote memory skills, and in the relative strength in visual processing. Children's strengths in processing visual information have been observed and used educationally in our TEACCH program for over two decades (Schopler, 1993). Moreover, the fact that visuospatial and sensory-motor processes are frequently spared or relatively well functioning has also been documented in several neurological studies (Courchesne, Lincoln, Kilman, & Galambos, 1985; Minshew, Furman, Goldstein, & Payton, 1990).

GUIDING TEACCH PRINCIPLES

Among the primary TEACCH principles (Schopler, 1994), two have most direct bearing on structured teaching. First, the primary purpose of our educational efforts is to improve each individual's adaptation. This is achieved by two different but related educational efforts. One is to improve each individual's level of skill, often using the student's special interests. The second is to modify or structure the environment to accommodate autism deficits. Both are essential components for teaching optimum development in autism.

In order to distinguish between skills to be developed directly and environmental accommodations that may be needed or individualized, diagnostic evaluation and assessment are needed. This is done formally with assessment instruments especially developed for autism. We use the

Childhood Autism Rating Scale (CARS) (Schopler, Reichler, & Renner, 1988) for identifying the features individuals share for the autism diagnosis. With the Psychoeducational Profile (PEP-R) (Schopler, Reichler, Bashford, Lansing, & Marcus, 1990) we assess unique characteristics of sociocognitive problems of learning. Although this is not part of the autism diagnosis, it is essential for any individualized educational program. This assessment is extended to adolescents and adults in order to evaluate their educational needs for vocational placement and living arrangements (Mesibov, Schopler, Schaffer, & Landrus, 1988). In addition to the data provided by these formal assessment procedures, equally important is the informal assessment data provided by informal observations of teachers, parents, and all others familiar with the individual. This information provides the basis for another major principle: providing structured teaching adjusted for the developmental level of autistic individuals at home, at school, or at the work place. Structured teaching is individualized according to particular patterns of emerging skills and relative deficits described earlier.

For students with autism, structured teaching offers learning opportunities not otherwise available. It is not a curriculum taught like communication or social skills and leisure activities, and so on, but it is the framework in which vocational, social, and living skills are taught. Emphasis is on the visual components of structure, because visual processing is a strength through which deficits in auditory processing and other deficits discussed earlier are minimized. The aim is to increase and maximize independent functioning and to reduce the frequent need for teacher correction and reprimands. This in turn has the effect of reducing student–teacher frustrations and communication barriers, which are associated with a large percentage of behavior problems. In addition to preventing behavior problems, different levels of structure can be adapted at every age and developmental level and individual need. Visual structures can also be faded or used by the nonhandicapped population.

THE FOUR MAJOR COMPONENTS OF STRUCTURED TEACHING

Physical Organization

Here we refer to the physical layout of a room or space used for teaching, working, leisure, or living activities. The emphasis is on consistent, visually clear areas and boundaries for specific activities. This enables students to identify and remember activities that take place here and the relationships between activities. Physical organization enhances the ability of students with autism to understand and function effectively in their environments.

Children with autism have difficulty differentiating between dissimilar events. A clearly organized class highlights the specific activities and reinforces the important concepts. For example, if a visually clear location in the room is always used for individualized learning tasks, a child will know what is expected when sent to that spot. Likewise, the child can better understand the relationship between work and play if successful completion of an individual work–study activity is followed consistently by play in a visually distinctive play area.

Visual structure of a classroom helps students with autism or similar learning problems by focusing their attention on the most relevant aspects of their tasks. These students are often distracted by sights and sounds, making it difficult for them to identify or attend to relevant cues. Blocking out as many extraneous sights and sounds as possible can help them focus on the most relevant dimensions of their activities. Dividers can minimize visual and auditory distractions. Bookshelves, window shades over outside distractions, the distribution of work areas around the classroom, and minimal use of decorations on the walls near individual study areas are other ways to minimize distractions. Independent study areas should not be placed near distracting mirrors or windows. It is helpful to have study areas near shelves or storage cabinets so that teaching materials are easily accessible. Built-in cabinets make ideal study area boundaries for this reason. For some students, having desks face blank walls eliminates distractions and helps them focus their attention on the relevant dimensions of their learning activities.

A classroom that is too small or cluttered or lacks adequate storage space is not only uncomfortable, making students crowded and on top of one another, it also makes it difficult for students to identify visual boundaries.

Nonvisual Physical Structure

It is often most productive to use other structures to facilitate learning, depending on the function of space. For example, the location of the bathroom is of critical importance. Toilet training preschoolers or lower functioning students is futile if there is a long distance between their classroom and the toilet. Even if students have independent bathroom skills, valuable classroom time can be more productively used than walking to and from the bathroom with each child. Places in the classroom where students spend independent time, such as play or leisure time, are best located away from exits through which a student may wander off. There are many considerations in arranging the physical structure of a classroom. For example, a classroom with multiple exits to the outside is undesirable for a student in a running off phase. A classroom for intermediate students should not be located on a kindergarten hall. This location complicates appropriate peer socialization opportunities and magnifies the handicaps of the bigger, older students. It must be kept in mind that no physical space is perfect and that most undesirable features can be modified.

Developmental Considerations

Appropriate space or classroom structure varies depending on the age and developmental level of the students. For preschool children, the pertinent learning areas generally include play, individual or independent work, social skills group, outside play, toilet, and self-help skills. For school age students, other areas similar to those for younger children are used, emphasizing the needs of this age group. These include a leisure area, a place for teaching prevocational skills, self-help focusing on domestic skills and grooming, and a snack area to replace the school cafeteria. For adults living in a group home, activities are often divided by rooms much as in any other home, but some visual delineations within the space may still be helpful.

Figure 13-1 shows a preschool play area delineated by a three-dimensional jungle gym with a movable exit. This is effective even before the child learns to recognize two-dimensional space. At that time, the play area can be recognized simply by the two-dimensional lines formed by a carpet. This is a delineation of space similar to that shown for the patio area of a group home in Figure 13-2. Like a carpet, the cement platform designates the picnic area. Related materials such as the table, the cooker, and chairs all support the visual and functional identification of this space.

Physical structure can be used in other contexts with adults. In Figure 13–3 chalk lines identify the space to be cultivated. The plastic cylinders show the area to be dug up first and keep the student from digging up the wrong location. The rod at the beginning of the bed is used to measure the width of the bed every time the cylinders are moved forward, and perpendicular tape fastened to the center of the rod shows the depth for turning the earth. This visual clarification of the gardening space enables the young adult to work independently very quickly.

Fig. 13-1. Physical space: preschool play area

Fig. 13-2. Physical space: group home patio area

Fig. 13-3. Physical structure used for planting a garden

Individualization

The unique needs of each student can be facilitated via the physical structure. For example, one desk might be opposite a blank wall with pieces of tape on the floor indicating where the chair is placed while the students are working. Another study area might be partitioned on two sides with dividers. One side could have shelves with materials for students who can secure their own teaching materials independently. A third desk could be without partition for students who have learned to study or work despite distractions. As students learn to function more independently, the amount and kind of physical structure can be adjusted or faded.

Transition Area

It is one of the defining characteristics of autism that such students tend to show marked distress over change, even in trivial aspects of their environment. Accordingly, we have found it most helpful to identify one area of a classroom as a transition area. A transition area is the location where all the schedules are placed. Students come here to learn what their next activity will be, enabling them to orient to the change. Transition areas are a concrete way mediated through visual schedules for introducing consistency to the many changes that occur during the school day. They are an important segment of the physical structure that prevents and reduces one of the common sources of agitation and behavior problems in autism. Figure 13-4 shows such a transition area with schedules at different levels of functioning.

Schedules

As physical structure helps the student understand the concept of where activities and functions take place, so schedules accommodate difficulties with the concept of when and what the activity will be. Schedules explain to each student which activities will occur and in what sequence. Schedules also help students anticipate and predict activities. Visually clear schedules do not require the same level of memory as do verbal schedule instructions. Autistic people often have a poorly developed sense of time, which makes relatively unpleasant tasks seem to last forever, while enjoyable activities may become unthinkable. Visually clear schedules help students with autism and similar problems for many reasons, including the following:

1. They minimize problems of impaired memory or attention.
2. They reduce problems with time and organization.
3. They compensate for problems with receptive language, which also cause obstacles to following verbal directions.
4. They foster student independence, especially from negative teacher-interactions over the repeated need to know what comes next.
5. They increase self-motivation by readily available visual reminders that "first comes work, then play".

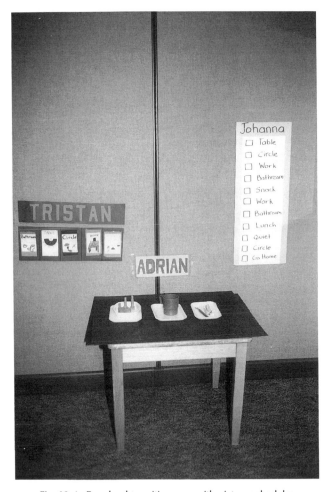

Fig. 13-4. Preschool transition area with picture schedules

As students learn to use schedules, they also learn to follow directions more independently. These are necessary skills for functioning in adult community placements, and schedules can be used more easily when needed in settings for adults.

Types of Schedules

Different time periods can be represented from yearly calendars to schedules of less than an hour, depending on the type of problem involved. In the case of a TEACCH classroom, two types of schedules are usually used simultaneously: the general classroom schedule and the individual student schedule. The overall classroom schedule outlines the day for the entire class. It shows general work times and break times. Table 13-1 is an example of a typical schedule for an intermediate age classroom.

This schedule shows where students are working and when they are engaged in other projects. Work times involve many different activities such as independent prevocational work, individual training for self-help skills, domestic chores, or jobs around the school. These specific activities are listed on the individual student's schedule and may differ for each student.

The general classroom schedule is relatively consistent from week to week except when field trips, special events, or community activities require adjustments. This schedule is usually posted for everyone to see and use. The daily schedule is often revised when students arrive in the morning. The format may be written as in Table 13-1, but some students may not comprehend a written schedule. For them the same schedule can be illustrated with pictures or drawings representing each activity. For example, a picture of a desk or table might depict an individual learning session. Such picture schedules can be arranged from top to bottom or from left to right. By posting both pictures and their word descriptions, the transition from pictures to words is facilitated.

Individual schedules help students understand and remember what to do during the activities listed on the general schedule. These may be created and administered by the teacher or made jointly with the student. Irrespective of who made up the schedule, it is essential that it is meaningful to the student and based on a thoughtful assessment of his or her curriculum needs. The schedule may involve a word or picture in envelopes for each item. The student removes the relevant picture from his

Table 13-1. Intermediate School Day Schedule

Time	Activity
8:30	Student arrival
8:45	Work Session 1
9:45	Work Session 2
10:15	Break
10:30	Leisure learning and school friends
11:00	Work Session 3
11:45	Prepare for lunch
12:00	Lunch
12:30	Outside or gym
1:00	Clean cafeteria tables and floors
1:45	Work Session 4
2:30	Dismissal

schedule envelope, takes it to the place where the activity takes place, and places the picture in a matching pocket or envelope. The student then moves on to the next schedule item. Tristan's schedule in Figure 13-4 shows such a daily work-picture schedule in which each unit is removed from its envelope, taken to the approximate physical space for completion, and then returned to its envelope. The child is then ready to pick up the next scheduled item.

Schedules for Level of Communication

Autistic children span a wide spectrum of reading or communication skills to which schedules can be accommodated. For low functioning nonverbal children the physical object schedule is the simplest. A child may be given a toothbrush as a reminder to go to the toilet area, or a coat as a reminder to go outside. Increasing levels of abstraction can be used with increasing levels of developmental functioning. For nonreaders color codes can be used. These may eventually be replaced by pictures, numbers, or words, depending on the current level of the student's communication. By coupling the schedule with the next level, a gradual transition to more abstract levels can be taught. Figure 13-4 shows examples of three levels of individual schedules. Adrian's schedule is at the simplest level and is represented by objects: a nut and bolt are his first objects and indicate work, followed by a cup for a snack, and toothpaste and a toothbrush for brushing teeth. Each object is taken to the appropriate area.

Tristan's schedule illustrates a communication level in which pictures are used to facilitate the transition to words. Johanna's schedule, at the highest level of communication, illustrates the use of words only. This is similar to a shopping list, in which the items are simply checked off.

The three schedules in Figure 13-4 came from a preschool-age group, but could easily be applied to an older age group by using the same levels of communication functions. This is illustrated by Figure 13-5, which shows a picture schedule for a young adult. However, even in this age group some may need schedules using objects, a color code, pictures, numbers, or words.

Here Mark's schedule goes from breakfast to tooth brushing, barn work, and washing hands. When Mark completes each task, he takes hi schedule card, which reminds him to return to his schedule, and places it in the envelope shown in the upper left corner.

Some schedules require two or three activities to be completed within a time period, while others require only one completed activity before a break or reward. Each individual schedule needs balance, alternating new

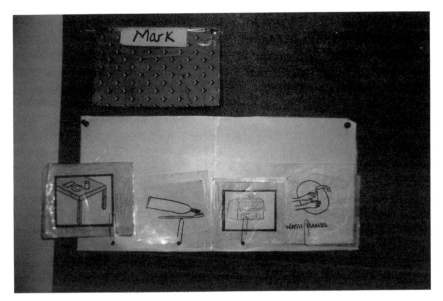

Fig. 13-5. Picture schedule for a young adult

or difficult tasks with more enjoyable or easier tasks. Physically demanding activities are alternated with less active ones.

Work Systems

Whereas a schedule tells each student the sequence of events during
the day, the work system informs students of what to do while in their
independent work areas. This aspect of structured teaching is essential for
students to learn how to work more independently of teacher supervision.
Work systems help children to know what is expected of them during an
activity, ways to organize themselves systematically, and how to complete
their tasks.

Individual work systems communicate at least three important pieces
of information to students. They indicate:

1. The task students are supposed to do, because they can easily see
   the items in each work study box.
2. How much there is to be done. The work-study box and its contents
   are always on the left, with the contents visible.
3. How students will know when they are finished, that is, when the

material in the work-study-area box has been processed and moved to the finish box, always on the right.

This consistency of visually accessible information helps to mitigate a frequent source of tension and behavior problems—the child's sense that difficult or undesirable tasks may last forever. It also provides a sense of closure, which is important to motivate students with autism. The reward is presented after the work is completed. This can be selected beforehand by the student and shown on the work-study table.

Developmental Considerations

Work systems can be designed for students at all levels of developmental function depending on a graduated use of symbolic complexity. At lower levels of functioning objects are used directly. The next levels involve color coding, pictures, numbers, and written words. Three examples of different developmental levels are shown below.

Adrian's work system (Fig. 13-6) is a left-to-right work system with a finished box on the right. Adrian uses physical objects corresponding to his

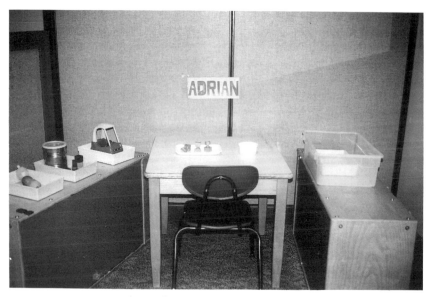

Fig. 13-6. Left-to-right work system

schedule shown in Figure 13-4. Figure 13-6 shows that the first work-study item is the plastic nuts and bolts, a piece of which was used as his object-schedule and transition piece. The next item involves two fine-motor exercises, assembling beads, and then the slightly more difficult task of placing blocks through a block-shaped opening. As he completes each task, the materials are placed in the finished box to his right. The fourth work-study container shows the toy car for a play time reward.

Tristan's work plan (Fig. 13-7) is also shown as the fourth item of his horizontal work-picture schedule item labeled "work" on Figure 13-4. Tristan follows a color-matching work system with a finished shelf to his right. This involves four work-study containers on the left that are color coded with different primary colored circles. He also has a work schedule over his desk, which shows him the sequence for completing each basket. After completion of the first work-study basket, he places the circle in the envelope on the basket, places the basket on the finished shelf, and goes on to the next basket.

Figure 13-8 shows Johanna's work system at the level of using numbers. Johanna matches the number cards to the corresponding numbered container. Her first container holds a coloring task in which she learns the word for each color while practicing control in coloring circles.

Fig. 13-7. Color-matching work system

Fig. 13-8. Work system using numbers

Individualization

Each of the work-system examples shown above can be individualized according to the educational needs and communication level of each student. Jigsaw puzzles could involve more pieces without insets, or be replaced entirely by different learning tasks. The main limiting factor is the teacher's knowledge of each student's learning needs and how best to translate these to fitting a work-study system. This same system can be adapted to adults living in the community or a group home. Figure 13-9 shows a work system for learning hygiene tasks. It also goes from left to right, beginning with brushing teeth and moving through sharing and applying deodorant.

Task Organization

Task organization is the fourth major component of structured teaching. The work system provides the student with visually clear information on what the learning task is about, how many things are to be done, how many things have already been completed, and the outcome to expect. Thus, the organization of materials provides visually clear guidelines on the positional relationship between the parts and task completion. Such

Fig. 13-9. Work system for hygeine tasks

jigs (or blueprints) are helpful to our students because they offer instructions in a way easiest for them to understand. They clarify task requirements, sequences, relevant concepts, and other important guidelines. A jig is an essential tool for teaching students with autism to function in community-based settings without direct adult supervision, just as clear directions are necessary to help nonhandicapped adults assemble complex Christmas presents.

An important advantage of appropriately designed jigs is that they are mechanisms for teaching our students to look for instructions rather than follow their general tendency to complete a task the way they think it should be done. Equally noteworthy, jigs, like the other components of structured teaching, can be adapted to different levels of developmental functions, and can also be individualized according to the needs of each student. As in the other structure components, these can involve objects, pictures, colors, numbers, or words.

Functional Levels of Jigs

Three different developmental levels are shown below. Figure 13-10 shows the first item in Tristan's work session shown on Figure 13-6. Here he learns how to match crayons with their appropriate colors and places

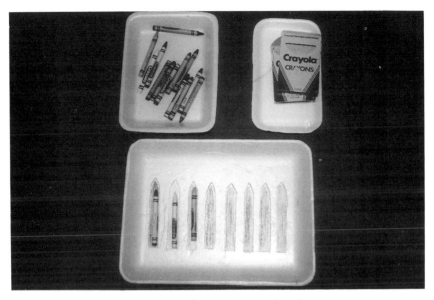

Fig. 13-10. Jig for sorting crayons by color

them in a crayon box. The jig has indented colored crayon molds, which help him to sort crayons in the right sequence.

Figure 13-11 shows the jig for Johanna's first task, shown in Figure 13-4. Like Tristan, she is learning not only to match colors but also the word for each color. A similar task organization can be used for adults learning housekeeping tasks.

Figure 13-12 shows a word-picture jig for the first step of baking bread. From left to right the cards depict, "Pour one cup warm water," "Pour one tablespoon of molasses," and then "Pour two packs of yeast." The appropriate materials are also provided from left to right.

At a somewhat more casual level, Figure 13-13 shows a jig for sorting dark from light laundry.

Individualization

Individual variations in these jigs are easily made depending on each student's educational assessment and curriculum requirements.

In the first example, crayons could be replaced by other colors or be presented without the mold. The second example could use different shapes and words. In the third, bread baking could be shown in a similar

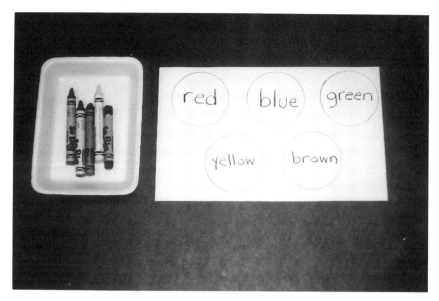

Fig. 13-11. Jig for sorting crayons by color and name

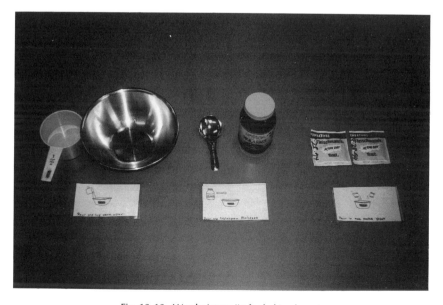

Fig. 13-12. Word-picture jig for baking bread

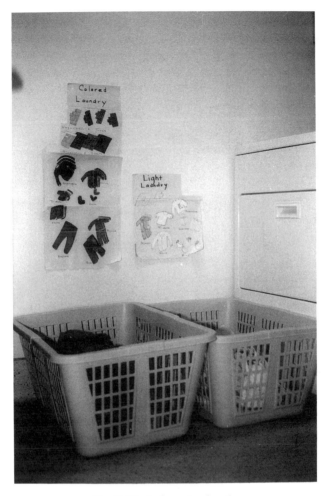

Fig. 13-13. Jig for sorting laundry

fashion for any other step in the baking process, or it could be replaced by sandwich preparation, doing dishes, or any other activity especially relevant for a particular student. Jigs usually go from left to right, but can also be presented up and down. They indicate a sequence to follow and show the completed task.

We have discussed both developmental variations and individualization; however, it should be kept in mind that with these variations, some aspects of task organization remain constant.

Constructive Routines

We have discussed the four main components of structured teaching, which represent environmental accommodations to expressions of a child's autism deficits. All four of these encourage a productive use of the autistic student's affinity for routines, and are consistent enough to compensate for the student's problem solving deficiencies, but flexible enough to change or fade as best helps each child.

The physical structure provides routines for location of function and activity. Schedules offer routines for sequence and activity changes. Work systems help to form habits for learning tasks, leisure activities, and routines for going from left to right or up and down. As most work systems show the reward after task completion, they also help establish a routine of "first work, then play." These routines are useful not only in the classroom and at home, but they also transfer to the workplace and other residential environments.

Left to Right and Top to Bottom are other routines with long-lasting and far-reaching consequences. Our students are frequently immobilized when confronting new tasks with unfamiliar demands. Learning to approach all assignments in a left to right or top to bottom sequence gives them a systematic approach applicable to a multitude of tasks such as collating, washing dishes, mopping floors, sorting, reading, writing, and so on.

Most children with autism develop stereotypical ways of approaching certain tasks. These are remarkably steadfast, although not generally productive. For example, one child might need to touch each window five times before entering a school bus. Because students with autism so often develop and follow routines in their activities, it is most useful to use this tendency in a positive way. By proactively developing productive and flexible routines for them in important situations, their routines can be changed from a distracting liability to a valuable asset.

OTHER STRUCTURED TEACHING CONCEPTS

In the preceding section, our emphasis was on the four main components of structured teaching. They also illustrate part of our first guiding principle, the educational aim of maximizing each child's adaptation either by environmental accommodation to the child's deficits or by teaching skills directly. These structural components represent primarily environmental accommodations to deficits. We have emphasized these components because they are too often ignored or casually improvised. They are important with autism and related communication handicaps because they reduce and prevent behavior problems. At the same time, they promote the students' independent functioning.

Here we review the second and equally important part of our goal, to increase adaptation by directly improving each student's skill level and making the classroom environment work. The concepts discussed here can also be found in the behavior modification literature. However, in our application these are subordinated to coordination with structured teaching. They include providing directions for tasks, offering prompts, and delivering reinforcers.

Directions

Directions explaining to students how to complete their tasks can be offered both verbally and nonverbally. The deciding mode of teacher communication should be what communicates most clearly to each student. For verbal directions this often means using minimal language. For example, the direction, "I want you to finish putting all these nuts and bolts together, and then when you finish, you can go over to the play area and choose a toy to play with" increases the chances many students will be confused. One could as easily say, "First finish nuts and bolts, then play." For students with difficulty processing language this telegraphic statement is more likely to be understood than the longer sentences more commonly used by teachers. Directions can also be given with gestures and contextual cues, facilitated by the visual structures discussed above.

Prompts

Teacher prompts can be helpful, especially when teaching new tasks. Our students learn more effectively when they accurately complete a task, because the gain in competence not only reinforces the learning process, but also the student's sense of confidence. Different types of prompts can be useful depending on the level of communication. Such prompts are a behavioral teaching aid, but do not replace the approach described in the TEACCH Communications Curriculum described by Watson, Lord, Schaffer, and Schopler (1989).

Physical prompts are used to guide student actions toward the completion of a task. For example, the teacher might assist a child in pulling up her pants after using the bathroom. A verbal prompt might remind a child with language to put a napkin in his lunch tray.

Accompanying verbal directions with gestures as prompts often increases students' understanding. A teacher might point to the nuts and bolts from a work task and then to the play area while giving the direction, "First work, then play." Before prompting it is important to have the student's attention. This does not mean that eye contact has to be established. Some of our students signal their attention by body orientation, a verbal response, or by stopping other activities. It is helpful to know how each student signals attention and to be sure it has been attained before delivering the prompt.

Prompts can also be gestural. For example, instead of telling the student to get a napkin, the teacher may point to the empty space on the student's lunch tray. Modeling or demonstrating how something is done is another type of prompt. The teacher saying "Hi" to a visitor can be a prompt to greet someone.

Teachers should be systematic in their use of prompts. If prompts are not offered clearly and consistently before a student responds incorrectly, they will be ineffective. For example, if a student is having difficulty adding the correct amount of detergent while washing dishes, the prompt is needed before an error is made.

Teachers also must be conscious that they might be prompting their students unintentionally. In these situations teacher and student positioning in the learning areas of the classroom can be crucial. Correct responses are frequently relayed to students by the slightest movement of the head or eyes of the teacher. Some students generally referred to as prompt-dependent will repeatedly glance at their teacher after each step of a task for validation and reassurance. While working with these students, teachers should position themselves beside or behind the students instead of in front of them. Thoughtful positioning minimizes the number of unintended prompts and cues.

Reinforcers

Reinforcers are another way of structuring tasks for students with autism. Most of us are motivated to work because of a combination of praise from others, intrinsic satisfaction, and remuneration. Students with autism are not always motivated by these. Teachers must discover what is motivating for their students and then teach them to work for these incentives. For example, if a teacher learns that a student is fascinated by sandpaper, then a student's work times can be arranged so that sandpaper can be used in the workshop area after work is completed. For this student, the sandpaper is a meaningful and more motivating reward than the motivators traditionally used with nonhandicapped students.

Reinforcers can include many different items or activities. Some students are motivated by food or toys that they especially like; others are motivated by preferred activities. Some students are able to earn money or tokens throughout the day and trade them for reinforcers later on. Some of our students are satisfied simply by completing their work accurately. These students need fewer external reinforcements as long as they are given social reinforcement, a meaningful way of understanding when their work is successfully completed. Whenever possible, the type of reinforcer should be a natural consequence of the activity. For example, if making requests is being reinforced, the natural reward is the requested item. Praise and social reinforcers always should accompany more tangible rewards for students with autism. Pairing social and tangible reinforcers increases the desirability of personal contact for these students and makes people greater sources of reinforcement in the future.

Reinforcements must be used systematically if they are to be effective teaching tools. The frequency as well as the type of reinforcement should be individualized; some students need continuous reinforcement, whereas others need it only intermittently. Reinforcements should immediately follow the behavior or skill being learned, at least initially, so that the relationship between the two is clear to the student. A teacher can determine if the type and frequency of reinforcement are effective by assessing student interest and progress in the behavior being reinforced.

SUMMARY AND CONCLUSIONS

We have reviewed the characteristics of autism and some of the special needs they present for both learning and teaching. From our 25 years of research and experience as a statewide program, we have reviewed some of the viable and enduring guiding principles over that period. Structured teaching, one of the most important of these, is a system for organizing space, change of activities with schedules, work-study systems to facilitate the learning task process, and material organization to promote student independence. Focusing on the strengths characteristically found in autism and related developmental disorders—skills with visual processing, reliance on rote memory routines, and special interests—structured teaching can be applied usefully in the classroom, at home, with leisure activities, and in the workplace. Structured teaching can be adapted to different levels of developmental function and according to individual needs. It has played an important role in overcoming or neutralizing autism deficits, preventing behavior problems, and promoting independence (Schopler, Mesibov, & Baker, 1982). For most people with autism to achieve their potential for community living and effective functioning, structured teaching strategies should be an integral part of their educational environment.

REFERENCES

American Psychiatric Association. (1980). *Diagnostic and statistical manual of mental disorders* (3rd ed.). Washington, DC: Author.
American Psychiatric Association. (1987). *Diagnostic and statistical manual of mental disorders* (3rd ed., rev.). Washington, DC: Author.
American Psychiatric Association (1994). *Diagnostic and statistical manual* (4th ed.). Washington, DC: Author.
Axline, V. M. (1947). *Play therapy.* New York: Houghton Mifflin.
Baron-Cohen, S., Leslie, A. M., & Frith, U. (1985). Does the autistic child have a theory of mind? *Cognition, 21,* 37–46.
Bartak, l. (1978). Educational approaches. In M. Rutter & E. Schopler (Eds.), *Autism: A reappraisal of concepts and treatment* (pp. 423–438). New York: NY: Plenum Press.
Bettelheim, B. (1967). *The empty fortress: Infantile autism and the birth of the self.* London: Collier-Macmillan.
Courchesne, E., Lincoln, A. J., Kilman, B. A., & Galambos, R. (1985). Event-related brain potential correlates of the processing of novel visual and auditory information in autism. *Journal of Autism and Developmental Disorders, 15,* 55–76.
Fischer, I., & Glanville, B. (1970). Programmed teaching of autistic children. *Archives of General Psychiatry, 23,* 90–94.
Frith, U. (1989). *Autism: Explaining the enigma.* Oxford: Blackwell.
Graziano, A. M. (1970). A group-treatment approach to multiple problem behaviors of autistic children. *Exceptional Children, 36,* 765–770.
Halpern, W. I. (1970). The schooling of autistic children: Preliminary findings. *American Journal of Orthopsychiatry, 40,* 665–671.
Itard, J. G. (1962). *The wild boy of Aveyron.* New York: Appleton-Century-Crofts.
Mesibov, G. B., Schopler, & Hearsey, K. A. (1994). Structured teaching. In E. Schopler & G. B. Mesibov (Eds.), *Behavioral Issues in Autism* (pp. 195–207). New York: Plenum Press.
Mesibov, G. B., Schopler, E., Schaffer, B., & Landrus, R. (1988). *Adult and adolescent psychoeducational profile (AAPEP).* Austin, TX: Pro-Ed.
Minshew, N. J., Furman, J. M., Goldstein, G., & Payton, J. B. (1990). The cerebellum in autism: Central role or epiphenomenon? *Neurology, 40*(1), 173.
Schopler, E. (1989). Principles for directing both educational treatment and research. In C. Gillberg (Ed.), *Diagnosis and treatment of autism* (pp. 167–183). New York, NY: Plenum Press.
Schopler, E.(1993). Neurobiologic correlates in the classification and study of autism. In S. H. Broman & J. Graham (Eds.), *Atypical cognitive deficits in developmental disorders: Implications for brain function* (pp. 87–100). Hillsdale, NJ: Erlbaum.
Schopler, E. (1994). Behavioral priorities for autism and related developmental disorders. In Schopler, E., & Mesibov, G. B. (Eds.), *Behavioral Issues in Autism.* New York: Plenum Press.
Schopler, E., Brehm, S., Kinsbourne, M., & Reichler, R. J. (1971). The effect of treatment structure on development of autistic children. *Archives of General Psychiatry, 24,* 415–421.
Schopler, E., Mesibov, G. B., & Baker, A. (1982). Evaluation of treatment for autistic children and their parents. *Journal of the American Academy of Child Psychiatry, 21,* 262–267.

Schopler, E., Mesibov, DeVellis, R. F., & Short, A. (1981). Treatment outcome for autistic children and their families. In P. Mittler (Ed.), *Frontiers of knowledge in mental retardation: Social, educational, and behavioral aspects* (pp. 293–301). Baltimore, MD: University Park Press.

Schopler, E., Reichler, R. J., Bashford, A., Lansing, M. D., & Marcus, L. M. (1990). *Psychoeducational profile-revised (PEP-R)*. Austin, TX: Pro-Ed.

Schopler, E., Reichler, R. J., & Renner, B. R. (1988). *The childhood autism rating scale (CARS)*. Los Angeles, CA: Western Psychological.

Sigman, M. (1994). What are the core deficits in autism? In S. H. Broman, & J. Grafman (Eds.), *Atypical cognitive deficits in developmental disorders: Implication for brain function.* (pp. 139–157). Hillsdale, NJ: Erlbaum.

Watson, L., Lord, C., Schaffer, B., & Schopler, E. (1989). *Teaching spontaneous communication to autistic and developmentally handicapped children.* Austin, TX: Pro-Ed.

Cognitive Education of
Young Children with Autism
An Application of Bright Start

GRETCHEN BUTERA and H. CARL HAYWOOD

INTRODUCTION

Autism presents persistent and frustrating problems in socialization and learning. Since the initial description of the syndrome by Kanner (1943), the literature on the effects of treatment and educational programs has been pessimistic with respect to long-term prognosis. Recent authors described the particular learning challenges and specific cognitive processing deficits that characterize children with autism and this more adequate description has led to the promise of more effective remedial procedures (see Schopler, 1987, 1989 regarding Treatment and Education of Autistic and Related Communication-Handicapped Children).

Tactics for changing the behavior of children with autism have been based heavily on an operant conditioning paradigm. Careful control of stimulus presentation and one-to-one teaching methods were first proposed for treatment of children with autism by Ferster (1961). Short-term gains from these teaching methods are often impressive, but they may not provide sufficient opportunity for social and language learning such as

GRETCHEN BUTERA • Department of Special Education, West Virginia University, Morgantown, West Virginia 26506-6122. H. CARL HAYWOOD • Peabody College, Vanderbilt University, Nashville, Tennessee 37203.

Learning and Cognition in Autism, edited by Eric Schopler and Gary B. Mesibov. Plenum Press, New York, 1995.

would occur in group instruction (Strain, 1983). Furthermore, they often fail to produce generalized treatment effects (R. Koegel, L. Koegel, & O'Neill, 1989), and they consume too much of a teacher's time (Myles & Simpson, 1990). Behavioral interventions focused on "pivotal behavior" (Koegel, et. al., 1989) that could restrict generalization of treatment effects may address some of these issues. The larger question is not whether the operant conditioning paradigm has specific problems that can be repaired, but whether it indeed provides the most productive conceptual system from which to design effective treatment. The paradigm is limited in several ways, including the following: (a) the operant conditioning paradigm deals with behavior rather than with the psychological roots of behavior; (b) stimulus control of behavior frequently does not generalize from setting to setting, from person to person, or beyond the contingent-reinforcement situations in which it was established; (c) by not taking into account the cognitive processing deficits frequently seen in children with autism, it does not offer a basis for their remediation. It is this last problem that constitutes the emphasis of the remainder of this chapter.

Wholistic perspectives on child development that acknowledge the integrated fashion in which the cognitive, linguistic, behavioral, and social affective domains develop are helpful for designing treatment programs. While we focus in this chapter on the *cognitive* processing deficits children with autism frequently display, we use a rather loose definition of *cognitive* and acknowledge the integrated nature of development. We mean to propose that theories of cognitive development provide a useful perspective from which interventions can be designed to treat cognitive processing deficits. The difficulties that children with autism encounter in thinking, perceiving, and problem solving can be directly addressed by activities designed specifically to develop cognitive processes that are necessary for optimal growth and development. It is useful, then, to examine commonly observed characteristics of children with autism, and then to address the question of the modifiability of deficient cognitive processes that may underlie these characteristics.

CHARACTERISTICS OF CHILDREN WITH AUTISM

Attention/Arousal Deficits

The parents of children with autism often describe them as being uncomfortable with human contact and interaction and nearly impossible to console in contrast to normally developing infants. Infants with autism are notoriously passive, staring into space while their normally developing peers are actively engaged in a visual, auditory, and tactile exploration of their environment. Taken together, these two characteristics, withdrawal from human contact and extreme passivity, suggest that children with autism are, from the beginning of their lives, both *less responsive* and *less differentially response* to external stimuli than are other children of the same age.

Arousal/attention deficits may be critical factors related to this lack of responsivity (e.g., Goldstein & Lancy, 1985; Ornitz & Ritvo, 1976; Rimland, 1964; Wetherby & Gaines, 1982). The central concept is that children with autism do not lack intellectual ability—or at least intellectual potential; rather, they do not process information adequately because the structures and neural networks involved in arousal, probably in the reticular activating system, malfunction because of genetic predisposition, disease, or trauma. Neurological studies of persons with autism support this view. For example, Yuweiler, Geller, and Ritvo (1975) found that children with autism have elevated serum levels of the neurotransmitter serotonin (implicated in arousal). Kennard (1960) found that their EEG patterns are more readily desynchronized. Koontz and Cohen (1981) found that persons with autism show several cardiovascular phenomena that are similar to those of nonautistic persons who are actively screening out sensory input, for example, when they are concentrating on some focused mental task. For children with autism, a low level of arousal seems to correspond to a low level of information processing. The effects of this low-level processing are cumulative in that additional disabilities result when people fail to engage their environment and to derive information effectively from it. Hence, children with autism fail to develop the knowledge base necessary for effective thinking, structured perception, learning, and problem solving because they do not attend initially to what information is available to be processed.

Perhaps because of arousal/attention deficits, children with autism fail to develop the processes that allow them to select the relevant features of a stimulus in learning tasks. Teachers and clinicians find, for example, that children are responding to an inadvertent hand gesture on the part of the teacher rather than to the stimulus of a written vocabulary word. Subsequently, students fail to "learn" when another teacher, omitting the hand gesture, asks the child the vocabulary word. Similarly, sorting tasks that require children to attend to more than one stimulus cue, such as putting various housekeeping toys away, for example, require children to attend to various aspects of each item. Kitchen items are put in the kitchen; clothing is hung, and blocks are put somewhere else entirely. From a Piagetian view, for children to adequately perform such tasks, they must not only attend to the relevant features of each item, they also must abstract a general rule about the relationship between each item (Ginsburg & Opper, 1978).

Haywood (1987a, 1989; Haywood, Tzuriel, & Vaught, 1992) has suggested a sharp distinction between "intelligence" and "cognitive processes." According to this distinction, intelligence is largely determined genetically and resistant to modification, but cognitive processes must be acquired (through learning, often with teaching), and are quite readily modifiable. This distinction between fluid and cognition is similar to Cattell's (1963) and Horn's (1972) distinction between fluid and crystallized intelligence. These authors attempted to group together those aspects of intelligence that seem to be constant and relatively immutable, and to contrast them with those that appear to be modifiable with experience. Haywood's distinction incorporates that contrast and adds the notion that the modifiable components are acquired through successive interactions with the environment.

From a cognitive-education perspective, children with autism do not necessarily lack intelligence; they lack adequately developed cognitive processes. Feuerstein (e.g., Feuerstein & Rand, 1974; Feuerstein, Rand, Hoffman, & Miller, 1980) has elaborated the essentially Piagetian constructivist notion that every child has the developmental task of *constructing* a personal logic system that can then serve that child as a set of tools for perceiving, ordering, understanding, and ultimately manipulating his or her world (see also Paour, 1992; Piaget, 1952). If a personal set of thinking and learning tools has to be constructed by every child, then it is especially important that children have available to them the means with which to take in information efficiently, relate incoming to stored knowledge, and reorganize their knowledge structures to reveal new levels of comprehension—and thus develop new tools for understanding and for learning. To the extent that their perceptual and perceptual-cognitive processes, being impaired, keep them from these tool-building activities, the performance of children with autism is increasingly deficient, creating the illusion of basically low intelligence and leading to cumulative deficiencies in knowledge and i the cognitive (and consequently motivational; see Haywood, 1992) tools of learning.

Social Deficits

Another critical feature of autism commonly mentioned in the literature is difficulty in processing social meaning. Social meaning in this sense includes both the ability to make sense out of information that is specifically social, such as facial expressions and voice intonations, and the ability to recognize and respond appropriately to more complex interpersonal data, such as the efforts of other children to initiate play (Lord, 1985; Rutter, 1983). Infants with autism have difficulty making and maintaining eye contact, and that foretells lifelong reluctance to engage in social interaction. Some of the earliest indications of autism include deficits in the earliest forms of social behavior, such as looking at or imitating caregivers. Such "social responses" are precursors to the nonlinguistic and linguistic strategies that normally developing infants use to communicate. The etiology of these difficulties in autistic persons remains unclear (but may indeed be related to the perceptual-cognitive difficulties discussed in the preceding paragraph). Lovaas, Koegel, Simmons, and Long (1973) suggested that, because of attentional and arousal deficits, children with autism respond to only a limited proportion of the stimuli that at any moment are available to them, and that objects or persons that usually acquire reinforcing qualities for young children thus fail to do so. This is a conceptually interesting blend of perceptual-cognitive etiology and its subsequent elaboration according to behaviorist principles—an approach that could be promising.

Communication Deficits

Children with autism are usually delayed in their sensorimotor development, most notably in the onset of speech. This deficiency leads to a pronounced deficiency in interpersonal communication, a difficulty that contributes to social deficits and continues to characterize persons with autism throughout their lives. Communication difficulty also constitutes a cognitive deficiency at the information-input level, because it limits the information that may be received, and that, in turn, limits the information available for cognitive processing.

Children with autism characteristically display a general delay in the acquisition of almost all language skills. Difficulties in expressive language are commonly one of the earliest and greatest sources of concern for most parents (DeMeyer, 1979). In addition, however, Bartak, Rutter, and Cox (1975) found that children with autism show greater deficits in general comprehension of language than children who have language disorders and are matched on chronological age, nonverbal IQ, and overall language skills. Lord (1985) and Schopler and Mesibov (1985) questioned whether this language difficulty is the primary deficit in children with autism or whether it represents some more central cognitive or social dysfunction. Regardless of the etiology of the language deficits of children with autism, it is apparent that deficits in symbolic representation, difficulties in ascertaining social meanings, and malfunctioning of the arousal/attentional mechanisms, interact. Language comprehension is not a discrete, self-contained process but the end product of a series of linguistic, cognitive, and social functions. The pervasive dysfunction resulting in difficulties in language comprehension requires teaching procedures that are highly individualized and especially intense.

Motivational Deficits

Children with autism are difficult to teach in part because they seem to have difficulties in motivation. Indeed it seems that frequently they choose not to perform a learning task more times than they are unable to perform the same task. Such children respond with anger when they are interrupted from their far more (apparently) enjoyable self-stimulatory behavior. They are more likely to engage in rocking, hand flapping, or head-banging than interact the environment in ways that promote optimal growth and development. Repeated experiences of failure due to the severity of their disability may further depress motivation. Learned helplessness (Koegel & Egel, 1979) may result when children conclude that rewards and responding are independent. Learned helplessness is described as an individual's being very slow or failing to respond to learning interactions (Miller & Seligman, 1975). This described behavior is very similar to that of many children with autism as they fail to engage in the learning environment. The motivation to learn requires that an individual assume reasonable risks by responding to learning tasks; children with autism are unwilling to do so, perhaps in part because of their learned helplessness. When this lowered motivation combines with the difficulties children with autism have in attending, the rate and acquisition of learning content or cognitive processes is quite depressed.

Theories about cognitive development have led in recent years to the development and use of instructional programs that focus on cognitive or "thinking" skills (Nickerson, 1988–1989). These programs generally describe students as "apprentice learners" (Collins, Brown, & Newman, 1989) who participate in collaborative learning activities as teachers model, demonstrate, and discuss mental strategies used in task completion. Although the use of such approaches is not common with children who have disabilities, this application has increased (Resnick, 1987). It is our contention that a cognitive approach may be especially suitable for children with autism, because instruction of this sort focuses on cognitive-processing skills children with autism may fail to develop without instructional procedures targeted to assist development.

BRIGHT START

Bright Start (previously known as Cognitive Curriculum for Young Children, or CCYC; Haywood, Brooks, & Burns, 1986, 1992) addresses the needs of those children who, because of environmental circumstances of disabilities, are at risk for academic failure in the primary grades. This curriculum is designed to help children develop those thinking, perceiving, and problem-solving abilities that underlie most academic and social learning. Bright Start's authors assume that what is commonly considered intelligent behavior is the result of a succession of transactions involving native ability (intelligence), learned processes of thought (cognition), and successive life experiences. Cognitive processes are taught in Bright Start in a systematic fashion. Fundamental cognitive processes, including comparison, classification, and class inclusion, relations (including seriation, transitivity, space, time, number, causality) conservation, and role taking, as well as strategies such as systematic search, analytic problem solving, and self-regulation, are taught through a series of cognitively focused lessons presented in seven cognitive "small-group" units of the curriculum.

Goals of Bright Start

Children's development of representational thought and accession to the developmental stage of concrete operations are important goals of Bright Start. In this regard, Bright Start is similar to other curricula based at least in part on Piaget's descriptions of cognitive development (e.g., Hohmann, Banet, & Weikart, 1979). Bright Start differs from other cognitive curricula in its emphasis on metacognitive development (thinking about one's own thinking, learning to generate, rather than merely to learn, cognitive strategies). In Bright Start, children are encouraged to reflect on their own thought processes, evaluate them, and consider whether alternative strategies might be equally effective. Metacognitive emphasis, from this perspective, leads to cognitive development and more effective learning.

The stated goals of Bright Start are as follows:

1. To enhance the development of basic cognitive functions, especially those necessary to accede to the stage of concrete operations
2. To identify and remediate deficient cognitive functions
3. To develop task-intrinsic motivation
4. To develop representational thought

5. To enhance learning effectiveness and readiness for school learning
6. To prevent unnecessary or inappropriate special education placement

Bright Start has three distinctive components: (1) a specified theoretical structure; (2) the mediational teaching style; (3) cognitive "small group" units, a series of lessons sharply centered on a specific participation program. The theoretical structure is provided in writing as well as in teacher-training workshops, and is supplemented with a number of focused papers on such topics as mediational teaching, intrinsic motivation, cognitive functions, and behavior management. Cognitive small-group lessons are provided in a teacher manual, with specific instructions for each lesson, but with room for the creativity of teachers themselves. There is a manual for parent participation, as well as a series of in-home activities that extend the classroom learning to the home.

Theoretical Base

Bright Start is based on four "sets" of theory about the intellectual and cognitive development of children. These include Haywood's *transactional perspective on development* (Haywood & Switzky, 1986a, 1992; Haywood et al., 1992); Piaget's *structural approach to cognitive development* (Piaget, 1952, 1960; Piaget & Inhelder, 1969); Vygotsky's emphasis on the *social context of cognitive acquisition* (Vygotsky, 1929, 1962, 1978); and Feuerstein's theory of *structural-cognitive modifiability* (Arbitman-Smith, Haywood, & Bransford, 1984; Feuerstein, 1970; Feuerstein & Rand, 1974).

The transactional perspective includes a view of human ability as multifaceted (contains many kinds of abilities) and multidetermined (the result of genetic, environmental, and personal transactions). Haywood and Switzky (1992) insisted both that learning ability (potential) can be enhanced by educational procedures and that it is specifically cognitive processes (rather than intelligence itself) that grow as a result of educational experiences. They asserted that "bad" experience does not destroy intelligence (short of actual destruction of brain cells), and that "good" experience does not create intelligence. According to the transactional perspective, cognitive education can help children to acquire fundamental and generalizable logic modes, which then help them to gain access to the intelligence they have and to apply their intelligence effectively to the tasks of perceiving their world and imposing structure on it, thinking systematically and consistently, learning, and problem solving. Cognitive processes and the personality trait of task-intrinsic motivation are said to develop in a transactional, mutually reinforcing fashion, so that as children become more cognitively competent they increasingly derive pleasure from the very activity of doing mental work: looking for and taking in new information; operating upon or "processing" that information; and developing novel expressions of the products of information processing. Increases in intrinsic motivation lead in turn to increased exploratory behavior, preference for novelty and complexity over familiarity and simplicity, and ultimately to greater learning and even greater cognitive competence. Behavior that results from a task-intrinsic motivational orientation such as exploration, novelty-seeking, and reasonable risk-taking is viewed as especially conducive to the acquisition of effective cognitive processes. Thus, procedures that promote the development of intrinsic motivation, especially in learning contexts, are essential in a cognitive classroom (Haywood, 1992; Haywood et al., 1986; Haywood & Burke, 1977).

Bright Start's authors acknowledge and emphasize the importance of the social environment for young children's acquisition of fundamental cognitive processes. Vygotsky (1978) held that much important cognitive learning must take place in a social context, and described interactions between children and adults that help children become more effective learners in a variety of ways: by reaching a better understanding of some of the task requirements of new learning; by acquiring a richer impression of the importance and excitement of learning; by enhancing their self-concepts as learners; and by experiencing success at learning. Teachers who use this curriculum adopt a teaching style that builds upon Vygotsky's description of the *zone of proximal development* (ZPD). The ZPD is defined as "the distance between the actual development as determined through problem solving under adult guidance or collaboration with more capable peers" (Vygotsky, 1978, p. 86).

Piaget's constructivism is clearly evident in Bright Start. If every child must construct his or her own personal logic system (a set of "understandings about the order of events in the world, a set of thinking habits, and a set of operations for doing cognitively important things), it is clear that some children require much more help than others. Early education can be especially helpful in this highly personal enterprise, because it is a time when individual differences can be more easily incorporated into classrooms than is possible later, with larger classes and more urgent content curricula. Bright Start's authors have emphasized as well Piaget's observations that cognitive development is *sequential* (in the sense that it is cumulative, with later acquisition depending on qualitatively new understanding based on prior accumulation of lower level knowledge). They derived from Piaget's observations also a strong emphasis on the specific criteria of concrete operatory thought (e.g., comparison, classification, conservation, seriation, and quantitative, spatial, and temporal relations) as the identifiable cognitive tools that need to be in place in order for children to accomplish the academic content learning of the primary and early elementary grades.

The remainder of the theoretical basis of Bright Start is taken directly from Feuerstein's Theory of Structural Cognitive Modifiability (SCM; see Arbitman-Smith et al., 1984; Feuerstein et al., 1980; Haywood et al., 1986, 1992). SCM assumes that there is a finite number (not yet known) of processes of logical thought that are so fundamental that they are required and applied in the understanding and learning of an infinite variety of contents. A further assumption is that these logic modes must be acquired by every child, in two quite different ways. Children learn some basic logical thinking through *direct exposure* (unmediated, direct interactions with their environment), that is, without any other person helping them. The other way in which they learn cognitively important things is through *mediated learning experience* (MLE). MLE refers to the manner in which parents, or any more cognitively competent person, help children to understand the broader, generalized meaning of their experiences. This is not simply a matter of information giving; it involves a particular style of adult–child interaction.

Mediational Teaching

Characteristics of mediated learning experiences include at least the following:

Intentionality: The adult intends to use the interaction to produce a change in the child.

Transcendence: The desired change must go beyond the content of the immediate situation toward generalizable rules, concept, or habit.

Communication of Meaning and Purpose: Every encounter has specific meaning and can be used to a generalized purpose, which should not be secret.

Mediation of Feelings of Competence: The child receives feedback on the outcomes of behavior (correct or incorrect, good or not so good), plus specification of the precise correct/incorrect elements (what was so good, or not).

Regulation of Behavior: The adult inhibits the child's impulsive responding and unblocks available but "unforthcoming" responses.

Shared Participation: The emphasis is on the adult-child partnership in seeking cognitive growth for the child, and the role of each participant in that quest is specified.

According to Feuerstein, almost any interaction between a child and an adult has the potential to be a MLE, to the extent that it fulfills at least the first three of these characteristics.

For a wide variety of reasons, many children do not get all the MLE they need in order to develop their cognitive processes and thus their intellectual potential. Reasons may include the absence of parent(s); low cognitive developmental and education levels of parents; poverty and social discrimination; emotional disturbance in the parents; or catastrophic conditions such as war, famine, and abrupt cultural transplantation. Another reason for getting less MLE than one needs (our interpretation, not necessarily Feuerstein's) is that the question of *how much MLE is enough* centers on the magnitude of a given child's need. Thus, a severely mentally retarded child with pronounced injury to the central nervous system will have such a great need for adult mediation that it might not be possible to fill that need entirely. Similarly, children with autism, because of the particular deficits in reviewing and processing information associated with the syndrome, may require especially intense and individualized mediational teaching procedures.

It is apparent that not all conditions can be overcome completely by increased MLE, but it can make a positive difference in every case. Failure to receive adequate MLE leads to inadequate cognitive development, and ultimately to ineffective thinking and learning and to such obvious outcomes as school failure and poor social adaptation. Arbitman-Smith et al. (1984) pointed out that professional teachers, as well as parents, provide MLE, but that the process differs in many important ways. Parents may wait for naturally occurring opportunities to mediate important cognitive principles and concepts and cultural aspects, but teachers must contrive opportunities. Parents usually have only one child at a given developmental level at a time, but teachers may have many. Teacher have a prescribed content domain that they must teach, so they must take advantage of the correspondence of content and process to teach both.

Thus, in Bright Start, teachers and children are partners in cognitive development as well as in everyday problem solving, using a *mediational teaching style* (Haywood, 1987b) that has been built upon SCM. Mediational teaching is an interactive process in which the developmental needs of the child and the criteria of MLE are used to design instruction. Mediational teachers seek cognitive-structural goals rather than immediate correct answers, and challenge both correct and incorrect answers in their attempts to elicit process-oriented responses. They use varied content as a means to teach cognitive strategies and processes. They emphasize throughout their teaching the order, structure, and predictability of the universe (Haywood, 1987b; Haywood et al., 1986).

Cognitive Small-Group Units

Bright Start includes 150 small-group lessons, varying from 14 to 28 lessons per unit (see Table 14-1). They are called "small-group" lessons because the authors advise teachers to divide the class and teach three to five children at a time on these lessons. Each lesson has a specified cognitive focus, which is then to be followed throughout the day, as well as

Table 14-1. Bright Start (CCYC) Small Group Units

Unit	Description and cognitive functions addressed
Self-regulation	First bring behavior under control of external stimulus Then under own control Then into social control Temporal summation Various cognitive aspects
Quantitative relations	Concepts number correspondence ordinal number cardinal number conservation counting as strategy
Comparison	Compare on single, then multiple, dimensions Compare in face of irrelevant variation Develop spontaneous comparative behavior
Role taking	Develop ability and disposition to take different perspectives Movie role-taking from physical to social realms
Classification	Group according to similarity Form classes and assign labels Identify by position within class Assign to multiple classes
Seriation	Introduces pattern and sequence
Distinctive feature	Bridge to first grade Identify letters of alphabet by their characteristics Generalize this understanding to other content domains

several activities that are recommended. These lessons require about 20–30 minutes per day.

The small-group lessons are focused on the direct teaching and learning of specific cognitive operations and concepts, with "content" used as a vehicle for teaching the cognitive operations. The authors have also recommended the teaching of daily content-oriented lessons (e.g., on colors, numbers, seasons, "community helpers") in which the day's "cognitive function" is applied systematically and used to assist in the content learning.

Cognitive-Mediational Behavior Management

Cognitive-mediational behavioral management (C-M) relies on the same principles as does the teaching of cognitive lessons: use of a mediational teaching style, confidence in the children's ability to behave in acceptable ways, a problem-solving approach to inappropriate behavior, and use of behavioral incidents to advance the learning of thinking modes and strategies. Principles and procedures are offered concerning the definition of unacceptable behavior (whatever interferes with learning), rules about rules, and promoting desired behavior and discouraging undesired behavior. This system is held to be generally incompatible with a contingent-reinforcement (C-R) approach to behavior management, for two important reasons: (a) a contingent-reinforcement system emphasizes correct responses, but Bright Start emphasizes correct processes (in a C-R system, a correct response often terminates engagement with that problem, but in a cognitive-mediational system any answer often stimulates further engagement with the problem, examining alternative processes and solutions, justifying processes and answers); and (b) C-R most often makes use of task-intrinsic incentives and reward, but C-M emphasizes task-intrinsic incentives, with problem solving as its own reward. In this latter case, the research literature suggests that use of extrinsic reinforcers may inhibit the development and expression of task-intrinsic motivation (e.g., Lepper, 1983).

Parent Participation Component

The *parent participation component* is unusually well developed and specific for a preschool program. There is an extensive summary of relevant theory and literature on parent participation (intended for the use of parent workers, not for parents themselves). The program is constructed to be entirely consistent with and supportive of the classroom curriculum, and consists of three major parts: (a) in-class parent participation; (b) parent organization (rather like the PTA); and (c) cognitive learning activities that are to be done at home by a parent and all children present in the home. These home activities are coordinated with the in-class small-group lessons, emphasizing the same cognitive processes but using easily understood activities and materials that are readily available at home.

Evaluation of Bright Start

Up to this writing, there have been nine evaluation studies on Bright Start, the first six of them already published. In general, they show that getting Bright Start results in greater gains in several domains of development than does getting an alternative (noncognitive) preschool curriculum. It has been applied with children between 3 and 8 years of age who have the following disabilities: autism, mental retardation, severe emotional disturbance, deafness and hearing impairments, language disorders and delays, and orthopedic handicaps. In addition, it has been used in Head Start programs and quite widely with normally developing children who come from poor and socially disadvantaged families. Implementation sites are in the United States, Canada, Mexico, Israel, Belgium, France, and Switzerland, so far. The curriculum is available in English, French, Spanish, Hebrew, and Flemish.

Evaluation studies have generally shown the following:

1. IQ increase greater than that found in comparison programs (Dale & Cole, 1988; Haywood et al., 1986; Samuels, Killip, MacKenzie, & Fagan, 1992)
2. Gains in cognitive processes themselves, such as analogical reasoning, verbal reasoning, and concept formation (Dale & Cole, 1988; Tzuriel & Kaniel, 1992; Vanden Wyngaert, 1991; Warnez, 1991)
3. Gains in task-intrinsic motivation (Haywood et al., 1986; Tzuriel & Kaniel, 1992);
4. Greater likelihood of regular class placement, and a substantial probability of retention in regular classes for up to 4 years following preschool Bright Start experience, by independent determination (Price, 1992)
5. Clear differentiation of teacher–child activities, compared to programs that come from a different theoretical base; that is, both teachers and children were doing what the theories said they should do (Dale & Cole, 1988)

6. Greater use of planning and organizational strategies (Tzuriel & Kaniel, 1992)
7. Increase in receptive language and in "higher quality answers to questions" (Vanden Wyngaert, 1991)

The long-term questions are just now being investigated, with follow-up cohorts in Canada and Israel. The data are not yet in, for example, on such questions as whether Bright Start at preschool is associated with higher school achievement scores in the primary grades. Price's (1992) follow-up study did show, however, that, averaged across four cohorts of children, about 50% of the children who had been identified initially as "in need of special education" are independently placed in regular classes following preschool Bright Start, and that they tend to stay there in roughly equal proportions. There is, thus, positive evidence on five of the six goals of the program, with no evidence in yet on the sixth (preparation for the content learning of the primary grades).

APPLICATION OF BRIGHT START TO CHILDREN WITH AUTISM

Bright Start presents an example of an alternative approach to currently advocated methods for teaching young children with autism. Its application is novel and evaluation data on its use with children with autism are difficult to obtain. The inherent difficulties in finding appropriate means of documenting cognitive change (Nickerson, 1988-1989), as well as the methodological difficulties in accessing the intellectual abilities of children with autism, make the collection of evaluation data difficult (Goldstein & Lancy, 1985). However, the use of this approach in education and treatment is theoretically sound and the value of such an approach can only be evaluated in application that becomes refined over time.

Remediation of Arousal/Attention Deficit

Difficulties that children with autism experience with attention/arousal are addressed in *Bright Start* in several ways. First, because mediational teaching focuses on the *processes* rather than the product of learning, it assists children in metacognitive development. Children with autism are asked to become reflective regarding their own thinking processes and are assisted in selecting strategies and problem-solving methods that helps focus attention on *how* to bring attentional resources to bear on intellectual tasks. Teachers are purposeful in asking children to reflect about their

Table 14-2. Mediational Questions

---

1. What do you need to do next?
2. Tell me how you did that?
3. What do you think what would happen if _____?
4. When have you done something like this before?
5. How do you feel if ?
6. Yes, that's right, but how did you know it was right?
7. When is another time you need to ?
8. Stop and look carefully at what you're doing.
9. What do you think the problem is ?
10. Can you think of another way we could do this?
11. Why is this one better than that one?
12. Where have you done that before to help you solve a problem?
13. Let's make a plan so we don't miss anything.
14. How can you find out?
15. How is different from (like)?

---

cognitive processes through active questioning (see Table 14-2). It is important to note that these procedures are designed to be individualized. It is apparent that the cognitive-linguistic "load" of processing questioning of this sort may be too great for some young children with autism.

Difficulties that children with autism experience in stimulus overselectivity are remediated by direct teaching of the processes of comparing, classifying, and extracting general rules. An entire unit of the curriculum is addressed to the processes of comparison as children practice attending to relevant cues, comparing to a model, using labels as a strategy for remembering, and using systematic search procedures to solve problems. Classification, class inclusion, and seriation are also directly addressed by lessons and units in the curriculum. Comparative behavior learned in the comparison unit is applied as children perform classification activities that are designed to demonstrate to children the efficiency and utility of such cognitive processes for problem solving. Finally, Bright Start presents an entire unit on Distinctive Features. This is the last unit in the curriculum and is designed in part to ready children for formal reading instruction in that it seeks to point out the distinctive features of the letters of the alphabet. The cognitive processes that underpin the successful performance of perceiving the essential visual components of letters are primary to all tasks that require perception of relevant stimulus properties. Failure to develop these cognitive processes may account in part for the developmental delays children with autism display. As Goldstein and Lancy (1985) pointed out, studies on concept attainment suggest that although children with autism may be delayed in their development of the abilities to use formal thought and classify stimuli, they are nevertheless capable of this level of cognitive functioning. It is necessary, therefore, for instruction to directly assist children in acquiring these cognitive processes.

Remediation of Social Deficits

Bright Start directly addresses the learning of social meanings. Two of the seven small-group units provide lessons about social meanings. Self-Regulation, the first unit of the curriculum, is directed toward helping children develop behavioral control by first asking them to play games that require large-muscle activity (Fast and Slow). Children bring their behavior under control of external stimuli. Definition of the limits of one's own body is established in the game called "Busy Bee." This definition is seen as a necessary prerequisite to activities that require the children to imitate (e.g., a game called "Copy Cat").

Throughout the 24 lessons of the Self-Regulation unit, children are asked to practice cognitive functions that include matching to a model, thinking about one's own behavior, listening or looking carefully and gathering clear and complete information, accommodating to changes, learning and using rules, role taking, and other basic cognitive processes that allow children to function effectively in social settings. Many of these cognitive functions are in a sense precognitive and prelinguistic in that they are necessary prerequisites to language learning and conscious planned thinking. It is at precisely this level of functioning that children with autism commonly begin to experience cognitive processing deficits.

The second unit of Bright Start that specifically addresses social learning is the Role Taking unit. This series of 17 lessons is designed to build on those skills learned in Self-Regulation and attempts to teach children that different people have different perspectives. Cognitive functions that are emphasized include comparing, thinking about things before acting, labeling, hypothetical thinking, and others. Activities that are clearly remedial to children with autism include those that involve labeling relevant cues that suggest someone else's feelings (e.g., facial expression). It is precisely the lack of this kind of awareness of relevant cues in social situations that contributes to the difficulties persons with autism having in discriminating, understanding, and responding appropriately to social meanings. Activities that involve role playing, wherein the teacher reads a story involving feelings and the children subsequently act out the feelings expressed by the story's characters, give children the opportunity to model, practice, and acquire the socially appropriate skills necessary to function effectively in social situations. It is interesting to note in this context that the clinical literature suggests that those persons with autism who eventually "recovered" were often urged, pressured, or instructed by their families to "act normal" and were given frequent, detailed instruction about what "acting normal" meant. In other words, the mediation involved in the learning of social meanings may need to be particularly intense and frequent for children with autism.

Remediation of Communication Deficits

Mediational teaching as it is used in Bright Start is clearly language-based. Research on the efficacy of Bright Start or earlier versions of it (Cole, Mills, & Dale, 1989; Dale & Cole, 1988; Haywood et al., 1986) revealed that children who use this approach make notable gains on various tests that measure language skill, such as Mean Length of Utterance and the Verbal and General Cognitive Index subscales of the McCarthy Scales. Thus, this approach addresses quite directly remediating the deficient processes of children with autism. It may be argued that the language and cognitive load required to perform adequately in a mediational interaction requires the ability to use language as a representational tool (Dale & Cole, 1988); however, given our limited ability to assess adequately the linguistic abilities of young children, it seems appropriate to err, if need be, in the direction of expecting that a young child with autism can use language representationally. Clearly, children will not learn the basic linguistic processes necessary for optimal cognitive and linguistic development unless they are given opportunity to do so.

Studies whose authors have used a natural language paradigm of treatment delivery (more similar to mediational teaching) with autistic children have been more successful than have repetitive practice paradigms (Bernard-Opitz, 1982; O'Dell and Koegel, 1981; Watson, Lord, Schaffer, & Schopler, 1989; Wetherby & Gaines, 1982). The language-enriched environment of mediational teaching presents opportunities for children with autism to acquire language in ways that are natural and more similar to normal development. Wetherby and Gaines (1982) found that children with autism were more likely to initiate conversation in a free-play setting with adults. Since this finding is inconsistent with anecdotal reports in the autism literature, the speculation was that because the adult in this setting was particularly nondirective, the child had some control and the ability to engage in topics of conversation that were child-selected. Similarly, Bernard-Opitz (1982) found that children with autism were more likely to engage in conversation with their parents when the parents were instructed not to initiate conversation but only to respond to child-initiated attempts to converse. Additional studies (Hart & Risley, 1980; O'Dell & Koegel, 1981; Watson, et al, 1989) demonstrated the overall effectiveness of "natural language" procedures in contrast to repetitive practice procedures in treatment of children with autism. Natural language procedures include turn-taking and shared control by the child and the teacher, and are highly suggestive of the shared participation seen in mediational-teaching procedures.

Remediation of Motivation Deficits

One of the six goals of Bright Start is the development of intrinsic motivation for learning (Haywood, Brooks, and Burns, 1992, p. 14). This goal is most appropriate for children with autism who often appear to lack this kind of motivational orientation. Mediational teachers who seek to develop task-intrinsic motivation realize that cognitive development is dependent on the mutual development of cognitive processes and enthusiasm (Butera, 1988). Teachers who use Bright Start provide children with learning tasks that are just beyond the level of competence of an individual child and then provide enough participation in the task by an adult or more competent peer so that success is assured. The mastery of tasks that children perceive as cognitively challenging appears to be directly related to task-intrinsic motivational development. Mediation teachers may reward children with further opportunity to engage in learning so as to convey the rewarding properties of learning activities. Mediational teachers are careful to consider the appeal of the learning environment so that children are more likely to engage in learning. Finally, to mediational teachers *feedback* means giving information on performance rather than rewarding performance. Opportunity for choice has been consistently found to increase motivation to engage in learning activities (Blackwell, 1975; Turner, 1978). Thus, mediational-teaching procedures that emphasize the development of intrinsic motivation and implicate the value of choice in teaching interactions serve to help with autism develop intrinsic motivation for learning.

SUMMARY

Pupils with autism are likely to spend a majority of their school years in a variety of public school placements, particularly if they exhibit higher functioning autistic disorders. Thus, children with autism may be seen in general educational classrooms, resource rooms, or classrooms for children with learning handicaps, as well as in classrooms for children with autism. An array of placements may be necessary because of the wide range of abilities and disabilities such children exhibit (Schopler, 1989; Webber, 1990). Teaching procedures that are more normalized and typical of instruction in general education facilitate the development of "mainstreaming" skills. Mediational-teaching procedures are more typical of instruction that is currently in use in early childhood settings in which teachers focus on child-initiated learning activities. Thus, mediational teaching in any educational setting will be likely to facilitate the successful "mainstreaming" of children with autism.

Mediational teaching and Bright Start represent an alternative to those who insist that teachers' roles have become increasingly "de-skilled" (Apple, 1982) or "de-professionalized" (Woodward, 1986). Informal surveys of teachers who have inquired about Bright Start revealed that teachers were initially interested in the curriculum because of the attractiveness of its theoretical structure (Haywood & Brooks, 1990). Teacher-training in Bright Start includes a fairly comprehensive review of the theoretical base of the curriculum. The notion here is that teachers who understand the reasons for recommended applied practice will be able to successfully modify curriculum for the individual needs of their students. The side-benefit of this perspective is that it recognizes the teacher as a skilled professional rather than a technician who delivers preprogrammed packages of instruction. This may be especially important for teachers who work with populations that are especially difficult, such as those represented by children who have autism.

The activities that are used to teach cognitive processes in Bright Start were developed by both teachers and the authors. In a process that the authors described as appearing far more orderly in retrospect than it did at the time, psychologists and teachers met and discussed plans for turning theory into practice and classroom activities. The response of the children to lessons that were not successful resulted in a great deal of revision, elimination, reordering, and combining by all involved. This process of curriculum development is quite compatible with currently employed effective teaching procedures. Good teaching involves the ability to reflect about oneself, children, content, and the relationship between school and society (Adler & Goodman, 1986). Teachers from this perspective included revision of instructional procedures as a key component of effective lesson planning. Mediational teaching requires this reflective practice and it provides a theoretical framework for such teaching.

Bright Start presents an alternative to currently advocated methods for teaching young children with autism. Its application with this population is effective because it provides instruction that is directly remedial for the kinds of cognitive-processing deficits children with autism frequently display. Further, mediational teaching, as employed as employed by those who use programs such as this one, involves teaching procedures that are more natural than those developed from an operant-teaching paradigm. Thus, mediational teaching is seen as more likely to produce generalizable learning for children with autism, who may very well receive much of their education in the general education setting. Finally, the theoretical base of the curriculum is thoroughly reviewed with teachers who are training to use Bright Start. The result of this training in theory is that teachers acquire a conceptual framework that allows them to modify instructional practice as necessary and encourages them to be primary decision makers in their classrooms.

ACKNOWLEDGMENTS

This chapter is based on a presentation given by the authors at the 12th Annual TEACCH Conference. "Learning and Cognition in Autism," Chapel Hill, North Carolina, May 23–24, 1991. An earlier version was published in *Focus on Autistic Behavior* (Butera & Haywood, 1992). The authors are grateful to Pro-Ed Publications for permission to exercise some degree of overlap between this chapter and the earlier journal article.

REFERENCES

Adler, S., & Goodman, J. (1986). Critical theory as a foundation for methods courses. *Journal of Teacher Education, 13,* 2–9.
Apple, M. (1982). *Education and power.* London: Routledge & Kegan Paul.
Arbitman-Smith, R., Haywood, H. C., & Bransford, J. D. (1984). Assessing cognitive change. In P. Brooks, R. Sperber, C. McCauley (Eds.), *Learning and cognition in the mentally retarded,* (pp. 433–471). Hillsdale, NJ: Erlbaum.
Bartak, L., Rutter, M., & Cox, A. (1975). A comparative study of infantile autism and specific developmental receptive language disorder: I. The children. *British Journal of Psychiatry, 126,* 127–145.
Bernard-Opitz, V. (1982). Pragmatic analysis of the communication behavior of an autistic child. *Journal of Speech and Hearing Disorders, 47,* 99–109.
Blackwell, L. R. (1975). *Student choice in curriculum, feelings of control and causality, and academic motivation and performance.* Unpublished doctoral dissertation, University of California, Santa Barbara.
Butera, G. (1988). Enhancing intrinsic motivation in the classroom. *The Thinking Teacher, 4,* 1–5.
Butera, G., & Haywood, H. C. (1992). A cognitive approach to the education of young children with autism. *Focus on Autistic Behavior, 6*(6), 1–14.
Cattell, R. B. (1963). Theory of fluid and crystallized intelligence: A critical experiment. *Journal of Educational Psychology, 18,* 165–244.
Collins, A., Brown, J. S., & Newman, S. E. (1989). Cognitive apprenticeship: Teaching the

crafts of reading, writing, and mathematics. In L. B. Resnick (Ed.), *Knowing, learning, and instruction* (pp. 453–494). Hillsdale, NJ: Erlbaum.

Cole, K. N., Mills, P. E., & Dale, P. S. (1989). A comparison of the effects of academic and cognitive curricular for young handicapped children one and two years postprogram. *Topics in Early Childhood Special Education, 9,* 110–127.

Dale, P., & Cole, K. (1988). Comparison of academic and cognitive programs for young handicapped children. *Exceptional Children, 545,* 469–447.

Danner, F., & Lonkey, E. (1981). A cognitive-developmental approach to the effects of reward on intrinsic motivation. *Child Development, 52,* 1043–1052.

Deci, E., & Ryan, R. (1985). *Intrinsic motivation and self-determination in human behavior.* New York: Plenum Press.

De Meyer, M. K. (1979). *Parents and children in autism.* Washington: Winston.

Ferster, C. B. (1961). Positive reinforcement and behavioral deficits of autistic children. *Child Development, 32,* 437–456.

Feuerstein, R. (1970). A dynamic approach to the causation, prevention, and alleviation of retarded performance. In H. C. Haywood (Ed.), *Social-cultural aspects of mental retardation* (pp. 341–377). New York: Appleton-Century-Crofts.

Feuerstein, R., & Rand, Y. (1974). Mediated learning experience: An outline of the proximal etiology for differential development of cognitive functions. *International Understanding, /10,* 7–37.

Feuerstein, R., Rand, Y., Hoffman, M. B., & Miller, R. (1980). *Instrumental enrichment.* Baltimore: University Park Press.

Ginsburg, H., & Opper, S. (1978). *Piaget's theory of intellectual development* (2nd ed.). Englewood Cliffs, NJ: Prentice-Hall.

Goldstein, G. I., & Lancy, D. F. (1985). Cognitive development in autistic children. In L. S. Siegel & F. J. Morrison (Eds.), *Cognitive development in atypical children,* (pp. 83–112). New York: Springer-Verlag.

Hart, B., & Risley, T. R. (1980). *In vivo* language intervention: Unanticipated general effects. *Journal of Applied Behavior Analysis, 13,* 407–432.

Haywood, H. C. (1987a). The mental age deficit: Explanation and treatment. *Uppsala Journal of Medical Science,* (Suppl. 44), 191–203.

Haywood, H. C. (1987b). A mediational teaching style. *The Thinking Teacher, 4,* 1–7.

Haywood, H. C. (1989). Multidimensional treatment of mental retardation. *Psychology in Mental Retardation and Developmental Disabilities, 15*(1), 1–10.

Haywood, H. C. (1992, February). The strange and wonderful symbiosis of cognition and motivation. Presidential address, International Association for Cognitive Education, Riverside, CA.

Haywood, H. C., & Brooks, P. H. (1990). Theory and curriculum development in cognitive education. In M. Schwebel, C. A. Maher, & N. S. Fagley (Eds.), *Promoting cognitive growth over the life span* (pp. 165–192). Hillsdale, NJ: Erlbaum.

Haywood, H. C., Brooks, P., & Burns, S. (1986). Stimulating cognitive development at developmental level: A tested, nonremedial preschool curriculum for preschoolers and older retarded children. In M. Schwebel & C. A. Maher (Eds.), *Facilitating cognitive development: Principles, practices, and programs* (pp. 127–147). New York: Haworth Press. Also in *Special Services in the Schools, 2,* 30.

Haywood, H. C., Brooks, P., & Burns, S. (1992). *Bright Start: Cognitive Curriculum for Young Children.* Watertown, MA: Charlesbridge.

Haywood, H. C., & Burke, W. P. (1977). Development of individual differences in intrinsic motivation. In I. C. Uzgiris & F. Weizman (Eds.), *The Structuring of experience.* New York: Plenum Press.

Haywood, H. C., & Switzky, H. N. (1986a). Intrinsic motivation and behavior effectiveness in retarded persons. In N. R. Ellis & N. W. Bray (Eds.), *International review of research in Mental Retardation* (Vol. 14, pp. 1–46). New York: Academic Press.

Haywood, H. C., & Switzky, H. C. (1986b). The malleability of intelligence: Cognitive processes as a function of polygenic-experiential interaction. *School Psychology Review, 15,* 245–255.

Haywood, H. C., & Switzky, H. C. (1992). Ability and modifiability: How, and how much can ability be changed? In J. Carlson (Ed.), *Advances in cognition and educational practice, Vol. 1A: Cognition and educational practice: An international perspective* (pp. 25–85). Greenwich, CT: JAI Press.

Haywood, H. C., Tzuriel, D., & Vaught, S. (1992). Psychoeducational assessment from a transactional perspective. In H. C. Haywood & D. Tzuriel (Eds.), *Interactive assessment* (pp. 38–63). New York: Springer-Verlag.

Hohmann, M., Banet, B., & Weikert, D. P. (1979). *Young children in transition: A manual for preschool educators.* Ypsilanti, MI: High/Scope Educational Research Foundation.

Horn, J. L. (1972). Structure of intellect: Primary abilities. In R. M. Dreger (Ed.), *Multivariate personality research.* Baton Rouge, LA: Clarton.

Kanner, L. (1943). Autistic disturbances of affective contact. *Nervous Child, 2,* 217–250.

Kennard, M. A. (1960). Value of equivocal signs in neurological diagnosis. *Neurology, 10,* 753–764.

Koegel, R. L., & Egel, A. L. (1979). Motivating autistic children. *Journal of Abnormal Psychology, 88,* 418–426.

Koegel, R. L., Koegel, L. K. & O'Neill, R. E. (1989). Generalization in the treatment of autism. In L. V. McReynolds & J. E. Spradlin (Eds.), *Generalization strategies in the treatment of communication disorders* (pp. 116–131). Toronto: Decker.

Koontz, J. P., & Cohen, D. J. (1981). Modulation of sensory intake in autistic children: Cardiovascular and behavioral indices. *Journal of the American Academy of Child Psychiatry, 20,* 692–701.

Lepper, M. R. (1983). Extrinsic reward and intrinsic motivation: Implications for the classroom. In J. M. Levine & M. C. Wang (Eds.), *Teacher and student perceptions: Implications for learning.* Hillsdale, NJ: Erlbaum.

Lord, C. (1985). Language comprehension and cognitive defroster in autism. In L. S. Siegel & F. J. Morrison (Eds.), *Cognitive development in atypical children* (pp. 67–82). New York: Springer-Verlag.

Lovaas, O. I., Koegel, R. L., Simmons, J. Q., & Long, J. S. (1973). Some generalization and follow-up measures on autistic children in behavior therapy. *Journal of Applied Behavior Analysis, 6,* 11–166.

Miller, W. R., & Seligman, M. E. P. (1975). Depression and learned helplessness in man. *Journal of Experimental Psychology, 84,* 228–238.

Myles, B. S., & Simpson, R. L. (1990). A clinical/prescriptive method for use with students with autism. *Focus on Autistic Behavior, 4*(6), 1–14.

Nickerson, R. S. (1988–1989). On improving thinking through instruction. *Review of Research in Education, 15,* 3–57.

O'Dell, M., & Koegel, R. L. (1981, April). *The differential effects of two methods of promoting speech in nonverbal autistic children.* Paper presented at the 1981 Annual Convention of the American Speech-Language-Hearing Association, Los Angeles, CA.

Ornitz, E.M., & Ritvo, E. (1976). The syndrome of autism: A critical review. *American Journal of Psychiatry, 133,* 609–621.

Paour, J. L. (1992). Piagetian approaches to mental retardation: Hopes, barriers, opportunities, and convergences. In J. S. Carlson (Ed.), *Advances in cognition and education practice,*

Vol. 1A: Theoretical issues: Intelligence, cognition, and assessment (pp. 87–111). Greenwich, CT: JAI Press.

Piaget, J. (1952) *The origins of intelligence in children*. New York & Paris: International Universities Press.

Piaget, J. (1960). *The language and thought of the child*. London: Routledge.

Piaget, J., & Inhelder, B. (1969). *The psychology of the child*. New York: Basic Books.

Price, M. A. (1992). Early cognitive education—and then what? *The Thinking Teacher, 7*(2), 8–11.

Resnick, L. B. (1987). *Education and learning to think*. Washington, DC: National Academy Press.

Rimland, B. (1964). *Infantile autism*. New York: Appleton-Century-Crofts.

Rutter, M. (1983). Cognitive deficits in the pathogenesis of autism. *Journal of Child Psychology and Psychiatry, 24*, 513–532.

Samuels, M. T., Killip, S. M., MacKenzie, H., & Fagan, J. (1992). Evaluating preschool programs: The role of dynamic assessment. In H. C. Haywood & D. Tzuriel (Eds.), *Interactive assessment* (pp. 251–271). New York: Springer-Verlag.

Schopler, E. (1987). TEACCH. In C. Reynolds & L. Mann, (Eds.), *Encyclopedia of special education* (pp. 1536–1537). New York: Wiley.

Schopler, E. (1989). Principles for directing both educational treatment and research. In C. Gillberg (Ed.), *Diagnosis and treatment of autism* (pp. 167–183). New York: Plenum.

Schopler, E., & Mesibov, G. B. (1985). Communication problems in autism. New York: Plenum Press.

Strain, P. (1983). Generalization of autistic children's social behavior change: Effects of developmentally integrated and segregated settings. *Analysis and Intervention in Developmental Disabilities, 3*, 23–24.

Turner, B. L. (1978). *The effects of choice of stimulus materials on interest in the remediation process and the generalized use of language training*. Unpublished master's thesis, University of California, Santa Barbara.

Tzuriel, D., & Kaniel, S. (1992, February). *The Cognitive Curriculum for Young Children: Evaluation of CCYC in Israel*. Paper presented at the 3rd International Conference of the International Association for Cognitive Education, Riverside, CA.

Vanden Wyngaert, R. (1991). Cognitive education with speech and language-disordered children. *The Thinking Teacher, 6*(3), 1–5.

Vygotsky, L. S. (1929). The problem of the cultural development of the child. *Journal of Genetic Psychology, 36*, 415–434.

Vygotsky, L. S. (1962). *Thought and language*. Cambridge, MA: MIT Press.

Vygotsky, L. S. (1978). *Mind in society: The development of higher psychological processes*. Cambridge, MA: Harvard University Press.

Warnez, J. (1991). Implementation of the CCYC in a therapeutic center. *The Thinking Teacher, 6*(1), 7–9.

Watson, L., Lord, C., Schaffer, B., & Schopler, E. (1989). *Teaching spontaneous communication to autistic and developmentally handicapped children*. New York: Irvington.

Webber, C. F. (1990). Mainstreaming a child with autism: One school's experience. *Focus on Autistic Behavior, 5*, 8–10.

Wetherby, A. M., & Gaines, B. (1982). Cognition and language development in autism. *Journal of Speech and Hearing Disorders, 47*, 63–70.

Woodward, A. (1986). Overprogrammed materials: Taking the teacher out of teaching. *American Educator, 10*(1), 22–25.

Yuweiler, A., Geller, E., & Ritvo, E. (1975). Uptake and efflux of serotonin from platelets of autistic and nonautistic children. *Journal of Autism and Childhood Schizophrenia, 5*, 83–98.

Educational Strategies in Autism

SANDRA L. HARRIS

INTRODUCTION

The mid-1960s witnessed a transformation in the education of children with autism. As we moved away from a psychodynamic conceptualization of this disorder and began to explore its biological roots (Rimland, 1964; Schopler & Reichler, 1971b), it became possible to construe treatment in new ways. This led to an appreciation of the value of such phenomena as a structured learning environment (Schopler, Brehm, Kinsbourne, & Reichler, 1971), operant teaching techniques (Lovaas, Berberich, Perloff, & Schaeffer, 1966), and the role of parents as cotherapists (Lovaas et al., 1973; Schopler & Reichler, 1971a).

In the two decades since those original innovations, researchers and educators have expanded and modified their initial discoveries, refining the technology to create increasing precision in educational procedures. Methods of treatment are used today that were only dimly visualized 10 years ago, and the next decade will doubtless witness changes that will make today's methods seem crude. Being open to this evolution, and ensuring that our services employ the best of current procedures is a responsibility of every person who serves children with autism and their families.

The present chapter provides an overview of some of the recent advances in educational strategies for children with autism. Although not

SANDRA L. HARRIS • Graduate School of Applied and Professional Psychology, Rutgers University, Piscataway, New Jersey 08855-0819.

Learning and Cognition in Autism, edited by Eric Schopler and Gary B. Mesibov. Plenum Press, New York, 1995.

comprehensive, the chapter attempts to introduce the reader to major current trends in educational technology. These trends focus on four areas: variations in the teaching context, including the ingredients in the discrete trial and naturalistic instructional formats; the teaching of social skills, including a concurrent emphasis on peer models and integration of persons with autism into the community; the development of speech and language, including the use of vocal and nonvocal augmentative techniques of communication; and the management of disruptive behavior, including functional assessment.

THE CONTEXT FOR INSTRUCTION

For many years the discrete trial format in which a stimulus was presented (time allowed for the child to respond, the response consequated, and data recorded), was probably the most common format recommended for teaching children with autism (e.g., Handleman & Harris, 1986; Koegel, Russo, & Rincover, 1977). This approach continues to be used and has undergone considerable refinement in recent years. In addition, there has been an emphasis on using more naturalistic instructional settings to promote generalization and maintenance of responding.

Reinforcement Techniques

The use of positive reinforcement to shape and maintain desirable behaviors has made substantial progress since the days of using M&Ms to reward good behavior. Although sweet treats continue to be used, a broad range of reinforcers are now known to be effective, and we have gained considerable sophistication in the delivery of these rewards. While food, tickles, hugs, praise, breaks from work, and time to play are widely used rewards, other innovative items have been demonstrated to be effective reinforcers, including sensory stimulation with music, vibration, or strobe lights (Ferrari & Harris, 1981; Murphy, 1982), and permitting the student a brief period for self-stimulatory or other aberrant behavior (e.g., Charlop, Kurtz, & Casey, 1990; Sugai & White, 1986; Wolery, Kirk, & Gast, 1985).

When working within a discrete trial format, it is preferable that the reinforcer be intrinsic to the behavioral chain rather than extrinsic (e.g., Koegel & J. A. Williams, 1980; J. A. Williams, Koegel, & Egel, 1981). For example, when learning colors a child might be required to "pick up the blue cup" (containing juice) in order to receive a drink, rather than being given juice by the teacher after making a correct response. In addition, using a variety of reinforcers is usually superior to the use of a single form of reinforcement (e.g., Egel, 1981).

Instructional Formats

The timing and pacing of instruction in the discrete trial format can influence acquisition. For example, a fast-paced instructional pattern, with only a brief interval between trials (Koegel, Dunlap, & Dyer, 1980), and variation of tasks within a session rather than focusing on a single task (Dunlap & Koegel, 1980) improve learning. Delaying the use of prompts has been found useful in increasing spontaneity (e.g., Charlop, Schreibman, & Thibodeau, 1985) and teaching the child to withhold his or her response for a few seconds helps to decrease impulsive answers (Dyer, Christian, & Luce, 1982).

Although some instruction may be more efficient in a discrete trial format, looser forms of learning such as incidental teaching techniques (e.g., McGee, Krantz, & McClannahan, 1984) and the natural language teaching paradigm (R. Koegel, O'Dell, & L. Koegel, 1987) are probably superior for enhancing motivation and ensuring that responses are generalized and spontaneous. The natural language teaching paradigm draws upon many of the same instructional principles as the discrete trial format, but also focuses on creating a learning situation in which the child has an opportunity for shared control over transactions, the activities are inherently attractive, reinforcers are a part of the adult–child interaction, and the learning trials are part of the natural interchange (Koegel et al., 1987).

ENHANCING SOCIAL AND INTERPERSONAL FUNCTIONING

Difficulties in establishing and maintaining relationships with other people are integral to the diagnosis of autistic disorder. Given the need of every student with autism for improved social skills, this domain should be a prominent component of each student's educational plan. Fortunately, the past decade has seen considerable research in this area, offering the classroom teacher an empirical basis from which to approach the social needs of his or her students.

Teaching Social Skills

Being socially adept demands a broad range of skills that grow increasingly complex with the age of the student. These social skills include the mechanics of how to play a game with another person (Coe, Matson, Fee, Manikam, & Linarello, 1990), expressing affection to another child (McEvoy et al., 1988), choosing leisure activities (Hawkins, 1982), using assertive conversational skills to make requests and to ensure that another person plays by the rules of a game, (McGee et al., 1984), learning how to engage someone else in an activity of interest (Gaylord-Ross, Haring, Breen, & Pitts-Conway, 1984), shopping in community stores (Haring, Kennedy, Adams, & Pitts-Conway, 1987), and being perceptive of the needs of others (Harris, Handleman, & Alessandri, 1990). Regardless of which specific social skill is being taught, giving children shared control over their activities may serve to diminish their socially avoidant responses and enhance the acquisition of adaptive social behaviors (Koegel, Dyer, & Bell, 1987).

An important first step in developing a social skills curriculum is to document the feasibility of teaching specific skills to persons with autism using well-controlled, single subject designs. Once this is accomplished, it is important that these discrete skills be integrated into a comprehensive curriculum. Although this ideal of inclusive training is not yet available, both Mesibov (1984) and T. I. Williams (1989) described social-skills-training packages for young people with autism. While less rigorous in their research base than some of the studies of discrete skills, these two reports have the virtue of describing a curriculum for helping people with autism acquire a range of important social behaviors.

T. I. Williams (1989) worked with higher functioning children with autism ages 9 to 16, who were being integrated into a normal school setting. Weekly group meetings initially focused on learning cooperative games, moved on to playing simple social roles, and grew increasingly complex as the youngsters learned to engage in conversations, modulate voice tone, terminate interactions, control inappropriate behavior, exhibit increased flexibility, and be assertive in social settings. Mesibov (1984) offered a similarly comprehensive curriculum for more impaired adolescents and young adults with autism with weekly meetings that addressed ways to meet people, improved attending skills, the identification and expression of emotion, the appreciation of humor, and turn taking in conversation.

Peer Models

One of the primary means of teaching social skills to children and adolescents with autism has been the use of peer models. Much of this work has employed normally developing preschool-age youngsters (e.g.,

Odom, Hoyson, Jamieson, & Strain, 1985; Odom & Strain, 1986), or older, elementary school-age peers (Blew, Schwartz, & Luce, 1985; Lord & Hopkins, 1986; Sasso & Rude, 1987), and a few studies have used mildly handicapped peers as models for youngsters with more severe impairments (e.g., Shafer, Egel, & Neef, 1984).

Perhaps the most programmatic use of preschool-age peers to teach social and play skills to young children with autism was done by Strain, Odom and their colleagues as part of their integrated preschool program (e.g., Odom et al., 1985; Odom & Strain, 1986; Strain, 1983). Their work documented the fact that preschool peers can learn to initiate interactions with the autistic child, and that such initiations increase the social responses of the children with autism. Other researchers have extended these findings to elementary-age children (e.g., Brady, Shores, McEvoy, Ellis, & Fox, 1987; Oke & Schreibman, 1990). Although an important contribution to the educational literature, this work is not without limitations, including the complexity of the demands imposed on teachers to carry out the procedures, the difficulty more impaired children have in benefiting from the exposure, and the limitations of generalized responding.

It is important that social skills learned under controlled training conditions be generalized both by the child with autism, and by the child's peers, to other settings. Several variables may contribute to this transfer. The work of Strain and his colleagues suggested that generalization sessions in integrated settings result in higher levels of social behavior on the part of the children with autism than do segregated settings (Strain, 1983). Carr and Darcy (1990) pointed to the importance of using multiple training objects in attracting attention to the peer model, and of ensuring that inherently reinforcing activities are available to enhance generalized responding. Another variable that may be important in facilitating the responses of untrained peers, is the use of high-social-status peers as the initial models for the children with autism. Sasso and Rude (1987) noted that when high-status peers in an elementary school were trained to initiate social interactions with autistic children, there were more initiations by untrained peers than when the trained peers were youngsters of low status.

The importance of adult involvement appears to vary with the age of the peers. For preschool-age children, teacher prompts to initiate social behaviors enhance the behavior of both the peers (Odom et al., 1985) and the children with autism (Odom & Strain, 1986). However, with older peers, Lord and Hopkins (1986) found the youngsters engaged in more interactions without adult prompting. They also found that older partners (ages 10 to 12) were more effective than younger children (ages 5 to 6) at adapting their interactions to the needs of the developmentally impaired youngsters. Meyer and her colleagues (1987) similarly found that for elementary-age children, teacher supervision was largely superfluous.

In addition to modeling play related behaviors, normally developing peers have been employed as models for helping children with autism master community-based skills such as checking out a library book or purchasing a snack (Blew et. al., 1985) and academic tasks such as color and shape discrimination (e.g., Egel, Richman, & Koegel, 1981), or language skills (Ihrig & Wolchik, 1988). Preliminary data from Lanquetot (1989) suggested that in addition to acquisition of the targeted skill, peer modeling may also have a beneficial effect on the behavior of the child with autism.

Powerful as it is for mastering some skills, peer modeling may not always be the optimal way for children with autism to learn new skills. Charlop and Walsh (1986) found that a time-delayed prompt was more effective than peer modeling to teach children with autism to emit spontaneous expressions of affection. They suggest that the structure of the modeling environment and the consequent stimulus control over the learner's behavior may be important determinants of whether a modeling approach is effective.

Mainstreaming and Integration

In discussing the introduction of children with autism to integrated educational settings it is useful to know that there is considerable variability in the use of the terms *integration* and *mainstreaming*. In response to this variation Odom and Speltz (1983) proposed that classes with mostly handicapped children and some peers be called *integrated special education* classes, while those that contain mostly children without handicapping conditions be called *mainstreamed special education* classes. Mainstreamed classes are essentially classes within the regular educational system, whereas the integrated special education classes are usually built around a more individualized educational model. Full participation in the same class appears most common at the preschool level (e.g., Harris, Handleman, Kristoff, Bass, & Gordon, 1990; Strain, 1983), with elementary-age and older children more likely to share some activities, but have a segregated classroom (e.g., Meyer et al., 1987; Sasso & Rude, 1987).

Perhaps the most important demonstrations of the benefits of an integrated or mainstreamed placement have been done at the preschool level. Early intervention programs for the most part include some form of integrated experience as an important component of treatment. Lovaas's (1987) report of recovery from autism by some of the young participants in his early intervention project, involved intensive behavioral-individual work with the child in the home during the first year, followed by mainstreaming the child into a regular preschool program during the second year. Replication with new samples to determine the range of children who can benefit from these techniques, and longitudinal research to explore how well the participants function over time will be important. Lovaas's work has brought critical concerns along with strong support (e.g., Lovaas, Smith, & McEachin, 1989; Schopler, Short, & Mesibov, 1989).

Strain and his colleagues (e.g., Odom et al., 1985; Odom & Strain, 1986; Strain, 1983) relied exclusively on an integrated preschool placement for their children, while Harris, Handleman, and Alessandri (1990) moved their children from a segregated to an integrated preschool class as the children became developmentally more advanced. There are no data comparing these approaches, and hence no empirical basis for choosing one approach over the other.

Integrating children with autism into public school settings is probably easier when they have been taught requisite social skills and when the normally developing youngsters have been educated about handicapping conditions and given a controlled opportunity to share activities with their developmentally impaired schoolmates (Sasso, Simpson, & Novak, 1985).

Egel and Gradel (1988) noted that the empirical basis for integration is not yet fully established, but that access to integrated activities appears to benefit children with autism in ways that cannot be achieved in segregated settings. The extent of this integration may vary according to the needs of the individual child, with some higher functioning youngsters able to function well in regular education classes with minimum support, with other children sharing some classes with their normally developing peers and returning to a separate class for other subjects, and with more impaired youngsters sharing cafeteria and recreational activities, but having their other needs met in a separate class.

DEVELOPING SPEECH AND LANGUAGE

Speech and language deficits are universal in students with autism. Although the nature of the deficit varies with the person's age and degree of disability, each person with autism requires specialized training in communication skills. The recent research on speech and language for persons with autism has examined both ways to facilitate speech acquisition, and techniques for developing communication for nonverbal students.

Enhancing Speech

A major focus in recent years has been to ensure that the speech skills being taught have immediate, pragmatic use for the student. In general the data suggest that enhancing the child's motivation by a careful arrangement of the learning environment, by rich reinforcement of efforts to communicate, and by giving the child an opportunity to share control of activities, facilitates the acquisition of functional speech (e.g., Beisler & Tsai, 1983). Wetherby (1986) recommended responding to the child's communicative intent as the initial focus of instruction, developing give-and-take joint interactions through turn-taking games, assessing aberrant behaviors for their communicative function, and encouraging the child to be both the initiator of communication and a respondent. She argued that, rather than in a discrete trial format, these goals can best be accomplished in a more naturalistic interaction that draws upon incidental teaching techniques.

Consistent with these goals, R. Koegel et al. (1987) developed a natural-language teaching paradigm in which a rich and varied array of stimulus items are employed, the reinforcers are those which occur naturally as part of the interaction and manipulation of the objects, the child's attempts at communication are reinforced, and the teaching trials occur as an integral part of a natural interchange between child and adult.

Research examining some of the specific components of the natural-learning context has provided support for the value of these strategies. For example, reinforcing a nonverbal child's attempts to speak, regardless of the quality of the attempt, leads to more speech than the more traditional approach of only reinforcing increasingly accurate approximations of a criterion model (Koegel, O'Dell, & Dunlap, 1988). Similarly, McGee, Krantz, Mason, and McClannahan (1983) relied on an interesting environment to motivate response when teaching receptive object labels to their adolescent students. During the course of lunch preparation, they employed a modified incidental-teaching strategy to teach the labels for foods as those items were being used in the preparation of the meal.

One technique for increasing the spontaneous use of speech by children with autism is use of a time-delay procedure when modeling an appropriate vocalization (e.g., Charlop, Schreibman, & Thibodeau, 1985). Using this technique, the teacher presents an item the child might want, such as cookie, and models the appropriate response, "I want cookie." Gradually, the teacher delays the amount of time before he or she offers the modeled response, allowing the child to respond prior to the model. This strategy increases the likelihood that children will initiate spontaneous requests for desired items. Matson and his colleagues (Matson, Sevin,

Fridley, & Love, 1990) similarly used a time-delay procedure to increase the use of the words "please," "thank you," and "you're welcome."

Sign and Other Augmentative Communication Methods

Some students are unable to learn speech within the constraints of our present technology. For these children a nonverbal means of communication is essential. For other students, who acquire speech gradually, the supplemental use of nonverbal communication may facilitate the acquisition of speech or may serve to reduce the child's frustration during the early years of mastering spoken language. Manual sign language has been the primary means of teaching communicative skills to these youngsters (Howlin, 1989), although other augmentative methods, including the use of computerized systems, are also used.

It would be useful to know early in their development which children are most likely to benefit from some form of nonvocal communication and which children will acquire speech without the need for this augmentative instruction. Although definitive data are not available to answer that question, in general children who are higher functioning and verbal do acquire more spoken language than those who have lower IQs and whose vocalizations are limited in number and distorted in quality (e.g., Konstantareas, 1987; Nishimura, Watamaki, Sato, & Wakabayashi, 1987). Early simultaneous-communication training might therefore be especially important for those youngsters less likely to master speech. Although the data are not yet conclusive, it appears that speech and sign should be taught simultaneously to most children, because sign alone may not facilitate speech (Howlin, 1989; Yoder & Layton, 1988).

Carr, Kologinsky, and Leff-Simon (1987) suggested that while specific signing skills might efficiently be taught in a traditional discrete-trial format, shifting the use of these skills to functional communication requires practice in an incidental-teaching format. Just as meaningful speech seems to be facilitated when children with autism learn in a natural context, so too does the acquisition of communicative sign benefit from a modified incidental-teaching approach (e.g., Carr & Kologinsky, 1983). Such techniques can include making an attractive object visible but inaccessible so that the student must use sign to request the item, incorporating opportunities to use sign during routine-care activities, and providing very brief mini-teaching sessions to help students master the motor acts for signs and apply them in the proper context (Schepis et al., 1982).

Although the bulk of research on nonvocal communication by persons with autism has focused on manual sign, other systems can be used as well. Lancioni (1983) taught low-functioning children with autism to use pictures to communicate preferences. Abrahamsen, Romski, and Sevcik (1989) used a computerized system of graphic symbols to teach nonverbal persons with autism and related disorders to communicate. Their data showed an increase in sociability and attending behaviors for participants who learned the symbol system.

Identification of the augmentative techniques to be used with a student need to be based on a careful assessment of that individual's skills. For some persons with autism, a picture board that graphically depicts desired items is appropriate, while for others, more complex boards that "speak" simple words or phrases, or ones that enable the student to create novel sentences provide flexible and relatively sophisticated communication.

The use of communication boards (Angelo & Goldstein, 1990) and portable computerized systems as augmentative means of communication for persons with autism has just begun to be explored, but holds promise as a means of interacting with a wide range of persons in the community. In addition to being difficult to master for many persons with autism, a notable limit of manual sign has been its restriction to other persons who sign. This works at counterpurposes to the goal of integrating persons with autism into the wider community. Small, hand-held computers might overcome this obstacle to a considerable degree.

MANAGING DISRUPTIVE BEHAVIOR

Much of the recent research on helping persons with autism control their disruptive or aberrant behaviors has focused on the functional and contextual analysis of these behaviors and on the development of creative interventions to help students learn more appropriate alternative behaviors. These techniques have diminished, but not eliminated, the need to rely upon aversive procedures to decrease potentially dangerous behaviors (Harris & Handleman, 1990).

Functional Assessment

Environmental complexity (Duker & Rasing, 1989), teacher demands (Edelson, Taubman, & Lovaas, 1983), and task difficulty (Weeks & Gaylord-Ross, 1981) all impact on the disruptive, aberrant behaviors of persons with autism. The notion that disruptive and aberrant behaviors may sometimes be a form of communication has led to an increased sensitivity on the part of educators to understanding the context in which these behaviors occur and how we might teach the student a more appropriate mode of expressing his or her needs.

Carr and Durand (1985) noted that disruptive behavior often involves an escape response with consequent negative reinforcement, or an attention-seeking response with consequent positive reinforcement of the behavior. If it can be determined which of these patterns is operative for a student, it may then be possible to teach the student an alternative mode of escaping from the task (e.g., asking for assistance or to take a break) or gaining an adult's attention (e.g., asking for feedback). Among the disruptive behaviors that have been addressed by a functional assessment coupled with the teaching of appropriate alternative responses have been aggressive, disruptive behavior (Carr & Durand, 1985), self-stimulation (Durand & Carr, 1987), and psychotic speech (Durand & Crimmins, 1987). Wacker and his colleagues (1990) suggested that mild negative consequences such as time out or graduated guidance enhance the use of functional communication training to diminish disruptive behavior.

In addition to the analysis of task demands and adult attention, other contextual factors should be considered in the assessment of disruptive or maladaptive behaviors. For example, the familiarity of the teacher and the stimulus materials can influence self-stimulation or echolalia (Charlop, 1986; Runco, Charlop, & Schriebman, 1986); eliminating sensory feedback associated with self-stimulation may reduce these behaviors (Maag, Wolchik, Rutherford, & Parks, 1986; Rincover, Newsom, Lovaas, & Koegel, 1977); and teaching a child how to point may reduce the frequency of inappropriate "leading" behavior (Carr & Kemp, 1989). The highly skilled application of differential reinforcement of other behavior (DRO; Cowdery, Iwata, & Pace, 1990), and allowing students to make choices about instructional activities (Dyer, Dunlap, & Winterling, 1990), have also been found to decrease aberrant behavior.

As research on functional assessment continues we are learning how complex the assessment must sometimes be. The variables that determine the function of an aberrant response in one setting may not hold true in another. Haring and Kennedy (1990) indicated that it is necessary to assess the disruptive behavior across settings to develop an optimal intervention package. For example, their research showed that when doing an instructional task, differential reinforcement of other behaviors (DRO) led to a reduction in problem behaviors and an increase in task performance, whereas time-out had no effect. By contrast, for the same participants in a leisure setting, time-out reduced the problem behaviors and DRO was ineffective. These data suggest that the leisure activity was reinforcing to the students and removal was therefore aversive, a situation that did not hold true in the classroom.

The Use of Aversive Techniques

Aversive procedures, when they must be used, tend to be less intrusive than was the case 10 or 15 years ago (e.g., Linscheid, Iwata, Ricketts, Williams, & Griffin, 1990). A number of techniques have been developed that are effective alternatives to electric shock or other physically painful punishers. For example, physical exercise (e.g., Allison, Basile, & MacDonald, 1991; Gordon, Handleman, & Harris, 1986), and brief restraint (Dorsey, Iwata, Reid, & Davis, 1982) have both proved effective for suppressing disruptive behaviors. The intense controversy surrounding the use of aversive procedures (Harris & Handleman, 1990), and the increased emphasis on development of nonaversive alternatives has probably served to diminish the frequency of research in this area.

SUMMARY

One of the major changes in recent years has been a broadening the instructional context to place greater value on teaching in naturalistic settings. Nonetheless, there remain situations in which the discrete-trial format may be the most efficient way to impart basic information. The technology underlying this format has undergone change, with an increasing emphasis on a rapid paced and varied instructional process that offers a variety of reinforcers.

Another important change in educational strategy has been an increased understanding of how to encourage the development of social behavior. This has included the use of normally developing peers as models for appropriate behavior, and the integration of students with autism into more normalized educational settings. For preschool-age children this integration may be a full-time placement in a class with normally developing peers, whereas for older children it is more typically a sharing of common resources with peers and some instruction in a segregated classroom.

Techniques for teaching communication continue to grow more sophisticated. A major change has been the emphasis on teaching language in naturalistic settings, rather than in a discrete-trial format. The naturalistic setting, if properly employed, seems to enhance motivation and facilitate generalization and maintenance of behavior. In spite of advances in technology for teaching speech, there are still children who remain nonverbal, and for these youngsters the use of manual sign or other augmentative methods hold promise for increasing communication, and in some cases for stimulating the development of speech.

The functional assessment of disruptive behavior and comprehensive examination of the impact of context on behavior have enabled us to diminish the extent to which it is necessary to rely on aversive procedures to cope with aberrant, dangerous behaviors. Nonetheless, it does appear that there are some persons with autism for whom the present nonaversive technology is insufficient, and who require sophisticated aversive procedures to gain control over their dangerous behaviors.

The changes in educational technology for children with autism over the past 20 years have been exciting for those of us who have witnessed that transformation. A chapter on the same topic another decade hence will doubtless describe even greater efficacy in our approach to treatment.

REFERENCES

Abrahamsen, A. A., Romski, M. A., & Sevcik, R. A. (1989). Concomitants of success in acquiring an augmentative communication system: Changes in attention, communication, and sociability. *American Journal on Mental Retardation, 93,* 475–496.

Allison, D. B., Basile, V. C., & MacDonald, R. B. (1991). Brief report: Comparative effects of antecedent exercise and lorazepam on the aggressive behavior of an autistic man. *Journal of Autism and Developmental Disorders, 21,* 89–94.

Angelo, D. H., & Goldstein, H. (1990). Effects of a pragmatic teaching strategy for requesting information by communication board users. *Journal of Speech and Hearing Disorders, 55,* 231–243.

Beisler, J. M., & Tsai, L. Y. (1983). A pragmatic approach to increase expressive language skills in young autistic children. *Journal of Autism and Developmental Disorders, 13,* 287–303.

Blew, P., Schwartz, I. S., & Luce, S. (1985). Teaching functional community skills to autistic children using nonhandicapped peer tutors. *Journal of Applied Behavior Analysis, 18,* 337–342.

Brady, M. P., Shores, R. E., McEvoy, M. A., Ellis, D., & Fox, J. J. (1987). Increasing social interactions of severely handicapped autistic children. *Journal of Autism and Developmental Disorders, 17,* 375–390.

Carr, E. G., & Darcy, M. (1990). Setting generality of peer modeling in children with autism. *Journal of Autism and Developmental Disorders, 20,* 45–59.

Carr, E. G., & Durand, V. M. (1985). Reducing behavior problems through functional communication training. *Journal of Applied Behavior Analysis, 18,* 111–126.

Carr, E. G., & Kemp, D. C. (1989). Functional equivalence of autistic leading and communicative pointing: Analysis and treatment. *Journal of Autism and Developmental Disorders, 19,* 561–578.

Carr, E. G., & Kologinsky, E. (1983). Acquisition of sign language by autistic children. II: Spontaneity and generalization effects. *Journal of Applied Behavior Analysis, 16,* 297–314.

Carr, E. G., Kologinsky, E., & Leff-Simon, S. (1987). Acquisition of sign language by autistic children. III: Generalized descriptive phrases. *Journal of Autism and Developmental Disorders, 17,* 217–229.

Charlop, M. H. (1986). Setting effects on the occurrence of autistic children's immediate echolalia. *Journal of Autism and Developmental Disorders, 16,* 473–483.

Charlop, M. H., Kurtz, P. F., & Casey, F. G. (1990). Using aberrant behaviors as reinforcers for autistic children. *Journal of Applied Behavior Analysis, 23,* 163–181.

Charlop, M. H., Schreibman, L., & Thibodeau, M. G. (1985). Increasing spontaneous verbal responding in autistic children using a time delay procedure. *Journal of Applied Behavior Analysis, 18,* 155–166.

Charlop, M. H., & Walsh, M. E. (1986). Increasing autistic children's spontaneous verbalizations of affection: An assessment of time delay and peer modeling procedures. *Journal of Applied Behavior Analysis, 19,* 307–314.

Coe, D., Matson, J., Fee, V., Manikam, R., & Linarello, C. (1990). Training nonverbal and verbal play skills to mentally retarded and autistic children. *Journal of Autism and Developmental Disorders, 20,* 177–187.

Cowdery, G. E., Iwata, B. A., & Pace, G. M. (1990). Effects and side effects of DRO as treatment for self-injurious behavior. *Journal of Applied Behavior Analysis, 23,* 497–506.

Dorsey, M. F., Iwata, B. A., Reid, D. H., & Davis, P. A. (1982). Protective equipment: Continuous and contingent application in the treatment of self-injurious behavior. *Journal of Applied Behavior Analysis, 15,* 217–230.

Duker, P. C., & Rasing, E. (1989). Effects of redesigning the physical environment on self-stimulation and on-task behavior in three autistic-type developmentally disabled individuals. *Journal of Autism and Developmental Disorders, 19,* 449–460.

Dunlap, G., & Koegel, R. L. (1980). Motivating autistic children through stimulus variation. *Journal of Applied Behavior Analysis, 13,* 619–627.

Durand, V. M., & Carr, E. G. (1987). Social influences on "self-stimulatory" behavior: Analysis and treatment application. *Journal of Applied Behavior Analysis, 20,* 119–132.

Durand, V. M., & Crimmins, D. B. (1987). Assessment and treatment of psychotic speech in an autistic child. *Journal of Autism and Developmental Disorders, 17,* 17–28.

Dyer, K., Christian, W. P., & Luce, S. C. (1982). The role of response delay in improving the discrimination performance of autistic children. *Journal of Applied Behavior Analysis, 15,* 231–240.

Dyer, K., Dunlap, G., & Winterling, V. (1990). Effects of choice on the serious problem behaviors of students with severe handicaps. *Journal of Applied Behavior Analysis, 23,* 515–524.

Edelson, S. M., Taubman, M. T., & Lovaas, O. I. (1983). Some social contexts of self-destructive behavior. *Journal of Abnormal Child Psychology, 11,* 299–312.

Egel, A. L. (1981). Reinforcer variation: Implications for motivating developmentally disabled children. *Journal of Applied Behavior Analysis, 14,* 345–356.

Egel, A. L., & Gradel, K. (1988). Social integration of autistic children: Evaluation and recommendations. *Behavior Therapist, 11,* 7–11.

Egel, A. L., Richman, G. S., & Koegel, R. L. (1981). Normal peer models and autistic children's learning. *Journal of Applied Behavior Analysis, 14,* 3–12.

Ferrari, M., & Harris, S. L. (1981). The limits and motivating potential of sensory stimuli as reinforcers for autistic children. *Journal of Applied Behavior Analysis, 14,* 339–343.

Gaylord-Ross, R. J., Haring, T. G., Breen, C., & Pitts-Conway, V. (1984). The training and generalization of social interaction skills with autistic youth. *Journal of Applied Behavior Analysis, 17,* 229–247.

Gordon, R., Handleman, J. S., & Harris, S. L. (1986). The effects of contingent versus noncontingent running on the out-of-seat behavior of an autistic boy. *Child and Family Behavior Therapy, 8,* 337–344.

Handleman, J. S., & Harris, S. L. (1986). *Educating the developmentally disabled. Meeting the needs of children and families.* Boston, MA: College-Hill.

Haring, T. G., & Kennedy, C. H. (1990). Contextual control of problem behavior in students with severe disabilities. *Journal of Applied Behavior Analysis, 23,* 235–243.

Haring, T. G., Kennedy, C. H., Adams, M. J., & Pitts-Conway, V. (1987). Teaching generalization of purchasing skills across community settings to autistic youth using videotaped modeling. *Journal of Applied Behavior Analysis, 20,* 89–96.

Harris, S. L., & Handleman, J. S. (Eds.). (1990). *Aversive and nonaversive interventions.* New York: Springer.

Harris, S. L., Handleman, J. S., & Alessandri, M. (1990). Teaching youths with autism to offer assistance. *Journal of Applied Behavior Analysis, 23,* 297–305.

Harris, S. L., Handleman, J. S. Kristoff, B., Bass, L., & Gordon, R. (1990). Changes in language development among autistic and peer children in segregated and integrated preschool settings. *Journal of Autism and Developmental Disorders, 20,* 23–31.

Hawkins, A. H. (1982). Influencing leisure choices of autistic like children. *Journal of Autism and Developmental Disorders, 12,* 359–366.

Howlin, P. (1989). Changing approaches to communication training with autistic children. *British Journal of Disorders of Communication, 24,* 151–168.

Ihrig, K., & Wolchik, S. A. (1988). Peer versus adult models and autistic children's learning: Acquisition, generalization, and maintenance. *Journal of Autism and Development Disorders, 18,* 67–79.

Koegel, R. L., Dunlap, G., & Dyer, K. (1980). Intertrial interval duration and learning in autistic children. *Journal of Applied Behavior Analysis, 13,* 91–99.

Koegel, R. L., Dyer, K., & Bell, L. K. (1987). The influence of child-preferred activities on autistic children's social behavior. *Journal of Applied Behavior Analysis, 20,* 243–252.

Koegel, R. L., O'Dell, M., & Dunlap, G. (1988). Producing speech use in nonverbal autistic children by reinforcing attempts. *Journal of Autism and Developmental Disorders, 18,* 525–538.

Koegel, R. L., O'Dell, M. C., & Koegel, L. K. (1987). A natural language teaching paradigm for nonverbal autistic children. *Journal of Autism and Developmental Disorders, 17,* 187–200.

Koegel, R. L., Russo, D. C., & Rincover, A. (1977). Assessing and training teachers in the generalized use of behavior modification with autistic children. *Journal of Applied Behavior Analysis, 10,* 197–205.

Koegel, R. L., & Williams, J. A. (1980). Direct versus indirect response-reinforcer relationships in teaching autistic children. *Journal of Abnormal Child Psychology, 8,* 537–547.

Konstanareas, M. M. (1987). Autistic children exposed to simultaneous communication training: A follow-up. *Journal of Autism and Developmental Disorders, 17,* 115–131.

Lancioni, G. E. (1983). Using pictorial representations as communication means with low-functioning children. *Journal of Autism and Developmental Disorders, 13,* 87–105.

Lanquetot, R. (1989). The effectiveness of peer modeling with autistic children. *Journal of the Multihandicapped Person, 2,* 25–34.

Linscheid, T. R., Iwata, B., Ricketts, R. W., Williams, D. E., & Griffin, J. C. (1990). Clinical evaluation of the self-injurious behavior inhibiting system (SIBIS). *Journal of Applied Behavior Analysis, 23,* 53–78.

Lord, C., & Hopkins, J. M. (1986). The social behavior of autistic children with younger and same-age nonhandicapped peers. *Journal of Autism and Developmental Disorders, 16,* 249–262.

Lovaas, O. I. (1987). Behavioral treatment and normal educational and intellectual functioning in young autistic children. *Journal of Consulting and Clinical Psychology, 55,* 3–9.

Lovaas, O. I., Berberich, J. P., Perloff, B. F., & Schaeffer, B. (1966). Acquisition of imitative speech by schizophrenic children. *Science, 151,* 705–707.

Lovaas, O. I., Koegel, R. L., Simmons, J. Q., & Long, J. S. (1973). Some generalization and follow-up measures on autistic children in behavior therapy. *Journal of Applied Behavior Analysis, 6,* 131–165.

Lovaas, O. I., Smith, T., & McEachin, J. J. (1989). Clarifying comments on the young autism study: Reply to Schopler, Short, and Mesibov. *Journal of Consulting and Clinical Psychology, 57,* 165–167.

Maag, J. W., Wolchik, S. A., Rutherford, R. B., & Parks, B. T. (1986). Response covariation of self-stimulatory behaviors during sensory extinction procedures. *Journal of Autism and Developmental Disorders, 16,* 119–132.

Matson, J. L., Sevin, J. A., Fridley, D., & Love, S. R. (1990). Increasing spontaneous language in three autistic children. *Journal of Applied Behavior Analysis, 23,* 227–233.

McEvoy, M. A., Nordquist, V. M., Twardosz, S., Heckaman, K. A., Wehby, J. H., & Denny, R. K. (1988). Promoting autistic children's peer interactions in an integrated early childhood setting using affection activities. *Journal of Applied Behavior Analysis, 21,* 193–200.

McGee, G. G., Krantz, P. J., Mason, D., & McClannahan, L. E. (1983). A modified incidental-teaching procedure for autistic youth: Acquisition and generalization of receptive object labels. *Journal of Applied Behavior Analysis, 16,* 329–338.

McGee, G. G., & Krantz, P. J., & McClannahan, L. E. (1984). Conversational skills for autistic adolescents: Teaching assertiveness in naturalistic game settings. *Journal of Autism and Developmental Disorders, 14,* 319–330.

Mesibov, G. (1984). Social skills training with verbal autistic adolescents and adults: A program model. *Journal of Autism and Developmental Disorders, 14,* 395–404.

Meyer, L. H., Fox, A., Schermer, A., Ketelsen, D., Montan, N., Maley, K., & Cole, D. (1987). The effects of teacher intrusion on social play interactions between children with autism and their nonhandicapped peers. *Journal of Autism and Developmental Disorders, 17,* 315–332.

Murphy, G. (1982). Sensory reinforcement in the mentally handicapped and autistic child: A review. *Journal of Autism and Developmental Disorders, 12,* 265–278.

Nishimura, B., Watamaki, T., Sato, M., & Wakabayashi, S. (1987). The criteria for early use of nonvocal communication systems with nonspeaking autistic children. *Journal of Autism and Developmental Disorders, 17,* 243–253.

Odom, S. L., Hoyson, M., Jamieson, B., & Strain, P. S. (1985). Increasing handicapped preschoolers' peer social interactions: Cross-setting and component analysis. *Journal of Applied Behavior Analysis, 18,* 3–16.

Odom, S. L., & Speltz, M. L. (1983). Program variations in preschools for handicapped and nonhandicapped children: Mainstreamed vs. integrated special education. *Analysis and Intervention in Developmental Disabilities, 3,* 89–103.

Odom, S. L., & Strain, P. S. (1986). A comparison of peer-initiation and teacher-antecedent interventions for promoting reciprocal interactions of autistic preschoolers. *Journal of Applied Behavior Analysis, 19,* 59–71.

Oke, N. J., & Schreibman, L. (1990). Training social initiation to a high-functioning autistic child: Assessment of collateral behavior change and generalization in a case study. *Journal of Autism and Developmental Disorders, 20,* 479–497.

Rimland, B. (1964). *Infantile autism.* New York: Appleton-Century-Crofts.

Rincover, A., Newsom, C. D., Lovaas, O. I., & Koegel, R. L. (1977). Some motivational properties of sensory stimulation in psychotic children. *Journal of Experimental Child Psychology, 23,* 312–323.

Runco, M. A., Charlop, M. H., & Schreibman, L. (1986). The occurrence of autistic children's self-stimulation as a function of familiar versus unfamiliar stimulus conditions. *Journal of Autism and Developmental Disorders, 16,*31–44.

Sasso, G. M., & Rude, H. A. (1987). Unprogrammed effects of training high-status peers to interact with severely handicapped children. *Journal of Applied Behavior Analysis, 20,* 35–44.

Sasso, G. M., Simpson, R. L., & Novak, C. G. (1985). Procedures for facilitating integration of autistic children in public school settings. *Analysis and Intervention in Developmental Disabilities, 5,* 233–246.

Schepis, M. M., Reid, D. H., Fitzgerald, J. R., Faw, G. D., Van Den Pol, R. A., & Welty, P. A. (1982). A program for increasing manual signing by autistic and profoundly retarded youths within the daily environment. *Journal of Applied Behavior Analysis, 15,* 363–379.

Schopler, E., Brehm, S., Kinsbourne, M., & Reichler, R. J. (1971). Effect of treatment structure on development in autistic children. *Archives of General Psychiatry, 24,* 415–421.

Schopler, E., & Reichler, R. J. (1971a). Parents as cotherapists in the treatment of psychotic children. *Journal of Autism and Childhood Schizophrenia, 1,* 87–102.

Schopler, E., & Reichler, R. J. (1971b). Psychobiological referents for the treatment of autism. In D. W. Churchill, G. D. Alpern, & M. K. DeMyer (Eds.), *Infantile autism* (pp. 243–264). Springfield IL: Thomas.

Schopler, E., Short, A., & Mesibov, G. (1989). Relation of behavioral treatment to "normal functioning": Comment on Lovaas. *Journal of Consulting and Clinical Psychology, 57,* 162–164.

Shafer, M. S., Egel, A. L., & Neef, N. A. (1984). Training mildly handicapped peers to facilitate changes in the social interaction skills of autistic children. *Journal of Applied Behavior Analysis, 17,* 461–476.

Strain, P. S. (1983). Generalization of autistic children's social behavior change: Effects of developmentally integrated and segregated settings. *Analysis and Intervention in Developmental Disabilities, 3,* 23–34.

Sugai, G., & White, W. J. (1986). Effects of using object self-stimulation as a reinforcer on the prevocational work rates of an autistic child. *Journal of Autism and Developmental Disorders, 16,* 459–471.

Wacker, D. P., Steege, M. W., Northup, J., Sasso, G., Berg, W., Reimers, T., Cooper, L., Cigrand, K., & Donn, L. (1990). A component analysis of functional communication training across three topographies of severe behavior problems. *Journal of Applied Behavior Analysis, 23,* 417–429.

Weeks, M., & Gaylord-Ross, R. (1981). Task difficulty and aberrant behaviors in severely handicapped students. *Journal of Applied Behavior Analysis, 14,* 449–463.

Wetherby, A. M. (1986). Ontogeny of communicative functioning in autism. *Journal of Autism and Developmental Disorders, 16,* 295–316.

Williams, J. A., Koegel, R. L., & Egel, A. L. (1981). Response-reinforcer relationships and improved learning in autistic children. *Journal of Applied Behavior Analysis, 14,* 53–60.

Wiliams, T. I. (1989). A social skills group for autistic children. *Journal of Autism and Developmental Disorders, 19,* 143–155.

Wolery, M., Kirk, K., & Gast, D. L. (1985). Stereotypic behavior as a reinforcer: Effects and side effects. *Journal of Autism and Developmental Disorders, 15,* 149–161.

Yoder, P. J., & Layton, T. L. (1988). Speech following sign language training in autistic children with minimal verbal language. *Journal of Autism and Developmental Disorders, 18,* 217–229.

Educational Approaches in Preschool
Behavior Techniques in a Public School Setting

ANDREW S. BONDY and LORI A. FROST

INTRODUCTION

Autism is a complex and often enigmatic developmental disability characterized by puzzling social communication. Whereas many people ponder how children with autism think about the world, others have studied how these children behave in the world they share with us. A behavioral approach to working with preschool children with autism emphasizes analyzing their actions in terms of the preceding circumstances and the ensuing consequences. This chapter addresses how one public school program integrated the technology associated with behavior analysis with the particular proclivities and aversions associated with children demonstrating this syndrome. We review both what is beneficial to teach such children and how their lessons can be effectively arranged.

THE DELAWARE AUTISTIC PROGRAM

We begin with a description of the Delaware Autistic Program (DAP), where each of the procedures to be discussed was developed. DAP is a

ANDREW S. BONDY • Delaware Autistic Program, 144 Brennen Drive, Newark, Delaware 19713. LORI A. FROST • Pyramid Educational Consultants, 5 Westbury Drive, Cherry Hill, New Jersey 08003.

Learning and Cognition in Autism, edited by Eric Schopler and Gary B. Mesibov. Plenum Press, New York, 1995.

full-year public school program serving all educationally classified autistic students ages 0–21 years. Delaware provides excellent fiscal support for a very strong staff–student ratio, including critical specialists, such as psychologists and speech and language pathologists (SLPs).

The program provides a wider range of services than most public school programs for autistic students. Among these are two community-based group homes, respite care, after-school community-based recreation programs, daily adaptive physical education, and in-home parent and family training. These services are available all year with an extended summer program and special respite days during major school vacations.

DAP serves over 150 students statewide, equivalent to an incidence rate of 9 per 10,000. There are three primary centers within the state. Many students are in team classes with less handicapped students, and some autistic students are in less restrictive settings, such as regular classrooms, where they receive supplemented services, such as speech therapy. The educational classification of autism used is similar to the DSM-III-R (American Psychiatric Association, 1987) diagnosis, but may include some children diagnosed as pervasive developmental disorder, not-otherwise-specified. As in other programs, the students vary widely in intellectual ability, although over 80% function in the retarded range. Of the children aged 5 years and younger entering the program, over 80% do not display functional speech.

The Educational Program

In this section, we describe how we begin the assessment of each child's strengths and weaknesses, how that information is used to identify what to teach a child, and how we actually teach a child critical skills. We then focus on two fundamental areas, behavior management and communication training, and describe several innovative systems designed to deal with these areas. The final section outlines how we approach the issues of student integration and parent involvement.

Intake Process

Parental permission is required to make a referral, because DAP is part of the public school system. However, a medical diagnosis of autism is not necessary for the school to conduct its own educational evaluation. Referrals are made by parents, family physicians, children's hospitals, social workers, child-screen teams, and other school personnel. During the intake process, the focus is on characteristics associated with autism rather than formal assessment of general intellectual functioning. The intake process for very young children combines standardized and nonstandardized procedures. Several staff, including a psychologist, a speech and language pathologist, and a teacher, directly observe the child within the school and in his or her home or day-care facility. Parents accompany the child to the school and are interviewed by several staff members. The parents also are observed and videotaped while interacting with their child in one unstructured situation, and one in which the parents are asked to direct the child toward specific activities. Various questionnaires are used with parents, including the Childhood Autism Rating Scale (Schopler, Reichler, & Renner, 1986) and the Autism Behavior Checklist (Krug, Arick, & Almond, 1980). We do not use exact cut-off scores to make the final classification recommendation to the Individualized Education Program (IEP) team.

When working with the child during this initial evaluation, staff members attempt to create situations during which the child may initiate communicative or social interactions. A variety of toys, snacks, and other materials are made available to the child. The child's interactions with these objects may help staff members assess play skills and potential reinforcers. Staff members also try to assess the child's reaction to being left alone or having simple routines interrupted.

Educational Programming

We describe the general educational philosophy for DAP because it is the basis for how we design each student's educational program. This philosophical orientation is combined with a functional approach to curriculum selection and activity selection.

Philosophical Orientation and Curriculum Guidelines

The long-term goal of the DAP is to teach students skills that enable them to function as independently as possible in the general community. We believe that each student should be served in a setting that provides the least restrictive effective environment. Therefore, one broad goal for our youngest students is to see them successfully function outside of a center-based program. We view the community as a teaching location equal in importance to the school (Squittiere, 1990; Squittiere & Bondy, 1988). Thus, even for these very young children, direct training in com-

We also believe that significant progress in communication skills must occur for long-term changes to develop in socialization and behavior management (Bondy, 1987). Therefore, communication programming occurs throughout the school day and is the shared responsibility of each member of the child's educational team.

We believe that long-term success with children's behavior-management problems depends upon the development of alternative actions by the children that essentially serve them in a manner similar to the problem behavior. For example, if a child were screaming out to gain a teacher's attention, part of the intervention would aim at teaching the child a more acceptable way of obtaining the teacher's attention. It is not appropriate to simply attempt to eliminate the screaming. These alternative responses can be developed only within an environment that ensures a rich array and schedule of reinforcers—as defined from the child's perspective.

Curriculum objectives are organized around key domains (Brown, Nietupski, & Hamre-Nietupski, 1976); objectives are categorized by aspects of a child's life (i.e., dressing, eating, playing with toys) rather than by supposed underlying abilities (i.e., fine- vs. gross-motor, cognitive). A young child's deficits in language and social orientation usually influence all facets of what young children do and learn and thus all aspect's of a child's life (in and out of school) must be considered in the development of the IEP.

Developing Initial Objectives

A new student's IEP and daily schedule are developed by a multidisciplinary team. Objectives are developed to provide services in areas where the child needs to display critical skills. For these very young children, many of their activities occur within a classroom setting but are not academically oriented. The classrooms are set up to promote frequent opportunities to play with toys, dolls, and other age-appropriate materials. Staff members, including specialists such as occupational and physical therapists, work with the children within the classroom (or out in the community, when appropriate). When specialists require materials or equipment that would not naturally fit into the classroom setting (e.g., adaptive physical education, certain occupational therapy or physical therapy activities), they remove the child from the primary setting.

The child's initial objectives are refined during the first month in DAP. To make the necessary adjustments, staff members are encouraged to use a variety of assessment instruments and work closely with parents to determine the child's unique needs. For example, parents may indicate determine the child's unique needs. For example, parents may indicate that they only go shopping at 1:00 A.M. when one parent can be assured that the child is asleep, because the parents cannot control their 3-year-old child in a supermarket or a mall. Depending on the magnitude of this type of problem, the team makes suggestions regarding an objective to teach the child how to accompany adults when shopping. Thus, the full IEP becomes one that has both functional objectives (either remedial or initial) and those that are derived from developmental inventories. As preschool children approach kindergarten or first-grade age, more academically oriented objectives are added.

Instructional Procedures

After staff members have identified *what* they will teach to a student, they begin to plan *how* they will teach the student. This section describes the types of educational procedures staff members can select and how they organize their teaching plans.

Contents of the Teaching Plans

The teaching plans developed within DAP address critical educational issues, including prompting strategies, error-correction procedures, and reinforcement systems (see Table 16-1 for the general content of lesson plans). After a student's objectives have been selected, staff members develop lesson plans using a system called Prescriptive Teaching Plans (PTPs; see DAP staff manual for details). These plans follow a standard behavior-analysis format in focusing upon the ABCs of teaching (i.e., the

Table 16-1. Lesson Plan Components

I.	Lesson format
II.	Prompt strategy
III.	Behavior specification (including task-analysis steps)
IV.	Reinforcement systems
	a. Within task
	b. Completed task
V.	Error correction strategy
VI.	Generalization
	a. Stimulus factors (i.e., people, places, etc.)
	b. Response factors (i.e., intensity, duration, etc.)
VII.	Data collection system and review

Source: Bondy (1991).

antecedents, behaviors, and consequences). We have assumed that there are a limited number of ways to teach, whereas there are an infinite number of skills that can be taught. Staff members begin their teaching plans by selecting designated prompting strategies and lesson formats.

Prompting Strategies

In this section we describe various prompting strategies. We broadly define prompts as actions taken by teachers before a child reacts during a lesson. Prompts may be verbal, such as asking a question or giving a direction; gestural, such as pointing to a door or tapping on a pencil; or modeling an entire behavior or part of that behavior. Finally, certain prompts involve physical assistance, either in part or throughout the entire student performance. The most common prompting strategy requires staff members to identify how intrusive each type of prompt may be for a student given a particular lesson. Staff members then arrange a prompt hierarchy from *Least Instrusive* to *Most Intrusive.* During a lesson, staff members begin with the least intrusive prompt. If a child does not perform the requisite response, then staff members provide the next level of prompt after a defined pause (e.g., 5 seconds). This process is repeated until the child completes the response.

One caveat is that while verbal prompts seem minimally intrusive to us, they are often the most difficult to remove once introduced. Many children become "prompt dependent" by the unnecessary inclusion of verbal prompts in routines that ultimately should not require verbal cues, as in many types of motor sequencing. For example, when teaching a girl to tie her shoes, if a staff member were to introduce each step in the sequence with a verbal cue (i.e., "now cross the laces," "now pull the laces," etc.) many children would wait for the verbal cue rather than learn each step as a function of the last motor step.

Another prompting strategy that involves sequencing of prompts is fading. Staff members begin with the most intrusive prompt and gradually reduce the degree of each prompt or the intrusiveness of the type of prompt over time. Another useful strategy involves delayed prompting (Halle, Baer, & Spralin, 1981), whereby staff members begin with the cue that should ultimately be associated with a response, and follow that prompt with a currently effective prompt. Over a period of lessons, staff members gradually increase the delay between the ineffective and the effective cue. For example, assume that a girl can imitate single words but cannot name a spoon. When using delayed prompting, the teacher would hold the spoon up and immediately say "spoon." Given the child's imitative skills, she is likely to imitate and say "spoon." Next, the teacher would hold up the spoon and pause for half a second before saying "spoon." Over a series of trials, the teacher would increase the delay between holding up the spoon and naming it. Many children begin to say "spoon" before the teacher says the word. Such responses are immediately rewarded and are more strongly rewarded than are imitative responses.

Lesson Formats

In this section we discuss how lesson arrangements are described in terms of their format. Lesson format refers to how the teacher presents a lesson with regard to repetition, sequence, and general conditions. A discrete trial format calls for isolating certain aspects of a lesson and repetition of small steps. For example, when teaching a child to name letters, the teacher could use index cards with different letters written on them with a child sitting at a desk. Asking the child to name each card constitutes a "trial" and the teacher can record success versus failure for each trial. On the other hand, an incidental format would rely upon letters naturally occurring in the classroom and lessons would focus on teaching these letters without creating a special lesson arrangement at a special desk. The advantages of discrete trial formats center on teacher control of materials and repetitions while incidental formats tend to offer advantages in terms of generalization and promoting child initiations.

An important aspect of teaching requires teachers to identify the independent steps that constitute a task. This process results in a task analysis. While we often identify complex behaviors with a single term, such as brushing teeth, getting dressed, etc., these actions actually consist of a series of steps. Many children learn certain steps more readily than other small steps. It is often important to note the exact steps that are presenting a problem and then consider altering the prompt strategy associated with teaching that particular step.

Furthermore, task sequences can be taught in several formats. Whole task presentation involves having the child engage in every step of the sequence with whichever level of prompt support is necessary. On the other hand, staff members may decide to use a backward-chaining procedure, wherein the initial steps are completely supported by the teacher, whereas only the last step is actually taught to the child. Once this last step is learned, then the teacher assists with all but the next-to-last step and attempts to teach this step. If this step is completed, the child generally continues with completing the already-learned last step. This format is often successful with tasks that have meaningful or noticeable outcomes for the child. For example, if a boy wants to go outside to play but does not have his shoes on, the teacher could help the boy with all aspects of putting on his shoes except for the last step. Once this step is completed, the child can go out to play. Over time, the child is expected to accomplish more of the task and always ends the sequence successfully and goes to play.

Another format is forward chaining, whereby the child is taught the initial steps and the teacher provides assistance for the remainder of the steps. This format is often used when a task has no important natural consequence for a child and the staff cannot easily link completion of the task to the start of another important task. To summarize, teachers must identify which prompts they expect to use while teaching a lesson, describe how these prompts are associated with each other, and plan how the steps of the lesson are to be arranged.

Reinforcement Strategies

After teachers have selected their prompt strategies, they next address how they will reward students for their positive performances. Teachers identify reinforcement strategies, noting the difference between within-task reinforcers and completed-task reinforcers. The long-term goal is to reduce within-task rewards and use completed-task reinforcers that are as naturally arranged as possible. Staff members describe the current schedule of reinforcement and how the current schedule can be modified over time to reduce the overall frequency of teacher-based rewards. The goal is not to eliminate the need for reinforcement systems, but to merge these school-based reward programs with those used in the community. For example, rather than seeking to eliminate all food- or drink-related rewards, we accept that most people in the real world self-arrange for reward schedules in which an hour or two of work is interrupted with the opportunity to buy a snack or a soda. We expect our older students to function under similar contingencies. Thus, we begin to gradually wean our younger students from their initially rich reward schedules to help prepare them eventually to function in the workplace under contingencies readily acceptable to society. Furthermore, it is crucial that staff members select rewards that are powerful from the student's perspective. For example, a staff member working with a child who likes to watch things spin would be encouraged to find toys that display the critical visual feedback from the child's point of view.

Error Correction

A unique aspect of our lesson plan structure is the requirement for staff members to predict and identify error-correction strategies appropriate for an individual's lessons (see Bondy, 1990). This section describes several error-correction strategies developed within DAP. Error-correction procedures arrange for a learning opportunity for the child following an error, rather than having staff simply "fix" the situation. For example, if a young boy left the bathroom and entered the classroom with his zipper open, the teacher could "fix" the situation by telling the child to pull up his zipper. However, after such a prompt, the child is unlikely to learn the appropriate skill and may, in fact, learn to depend upon this teacher's prompt. Instead, the teacher could "backstep" (Bondy, Peterson, & Newman, 1990) by prompting the child to return to the bathroom (i.e., the place before the error occurred), pull down his pants, start from that step, and avoid the error. This procedure places the correction under the appropriate stimulus and is likely to help the child learn the proper behavior. Use of this strategy does take a little more of the teacher's time when the error occurs, but it is likely to save time and effort in the long run.

Another error-correction strategy, often used in teaching language skills, is called model-prompt-switch-repeat. When teaching a child to name a coin, the teacher holds up a quarter and says, "What's this?" If the child incorrectly answers "dime," the teacher would *model* the correct answer: "quarter." The child is likely to correctly imitate the answer. However, at this point we cannot say if the child can answer the original question. Therefore, the teacher *switches* to another (usually simple) task, such as asking, "What's your name?" or "Touch your nose." The child, if truly attending to each teacher prompt, responds correctly. Now the teacher *repeats* the original prompt, saying, "What's this?" while holding up the quarter. If the child answers correctly, praise is provided along with any other reward associated with the lesson. This sequence assures the teacher that the child responded to the combination of the quarter and the question and not to some other superficial aspect of the lesson.

Finally, when errors occur at the same point in a task sequence over a period of time, the teacher may use *anticipatory prompting* to prevent potential errors. For example, if a girl does not put the cap back on a toothpaste container after rinsing her mouth, a typical reaction would be to prompt the child after this error. If the error occurred on a regular basis, however, the teacher could tap the top while the girl was still rinsing, thus cuing the child before the error occurs. The child is likely to complete rinsing as usual and is more likely to continue with the sequence without further prompts. Over time, the anticipatory prompt can be faded in magnitude or be moved farther back into the sequence until it is unnecessary.

Completing the Lesson Plan

The final sections of the PTP involve issues associated with generalization (both stimulus-related and response-related) and data collection. In this section the staff members link one particular objective to another and plan for long-term modifications in the response requirements. Data-collection decisions include how often data should be taken and how frequently the team should review the data. The program's guideline is that data should be useful to staff members in making teaching decisions and should not be collected merely to generate a set of numbers.

BEHAVIOR MANAGEMENT

The vast majority of the young children who enter DAP display one or more serious behavior-management problems. This section addresses how DAP designs intervention programs to help both children with serious behavior problems and the adults who work and live with them.

Behavior-management problems (i.e., aggression, tantrums, self-stimulation, property destruction, etc.) are often linked to the limited communicative repertoires of autistic children. As noted earlier, the long-range goal is to teach alternative responses that will be useful to the child. However, while a replacement repertoire is being identified and established, we must deal with the child's immediate responses, especially those that may be dangerous to the child or to other people.

Within DAP, there is a statewide system to review all behavior-management procedures via a Peer Review Committee and a Human Rights Committee process. These committees annually review all potential behavior-management procedures, including those considered benign. These committees, rather than program staff members, determine how restrictive, aversive, or ethically sound is a particular procedure. *Behavior-management procedures* are defined as any systematic attempt to reduce or eliminate behavior-management targets, such as self-injury, aggression, significant tantrums, or other behaviors that significantly interfere with traditional educational programming.

The committees categorize all behavior-management procedures as: a) procedures that may be utilized without further review; b) procedures for which data must be periodically reviewed after the fact; and c) procedures that should not be implemented without specific, prior-case review by the Peer Review Committee. A procedure for Emergency Review permits quick committee review to consider implementation of c-level or other emergency procedures given a rapidly developing crisis (e.g., a new and potentially dangerous form of self-injury suddenly appears in a student's repertoire).

COMMUNICATION TRAINING

Language, communication and social deficits are the most pervasive and handicapping deficits common to autism (Watson & Marcus, 1988). Within this section, we describe how DAP teaches nonvocal children a functional communication system and how we address the communication needs of children who display some functional speech.

Communication deficits include general delays in the development of language; atypical features such as total absence of speech (mutism), echolalia, perseverative language, and idiosyncratic use of language; and difficulties with conversation and discourse (Prizant, 1988). Children with autism typically display a wide array of problems related to the comprehension of language. The social deficits can range from problems with eye contact to a more global insistence on avoiding any form of social contact or interaction. Consequently, comprehensive programming for the preschool student's needs within these areas is crucial from the first day the student enters the program. As specific needs are identified and prioritized, team members work together to develop a plan for addressing communication goals within the student's activities.

Because of the need to address communication skills throughout the day, rather than in isolated or discrete instances, all speech/language intervention services are integrated into the classroom via a collaborative service-delivery model. The SLP works directly with each student, either individually or in groups, within the context of the student's regular daily activities. This model includes working with the students not only in the classroom, but at various community-based sites such as grocery stores, restaurants, shopping malls, and preschools. Furthermore, the SLP observes the teaching staff at work with the students and makes recommendations regarding teaching strategies. For example, if a student were learning to request a desired item, the SLP would recommend that the teacher arrange the classroom so that the desired items were visible but not readily accessible (e.g., out of reach or in a tightly closed, clear container). The SLP would suggest prompt strategies for the teaching staff to use that would help the child to appropriately request the item and that ultimately would lead to spontaneous requesting.

The format for teaching communication skills includes a blend of one-to-one teaching and naturalistic teaching strategies. One-to-one or discrete-trial training episodes initially may be necessary to teach a new communicative skill. The goal is to teach the student to use these skills in response to naturally occurring cues. Thus, staff members quickly switch from more structured teaching formats to increasingly child-directed strategies.

Communication Programming for Nonverbal Students

In this section, we describe our approach to working with very young children who do not have conventional speech. We describe a unique communication system that has had broad success with these children. Approximately 80% of the students entering DAP before the age of 6 have no functional verbal skills. They are either completely mute or do not use speech to affect the behavior of those around them. This group includes students who are extremely echolalic or students whose noncompliance interferes with adequate or effective communication. These students, from the first day at DAP, are taught to use a picture-based augmentative-communication system. This system, the Picture Exchange Communication System (PECS) teaches very young students a means of communicating within a social context (Bondy, 1987, 1988, 1989; Ryan & Bondy, 1988). To the best of our knowledge, DAP is the only program to use a picture-based system with autistic children as young as 2 years of age and to promote this system as the student's initial mode of communication. Children using PECS are taught to *give* a picture of a desired item to a communicative partner in exchange for the item. By doing so, the student initiates a communicative act for a concrete outcome within a social context.

PECS differs sharply from several other language-training approaches. A variety of language programs, both verbal (Lovaas, 1977; Guess, Sailor, & Baer, 1976; Kozloff, 1974) and sign language (Carr, Binkoff, Kologinsky, & Eddy, 1978), have several common characteristics. Each program assumes that attending (including eye contact), and motor and verbal imitation skills are prerequisites to teaching functional language. Normal children learn each of these skills because of the associated social consequences for them. Very young autistic children are not highly responsive to these types of rewards, and thus, these programs must provide nonsocial rewards to the child. For example, an autistic child may be given candy for looking into the eyes of his or her teacher. Such training may require weeks or months and is to be completed before functional communication training is formally begun. While such attending may have the form of normal eye contact, because it does not have the same consequences, it does not have the same function. Such training also does not teach the child to initiate social contacts, but rather focuses upon how the child should respond to the social approach of teachers.

Some augmentative or alternative communication systems (Reichle & Sigafoos, 1991) for language-deficient children have involved the use of pictures, thus avoiding the issues associated with teaching eye-contact and imitative skills. These picture-based systems have relied upon pointing to pictures (or touching and/or tapping them). Traditionally, pointing to pictures has followed a matching-to-sample format involving matching objects to objects, objects to pictures, and then pictures to objects. Training also generally involves teaching children to respond to verbal prompts such as "Point to the picture of the cup," or "Show me the cup." This type of responding may be relatively easy for nonautistic children because these actions are primarily rewarded and maintained by social reactions. However, such consequences are weak motivators for preschool-aged autistic children. Another difficulty sometimes encountered when attempting to teach autistic preschoolers to point to pictures is the self-stimulatory actions that may be engendered by such stimuli. Some children may tap upon the picture of a cookie while staring out the window. Teachers may rightfully wonder whether the child had engaged in a form of communication. Finally, pointing to pictures does not ensure that someone is there to "listen" to the child; that is, the child can point to a picture while alone (Ryan, 1990; Ryan, Bondy, & Finnegan, 1990).

Programs that involve speech-, sign-, or picture-point systems commonly teach labeling as the first communicative function (Carr, 1982; Powers & Handleman, 1984). We believe that labeling is not the appropriate initial communicative function to teach autistic children, because it fails to incorporate the types of reinforcers to which preschool autistic children are sensitive (Bondy, Finnegan, Ryan, & Wachowiak, 1989). As Skinner (1957) pointed out, labeling is maintained by "educational" or social reinforcers. Another communicative function, requesting, is maintained by its specified consequences. This verbal skill does not require socially based reinforcers and, therefore, can be learned immediately by autistic children. Eye contact, imitation, matching-to-sample, and labeling are all skills that are reinforced by social reactions from adults and are thus very difficult as initial behaviors to teach autistic children. The very first skill taught within PECS, therefore, is requesting, because this skill is maintained by specified, typically concrete reinforcers (Bondy & Ryan, 1991). The student learns to give a picture of a desired item to an adult in order to receive a highly desired item. This step can be learned because the child immediately receives what she or he wants. If the receipt of the item is also accompanied by social reinforcement (e.g., "Good!" "You want a cookie"), it initially is not this socially based praise that increases the likelihood that the student will repeat the behavior. Rather, the student learns that the behavior (giving a picture) is likely to result in obtaining a desired item and will repeat the behavior for that reason. Hopefully, over a period of time, social praise will begin to function as an effective reinforcer for the child's communicative attempts.

Steps of PECS

Training in PECS begins with teachers assessing potential reinforcers for each particular child. Items that the child persistently reaches for and takes are selected. The first phase of PECS (Ryan et al., 1990) involves teaching a child to pick up a single picture, place it into the open hand of the teacher, and thus exchange the picture for individual objects. While physical and gestural prompts are used in this phase, no verbal prompts should be provided lest the child become immediately dependent upon a verbal prompt. Next, when the child picks up the picture, the teacher gradually moves away from the child while keeping his/her hand open, so that the child is taught to get the picture and walk to the teacher to give him or her the picture. Gradually, additional pictures of unique reinforcers. Procedures consistent with various forms of discrimination training are used at this stage.

Once the student is able to use 10 to 20 pictures, the phrase "I want _____" is taught. In order to maintain the exchange, a "sentence strip" card is added to the communication board, so that the student places a single picture depicting "I want" and another picture corresponding to the desired item on the strip, and then gives the entire strip to the communicative partner. Next in the training sequence, the student learns to respond to the question: "What do you want?" This question is not taught earlier in order to reduce the likelihood of verbal-prompt dependency.

We also teach the child to respond to the words, "Do you want this?"—either concurrently with the prior step or independently. Teaching this specific "yes/no" question form involves another example of distinguishing between communicative function and form. The lessons involving "Do you want a cookie?" are of a different form than "Is this a cookie?" Although the answer to each involves the same form (i.e., "yes" or "no"), the corresponding reinforcers are different (i.e., the cookie in the former lesson, praise in the latter).

The next major step in the PECS sequence is teaching the student to label or "tact" items (Skinner, 1957). The student learns to answer the question "What is this?" by forming the phrase "It's a _____" on the sentence strip where "It's a" is a single picture. Spontaneous commenting or labeling then can be taught by combining modeling and prompt-fading techniques. Subsequent steps in PECS involve teaching additional vocabulary and concepts, along with new communicative functions. Further details regarding PECS are available in Bondy and Frost (1994).

Communication Programming for Verbal Students

In this section, the approach to working with students who have some functional speech is described. Communication programming for students entering DAP with some functional verbal skills focuses on ameliorating language delays and replacing atypical-language features with acceptable forms. These students often exhibit some use of appropriate communicative functions (e.g., requesting), but express these functions in nonconventional or atypical manners. For example, a student might request a drink by saying, "Do you want a drink?" For this student, intervention strategies would involve both reactions to the student when such a phrase is used (i.e., staff responding in a natural manner, "No I don't want a drink"), and preventative techniques (i.e., anticipatory prompting or modeling prior to an error). Young students with autism use a narrow range of words or phrases for expressing communicative functions, and these phrases often are learned and used in rote fashion. For such students, the SLP develops a series of goals involving new functions and forms, and the team develops a plan for teaching those functions throughout the student's day. For example, a student who requests reinforcing items only within familiar routines or contexts can be taught different means in different environments to request a wider variety of items, and can be taught to label or comment on those items in a social context.

In addition to the difficulties in the use of language, young students with autism demonstrate difficulties in their response to the communication of others. When children show difficulty in responding to even very simple directions, we teach them to respond to directions in which context or situational cues are highlighted. Instead of initially teaching a student to follow directions given in isolation during "training episodes," we teach those directions during familiar routines and activities in which the student is motivated to participate. For example, when sitting down to eat breakfast, a student might be shown his cereal and milk, and then be told to "get a spoon." Over time, the complexity of instructions is increased and contextual cues are reduced so that the student can respond to directions that are typical of those used in preschools and other settings. Students are taught to respond both to directions given individually and during group instruction.

APPROACHES TO INTEGRATION

Critical to the success of any program working with autistic children is its ability to teach behaviors that the students can use with peers, as well as with new adults. This section describes how DAP approaches teaching skills in integrated situations. The initial communication training with the nonvocal children via PECS puts an emphasis on the child successfully communicating with adults. As communication skills develop (both for children using PECS and children who speak), it is important to ensure that the new skills can be used with other children. Thus, as communication skills emerge, so also new social skills begin to appear if the appropriate context is provided. Within the classroom setting at DAP, however, a very young child will generally have only a few classmates, some of whom speak and some of whom may use other communication systems. Therefore, we seek appropriate communicative peers for these children as their communication repertoires expand.

In support of the principle of the least restrictive environment, one difficulty faced by a public school program for autistic preschoolers is the absence of pre-schooler classes in public schools. We have arranged for mainstreaming and reverse-mainstreaming with local kindergarten classes, but these classes often have too large a proportion of time devoted to academic tasks than is appropriate for our students. One unique solution has been for DAP to obtain student positions in local day-care or preschool programs, for which DAP pays the tuition. Staff members plan for a student to spend from 1 to 3 half-days within a center, and arrange for the student to be accompanied by staff (e.g., teacher, SLP, psychologist, or paraprofessional). The extent of time that the child will be accompanied by staff is largely a function of the wishes of the day-care staff. Although staff members work with all children within the day-care setting, at times the day-care workers prefer to continue to operate their programs without outside assistance. The goals for the child with autism in this setting focus on socialization and communication skills. Staff members note the child's initiation of language and other social skills, and also track the student's reactions to approaches by other children and group instructions by day-care personnel. Whereas traditional "preschool skills," (e.g., lessons related to numbers and letters) are monitored, they are not the basis upon which early success of the placement is judged. All of the children who have had successful preschool placements have had subsequent success in programs for mildly handicapped or nonhandicapped children.

PARENTAL INVOLVEMENT

Central to educating autistic preschoolers is involving parents with their children's education and development. In this section, we describe some of the strategies staff members use to teach parents new skills regarding interactions with their children. Our contact with parents begins during the intake process and remains important throughout the program. Staff communicate daily with parents via a home–school notebook and encourage daily comments from parents. Each IEP team assesses the family's need for formal training and recommends the type and amount of in-home as well as in-school training that a family should receive. The team also recommends which team members would best work with parents on particular issues in the home. Staff members work with the student until a successful protocol is developed. For example, for several years, one young child awoke at 2 or 3 o'clock in the morning, nagging his mother to make him oatmeal. For various reasons, his parents were not successful in their attempts to deal with this problem. Paraprofessional staff members went to the child's home at the critical wake-up time and directly intervened when the child got out of bed. The parents were able to continue the program to maintain the changes introduced by program staff. Several other forms of parental involvement are used by DAP (Bondy & Battaligni 1992), ranging from group discussions led by staff or nonprogram experts to parent "rap" sessions. Staff members have held special monthly sessions aimed at parents of preschoolers, and have reviewed a wide range of topics, including medical concerns, dietary issues, legal issues, sibling concerns, and post-school planning.

The program also operates a respite program that affords parents in- or out-of-home opportunities to partake in activities while their child is watched by trained personnel. This program is primarily paid by State funds but is partially paid by parents. Emergency respite in staff members' homes or a group home also is available to parents.

OUTCOME MEASURES

PECS Outcome Data

The outcome data for children taught via PECS has been very encouraging (Bondy & Peterson, 1990). Over the past 5 years, 66 children 5 years of age and younger have entered DAP without functional speech or other alternative communication systems. This group does not include children with speech difficulties such as echolalia, perservation, or similar unusual speech features if the child also displayed functional speech skills.

Although the absence of language makes estimations of overall intellectual functioning difficult with such young children, the range of such functioning has been from near normal to profoundly retarded. All of these children lived with their parents or guardians. Each child learned to exchange at least one picture for a potent reinforcer within 1 month of initiating PECS.

A typical pattern of picture use and speech acquisition is depicted in Figure 16-1. This child, as has been the case with over half of this group, demonstrated rapid acquisition of picture use. The child's first spoken words did not appear until several months after the introduction of PECS. During the next few months, the child acquired the use of additional pictures and used more spoken words. When the picture repertoire was about 80 items, the child's use of speech permitted staff to begin to put away some pictures. Twelve months after starting PECS, the child used only speech to communicate with adults and peers.

Of the total group begun on PECS, 34 children now use functional speech without any augmentation by a picture or symbol-based system. Of the other children, 14 use a combination of speech and pictures or written words. Within this group with a "mixed" outcome, 10 children have been

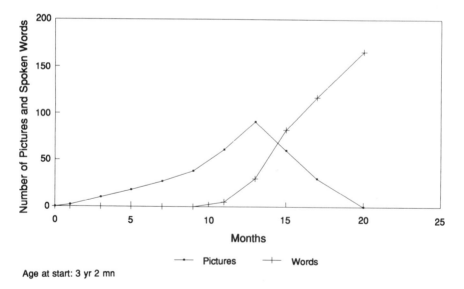

Age at start: 3 yr 2 mn

Fig. 16-1. The month-by-month acquisition of picture use and spoken-word use by a student (aged 3 years 2 months) started on the Picture-Exchange Communication System (PECS) (Bondy & Peterson, 1990).

in the program less than 2 years. Thus, of the total group, 73% have come to use speech solely or in combination with an augmentative system following initial training with PECS. Of the 19 children who have stayed on a picture-based system, the large majority perform in the severely and profoundly retarded range of intellectual functioning.

The changes in communication skills also have been associated with changes in behavior-management problems and various idiosyncratic behaviors of the children. For example, the Autistic Behavior Checklist (Krug et al., 1980) provides a listing of various unusual behaviors often associated with autism. The higher the score on this checklist, the greater the number of unusual or problematic behaviors have been described for a child. Children who have been placed on PECS have shown different degrees of changes in their ABC scores associated with different communication modalities (see Fig. 16-2). Children who stayed on picture-based systems displayed a very small reduction in their ABC scores, whereas students who used speech augmented by pictures displayed modest overall reductions. However, those children who learned to speak following PECS demonstrated a very large reduction in their ABC score. The mean scores for these three groups were comparable upon intake and were not

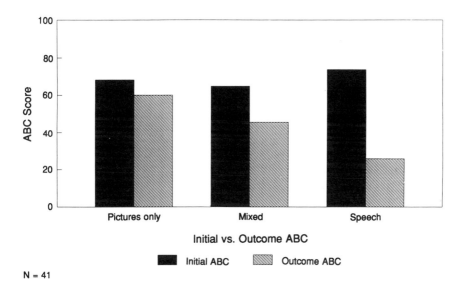

Fig. 16-2. The Autism Behavior Checklist (ABC) scores for students who started on the Picture-Exchange Communication System (PECS) by their initial scores and their score associated with their communication modality outcome (Krug et al., 1980).

associated with the communication-modality outcome for these students. While these outcomes are encouraging, they alone cannot support a causal relationship between the development of effective communication skills and the reduction of behavior-management targets.

General Outcome Data

We believe that one important purpose of our federal mandate to provide special students with a free and appropriate education is to provide them with a range of placement options in which they can maximize their potential. One such option is a center-based program. Such placement options are appropriate only if they are selected because they can meet the needs of some children (and are thus not mandatory for all children with a specific educational classification) and can be demonstrated to be educationally effective. When students are placed within a center-based program, there must be an emphasis upon getting those children into other types of placement options. All children who have entered DAP at age 5 or under and were speaking are now placed in either an integrated setting or have been de- or reclassified. Of the children entering DAP and placed upon the PECS program, 75% of those who have been in DAP for more than 1 year are now in integrated settings, or have been de- or reclassified. We believe such an outcome supports the overall success of DAP and its approach to educating preschool children with autism.

CONCLUSIONS

The Delaware Autistic Program, a public school organization, provides a wide range of education services to preschool children with autism. The program combines educational, behavioral, and communicative technology in the design of programs to develop critical skills that very young children with autism rarely develop without formal intervention. The program emphasizes using the Picture-Exchange Communication system to rapidly introduce functional communication skills to nonvocal children in a manner that eventually promotes the development of speech. Lesson plans follow a behavior-analytic framework to address prompting and reinforcement strategies, error correction, and long-term goal setting. Behavior-management plans focus on completing a functional analysis of critical behaviors and developing strategies to promote functionally equivalent alternative responses. There is a program-wide emphasis on community and other real world-oriented le₎ gram is fully involved with all levels of educational oppo each school district and has seen a large proportion ₍ children become successful students in a variety of classes ₁ᵤ₋ handicapped or nonhandicapped students. We hope to continue in our efforts to rapidly introduce language skills to these children and to expand upon their social-orientation-related skills. We also hope that in the near future, many more public schools' administrators will see the benefits and feasibility of directly operating preschool programs for very young children with autism.

REFERENCES

American Psychiatric Association. (1987). *Diagnostic and statistical manual of mental disorders* (3rd ed., rev.). Washington, DC: Author.

Bondy, A. (chair) (1987, May). Alternative and augmentative communication systems for autistic students. Symposium conducted at the Association for Behavior Analysis Convention, Nashville, TN.

Bondy, A. (chair) (1988a, May). Introducing picture-based communication systems with autistic students. Symposium conducted at the Association for Behavior Analysis Convention, Philadelphia, PA.

Bondy, A. (1988b, May). Autism and initial communication training: How long have we been wrong? Paper presented at the Association for Behavior Analysis Convention, Philadelphia, PA.

Bondy, A. (1989, May). The development of language via a picture exchange system with very young autistic children. Paper presented at Association for Behavior Analysis Convention, Milwaukee, WI.

Bondy, A. (Chair) (1990, May). Error correction: Three novel approaches. Symposium conducted at the Association for Behavior Analysis Convention, Nashville, TN.

Bondy, A. (Ed.). (1991). *Delaware Autistic Program Staff Manual*. Newark, DE: Delaware Autistic Program.

Bondy, A., & Battaglini, K. (1992). Strengthening the home-school-community interface for students with severe disabilities. In S. Christenson & J. C. Conoley (Eds.), *Home-school collaboration: Building a fundamental educational resource* (pp. 423–441). Silver Spring, MD: National Association of School Psychologists.

Bondy, A., Finnegan, C. S., Ryan, L. F., & Wachowiak, J. E. (1989, May). Novel augmentative communication strategies with young adolescent autistic students. Paper presented at the American Speech and Hearing Association Convention, St. Louis, MO.

Bondy, A. & Frost, L. (1994). The picture exchange communication system. *Focus on Autistic Behavior, 9*, 1–19.

Bondy, A., & Peterson, S. (1990, May). The point is not to point: Picture-exchange communication system with young students with autism. Paper presented at the Association for Behavior Analysis Convention, Nashville, TN.

Bondy, A., Peterson, S., Frangia, S., & Tarleton, R. (1990, May). Error correction procedures: Model, prompt, switch, repeat. Paper presented at the Association for Behavior Analysis Convention, Nashville, TN.

Bondy, A., Peterson, S., & Newman, P. (1990, May). Error correction procedures: Backstep. Paper presented at the Association for Behavior Analysis Convention, Nashville, TN.

Bondy, A., & Ryan, L. (1991, May). Picture-exchange communication system: Its relationship to *Verbal Behavior*. Paper presented at the Association for Behavior Analysis Convention, Atlanta, GA.

Brown, L., Nietupski, J., & Hamre-Nietupski, S. (1976). The criterion of ultimate functioning and public school services for severely handicapped students. In M. A. Thomas (Ed.), *Hey, don't forget about me: Education's investment in the severely, profoundly, and multiply handicapped* (pp. 2–15). Reston, VA: Council for Exceptional Children.

Carr, E. (1982). Sign language. In R. Koegel, A., Rincover & A., Egel (Eds.), *Educating and understanding autistic children* (pp. 142–157).

Carr, E., Binkoff, J., Kologinsky, E., & Eddy, E. (1978). Acquisition of sign language by autistic children. I: Expressive labeling. *Journal of Applied Behavior Analysis, 11,* 489–501.

Finnegan, C., Mclaughlin, D., Ryan, L., Wachowiak, J., Swanson, C., & Bondy, A. (1987). The impact of alternative/augmentative communication systems on inappropriate behaviors. Paper presented at the Association for Behavior Analysis convention, Nashville, TN.

Guess, D., Sailor, W., & Baer, D. (1976). *Functional speech and language training for the severely handicapped* (Vols. 1–4). Lawrence, KS: H & H Enterprises.

Halle, J. W., Baer, D., and Spradlin, J. E. (1981). Teacher's generalized use of delay as a stimulus control procedure to increase language use in handicapped children. *Journal of Applied Behavior Analysis, 14,* 389–409.

Kozloff, M. A. (1974). *Educating children with learning and behavior problems*. New York: Wiley.

Krug, D. A., Arick, J. R., & Almond, P. J. (1980). Behavior checklist for identifying severely handicapped individuals with high levels of autistic behavior. *Journal of Child Psychology and Psychiatry, 21,* 221–229.

Lovaas, O. I. (1977). *The autistic child: Language development through behavior modification*. New York: Irvington.

Powers, M. (1989). *Children with autism: A parent's guide*. Rockville, MD: Woodbine House.

Powers, M., & Handleman, J. (1984). *Behavioral assessment of severe developmental disabilities*. Rockville, MD: Aspen Press.

Prizant, B. (1988). Communication in the autistic client. In N. Lass, L. Reynolds, J. Northern, and D. Yoder (Eds.), *Handbook on speech, language, and hearing*. Toronto: D.C. Decker, Inc.

Reichle, J., & York, J., & Sigafoos, J. (1991). *Implementing augmentative and alternative communication strategies for learners with severe disabilities*. Baltimore, MD: Brooks.

Ryan, L. (1990, February). Picture-based augmentative communication systems for autistic students. Paper presented at the Mid-South Conference on Communicative Disorders. Memphis, TN.

Ryan, L., & Bondy, A. (1988, May). Beginning picture-based communication systems with very young autistic children. Paper presented at the Association for Behavior Analysis Convention, Philadelphia, PA.

Ryan, L., Bondy, A., & Finnegan, C. (1990, May). Please don't point! Interactive augmentative communication systems for young children. Paper presented at the American Speech-Language-Hearing Association. Seattle, WA.

Schopler, E., & Mesibov, G. B. (1988). *Diagnosis and assessment in autism*. New York: Plenum Press.

Schopler, E., Reicherler, R., & Renner, B. (1986). *The childhood autism rating scale (CARS)*. New York: Irvington.

Skinner, B. F. (1957). *Verbal behavior*. Englewood Cliffs, NJ: Prentice-Hill.

Squittiere, D. (1990, May). The community is not just a big classroom: The new role for teachers. Paper presented at the Association for Behavior Analysis Convention, Nashville, TN.

Squittiere, D., & Bondy, A. (Chairs). (1988). Autistic students as consumers and providers of community service: Implementing community-based training within a public school system. Conducted at the Association for Behavior Analysis Convention, Philadelphia, PA.

Watson, L. R., & Marcus, L. M. (1988). Diagnosis and assessment of preschool children. In E. Schopler & G. B. Mesibov (Eds.), *Diagnosis and Assessment in Autism* (pp. 271–301). New York: Plenum Press.

Index

Aberrant behavior
  communicative function of, 300, 302–303
  as reinforcement technique, 294
Abstract thought, 15–16, 145–147
Achievement discrepancy theory, of learning disabilities, 62–63
Acquisition tasks, in communication motivation treatment, 77–78
Affect
  relationship to cognition, 25–26
  in social behavior development, 24
Affective impairment, cognitive ability deficits and, 159–176
  ability to describe emotions, 163–165
  ability to label affect in others, 166
  conservation ability, 170, 171–172, 173–174
  emotional responsiveness, 168–170
  empathy, 166–167
  perceptual perspective taking, 170, 171, 175
  seriation ability, 172
Affective perspective taking, 166–167
After-school integrated social groups, 231, 232–238
Aggressive behavior
  functional assessment of, 303
  motivation and, 74
Agnosia
  facial, 45–46, 148, 208–208
  spatial, 46–47, 209
Agraphia, 39
Alcohol abuse, as fetal damage cause, 138
Alexia, 39
Anafranil (clomipramine), 146
Anarithmetica, 39
Anathria, 41

Antidepressant therapy, 146
Aphasia, 35
  expressive, 41
  in nonautistic children, 43
  receptive, 40–41
  seizure medication use in, 48
Apraxia, 37, 41
Arousal deficits, 270–272
  Bright Start remedial program for, 283–285
  hyperarousal, 14, 17, 22, 138
  neurobiological basis of, 112, 113
Artistic ability, 15
Associative memory, 15–16
Attention deficits, 16–18, 270–272
  auditory processing impairment and, 4
  Bright Start remedial program for, 283–285
  frontal lobe dysfunction in, 213
  hyperactivity disorder, 203
  neurobiological basis of, 112, 113
  See also Joint attention deficits; Stimulus overselectivity
Attention-shift problems, 152–153
Auditory stimuli processing, memory, functioning and, 107, 109
Autism
  causes of, 178
  definitions of, 57–61
    of Autism Society of America, 58–59
    of Diagnostic and Statistical Manual of Mental Disorders, 3–4, 59–61, 244
  diagnosis of
    as dual diagnosis, 67–68
    increasing frequency of, 60
  early conceptualizations of, 57–58

Autism (*Cont.*)
  learning disabilities relationship to, 34–
    35, 64–68
  neurological factors in, 271
  primary deficits of, 199, 200
  regressive/epileptic, 138, 139, 140
    IQ test performance in, 150–151
    sensory-processing problems of, 150–
    152
  "residual state" classification of, 59–60
  subtypes of, 138–141, 153
  symptoms of, 270–274
    appearance during infancy, 191
    as continuum, 138, 139, 178
    neurological disorders-related, 138
    triad of, 178, 179, 192–193
  See also High-functioning autism
Autism Behavior Checklist, 313, 329
Autism Society of American, autism definition of, 58–59
Autistic children, characteristics of, 270–274
Autistic traits, in relatives of autistic in-
  dividuals, 148
Aversive techniques, 304

Bayley Scale, 111
Behavior difficulties, of autistic individuals,
  73
  compared with learning-disabled in-
    dividuals, 67
  interrelatedness of, 73–74
Behavior management
  contingent-reinforcement approach in,
    281
  in Delaware Autistic Program, 320–321,
    329–330
Binet, Alfred, 111
Brain dysfunction
  as autism cause, 48–50, 90, 178
  as learning disabilities cause, 47–50, 61–
    62
  See also Brain stem abnormalities; Cer-
    ebellum abnormalities; Limbic sys-
    tem abnormalities
Brain imaging, 48, 141, 211–212
Brain stem abnormalities, 141
Bright Start, 269–292
  applications to autistic children, 283–289
    for arousal/attention deficit remedia-
    tion, 283–285

Bright Start (*Cont.*)
  applications to autistic children (*Cont.*)
    for communication deficit remediation,
    286–287
    for motivation deficit remediation, 287
    for social deficit remediation, 285–286
  cognitive-mediational behavior manage-
    ment in, 281
  cognitive small-group units in, 275, 276,
    280–281
  goals of, 275–276
  mediational teaching in, 278–280, 288–
    289
  parent participation in, 276, 281–282
  teacher training in, 288
  theoretical basis of, 276–278
Buddies program, in peer intervention,
  225, 226–232

California Verbal Learning Test, 125
Categorization abilities
  in autism, 119–122, 124–133, 160
    comparison with mentally-retarded in-
    dividuals, 125–126
    prototype-based strategies in, 129–131,
    132
    rule-based strategies in, 127–129, 130,
    131, 133
    theory-of-mind deficits and, 126–127
  definition of, 119
  in Down's syndrome individuals, 128–
    131, 133
  in normal development, 122–124
Cerebellum abnormalities, 112, 140–141,
  211
Cerebral hemispheric lateralization, 48,
  147
  echolalia and, 42
  functions of, 34
  information-processing deficits and, 99
  language development and, 40
  learning disabilities and, 7, 34, 43
  mathematical ability and, 39
  nonverbal learning disabilities and, 43
  reading abilities and, 36
  sequential processing and, 113
Childhood Autism Rating Scale, 245–246,
  313
Classification skills, 5–6. See also Categorization abilities

Classroom placement, of autistic children, 82–84. *See also* Cognitive education; Educational strategies
Cognition
  crystallized, 95, 96, 272
  fluid, 95, 96, 272
  functional systems of, 112–113
  integration with social activity, 160–161
Cognitive abilities, 5–6, 7, 14–16, 245
  assessment and interpretation of, 89–117
    of memory functioning, 107–110
    motivation and, 110–111
    practical considerations in, 110–112
    relationship to developmental assessment, 111
    sequential and simultaneous abilities assessment, 99, 101–107
  development of
    early, 16
    Piagetian theory of, 275, 276, 277–278
    transactional theory of, 276–277
  See also Cognitive processes
Cognitive ability deficits, 66
  adaptation to, 90–91
  affective impairment and, 159–176
    ability to describe emotions, 163–165
    ability to label affect in others, 166
    conservation ability, 170, 171–172, 173–174
    emotional responsiveness, 168–170
    empathy, 166–167
    perceptual perspective taking, 170, 171, 175
    seriation ability, 170, 172
  in autism subtypes, 138–141
  developmental brain lesions and, 90
  in learning-disabled children, 65–66
  process-oriented model of, 99, 101–105
  social cognition deficits, 22–25
Cognitive acquisition, social context of, 276, 277
Cognitive Curriculum for Young Children (CCYC). *See* Bright Start
Cognitive education, 269–292
  Bright Start program in, 10, 275–289
    application to autistic children, 283–289
    for arousal/attention deficit remediation, 283–285

Cognitive education (*Cont.*)
  Bright Start program in (*Cont.*)
    cognitive-mediational behavior management in, 281
    cognitive small-group units in, 275, 276, 280–281
    for communication remediation, 286–287
    evaluation of, 282–283
    goals of, 275–276
    mediational teaching in, 278–280
    for motivation remediation, 287
    parent participation in, 276, 281–282
    for social deficit remediation, 285–286
    theoretical basis of, 276–278
Cognitive-perceptual deficits, 245
  logic systems development and, 272
  relationship to social deficits, 273
Cognitive processes, 13–31, 137–156
  assessment of, 8
  differentiated from intelligence, 272
  general intellectual functioning, 14–16
  heterogeneity of, 25
  relationship to social thinking, 4
  relationship to task achievement ability, 121–122
  visual thinking, 141–148
    abstract thought in, 15–16, 145–147
    implications of, 144–148
    language ability in, 143–144
    nonvisual information in, 143
Communication boards, 302, 324
Communication deficits, 16, 65, 205, 273–274, 321
  DSM-III-R definition of, 59
  of learning-disabled individuals, 65, 67
  pragmatic, social relationships development and, 23
  prevalence of, 67
  types of, 5
  See also Language deficits
Communication training, 299–302, 304–305
  Bright Start remedial program for, 286–287
  in conversational skills, 8, 75–76
  in Delaware Autistic Program, 321–322
    for nonverbal students, 322–325, 326–330
    for verbal students, 325–326

Communication training (*Cont.*)
  motivation treatment, 7–8, 73–87
    child's choice of stimulus materials
      used in, 75–76
    deictic question use in, 80–82
    educational diagnostic testing and, 82–
      85
    interspersing maintenance skills in,
      77–78
    motivational treatment packages in,
      79–82
    natural reinforcers in, 78
    reinforcement of communicative at-
      tempts in, 76–77
    for spontaneous language and in-
      formation seeking, 80–82
    natural-language teaching paradigm,
      286–287, 295, 300
    for nonverbal students, 301–302, 322–325,
      326–330
    sign language, 43, 301, 302
Computed tomography (CT), 211
Computerized systems, for nonverbal communication, 302
Conservation ability, 170, 171–172, 173–174
Conversational deficits, 21–22
  skills training for, 8, 75–76
Crystallized intellectual abilities, 95, 96, 272
Cues
  acoustic, 109
  environmental
    internal mental representations versus,
      206, 207
    in pretend play, 209–210
  graphemic, 109
  semantic, 109
Curiosity
  lack of, in autistic children, 80
  use in language learning, 81

Daycamps, integrated programs in, 231,
  232–238
Daycare programs, mainstreaming in, 326
Deception, strategic, 208–209
Delaware Autistic Program, 10, 311–333
  behavior management in, 320–321
  communication training in, 321–326
    for nonverbal students, 6, 322–325,
      326–330
    for verbal students, 325–326

Delaware Autistic Program (*Cont.*)
  educational program of, 312–315
    curriculum objectives of, 314
    educational programming in, 313
    initial objectives development in, 314–
      315
    intake process for, 312–313
    philosophical orientation of, 313–314
  Individualized Education Program in,
    313, 314, 315
  instructional procedures of, 315–320
    error correction, 319–320
    lesson formats, 317–318
    lesson plan completion, 320
    prompting strategies, 316–317
    reinforcement strategies, 318
    teaching plans content of, 315–316
  integration approaches in, 326
  outcome measures of, 327–330
  parental involvement in, 313, 327
  Picture Exchange Communication Sys-
    tem of, 322–325, 326
    outcome data, 327–330
  Prescriptive Teaching Plans of, 315–316
  referrals to, 312–313
  respite care in, 327
Delayed prompting, 295, 316–317
Developmental lag theory, of learning dis-
  abilities, 63
Diagnostic and Statistical Manual of
  Mental Disorders, Third Edition
  (DSM-III)
  autism diagnostic criteria of, 59–60, 244
Diagnostic and Statistical Manual of Men-
  tal Disorders, Third Edition, Revised
  (DSM-III-R)
  autism diagnostic criteria of, 3–4, 60, 244
  learning disabilities diagnostic criteria of,
    61
Diagnostic and Statistical Manual of
  Mental Disorders, Fourth Edition
  (DSM-IV)
  autism diagnostic criteria of, 244
Differentiated reinforcement of other be-
  havior (DRO), 303–304
Directions
  autistic children's inability to follow, 110
  use in structured teaching, 264
  written versus verbal, 144–145
Discrete-trial format, 295, 317, 322

Disruptive behavior
    management of, 302–304
        in Delaware Autistic Program, 320–321
    motivation and, 74
    question use as alternative to, 80–82
Down's syndrome individuals
    categorization ability of, 128–131, 133
    strategic deception ability of, 208
    theory of mind of, 183, 187
Drug abuse, as fetal damage cause, 138
Dual diagnosis, of autism/learning disabilities, 67–68
Dyscalculia, 35, 38–39
Dysgraphia, 35, 37–38, 48
Dyslexia, 34, 36–37, 37
Dysphasia, 39–40
    auditory memory in, 109
    sequential and simultaneous processing assessment in, 101–105, 106
Dysthymia, Wechsler intelligence scales scores in, 100

Echoic memory capacity, 108
Echolalia, 19–20, 41–43, 67, 303
Educational strategies, for autistic children, 293–309
    for executive function deficits remediation, 214
    instructional formats of, 295
    mainstreaming and integration, 84, 288, 298–300, 304
    naturalistic instructional settings, 294, 304
    operant teaching technique, 269, 270, 293
    parents as cotherapists, 293
    peer intervention program, 221–240
        integrated social groups/daycamps, 231, 232–238
        peer-tutor/buddies programs, 9, 225, 226–232, 296–298, 304
    reinforcement techniques, 294–295
    for speech and language development, 299–302, 304–305
        nonverbal communication, 6, 301–302, 322–325, 326–330
        speech enhancement, 300–301
    structured teaching, 293
        efficacy of, 66
        historical background of, 243–244
        task organization in, 258–262

Educational testing
    motivation and, 82–84
    See also Cognitive abilities, assessment and interpretation of
Einstein, Albert, 148
Electroencephalographic (EEG) abnormalities
    in autistic children, 271
    in learning-disabled children, 47–48
Embedded Figures Test, 17
Emotional expression
    autistic children's understanding of, 166–170, 172
    personal narrative of, 148–150
    parental reports of, 165, 173
    See also Affect; Affective impairment; Affective perspective taking
Emotional perception deficits, strategic deception ability in, 208–209
Emotion-eliciting experiences, autistic children's description of, 163–165, 172–173
Empathy, 23, 166–167, 207
    personal experience of, 149–150
Environmental cues
    internal mental representations versus, 206, 207
    in pretend play, 209–210
Epilepsy, with autistic symptoms, 151
Error-correction strategies, 319–320
Escape response, in disruptive behavior, 303
Evoked potentials, 18, 150
Exclusion approach, to learning disabilities, 63–64
Executive function, 18–19
    definition of, 205
Executive function deficits, 9, 25, 199–219
    frontal lobe injury hypothesis of, 201, 205–215
        emotional perception impairment and, 208–209
        imitation deficits and, 209
        limitations of, 212–214
        neurological basis of, 210–212
        pretend-play deficits and, 209–210
        relationship to autism symptoms, 207–210
        spatial reasoning deficits and, 209
        theory-of-mind deficit and, 207–208
        treatment implications of, 214

Executive function (*Cont.*)
  neurological basis of, 112–113, 210–212
  studies of, 201–204
Eye contact avoidance
  by autistic infants, 210, 273
  management of, 322–323
    intrusive, 151

Face recognition deficits, 45–46, 148
Facial expression interpretation deficits, 24, 208–209
Facial-prototype learning, 124, 132
Fading, 316, 320
False beliefs testing, of theory-of-mind deficits, 23–24, 181–183, 184, 188–189
False photograph test, 212–213
Faraday, Michael, 148
Federal Register, learning disabilities definition of, 63, 65
Fever, as autistic symptom cause, 138
Fluid intellectual ability, 95, 96, 272
Foreign languages, autistic individuals' acquisition of, 143–144
Forward chaining, 318
Fragile X syndrome, 138
Freud, Sigmund, observing ego theory of, 5
Frontal lobe
  functions of, 205–206
  maturation of, 210
Frontal lobe dysfunction
  in attention deficit disorder, 213
  as executive function deficit cause, 8, 19, 200, 201, 205–215
    emotional perception impairment and, 208–209
    imitation deficits and, 209
    neurological basis of, 210–212
    pretend-play deficits and, 209–210
    relationship to autism symptoms, 207–210
    spatial reasoning deficits and, 209
    theoretical limitations of, 212–214
    theory-of-mind deficits and, 207–208
    treatment implications of, 214
  in phenylketonuria, 213
Functional assessment, of disruptive behavior, 302–304

Gaze deficits, 210
Generalization, of social skills, 297
  in peer tutor/buddies programs, 228

Generalized impairment, category-learning impairment and, 120, 121
Gestures
  autistic children's lack of, 188
  imitative use of, 42
  as prompts, 264–265
    inadvertent, 271
Graphic skills deficits: *see* Dysgraphia
Graphic symbol system, of nonverbal communication, 302

Head Start, 282
High-functioning autism
  cognitive abilities of, 5–6, 170–172, 173–174
    conservation ability, 170, 171–172, 173–174
    perceptual perspective taking ability, 170, 171, 175
    seriation ability, 170, 172
  relationship to learning disabilities, 64–66
  social understanding in, 159–170, 172–173
    ability to describe emotions, 163–165
    ability to label affect in others, 166
    empathy, 166–167
    parental reports of, 165
    relationship to cognitive abilities, 170–172, 173–174
    relationship to emotional responsiveness, 168–170
    theory of mind deficits and, 174
Hippocampal dysfunction, as autism basis, 22
Hyperarousal theory, of autism, 14, 17, 22, 138
Hypersensitivity, sensory, 140, 141, 150–151

Imitation
  in communication training, 322, 323
  deficits in, 160, 273
    in gesture use, 42
    prefrontal dysfunction and, 209
Inanimate objects, autistic children's attachment to, 45
Incidental-teaching format, 295, 300, 301
Infants
  autistic
    characteristics of, 270–271
    eye contact avoidance by, 273
  categorization abilities of, 123–124
  social understanding in, 161

Information-processing deficits, 15, 271
    cerebral hemispheric lateralization and,
        99
    complex-information processing deficits,
        17
    in frontal lobe-injured individuals, 201
    sequential mode versus simultaneous
        mode in, 99–105
    transactional theory of, 276–277
Information-seeking behavior, 80–82
Instructions. *See* Directions
Integration, of autistic children, 298–299
    in Delaware Autistic Program, 326
    See also Mainstreaming
Intellectual giftedness, 148
Intelligence
    differentiated from cognitive processes,
        272
    relationship to logic systems, 276–277
    Wechsler's definition of, 91
Intelligence quotient (IQ), in autism
    relationship to memory deficits, 22
    stability over time, 15
    See also Wechsler Intelligence Scale for
        Children—Revised
Intervention strategies, in autism, 6
Introspective thinking, 8

Japanese children, dyslexia in, 36
Jigs, 258–262
    functional levels of, 259–260, 261, 262
    individualization of, 260, 262
Joint attention
    autism-related deficits in, 5, 191–192, 210
    categorization impairment and, 133
    cognitive factors in, 161
    emotional factors in, 161
    neurobiological basis of, 112
    relationship to metarepresentation,
        191–192
    in infants, 161

Kaufman Assessment Battery for Children,
    Sequential and Simultaneous Pro-
    cessing Scales of, 15, 89, 101–107

Labeling
    of affect of others, 166, 167
    in communication and language train-
        ing, 144, 323, 324–325
Language, meaning and, 39–43

Language ability, testing of, motivational
    obstacles to, 82–84
Language deficits, 15–16, 19–22, 25, 33–34,
        273–274
    aphasia, 35
    expressive, 41
    in non-autistic children, 43
    receptive, 40–41
    seizure medication use in, 48
    cognitive deficits and, 15
    conversational deficits, 8, 21–22, 75–76
    dyscalculia, 38–39
    dysgraphia, 35, 37–38, 48
    dyslexia, 34, 36–37
    dysphasia, 39–40
    auditory memory in, 109
    sequential and simultaneous process-
        ing assessment in, 101–105, 106
    echolalia, 19–20, 41–43, 67, 303
    grammatical morphology, 20, 21
    memory functioning and, 107–108, 109–
        110
    motivation to communicate and, 73
    phonological processes deficits, 20, 76, 77
    qualitative deficits, 79
    quantitative deficits, 79
    syntax, 20–21
Language development, 37, 40–41
    in autism, 139, 140
    left cerebral hemisphere in, 49
    personal experience of, 143–144
Learned helplessness, 274
Learning
    clinical assessment methods for, 111–112
    spatial, 47
Learning disabilities, 57–70
    achievement discrepancy theory of, 62–63
    brain dysfunction and, 47–50
    developmental lag theory of, 63
    as dual diagnosis, 67–68
    early conceptualizations of, 61–63
    exclusion principle of, 63–64
    Federal Register definition of, 63, 65
    hemispheric lateralization and, 7, 34
    medical theory of, 61–62
    nonverbal, 43–47
        facial agnosia, 45–46, 148
        spatial agnosia, 46–47
        way-finding disorders, 46–47
    nonverbal intelligence quotient scores in,
        44

Learning disabilities (*Cont.*)
  relationship to high-functioning autism,
    64–66
  relationship to learning disabilities, 34–
    35, 66–68
  symptom cluster theory of, 62
  verbal. *See* Language deficits
Learning-disabled children
  participation in peer intervention pro-
    grams, 225–226
  social status of, 64
Learning discrepancy, 66
Learning Quotient, 35
Leiter International Performance Scale, 111
Letter Completion Test, 36
Limbic system abnormalities, 140–141, 211
Listening ability, 41
Listening tasks, dichotic, 17
Logic systems, 272
  relationship to intelligence, 276–277

Magnesium therapy, 151
Magnetic resonance imaging (MRI), 48,
  141, 211
Mainstreaming, 288, 298–300, 304
  in Delaware Autistic Program, 326
  negative effects of, 84
Maintenance trials, in communication motivation treatment, 77–78
Matching tests, 42
Mathematical ability impairment, 38–39
Maxwell, James, 148
Meaning
  acquisition of, 49
  language and, 39–43
Mediated learning experience (MLE)
  characteristics of, 278–280
  definition of, 278
  inadequate, 279
  See also Bright Start
Memory, 22, 107–110, 112
  associative, 15–16
  auditory stimuli processing and, 107,
    109
  echoic, 108
  emotional, 149
  language deficits and, 107–108, 109–110
  long-term, 107, 109–110
  non-language-based, 143
  short-term, 22, 107–108, 109, 110

Memory (*Cont.*)
  visual stimuli processing and, 107, 108–
    109
Mentally-retarded autistic individuals
  categorization ability of, 132
  cognitive abilities of, 15
Mental representation deficits. *See* Exec-
  utive function deficits
Mental states attribution deficits. *See* Theo-
  ry-of-mind deficits
Metacognitive development, 283
Metarepresentation, 23–24
  definition of, 180
  in play, 160
  relationship to pretense, 180–181, 191–
    192
M&Ms (Smarties) test, 182–183, 207–208
Model-prompt-switch-repeat, 319
Motivation
  to communicate. *See* Communication
    training, motivation treatment
  task-intrinsic, 276–277, 281, 282, 287
Motivation deficits, 274
  Bright Start remedial program for, 287
Motor learning, 14–15. *See also* Sensorimo-
  tor abilities
Motor skills. *See* Sensorimotor abilities
Musical ability, 15
Mutism, 41
Myelinization defects, 150–151

National Autism Society, 58
National Society for Children and Adults
  with Autism. *See* Autism Society of
  America
Natural-language teaching paradigm, 295,
  300
  comparison with repetitive practice ap-
    proach, 286–287
Neurofibromatosis, 138
Neurological disorders, autistic symptoms
  associated with, 138
Noise confusion, 138

Object permanence, 16, 160, 212
Observing ego theory, 5
One-to-one teaching methods, 269–270
Operant conditioning, 269, 270, 293
Oppositional disorder, Wechsler in-
  telligence scales scores in, 100

Parents
  as co-therapists, 293
  involvement in Bright Start program, 276, 281–282
  involvement in Delaware Autism Program, 313, 327
Parietal lobe, interaction with frontal lobe, 212
Peer intervention programs, 221–240
  integrated social groups/daycamps, 231, 232–238
    activities in, 235–238
    preparation of peers, 234
    recruiting peers, 232–234
    scheduling in, 235
  peer-tutor/buddies program, 9, 225, 226–232, 296–298, 304
    activities in, 229–231
    preparation of peers in, 227–228
    recruiting/selecting peers for, 226–227
    scheduling in, 228–229
  principles of, 222–226
  siblings' participation in, 238
Perception, in autism, 16–18
Perceptual perspective taking, 170, 171
Perseveration, as attention-shifting dysfunction, 153
Person perception, 44
Phenylketonuria, 138, 213
Phonology/phonics, 20, 76, 77
  use in reading, 145
Piagetian theory, of cognitive development, 275, 276, 277–278
Pictures, as nonverbal communicaiton technique, 302
Picture Exchange Communication System, 322–325, 326, 327–330
Picture schedules, 253–254, 255
Picture Story test, 37
Play
  use in peer-tutor/buddies programs, 230–231
  symbolic, impairment of, 5, 16, 23, 160, 179–181
    Block Design subtest of, 209–210
Play items, in communication motivation treatment, 76
Pointing
  referential, 210
  See also Gestures

Positron emission tomographic (PET) scans, 212
Preschool programs
  integrated and mainstreamed, 298–299
  peer modeling in, 297
  See also Delaware Autism Program
Pretense, relationship to metarepresentation, 180–181, 191–192
Pretend-play deficits. See Play, symbolic, impairment of
Problem-solving ability, 160
Prompts
  anticipatory, 319–320
  definition of, 316
  delayed use of, 295, 316–317
  with error correction, 319–320
  gestural, 264–265
    inadvertent, 271
  physical, 264
  strategies for, 316–317, 318
  verbal, 264–265
Proteus Mazes, 202
Psychoeducational Profile, 246
Psychometric assessment, 8. See also Cognitive abilities, assessment and interpretation of
Psychotic speech, 303

Question-asking, 80–82
  in mediational teaching, 283–284

Reading ability
  childhood development of, 37
  hemispheric lateralization and, 36
  word-calling impairment in, 42
Reading instruction
  phonics use in, 145
  preparation for, 284
Reasoning ability, 15, 17
Reinforcement
  in communication motivation treatment, 76–77, 78
  in Delaware Autistic Program, 318
  in speech skills training, 300
  in structured teaching, 265–266
  effect on task-intrinsic motivation, 7–8, 281
  techniques for, 294–295
  types of, 265–266

Repetitive behavior
  attention and, 18
  category-learning impairment and, 120
  as coping mechanism, 120
  verbal. *See* Echolalia
Representation, primary, 180. *See also* Metarepresentation
Requesting, in communication training, 323–324
Reticular activating system, 112, 113, 271
Rey Complex Figure Test, 203
Rey-Osterrieth Complex Figure test, 19
Rhett syndrome, 138
Ritualized behavior, category-learning impairment and, 120
Role playing, 285–286
Rote-memory, 124–125, 132–133

St. Paul Public Schools, peer tutor program of, 226
Sally-Ann false-belief test, 183, 184, 185, 186, 187
Savant skills, 73
Schedules, use in structured teaching, 251–255, 263
Seizures, as autism symptom cause, 140, 150–151
Self-injurious behavior, 73
  motivation and, 74
Self-stimulation, 274
  attention and, 18
  control of, 303
  motivation and, 74
  as reinforcement technique, 294
Sensorimotor abilities, 14–15, 25, 245
Sensory-processing deficits, personal narrative of, 151–153
Sensory stimulation, autistic children's responses to, 16–18
  as reinforcment technique, 294
  See also Stimulus overselectivity
Sequential processing, 99, 101–105, 112
  hemispheric lateralization and, 113
  Kaufman Assessment Battery for Children scales for, 15, 89, 101–107
  visual thinking methods for, 143, 145
  Wechsler Intelligence Scale for Children-Revised scales for, 15, 89, 101–107
Seriation ability, 170, 172
Serotonin levels, in autism, 271

Sign language, 43, 301, 322
Simultaneous processing, 99, 101–105, 112
  Kaufman Assessment Battery for Chidlren-Revised scales for, 15, 89, 101–107
  Wechsler Intelligence Scale for Children-Revised scales for, 15, 89, 101–105, 107
Singing, as learning method, 145
Social-avoidance behavior
  communication motivation treatment and, 76
  question use as alternative to, 80, 82
Social behavior development, affect and, 24
Social cognition, 22–25, 44
  See also Theory of mind
Social deficits, 4–5, 44–46, 65, 244–245, 272–273, 321
  causes of, 178
  categorization ability impairment and, 132
  co-occurence with communication and cognitive deficits, 45, 179
  frontal lobe injury-related, 205
  Diagnostic and Statistical Manual of Mental Disorders definition of, 59
  in learning-disabled individuals, 64–67
  situational predictability and, 120–121
Social groups, integrated, 231, 232–238
Social relationships, object permanence and, 16
Social skills
  generalization of, 297
  visual thinking approach to, 146–147
Social skills training, 9, 295–298, 304
  with Bright Start, 285–286
  in integrated social groups, 236–237
Sorting task ability, 160
  generalized deficits in, 271–272
Spatial learning, 47
Spatial perception disorders, 46–47
  in learning-disabled children, 44–45
Spatial reasoning deficits, prefrontal dysfunction and, 209
Spatial reversal task, 203, 204
Special education, integrated and mainstreamed, 298–299
Speech enhancement skills, 300–301

Stereotypical behavior
    communicative alternative to, 74
    use in TEACCH program, 263
Stimulus overselectivity, 16, 17
    Bright Start remedial program for, 284
    categorization impairment and, 133
    generalization impairment and, 121
    social behavior implications of, 273
Stimulus presentation control, 269–270
Structural-cognitive modifiability, 276, 278, 279
Structured teaching, 293
    efficacy of, 66
    historical background of, 243–244
    task organization in, 258–262
    See also TEACCH
Symbol system, of nonverbal communication, 302
Symptom cluster theory, of learning disabilities, 62

Tantrums, 74
Task analysis, 317
Task interspersion, in communication motivation treatment, 77–78
Task organization, in structured teaching, 258–262
TEACCH, 9–10, 243–268
    assessment procedures in, 245–246
    constructive routines in, 263
    directions use in, 264
    language training methods in, 144
    Left to Right routine in, 263
    physical organization in, 246–251, 252, 263
    principles of, 245–246
    prompts use in, 264–265
    reinforcers use in, 265–266
    schedules in, 251–255
    stereotypical behavior use in, 263
    task organization in, 258–263
    Top to Bottom routine in, 263
    visual-processing skills in, 6
    work systems in, 255–258
Theory of mind, 23–24
    definition of, 177
    delayed acquisition of, 190
    in normal development, 23
    precursor behavior, 161

Theory-of-mind deficits, 5, 8–9, 19, 138, 177–197, 200
    of Down's syndrome individuals, 183, 187
    false beliefs testing of, 23–24, 181–183, 184, 188–190
    frontal lobe dysfunction and, 207–208
    "hot", 174
    impairment triad and, 178–179, 192–193
    metarepresentation and, 23–24, 192
    pretense and, 179–181
    as primary emotional deficiency, 192
    relationship to verbal IQ, 203
    testing results in, 181–187, 188–189
    visual thinking and, 144
Thinking, rigid, 138, 139
Time-delay procedure, for speech skills training, 300–301
Time-out, 303–304
Toilet training, 247, 248
Token manipulation, as question-asking behavior motivation, 80–81
Tool use ability, 160
Tower of Hanoi, 19, 174, 203, 206–207
Toys, use in peer-tutor/buddies programs, 230–231
Trail-Making Test, 19
Transactional theory, of cognitive development, 276–277
Tuberous sclerosis, 138

Verbal reasoning, 15–16
Verbal skills, Wechsler intelligence scale scores of, 92, 93–99
Vinci, Leonardo da, 148
Vineland Adaptive Behavior Scales, 173
Visual discrimination learning, 14–15
Visual fixation patterns, 17
Visual-motor skills, Wechsler intelligence scale scores of, 93, 94, 95 97–99
Visual-spatial skills, 5, 14–15, 25
    compensatory role of, 147–148
    Wechsler intelligence scale scores of, 93, 97–99
Visual stimulation, 152
Visual stimuli processing, 6, 7
    memory functioning and, 107, 108–109
Visual thinking, 141–148
    abstract thought in, 15–16, 145–147

Visual thinking (*Cont.*)
  implications of, 144–148
  language ability in, 143–144
  nonvisual information in, 143
Vitamin B6 therapy, 151
Vocabulary development, 76

Way-finding deficits, 44–47
Wechsler intelligence scale(s), 14–15, 89,
    91–99, 100
  Block Design subtest, 14, 94, 95, 96, 97,
    99, 101, 106, 107, 209
  Coding subtest, 101, 106, 107
  comparison with Kaufman Assessment
    Battery for Children, 101, 102, 103–
    105
  Comprehension subtest, 15, 94, 95, 96,
    106
  as crystallized intellectual ability mea-
    sure, 95
  development of, 91–92
  Digit Span subtest, 15, 101
  factor solutions for, 96–99
  as fluid intellectual ability measure, 95
  Freedom from distractibility factor, 92,
    93–95
  Hand Movements subtest, 106
  Mazes subtest, 101

Wechsler intelligence scale(s) (*Cont.*)
  Object Assembly subtest, 14, 94, 95, 96,
    97, 99, 101, 106, 107
  Perceptual Organization factor, 92, 93–95
  Performance IQ scores, 14, 106–107, 111
    relationship to developmental quo-
    tients, 111
  Picture Arrangement subtest, 97, 101,
    106, 107
  Picture Completion subtest, 97, 101
  scaled score profiles of, 96–99
  sequential and simultaneous processing
    scales, 15, 89, 101–107
  Similarities subtest, 15, 101
  Verbal Comprehension factor, 92, 93–95
  Verbal IQ/Performance IQ discrepancy
    of, 92–95
  Vocabulary subtest, 15, 94, 95, 96, 100,
    106
Wisconsin Card Sorting Test, 19, 125, 174,
    202, 204
Word-calling, 42
Work systems, in structured teaching, 255–
    258, 259, 263

Zarontin (ethosuxiomide), 151
Zone of proximal development, 277